CliffsNotes

ASVAB AFQT CRAM PLAN™

by

*Colonel Pat Proctor, Carolyn C. Wheater,
and Jane R. Burstein*

Houghton Mifflin Harcourt
Boston • New York

About the Authors

COLONEL PAT PROCTOR is an Iraq war veteran who has written for the U.S. Army War College Quarterly, *Parameters,* and *Armchair General.*

CAROLYN C. WHEATER was a math instructor at the Nightingale-Bamford School in New York City for 25 years and taught at other high schools around the area for another 18 years. She writes extensively on middle school and high school math and standardized tests.

JANE R. BURSTEIN has been a high school English teacher, an ACT and SAT tutor, and is currently an Adjunct Instructor and Student Teaching Supervisor in the School of Education at Hofstra University. She has written several test-prep books, including Cram Plans for the ACT, SAT, GRE, and GMAT.

Dedication

This book is dedicated to all the brave women and men who serve in the armed forces. We appreciate your service to this country.

—Jane R. Burstein

Editorial

Executive Editor: Greg Tubach
Senior Editor: Christina Stambaugh
Production Editor: Jennifer Freilach
Technical Editors: Mary Jane Sterling and Tom Page
Proofreader: Susan Moritz

CliffsNotes® ASVAB AFQT Cram Plan™, 2nd Edition

Copyright © 2019 by Houghton Mifflin Harcourt Publishing Company

All rights reserved.

Library of Congress Control Number: 2019939013
ISBN: 978-1-328-57365-0 (pbk)

Printed in the United States of America
DOC 10 9 8 7 6 5 4 3 2 1   4500770965

For information about permission to reproduce selections from this book, write to trade.permissions@hmhco.com or to Permissions, Houghton Mifflin Harcourt Publishing Company, 3 Park Avenue, 19th Floor, New York, New York 10016.

www.hmhco.com

Table of Contents

Introduction

So, you've decided to serve your country. Congratulations! You're about to join a very distinguished group. Less than 2 percent of your fellow Americans have made the same commitment you're about to make. Whether you choose to serve only a single term of enlistment or you decide to make it a career; whether you serve in the guard, reserves, or active forces; whether you serve at home or overseas, for the rest of your life you'll be a member of this proud tradition, America's veterans.

But before you can raise your hand and swear an oath to support and defend the Constitution, there is one big hurdle in your path, the Armed Services Vocational Aptitude Battery (ASVAB). You must especially do well on the Armed Forces Qualifying Test (AFQT), the four key subtests of the ASVAB that the services use to measure you against your fellow recruits.

That's right. Your recruiter might not have told you, but as soon as you said you were interested in joining, the military began measuring you against all its other potential recruits. Just like any other employer, Uncle Sam is trying to get the best and the brightest people. And once he gets the best and the brightest, he sizes them up and puts only the best of the best in the most sought-after positions. Do you want to be a jet or helicopter mechanic? Do you want to be a medical technician? Those jobs require a lot of expensive and time-consuming training. The military is going to use your AFQT score to decide whether it wants to spend all that money and time on you!

Maybe you're joining the military for the adventure. You want to be an Airborne Ranger. You want to get into the action. You might be thinking right now that the AFQT doesn't matter to you. You'd be dead wrong! Your AFQT score doesn't get thrown away as soon as you sign your enlistment contract and have your job locked in. Whether you enlist for a single term or stay until retirement, your AFQT score follows you for the rest of the time you're in the military. Do poorly on the AFQT and you could be crippled in your ability to get promotions, choice assignment locations, or reenlistment bonuses later.

If the AFQT sounds like serious business, that's because it is. But don't worry—you've made a great decision: you chose to pick up this book. And choices are what this book is all about. Choose to follow one of the programs in this book—the two-month, one-month, or one-week cram plan—and you'll be successful on the AFQT. And that will open the door to a whole world of more choices, because a good AFQT score gives you the freedom to choose what you want to do in the military, where you want to do it, and for what amount of money. So let's get started!

About the Armed Services Vocational Aptitude Battery (ASVAB)

The first thing to understand about the ASVAB (the larger test that includes the AFQT) is that it's made for regular people, just like you. It isn't designed to test service members—it's designed to test people with no experience in the military. Moreover, this test is not designed just for high school or college students or for graduates—it's also designed to be taken by people who have been out of school for quite some time. The military is a big organization, and it needs people from all walks of life. So there is no reason to be intimidated by the ASVAB—it was written for you!

There are two kinds of ASVABs: the paper-and-pencil ASVAB and the computer adaptive test ASVAB (CAT-ASVAB). One test is not harder than the other; they ask the same kinds of questions. However, because of differences in the way each test is administered, you'll want to apply different strategies when taking each. For this reason, it's important to know which kind of test you're going to take.

And that leads to the second thing you need to understand about the ASVAB: Your recruiter wants you to be successful. He's graded based on the quality of recruits he brings into his service. The better you do on the ASVAB, the better the grade *he* gets. So if you need help or have questions, ask your recruiter! He'll be happy to help. And the first question you need to ask your recruiter is which kind of test you're taking—the paper-and-pencil or CAT-ASVAB.

Before we look at the two different kinds of ASVABs, there are some strategies that apply regardless of the type of test you're taking:

- **Be familiar with the test questions and format.** You're doing that right now! Complete one of the cram plans in this book, and you'll be ready.
- **Read every question carefully before you answer.** Make sure you understand what you're being asked.
- **Read all the answer choices.** Some answer choices are obviously wrong, but others look right, at least until you see the real right answer.
- **Stay alert.** A few hours doesn't seem like a long time until you spend it concentrating. Get a good night's sleep the night before the test. During the test, stretch in place or take deep breaths—whatever it takes to stay alert. *Remember:* This test is really important.

Now here's a look at the two different types of ASVABs.

Paper-and-Pencil ASVAB

This is a classic, standardized test. If you've ever taken tests like the Scholastic Aptitude Test (SAT) or the American College Test (ACT), then the format of the ASVAB will be immediately familiar. You get a test booklet, optical scan answer sheets, and a pencil. This test is usually given at locations called Military Entrance Test sites, but it's also sometimes administered at high schools.

The paper-and-pencil ASVAB is divided into nine subtests. You complete one part before you move on to the next. You can't go back to a previous subtest once you've started the next subtest, but you can go back and review your answers in the current subtest while there is still time remaining. Here are the sections of the paper-and-pencil ASVAB, along with the number of questions and minutes allowed for each. (Note the four boldface AFQT subtests—those are the ones that combine to form your AFQT score.)

Subtest	Number of Questions	Number of Minutes Allotted
General Science	25	11
Arithmetic Reasoning	**30**	**36**
Word Knowledge	**35**	**11**
Paragraph Comprehension	**15**	**13**
Mathematics Knowledge	**25**	**24**
Electronics Information	20	9
Auto and Shop Information	25	11
Mechanical Comprehension	25	19
Assembling Objects	25	15

Altogether, the test will take about 2½ hours to complete. Once you're done with the whole test, your answer sheets are sent off to be scanned and graded. You'll get your complete score in a few days, but your recruiter will probably get your AFQT score before you leave the test site. Don't be afraid to ask him how you did.

Here are a couple strategies that will help with the paper-and-pencil version of the ASVAB:

- **Watch the time.** Once you're out of time for a section, you aren't allowed to go back.
- **Answer everything.** There is no penalty for guessing. If you have 30 seconds left and you still have 10 unanswered questions, just fill in anything. Each question has four choices, so a guess will be right 25 percent of the time; odds are that out of 10 questions you'll get two or three questions correct. That's better than zero, right?

Computer Adaptive Test ASVAB (CAT-ASVAB)

The CAT-ASVAB is given at a Military Entrance Processing Station (MEPS). That's the same place where you get your physical, haggle with military personnel managers over your enlistment contract, and travel to your service's basic training site. (You might take the test on one day and come back to do all this other stuff on one or more other days.) As the name suggests, you take the computer adaptive test on a computer. The questions and answers appear on a computer screen and you use a mouse and/or keyboard to answer the questions. You'll also be given a pencil and as much scratch paper as you need. What is most interesting about this test is that it adapts to you as you take it. If you get a question wrong, the next one will be easier. Get a question right, and the next one will be harder. But you get more points for the harder questions than you do for the easier ones.

Roughly 70 percent of military applicants take the test via computer. You are allowed to complete the CAT-ASVAB at your own pace. This means that when you complete a test in the battery, you can immediately move on to the next section. You don't have to wait for everyone else to finish. As soon as you are finished with all the tests, you may leave the test room.

The CAT-ASVAB is divided into ten, rather than nine, subtests, though the actual questions are the same as in the paper-and-pencil ASVAB. (The four AFQT subtests are in boldface.)

Subtest	Number of Questions	Number of Minutes Allotted
General Science	16	8
Arithmetic Reasoning	**16**	**39**
Word Knowledge	**16**	**8**
Paragraph Comprehension	**11**	**22**
Mathematics Knowledge	**16**	**20**
Electronics Information	16	8
Auto Information	11	7
Shop Information	11	6
Mechanical Comprehension	16	20
Assembling Objects	16	16

A few other things are different about the CAT-ASVAB:

- Once you confirm an answer to a question, you can't go back and review or change your answer.
- You don't have to wait for all the time to elapse for a section—you move to the next subtest as soon as you're done with the previous one.

- The CAT-ASVAB usually takes less time to complete than the paper-and-pencil ASVAB because the questions adapt to your ability level—about an hour and a half.
- You don't have to wait for your score—you get it at the end of the test.

Because the test is adaptive, there are some strategies that are unique to the CAT-ASVAB:

- **Take your time on the first few questions in each section.** The harder questions are worth more than the easier ones. You want to get to the hard questions quickly so you can complete as many of them as possible. The only way to get to harder questions is to answer the easier ones right first.
- **Don't guess unless you have to!** Wrong answers bump you down to the easier questions, which aren't worth as much. Unless you're sure you don't know how to answer the question, take the time to find the right answer.
- **Answer every question.** Guessing is worse than knowing the right answer, but not answering at all is worse than guessing. Just as in the paper-and-pencil test, each question has four possible answer choices, so a guess will be right 25 percent of the time. If you can eliminate one or more of the answer choices as definitely wrong, those odds go up.

Your Score

No matter which type of ASVAB you take—the paper-and-pencil ASVAB or the CAT-ASVAB—you'll get two scores:

- A compilation of your scores for all the subtests of the ASVAB
- A score indicating how well you did on the four core subtests of the AFQT

Both scores are a percentile, between 1 and 99. They indicate the percentage of people who took the test in 1997 who did worse than you. So, if you get an 80, that means 80 percent of people who took the test in 1997 did worse than you. Congratulations! You finished in the top 20 percent!

This population-based scoring method is both good news and bad news. It's good news because you don't have to do perfect on the test to do well. You just have to do better than most of the people who took the test in 1997. It's bad news, however, because this scoring method makes it difficult to know how many questions you have to answer correctly to score well. There are some good estimates available on the Internet. (Rod Powers provides an excellent estimate system at www.thebalance.com/how-the-asvab-afqt-score-is-computed-3354094.) Unfortunately, there is no foolproof way to convert your number of right answers on any given section to your final AFQT score; the U.S. military has never published its scoring system. This is why the diagnostic and practice tests in this book don't include a grading scale.

Of the two scores you'll receive after taking the ASVAB, the AFQT score is, by far, the more important score. It determines which services and jobs you're eligible for. The other subtests in the ASVAB just help the recruiter and the personnel manager at the MEPS understand what things you're good at. If you walk into the MEPS with no idea what job you want to do in the military, your recruiter and the personnel manager will use your scores in the other, non-AFQT subjects of the ASVAB to help you decide. But if you don't do well enough on the AFQT, many doors will be closed to you, because the best jobs go only to the best and the brightest—those with the highest AFQT scores.

If you aren't happy with your score, you can take the ASVAB again, but you have to wait 1 month. If you want to take the test again after that, you have to wait another 6 months.

What score do you need to "pass" the AFQT? Well, just to get into a branch of service, these are the minimum scores.

Service	Minimum AFQT Score
Air Force	36
Army	31
Coast Guard	36
Marines	32
Navy	35

Note: These minimum scores change all the time based on the needs of the services; the minimum scores shown here were those at the time this book was written. Ask your recruiter for the most current information.

ASVAB scores are used primarily to determine enlistment eligibility, assign applicants to military jobs, and aid students in career exploration.

Remember: You bought this book because you want to do a lot better than just pass. You want to excel so you walk into MEPS with every door open to you, and every job, assignment location, and bonus available. To have those choices, you're going to have to do well on the AFQT.

About the Armed Forces Qualifying Test (AFQT)

Whether you're taking the paper-and-pencil ASVAB or the CAT-ASVAB, the AFQT consists of four topics:

- **Arithmetic Reasoning:** This section is a test of your ability to read and solve math problems. You'll be required to do addition, subtraction, multiplication, and division as you solve one-step and multistep word problems. Each question is multiple choice with four possible answers.

- **Word Knowledge:** This section is a vocabulary test. You'll be presented with a word, either alone or in a sentence. You'll then be given four choices and asked to choose the word that is most similar in meaning to the word in the question.

- **Paragraph Comprehension:** This is a reading comprehension test. You'll be asked to read short paragraphs on a variety of topics. After each paragraph, you'll have to answer one or more questions about the material you've just read. Again, each question is multiple choice with four possible answers.

- **Mathematics Knowledge:** This section is a test of high school-level mathematics. You'll be presented with math problems and have four answer choices from which to choose.

The rest of this book focuses on the AFQT, the four subtests of the ASVAB, because they're the ones that really matter. How you do in these four subjects will have a greater impact on your military career than anything else you do before you enter the military.

How to Use This Book

It's time to get to work. You need to begin by answering two questions:

- **How much time do you have before you take the ASVAB?** Don't worry if you don't have much time. This is a cram plan! This book will help you maximize the time you have to prepare. It includes two-month, one-month, and one-week plans that are tailored to the amount of time you have. Choose the one that fits your timeline.

- **Where are you now? What are your strongest and weakest subjects?** This book will help you answer that question so you can focus your efforts on improving in your weakest areas. Chapter 4 begins with a diagnostic test to help you decide what areas you need to work on.

Let's get started. Good luck!

Chapter 1

Two-Month Cram Plan

Two-Month Cram Plan			
	Arithmetic Reasoning	**Word Knowledge**	**Paragraph Comprehension**	**Mathematics Knowledge**
8 weeks before the test	**Study Time:** 2½ hours ❑ Take the **Diagnostic Test** and review the answer explanations. ❑ Based on your errors on the Diagnostic Test, identify difficult topics and their corresponding chapters. These chapters are your targeted areas.		
7 weeks before the test	**Study Time:** 2 hours ❑ **Word Problems:** Chapter 5 ❑ Read sections A–G. ❑ Do the odd-numbered practice questions in each section.	**Study Time:** 1–2 hours ❑ **Building Word Power:** Chapter 8 ❑ Read sections A–B. ❑ Review prefixes. ❑ Make flash cards for synonym clusters. If this is a targeted chapter, make flash cards for prefixes. ❑ **Testing Your Vocabulary:** Chapter 9 ❑ Study *aberration* through *draconian* in Section C.	**Study Time:** 1 hour ❑ **Improving Your Reading Skills:** Chapter 10 ❑ Read Section A. ❑ Do all the example questions in the section.	**Study Time:** 2 hours ❑ **Algebra:** Chapter 12 ❑ Read sections A–F. ❑ Do the odd-numbered practice questions in each section. ❑ **Probability and Statistics:** Chapter 15 ❑ Read sections A–C. ❑ Do the odd-numbered practice questions in each section.
6 weeks before the test	**Study Time:** 2 hours ❑ **Whole Numbers and Decimals:** Chapter 6 ❑ Read sections A–E. ❑ Do the odd-numbered practice questions in each section.	**Study Time:** 1–2 hours ❑ **Building Word Power:** Chapter 8 ❑ Review roots and suffixes. ❑ Study synonym cluster flash cards. ❑ Make flash cards for roots and suffixes. ❑ Do the practice questions at the end of the chapter. ❑ **Testing Your Vocabulary:** Chapter 9 ❑ Study *dubious* through *intrepid* in Section C.	**Study Time:** 1 hour ❑ **Improving Your Reading Skills:** Chapter 10 ❑ Read Section B. ❑ Do all the example questions in the section. ❑ Do half the practice questions at the end of the chapter. If this is a targeted chapter, do all the practice questions at the end of the chapter.	**Study Time:** 2 hours ❑ **Algebra:** Chapter 12 ❑ Read sections G–K. ❑ Do the odd-numbered practice questions in each section.

continued

	Arithmetic Reasoning	Word Knowledge	Paragraph Comprehension	Mathematics Knowledge

5 weeks before the test	**Study Time:** 2 hours
	❑ **Fractions:** Chapter 7
	  ❑ Read sections A–F.
	  ❑ Do the odd-numbered practice questions in each section.
		Study Time: 1–2 hours
		❑ **Testing Your Vocabulary:** Chapter 9
		  ❑ Read Section A and do half the practice questions in the section.
		  ❑ If this is a targeted chapter, do all the practice questions in the section.
		❑ **Testing Your Vocabulary:** Chapter 9
		  ❑ Study *introspection* through *preclude* in Section C.
			Study Time: 1 hour
			❑ **Answering the Reading Questions:** Chapter 11
			  ❑ Read Section A.
			  ❑ Read Section B, general overview questions, inference questions, and sequence of events questions.
			  ❑ Do all the example questions in each section.
				Study Time: 2 hours
				❑ **Geometry:** Chapter 13
				  ❑ Read sections A–E.
				  ❑ Do the odd-numbered practice questions in each section.

4 weeks before the test	**Study Time:** 1 hour
	❑ **Word Problems:** Chapter 5
	  ❑ Reread sections A–C.
	  ❑ Do the even-numbered practice questions in each section.
		Study Time: 1–2 hours
		❑ **Testing Your Vocabulary:** Chapter 9
		  ❑ Read Section B.
		  ❑ Do half the practice questions in the section. If this is a targeted chapter, do all the practice questions.
		  ❑ Study *precocious* through *whimsical* in Section C.
		  ❑ Do the practice questions in Section C.
			Study Time: 1 hour
			❑ **Answering the Reading Questions:** Chapter 11
			  ❑ Read Section B, structure questions, and style and tone questions.
			  ❑ Do all the example questions in each section.
				Study Time: 2 hours
				❑ **Geometry:** Chapter 13
				  ❑ Read sections F–I.
				  ❑ Do the odd-numbered practice questions in each section.
				❑ **Trigonometry:** Chapter 14
				  ❑ Read sections A–C.
				  ❑ Do the odd-numbered practice questions in each section.

3 weeks before the test	**Study Time:** 2½ hours ❑ Take the **Practice Test** and review the answer explanations. ❑ Based on your errors on the Practice Test, identify difficult topics and their corresponding chapters. These chapters are your targeted areas for further review.			

2 weeks before the test	**Study Time:** 1 hour
	❑ **Whole Numbers and Decimals:** Chapter 6
	  ❑ Reread sections A–C, focusing on your target area.
	  ❑ Do the even-numbered practice questions in each section.
		Study Time: 1–2 hours
		❑ **Building Word Power:** Chapter 8
		  ❑ Reread sections A–B.
		  ❑ Review prefixes, roots, and suffixes.
		❑ **Testing Your Vocabulary:** Chapter 9
		  ❑ Reread sections A–B.
		  ❑ Re-study *aberration* through *preclude* in Section C.
			Study Time: 1 hour
			❑ **Improving Your Reading Skills:** Chapter 10
			  ❑ Reread sections A–B.
			  ❑ If this is a targeted chapter, redo all the example questions.
				Study Time: 1½ hours
				❑ **Trigonometry:** Chapter 14
				  ❑ Reread sections A–C.
				  ❑ Do the even-numbered practice questions in each section.
				❑ **Probability and Statistics:** Chapter 15
				  ❑ Reread sections A–C.
				  ❑ Do the even-numbered practice questions in each section.

	Arithmetic Reasoning	Word Knowledge	Paragraph Comprehension	Mathematics Knowledge

7 days before the test	**Study Time:** 1 hour
	❑ **Fractions:** Chapter 7
	  ❑ Reread sections A–C, focusing on your target area.
	  ❑ Do the even-numbered practice questions in each section.
		Study Time: 1 hour
		❑ **Building Word Power:** Chapter 8
		  ❑ Re-study flash cards for synonym clusters.
		❑ **Testing Your Vocabulary:** Chapter 9
		  ❑ Re-study *precocious* through *sardonic* in Section C.
			Study Time: 45 minutes
			❑ **Improving Your Reading Skills:** Chapter 10 and
			❑ **Answering the Reading Questions:** Chapter 11
			  ❑ Choose a news article from the newspaper or online and read it carefully.
			  ❑ If either of these is a targeted chapter, write a summary of what you learned from reading the article.
				Study Time: 1½ hours
				❑ **Algebra:** Chapter 12
				  ❑ Reread sections A–B.
				  ❑ Do the even-numbered practice questions in each section.
				❑ **Geometry:** Chapter 13
				  ❑ Reread sections A–B in each chapter.
				  ❑ Do the even-numbered practice questions in each section.

6 days before the test	**Study Time:** 1 hour
	❑ **Word Problems:** Chapter 5
	  ❑ Reread sections D–F.
	  ❑ Do the even-numbered practice questions in each section.
		Study Time: 1 hour
		❑ **Building Word Power:** Chapter 8
		  ❑ Review prefixes, roots, and suffixes.
		❑ **Testing Your Vocabulary:** Chapter 9
		  ❑ Re-study *satiate* through *whimsical* in Section C.
			Study Time: 45 minutes
			❑ **Improving Your Reading Skills:** Chapter 10 and
			❑ **Answering the Reading Questions:** Chapter 11
			  ❑ Choose a science article from the newspaper or online and read it carefully.
			  ❑ If either of these is a targeted chapter, write a summary of what you learned from reading the article.
				Study Time: 1½ hours
				❑ **Algebra:** Chapter 12
				  ❑ Reread sections C–D.
				  ❑ Do the even-numbered practice questions in each section.
				❑ **Geometry:** Chapter 13
				  ❑ Reread sections C–D.
				  ❑ Do the even-numbered practice questions in each section.

5 days before the test	**Study Time:** 1 hour
	❑ **Whole Numbers and Decimals:** Chapter 6
	  ❑ Reread sections D–E, focusing on your target area.
	  ❑ Do the even-numbered practice questions in each section.
		Study Time: 1 hour
		❑ **Building Word Power:** Chapter 8
		  ❑ Study flash cards for roots and suffixes.
		❑ **Testing Your Vocabulary:** Chapter 9
		  ❑ Re-study *aberration* through *draconian* in Section C.
			Study Time: 45 minutes
			❑ **Improving Your Reading Skills:** Chapter 10 and **Answering the Reading Questions:** Chapter 11
			  ❑ Choose a short story from the library or online and read it carefully.
			  ❑ If either of these is a targeted chapter, write a summary of the plot of the story.
				Study Time: 1½ hours
				❑ **Algebra:** Chapter 12
				  ❑ Reread sections E–F.
				  ❑ Do the even-numbered questions in each section.
				❑ **Geometry:** Chapter 13
				  ❑ Reread sections E–F.
				  ❑ Do the even-numbered practice questions in each section.

continued

	Arithmetic Reasoning	Word Knowledge	Paragraph Comprehension	Mathematics Knowledge

4 days before the test	**Study Time:** 1 hour
	❏ **Fractions:** Chapter 7
	  ❏ Reread sections D–F, focusing on your target area.
	  ❏ Do the even-numbered practice questions in each section.
		Study Time: 1 hour
		❏ **Building Word Power:** Chapter 8
		  ❏ Review prefixes, roots, and suffixes.
		❏ **Testing Your Vocabulary:** Chapter 9
		  ❏ Re-study *dubious* through *intrepid* in Section C.
			Study Time: 45 minutes
			❏ **Improving Your Reading Skills:** Chapter 10 and
			❏ **Answering the Reading Questions:** Chapter 11
			  ❏ Choose a history article from the newspaper or online and read it carefully.
			  ❏ If either of these is a targeted chapter, write a summary of what you learned from reading the article.
				Study Time: 1½ hours
				❏ **Algebra:** Chapter 12
				  ❏ Reread sections G–H.
				  ❏ Do the even-numbered practice questions in each section.
				❏ **Geometry:** Chapter 13
				  ❏ Reread sections G–H.
				  ❏ Do the even-numbered practice questions in each section.

3 days before the test	**Study Time:** 1 hour
	❏ **Word Problems:** Chapter 5
	  ❏ Reread Section G.
	  ❏ Do the even-numbered practice questions in each section.
		Study Time: 1 hour
		❏ **Building Word Power:** Chapter 8
		  ❏ Re-study roots and suffixes flash cards.
		❏ **Testing Your Vocabulary:** Chapter 9
		  ❏ Re-study *introspection* through *preclude* in Section C.
			Study Time: 45 minutes
			❏ **Improving Your Reading Skills:** Chapter 10 and
			❏ **Answering the Reading Questions:** Chapter 11
			  ❏ Choose a technical article from the newspaper or online and read it carefully.
			  ❏ If either of these is a targeted chapter, write a summary of what you learned from reading the article.
				Study Time: 1½ hours
				❏ **Algebra:** Chapter 12
				  ❏ Reread sections I–K.
				  ❏ Do the even-numbered practice questions in each section.
				❏ **Geometry:** Chapter 13
				  ❏ Reread Section I.
				  ❏ Do the even-numbered practice questions in each section.

2 days before the test	**Study Time:** 1 hour
	❏ **Whole Numbers and Decimals:** Chapter 6
	  ❏ Rework any practice questions you missed earlier.
	❏ **Fractions:** Chapter 7
	  ❏ Rework any practice questions you missed earlier.
		Study Time: 1 hour
		❏ **Building Word Power:** Chapter 8
		  ❏ Review prefixes, roots, and suffixes.
		  ❏ Review all flash cards.
		❏ **Testing Your Vocabulary:** Chapter 9
		  ❏ Re-study *precocious* through *whimsical* in Section C.
			Study Time: 45 minutes
			❏ **Improving Your Reading Skills:** Chapter 10 and **Answering the Reading Questions:** Chapter 11
			  ❏ Choose any interesting article from the newspaper or online and read it carefully.
			  ❏ If either of these is a targeted chapter, write a summary of what you learned from reading the article.
				Study Time: 30 minutes
				❏ **Algebra:** Chapter 12; **Geometry:** Chapter 13; **Trigonometry:** Chapter 14; **Probability and Statistics:** Chapter 15
				  ❏ Review your target areas.
				  ❏ Rework any practice questions you missed earlier.

1 day before the test	❏ Relax. . . . You're well prepared for the test. ❏ Have confidence in your ability to do well.			

The day of the test	**Reminders:**
	❏ Have a good breakfast.
	❏ Bring these items with you to the test:
	  ❏ Photo ID
	  ❏ A watch
	❏ Try to go outside for a few minutes and walk around before the test.
	❏ ***Most important:*** Stay calm and confident during the test. Take deep slow breaths if you feel at all nervous. You can do it!			

Chapter 2

One-Month Cram Plan

One-Month Cram Plan				
	Arithmetic Reasoning	**Word Knowledge**	**Paragraph Comprehension**	**Mathematics Knowledge**
4 weeks before the test	**Study Time:** 2½ hours ❑ Take the **Diagnostic Test** and review the answer explanations. ❑ Based on your errors on the Diagnostic Test, identify difficult topics and their corresponding chapters. These chapters are your targeted areas.			
3 weeks before the test	**Study Time:** 2 hours ❑ **Word Problems:** Chapter 5 ❑ Read sections A–G. ❑ Do the odd-numbered practice questions in each section.	**Study Time:** 1½–2½ hours ❑ **Building Word Power:** Chapter 8 ❑ Read sections A–B. ❑ Review prefixes, roots, and suffixes. ❑ Make flash cards for synonym clusters. ❑ If this is a targeted chapter, make flash cards for prefixes, roots, and suffixes. ❑ **Testing Your Vocabulary:** Chapter 9 ❑ Read sections A–B. ❑ Do half the practice questions in these sections. If this is a targeted chapter, do all the practice questions in these sections. ❑ Study *aberration* through *noisome* in Section C.	**Study Time:** 1½–2 hours ❑ **Improving Your Reading Skills:** Chapter 10 ❑ Read sections A–B. ❑ Do all the example questions in each section. ❑ Do half the practice questions at the end of the chapter. If this is a targeted chapter, do all the practice questions at the end of the chapter.	**Study Time:** 2½ hours ❑ **Algebra:** Chapter 12 ❑ Read sections A–K. ❑ Do the odd-numbered practice questions in each section.
2 weeks before the test	**Study Time:** 3½ hours ❑ **Whole Numbers and Decimals:** Chapter 6 ❑ Read sections A–E. ❑ Do the odd-numbered practice questions in each section. ❑ **Fractions:** Chapter 7 ❑ Read sections A–F. ❑ Do the odd-numbered practice questions in each section.	**Study Time:** 1½–2½ hours ❑ **Building Word Power:** Chapter 8 ❑ Study synonym cluster flash cards. ❑ Study prefixes, roots, and suffixes flash cards. ❑ Do half the practice questions at the end of the chapter. If this is a targeted chapter, do all the practice questions at the end of the chapter. ❑ **Testing Your Vocabulary:** Chapter 9 ❑ Do half the practice questions in Section C. If this is a targeted chapter, do all the practice questions in Section C. ❑ Study *nondescript* through *whimsical* in Section C.	**Study Time:** 1½–2 hours ❑ **Answering the Reading Questions:** Chapter 11 ❑ Review sections A–B. ❑ Do all the example questions in each section. ❑ Do half the practice questions at the end of the chapter. If this is a targeted chapter, do all the practice questions.	**Study Time:** 2½ hours ❑ **Geometry:** Chapter 13 ❑ Read sections A–I. ❑ Do the odd-numbered practice questions in each section.

continued

	Arithmetic Reasoning	Word Knowledge	Paragraph Comprehension	Mathematics Knowledge
7 days before the test	**Study Time:** 2½ hours ❏ Take the **Practice Test** and review the answer explanations. ❏ Based on your errors on the Practice Test, identify difficult topics and their corresponding chapters. These chapters are your targeted areas for further review.			
6 days before the test	**Study Time:** 1½ hours ❏ **Word Problems:** Chapter 5 ❏ Reread sections A–D. ❏ Do the even-numbered practice questions in each section.	**Study Time:** 1 hour ❏ **Building Word Power:** Chapter 8 ❏ Review prefixes, roots, and suffixes. ❏ **Testing Your Vocabulary:** Chapter 9 ❏ Re-study *aberration* through *draconian* in Section C.	**Study Time:** 45 minutes ❏ **Improving Your Reading Skills:** Chapter 10 and **Answering the Reading Questions:** Chapter 11 ❏ Choose a science article from the newspaper or online and read it carefully. ❏ If either of these is a targeted chapter, write a summary of what you learned from reading the article.	**Study Time:** 1 hour ❏ **Probability and Statistics:** Chapter 15 ❏ Read sections A–C. ❏ Do the odd-numbered practice questions in each section.
5 days before the test	**Study Time:** 1½ hours ❏ **Whole Numbers and Decimals:** Chapter 6 ❏ Reread sections A–E. ❏ Do the even-numbered practice questions in each section.	**Study Time:** 1 hour ❏ **Building Word Power:** Chapter 8 ❏ Study flash cards for synonym clusters. ❏ **Testing Your Vocabulary:** Chapter 9 ❏ Re-study *dubious* through *intrepid* in Section C.	**Study Time:** 45 minutes ❏ **Improving Your Reading Skills:** Chapter 10 and **Answering the Reading Questions:** Chapter 11 ❏ Choose a short story from the library or online and read it carefully. ❏ If either of these is a targeted chapter, write a summary of the plot of the story.	**Study Time:** 1 hour ❏ **Trigonometry:** Chapter 14 ❏ Read sections A–C. ❏ Do the odd-numbered practice questions in each section.

	Arithmetic Reasoning	Word Knowledge	Paragraph Comprehension	Mathematics Knowledge

4 days before the test	**Study Time:** 1½ hours
	 ❑ **Fractions:** Chapter 7
	  ❑ Reread sections A–F.
	  ❑ Do the even-numbered practice questions in each section.
		Study Time: 1 hour
		 ❑ **Building Word Power:** Chapter 8
		  ❑ Study flash cards for prefixes, roots, and suffixes.
		 ❑ **Testing Your Vocabulary:** Chapter 9
		  ❑ Re-study *introspection* through *noisome* in Section C.
			Study Time: 45 minutes
			 ❑ **Improving Your Reading Skills:** Chapter 10 and **Answering the Reading Questions:** Chapter 11
			  ❑ Choose a history article from the newspaper or online and read it carefully.
			  ❑ If either of these is a targeted chapter, write a summary of what you learned from reading the article.
				Study Time: 2 hours
				 ❑ **Algebra:** Chapter 12
				  ❑ Reread sections A–K.
				  ❑ Do the even-numbered practice questions in each section.

3 days before the test	**Study Time:** 1½ hours
	 ❑ **Word Problems:** Chapter 5
	  ❑ Reread sections E–G.
	  ❑ Do the even-numbered practice questions in each section.
		Study Time: 1 hour
		 ❑ **Building Word Power:** Chapter 8
		  ❑ Study flash cards for synonym clusters.
		 ❑ **Testing Your Vocabulary:** Chapter 9
		  ❑ Re-study *nondescript* through *preclude* in Section C.
			Study Time: 45 minutes
			 ❑ **Improving Your Reading Skills:** Chapter 10 and **Answering the Reading Questions:** Chapter 11
			  ❑ Choose a technical article from the newspaper or online and read it carefully.
			  ❑ If either of these is a targeted chapter, write a summary of what you learned from reading the article.
				Study Time: 2 hours
				 ❑ **Geometry:** Chapter 13
				  ❑ Reread sections A–I.
				  ❑ Do the even-numbered practice questions in each section.

continued

	Arithmetic Reasoning	Word Knowledge	Paragraph Comprehension	Mathematics Knowledge
2 days before the test	**Study Time:** 1 hour ❑ **Word Problems:** Chapter 5; **Whole Numbers and Decimals:** Chapter 6; **Fractions:** Chapter 7 ❑ Rework any practice questions you missed earlier, with focus on your target sections.	**Study Time:** 1 hour ❑ **Building Word Power:** Chapter 8 ❑ Review flash cards for prefixes, roots, and suffixes. ❑ Review flash cards for synonym clusters. ❑ **Testing Your Vocabulary:** Chapter 9 ❑ Re-study *precocious* through *whimsical* in Section C.	**Study Time:** 45 minutes ❑ **Improving Your Reading Skills:** Chapter 10 and **Answering the Reading Questions:** Chapter 11 ❑ Choose any interesting article from the newspaper or online and read it carefully. ❑ If either of these is a targeted chapter, write a summary of what you learned from reading the article.	**Study Time:** 1 hour ❑ Focus on your target areas. ❑ Reread applicable sections. ❑ Rework any practice questions you missed earlier, with focus on your target areas.
1 day before the test	❑ Relax. . . . You're well prepared for the test. ❑ Have confidence in your ability to do well.			
The day of the test	**Reminders:** ❑ Have a good breakfast. ❑ Bring these items with you to the test: ❑ Photo ID ❑ A watch ❑ Try to go outside for a few minutes and walk around before the test. ❑ ***Most important:*** Stay calm and confident during the test. Take deep slow breaths if you feel at all nervous. You can do it!			

Chapter 3

One-Week Cram Plan

One-Week Cram Plan			
	Arithmetic Reasoning	**Word Knowledge**	**Paragraph Comprehension**	**Mathematics Knowledge**
7 days before the test	**Study Time:** 2½ hours ❑ Take the **Diagnostic Test** and review the answer explanations. ❑ Based on your errors on the Diagnostic Test, identify difficult topics and their corresponding chapters. These chapters are your targeted areas.			

6 days before the tests	**Study Time:** 2 hours
	 ❑ **Word Problems:** Chapter 5
	   ❑ Read sections A–G.
	   ❑ Do the practice questions in each section.
		Study Time: 2–3 hours
		 ❑ **Building Word Power:** Chapter 8
		   ❑ Read sections A–B.
		   ❑ Review prefixes, roots, and suffixes.
		   ❑ Make flash cards for synonym clusters and study them.
		   ❑ Do half the practice questions at the end of the chapter. If this is a targeted chapter, do all the practice questions.
		 ❑ **Testing Your Vocabulary:** Chapter 9
		   ❑ Study *aberration* through *heed* in Section C.
			Study Time: 1½–2 hours
			 ❑ **Improving Your Reading Skills:** Chapter 10
			   ❑ Read sections A–B.
			   ❑ Do all the example questions in each section.
			   ❑ Do half the practice questions at the end of the chapter. If this is a targeted chapter, do all the practice questions.
				Study Time: 2½ hours
				 ❑ **Algebra:** Chapter 12
				   ❑ Read sections A–K.
				   ❑ Do the practice questions in each section.

5 days before the test	**Study Time:** 2½ hours
	 ❑ **Whole Numbers and Decimals:** Chapter 6
	   ❑ Read sections A–E.
	   ❑ Do the practice questions in each section.
		Study Time: 2½ hours
		 ❑ **Testing Your Vocabulary:** Chapter 9
		   ❑ Read sections A–B.
		   ❑ Do half the practice questions in these sections.
		   ❑ If this is a targeted chapter, do all the practice questions in these sections.
		   ❑ Study *heinous* through *preclude* in Section C.
			Study Time: 1½–2 hours
			 ❑ **Answering the Reading Questions:** Chapter 11
			   ❑ Read sections A–B.
			   ❑ Do all the example questions in each section.
			   ❑ Do half the practice questions at the end of the chapter. If this is a targeted chapter, read two news articles in a newspaper or online.
				Study Time: 2½ hours
				 ❑ **Geometry:** Chapter 13
				   ❑ Read sections A–I.
				   ❑ Do the practice questions in each section.

continued

9

	Arithmetic Reasoning	Word Knowledge	Paragraph Comprehension	Mathematics Knowledge

4 days before the test	**Study Time:** 2 hours
	❑ **Fractions:** Chapter 7
	  ❑ Read sections A–F.
	  ❑ Do the practice questions in each section.
		Study Time: 2½ hours
		❑ **Testing Your Vocabulary:** Chapter 9
		  ❑ Do half the practice questions in Section C.
		  ❑ If this is a targeted chapter, do all the practice questions in Section C.
		  ❑ Study *precocious* through *whimsical* in Section C.
			Study Time: 2½ hours
			❑ **Improving Your Reading Skills:** Chapter 10
			  ❑ Review sections A–B.
			  ❑ Do any practice questions at the end of the chapter that you haven't yet completed.
			  ❑ If this is a targeted chapter, read one science article in a newspaper or online.
				Study Time: 2½ hours
				❑ **Trigonometry:** Chapter 14
				  ❑ Read sections A–C.
				  ❑ Do the practice questions in each section.
				❑ **Probability and Statistics:** Chapter 15
				  ❑ Read sections A–C.
				  ❑ Do the practice questions in each section.

3 days before the test	**Study Time:** 2½ hours ❑ Take the **Practice Test** and review the answer explanations. ❑ Based on your errors on the Practice Test, identify difficult topics and their corresponding chapters. These chapters are your targeted areas for further review.			

2 days before the test	**Study Time:** 1½ hours
	❑ **Word Problems:** Chapter 5; **Whole Numbers and Decimals:** Chapter 6; **Fractions:** Chapter 7
	  ❑ Reread your target sections.
	  ❑ Rework any practice questions you missed earlier.
		Study Time: 2½ hours
		❑ **Building Word Power:** Chapter 8
		  ❑ Review prefixes, roots, and suffixes flash cards.
		  ❑ Review synonym cluster flash cards.
		❑ **Testing Your Vocabulary:** Chapter 9
		  ❑ Review all the words in Section C.
			Study Time: 1½ hours
			❑ **Answering the Reading Questions:** Chapter 11
			  ❑ Review sections A–B.
			  ❑ Do any practice questions at the end of the chapter that you haven't yet completed.
				Study Time: 1½ hours
				❑ **Algebra:** Chapter 12; **Geometry:** Chapter 13; **Trigonometry:** Chapter 14; **Probability and Statistics:** Chapter 15
				  ❑ Reread your target sections.
				  ❑ Rework any practice questions you missed earlier.

1 day before the test	❑ Relax…. You're well prepared for the test. ❑ Have confidence in your ability to do well.			

The day of the test	**Reminders:**
	❑ Have a good breakfast.
	❑ Bring these items with you to the test:
	  ❑ Photo ID
	  ❑ A watch
	❑ Try to go outside for a few minutes and walk around before the test.
	❑ *Most important:* Stay calm and confident during the test. Take deep slow breaths if you feel at all nervous. You can do it!			

Chapter 4

Diagnostic Test

You'll need 1 hour and 24 minutes to complete the Diagnostic Test. The AFQT Diagnostic Test consists of four sections:

Section Number	Section	Number of Questions	Time
1	Arithmetic Reasoning	30	36 minutes
2	Word Knowledge	35	11 minutes
3	Paragraph Comprehension	15	13 minutes
4	Mathematics Knowledge	25	24 minutes

Section 1: Arithmetic Reasoning

Time: 36 Minutes

30 Questions

Directions: These questions can be answered using basic arithmetic. No calculators are permitted. Choose the best answer for each question from the four choices presented.

1. The local paper sold 400 classified ads at $7.50 each. How much was received from the sale of all these ads?

   A. $30
   B. $300
   C. $330
   D. $3,000

2. If 48 pounds of popcorn are packed into bags, each holding $\frac{3}{4}$ of a pound, how many bags will be needed?

   A. 12
   B. 16
   C. 36
   D. 64

3. If the speed of sound is slightly more than 900 ft./sec., how fast would you be traveling if you reached Mach 4, or four times the speed of sound?

   A. 225 ft./sec.
   B. 360 ft./sec.
   C. 3,600 ft./sec.
   D. 36,000 ft./sec.

4. In last week's primary election, the incumbent received 15,412 votes and the challenger received 9,962 votes. By how many votes did the incumbent win?

   A. 545
   B. 5,450
   C. 6,550
   D. 25,374

5. A recipe for three dozen cookies calls for two eggs. If you have a dozen eggs, how many cookies can you make?

   A. 18 cookies
   B. 36 cookies
   C. 216 cookies
   D. 432 cookies

6. Tulip bulbs are planted in three rows with eight bulbs in each row. If bulbs cost four for $3, how much will this planting cost?

   A. $6
   B. $12
   C. $18
   D. $36

7. The washers at Phil's Laundromat cost $1.50 per wash load, and the dryers give 6 minutes of time for 25¢. Phil generally runs one load of colored clothes and one of whites, but he finds he can put both loads into one dryer if he runs it for at least 45 minutes. If Phil picks up a roll of $10 worth of quarters before heading to the Laundromat, how much money will he have left when the laundry is done?

   A. $5
   B. $6.50
   C. $6.75
   D. $8.25

8. During contract negotiations, $\frac{7}{8}$ of the union members voted on a new contract proposal. Of those voting, $\frac{2}{3}$ voted to approve the contract. If there are 3,600 members in the union, how many voted to approve?

   A. 1,200
   B. 1,500
   C. 2,100
   D. 2,400

9. Mrs. Zhang drives 60 miles at a constant speed. If the trip takes 72 minutes, what is her speed in miles per hour?

   A. 40
   B. 50
   C. 60
   D. 70

10. In a recent survey, voters in a town were asked what political party they voted for most often. Six hundred people indicated they voted Republican. If this represents about three-fifths of the town's voters, how many voters are there in the town?

   A. 200
   B. 360
   C. 1,000
   D. 1,800

11. If a charter airline flies planes, each of which holds 220 people, how many planes will it need for a charter group of 1,100 passengers?

   A. 3
   B. 4
   C. 5
   D. 6

12. If one package of frozen lasagna serves 4 people, how many packages will be needed to serve 20 people?

   A. 5
   B. 10
   C. 20
   D. 80

13. If your heart beats 65 times a minute, how many times does it beat in an hour?

    A. 108
    B. 125
    C. 3,900
    D. 23,400

14. A car that sells for $20,000 loses 17 percent of its value in the first year. What is the value of the car after 1 year?

    A. $3,000
    B. $3,400
    C. $16,600
    D. $17,000

15. What is the cost of carpeting a room that measures 12 feet by 18 feet, if carpet costs $15 per square yard?

    A. $3,240
    B. $1,080
    C. $360
    D. $120

16. A recipe calls for $4\frac{2}{3}$ cups of flour. If you have $3\frac{1}{2}$ cups, how much more flour do you need?

    A. $1\frac{1}{2}$ cups

    B. $1\frac{1}{3}$ cups

    C. $1\frac{1}{6}$ cups

    D. $\frac{1}{6}$ cup

17. If Mary earns $12.30 per hour, how much will she earn by working a 40-hour week?

    A. $307.50
    B. $375
    C. $482
    D. $492

18. Hector's uncle gave him a baseball-card collection from the 1950s. Half of the cards were from the Brooklyn Dodgers, and one-fourth were from the New York Giants. The rest were evenly divided among the Philadelphia Athletics, the St. Louis Browns, and the Washington Senators. If there were 15 cards from the Browns, how many Dodgers cards did Hector's uncle give him?

    A. 15
    B. 45
    C. 60
    D. 90

19. A DVD player was marked at a reduced price that was 40 percent off the original list price. With a coupon for a special sale, you could receive an additional 10 percent off the reduced price. If the original list price of the DVD player before any markdowns was $150, what would you actually pay?

    A. $54
    B. $75
    C. $81
    D. $90

20. Glendally finds a $40 sweater on sale for 15 percent off, but she must pay 5 percent sales tax. If she hands the cashier $50, how much change will she receive?

    A. $18
    B. $16
    C. $14.30
    D. $2

21. The city-council bylaws require that 60 percent of the residents vote in favor of a proposal before it can become part of the city's constitution. An initiative to repeal the sales tax did not pass in the last election. If there are 4,000 residents in the city and everyone voted, what is the minimum number that could have voted against the proposal?

    A. 1,333
    B. 1,601
    C. 2,401
    D. 2,666

22. Five workers were observed packing boxes. Two of them could pack four boxes per minute, one could pack five boxes per minute, and the others could pack three boxes per minute. What is the average number of boxes packed per minute?

   A. 4
   B. 3.8
   C. 3.2
   D. 2.4

23. If 360 students can be transported on eight school buses, how many students can be transported on three buses?

   A. 45
   B. 135
   C. 960
   D. 1,080

24. Women make up $\frac{2}{3}$ of the workforce at a particular company. If there are 67 men in the company workforce, how many people does the company employ?

   A. 201
   B. 100
   C. 45
   D. 33

25. Jamal bought a CD for $9 and a DVD for $23. If he hands the cashier two $20 bills, how much change will he get back?

   A. $4
   B. $6
   C. $8
   D. $17

26. A refrigerator sells for $520, but the customer must pay 6 percent sales tax and a $50 delivery and installation fee. What is the total cost of the refrigerator?

   A. $81.20
   B. $601.20
   C. $604.20
   D. $882

27. If you invest $8,000 at 4 percent simple interest per year, how much will your total investment be worth after 5 years?

   A. $8,320
   B. $9,600
   C. $11,200
   D. $41,600

28. Charles has determined that his ideal workout schedule includes aerobics and weight training in a ratio of 3:5. If Charles has 2 hours per day to devote to working out, how many minutes should he spend on weight training?

   A. 15
   B. 24
   C. 45
   D. 75

29. A recipe calls for $\frac{1}{2}$ cup shortening, 1 cup brown sugar, 2 eggs, $\frac{1}{3}$ cup milk, and $2\frac{3}{4}$ cups oatmeal. If the recipe is recalculated to use a dozen eggs, how much oatmeal will be needed?

   A. $16\frac{1}{2}$ cups
   B. $12\frac{3}{4}$ cups
   C. 6 cups
   D. 3 cups

30. In a certain town, the ratio of Democrats to Republicans is 5:4. If there are 18,000 people in the town, how many are Democrats?

   A. 4,500
   B. 2,000
   C. 5,000
   D. 10,000

IF YOU FINISH BEFORE TIME IS CALLED, CHECK YOUR WORK ON THIS SECTION ONLY. DO NOT WORK ON ANY OTHER SECTION IN THE TEST.

STOP

Section 2: Word Knowledge

Time: 11 Minutes

35 Questions

Directions: Select the word or phrase that is nearest in meaning to the italicized word.

1. *Trivial* most nearly means
   - **A.** astonishing
   - **B.** insignificant
   - **C.** irrevocable
   - **D.** objective

2. *Irksome* most nearly means
   - **A.** careless
   - **B.** furious
   - **C.** varied
   - **D.** annoying

3. The police officer's attempt to rescue the toddler from the roof was *laudable*.
   - **A.** punitive
   - **B.** banal
   - **C.** ascetic
   - **D.** admirable

4. In the face of danger, the major remained *serene*.
   - **A.** energetic
   - **B.** calm
   - **C.** authoritative
   - **D.** frenzied

5. *Triumph* most nearly means
   - **A.** victory
   - **B.** endeavor
   - **C.** improvement
   - **D.** admiration

6. The *conflagration* could be seen from miles away.
   - **A.** incipient conflict
   - **B.** fortified compound
   - **C.** high-level meeting
   - **D.** large fire

7. A synonym for *spurious* is
   - **A.** amazed
   - **B.** spontaneous
   - **C.** false
   - **D.** speedy

8. *Incessant* most nearly means
   - **A.** without merit
   - **B.** unskillful
   - **C.** incapable of change
   - **D.** without stopping

9. A synonym for *gargantuan* is
   - **A.** huge
   - **B.** tough
   - **C.** generous
   - **D.** impolite

10. As they examined the project, all the observers were *incredulous*.
    - **A.** embarrassed
    - **B.** disbelieving
    - **C.** ignorant
    - **D.** silent

11. The candidate's speech was *impassioned.*

   A. fervent
   B. unemotional
   C. painful
   D. bland

12. The last day of vacation left everyone feeling *melancholy.*

   A. sad
   B. lazy
   C. rejuvenated
   D. forgetful

13. *Vacillate* most nearly means

   A. commemorate
   B. estimate
   C. waver
   D. conclude

14. *Hedonist* most nearly means

   A. underachiever
   B. pleasure-seeker
   C. time-waster
   D. go-getter

15. *Torpid* most nearly means

   A. fast
   B. slow
   C. dangerous
   D. plentiful

16. A synonym for *extrinsic* is

   A. external
   B. excited
   C. excellent
   D. exalted

17. Once she had seen the results of the experiment, the doctor was no longer *dubious.*

   A. certain
   B. complicit
   C. doubtful
   D. arrogant

18. Walking on a sprained ankle will *exacerbate* the injury.

   A. heal
   B. pinpoint
   C. stabilize
   D. worsen

19. *Lucrative* most nearly means

   A. timid
   B. progressive
   C. thrifty
   D. profitable

20. *Malignant* most nearly means

   A. hateful
   B. unsophisticated
   C. thoughtful
   D. elementary

21. We were surprised to find that our plumber was *inept.*

   A. skillful
   B. guilty
   C. incompetent
   D. unrealistic

22. *Benevolent* most nearly means

   A. kindly
   B. harmful
   C. complete
   D. brave

23. A synonym for *bellicose* is

   A. excitable
   B. combative
   C. futile
   D. lovely

24. The wise man was *revered* by the members of the tribe.

   A. respected
   B. secluded
   C. selected
   D. reprimanded

25. Most of the viewers found the movie *enigmatic.*

    A. endless
    B. puzzling
    C. disappointing
    D. frightening

26. Some of the test-takers were *apprehensive* about the exam.

    A. worried
    B. confident
    C. eager
    D. vicious

27. *Succinct* most nearly means

    A. trapped
    B. impersonal
    C. irrelevant
    D. concise

28. *Groundbreaking* most nearly means

    A. prophetic
    B. monotonous
    C. revolutionary
    D. strenuous

29. The captain was *diligent* in his efforts.

    A. negligent
    B. hard-working
    C. slow-moving
    D. glorious

30. The reviewers were surprised to find that the biography was *terse.*

    A. brief
    B. biased
    C. bogus
    D. brilliant

31. Many people find my father to be *laconic.*

    A. extremely long-winded
    B. not talkative
    C. physically overpowering
    D. genuinely compassionate

32. A synonym for *diffident* is

    A. different
    B. sentimental
    C. hypocritical
    D. shy

33. *Awe* most nearly means

    A. anxiety
    B. ease
    C. wonder
    D. humor

34. *Meticulous* most nearly means

    A. careful
    B. friendly
    C. sloppy
    D. extraordinary

35. *Hypothesis* most nearly means

    A. tendency
    B. illness
    C. theory
    D. technique

IF YOU FINISH BEFORE TIME IS CALLED, CHECK YOUR WORK ON THIS SECTION ONLY. DO NOT WORK ON ANY OTHER SECTION IN THE TEST.

Section 3: Paragraph Comprehension

Time: 13 Minutes

15 Questions

Directions: Read each passage below and answer the questions based on what is stated in or implied by the information in the passage.

Question 1 is based on the following passage.

The beautiful spotted leopard is the smallest of the "big cats" and one of the hardest to find in the wild. It is primarily nocturnal, but sometimes it can be seen hunting during twilight hours or on overcast days. It is often confused with its smaller cousin, the cheetah; however, the two animals have different patterns of spots.

1. In the passage, the leopard and the cheetah are contrasted in their
   A. mating habits
   B. preferred prey
   C. appearance
   D. habitat

Question 2 is based on the following passage.

Every year, millions of fish—salmon, steelhead trout, shad, alewives, and sturgeon, among others—migrate to their spawning and rearing habitats to reproduce. Some fish need to swim thousands of miles through oceans and rivers to reach these freshwater destinations. They are often blocked from completing their journey by human-made barriers, such as dams and culverts. When fish can't reach their habitat, they can't reproduce and maintain or grow their populations. Fish passage is important for the protection and restoration of migrating fish and their habitats

2. According to the passage, a major obstacle many fish face in trying to reach spawning grounds is

   A. the enormous distances they must swim to reach spawning habitats
   B. man-made constructions that function as blockades to prevent completion of the spawning journeys
   C. the loss of hospitable habitats due to ongoing human encroachment
   D. the reproductive faculties of the fish, which are damaged by environmental pollutants

Question 3 is based on the following passage.

A tornado is a violently rotating column of air that extends from a thunderstorm to the ground and is often—although not always—visible as a funnel cloud. Lightning and hail are common in thunderstorms that produce tornadoes. Tornadoes cause extensive damage to structure and disrupt transportation, power, water, gas, communications, and other services in their direct path and in neighboring areas. Related thunderstorms can cause heavy rains, flash flooding, and hail. About 1,200 tornadoes hit the United States every year, and every state is at risk. Most tornadoes in the United States occur east of the Rocky Mountains, with concentrations in the central and southern plains, the Gulf Coast, and Florida.

3. Based on the information in the passage, which of the following is true?

    A.   A tornado will never occur in New Jersey.

    B.   Tornadoes occur with the greatest frequency west of the Rocky Mountains.

    C.   About 1,200 tornadoes hit the United States every month.

    D.   Tornadoes are often accompanied by flash flooding and hail.

Question 4 is based on the following passage.

The tuxedo-clad flightless penguins, always fascinating to human beings, have become pop-culture icons. No fewer than five films in the past five years have featured the birds. It is not hard to understand the popularity of penguins: they are "well dressed," playful, and unafraid of people. Indeed, these striking birds with their distinct waddle have become synonymous with winter fun.

4. The best title for this passage is

    A.   The Lifestyle of the Penguins

    B.   Trendy and Playful Penguins

    C.   Natural Symbols of Winter

    D.   Popular Movies about Birds

Question 5 is based on the following passage.

We sat in the dimly lighted room and gazed out the foggy windows. It was the fourth straight day of rain, and the puddles on the lawn were beginning to look like lakes. Wearily, we looked at each other and sighed. This was supposed to have been a fun-filled week at the cabin, but so far, all we had done was watch old movies and play Monopoly.

5. The tone of this passage is best described as

    A.   optimistic

    B.   furious

    C.   gloomy

    D.   frantic

Questions 6 and 7 are based on the following passage.

Winds, which are caused by the uneven heating of the earth's atmosphere by the sun, can be harnessed to provide energy. We can use the available raw power of wind to propel kites or sailboats, but wind turbines can economically convert the raw energy into mechanical power. Mechanical power can be used to pump water or grind wheat. With the use of a generator, mechanical energy can be converted into electricity.

6. According to the passage, raw wind power

    A. is a result of the invariable heating of the atmosphere by the sun
    B. causes electrical energy to be converted into mechanical energy
    C. is a form of solar power that can be utilized as a source of electricity
    D. has been too expensive to be a viable source of energy

7. With which of the following statements would the author most likely agree?

    A. The United States is underutilizing an inexpensive form of energy.
    B. Wind power is a virtually limitless source of energy.
    C. Mechanical generators are too costly to be of value in the search for alternative energy sources.
    D. All fossil fuels will eventually be replaced by solar energy.

Questions 8 and 9 are based on the following passage.

In the early period of human history, when voyages and travels were not undertaken for amusement or instruction or for political or commercial motives, the discovery of adjacent countries was chiefly brought about by war. The wars of the Egyptians with the Scythians, mentioned in the pages of early history, must have opened faint sources of information concerning the neighboring tribes. Under the Grecian empire of Alexander and his successors, the progress of discovery by war is first marked on the page of history, and science began to accompany the banners of victory.

8. The main idea of this passage is

    A. The search for scientific information gave rise to the desire to travel.
    B. The wealth of the western world was mostly derived from looting conquered regions.
    C. The systematic conquest of weaker tribes united the ancient world.
    D. An increase in knowledge was a corollary of warfare.

9. The author suggests that science and warfare are

    A. equally important motivations for nations to undertake exploration
    B. mutually exclusive
    C. painful reminders of mankind's desire to destroy that which is unfamiliar
    D. related in that scientific knowledge is increased by the contact that comes along with conquest

Question 10 is based on the following passage.

On every worker's desk in every worker's cubicle in every major corporation in the United States, there sits a computer. To many of us, it is inconceivable that having a computer was once considered a luxury. Now we cannot imagine doing business without data programs, e-mails, video conferencing, and the Internet. Along with this boon in technology, however, has arisen a rather surprising issue: privacy in the workplace. With easy access to the Internet, many workers cannot resist the temptation to send personal e-mails, do some Internet browsing, and maybe even shop a bit on company time. Concerned by this use of company technology and waste of employee time, corporations are fighting back by installing monitoring devices. In 1986, Congress passed the Electronic Communications Privacy Act, which gave employers the right to monitor electronic communications in the workplace. Now companies can be sure all the "work" employees are doing on their computers is truly work related.

10. By repeating the word *every* in the first sentence, the author suggests that

  A. Corporations are relying too heavily on technology and ignoring the value of human-to-human contact.
  B. Computers have become visible and tangible symbols of the role of technology in modern businesses.
  C. Employers are correct in their assumption that too much time is being wasted by employees who use computers for personal affairs.
  D. The United States is unique in its reliance on computers to handle financial transactions.

Question 11 is based on the following passage.

Amory Blaine inherited from his mother every trait, except the stray inexpressible few, that made him worth while. His father, an ineffectual, inarticulate man with a taste for Byron and a habit of drowsing over the Encyclopedia Britannica, grew wealthy at thirty through the death of two elder brothers, successful Chicago brokers, and in the first flush of feeling that the world was his, went to Bar Harbor and met Beatrice O'Hara. In consequence, Stephen Blaine handed down to posterity his height of just under six feet and his tendency to waver at crucial moments, these two abstractions appearing in his son Amory.

11. Which of the following can be inferred from the passage?

  A. Amory Blaine had a tendency to be meek when in the company of wealthy relatives.
  B. Beatrice O'Hara was primarily attracted to Stephen Blaine for his height and the ambition that led him to earn great wealth.
  C. In his tendency towards indecisiveness, Amory Blaine was more like his father than like his mother.
  D. Stephen Blaine lived his whole life with the confidence that one day greatness would be his.

Question 12 is based on the following passage.

In 1913, physicist Niels Bohr introduced his model of the structure of the atom, a model that has lasted until the present day. Bohr used a structure similar to that of the solar system to depict the atom. He envisioned a central nucleus surrounded by electrons traveling in circular orbits. Because his model is so simple and easy to visualize, it is still taught to students as an introduction to atomic structure.

12. According to the passage, which of the following is true?

   A. Scientists are often forced to reject oversimplified models that don't hold up over time.
   B. The central electron in Bohr's model is surrounded by rotating protons.
   C. Bohr's model of the solar system is popular today as a way to help student visualize the planetary orbits.
   D. By comparing a new concept to a familiar concept, students can comprehend more easily.

Question 13 is based on the following passage.

In many cultures, the elephant is a symbol of wisdom and is famed for its long memory. These huge creatures, the largest land animals now living, can live for 50 to 70 years. Full-grown elephants have no predators other than human poachers. With new anti-poaching laws in effect in many African countries, their previously dwindling numbers have increased in recent years. In fact, some African nations are now dealing with an unanticipated overpopulation of these once endangered animals.

13. According to the passage, which of the following is true?

   A. Serious problems with poachers have led to the current crises in dwindling elephant populations.
   B. The oldest documented elephant is 65 years old.
   C. Other than human beings, the only predators that elephants face are lions.
   D. Some African countries face a new and unexpected problem: too many elephants.

Question 14 is based on the following passage.

Yawning, the wide opening of the mouth with a deep inhalation of air and a smaller exhalation, is a sign of more than just sleepiness. Sleep researchers have found that people yawn for a variety of reasons. Yawning can be a sign of boredom or even stress. In some cases, yawning is contagious. In close quarters, one person who yawns can set off a whole epidemic of yawns.

14. According to the passage, which of the following statements is true?

   A. Yawning is the definitive sign of tiredness.
   B. All people yawn when they are sleep-deprived.
   C. People will yawn most frequently right before they fall asleep.
   D. Sleepiness is not the only reason people yawn.

Question 15 is based on the following passage.

The president of the United States is the head of the executive branch of the government and commander-in-chief of the armed forces. To be elected president, a person must be a natural-born citizen of the United States, be at least 35 years old, and have been a permanent resident of the United States for at least 14 years. The president can serve for only two four-year terms of office.

15. According to the passage, which of the following statements is true?

    A. A man born in England who has lived in the United States for 20 years is eligible to become president.

    B. A 37-year-old woman who was born in Chicago, moved to France for 5 years, and has lived in Omaha, Nebraska, for 15 years, can be elected president.

    C. A 75-year-old man who was born in Houston, Texas, and has lived his whole life there is not eligible to be president.

    D. A 50-year-old woman who has lived her entire life in California can be elected president and serve for 9 years.

IF YOU FINISH BEFORE TIME IS CALLED, CHECK YOUR WORK ON THIS SECTION ONLY. DO NOT WORK ON ANY OTHER SECTION IN THE TEST.

Section 4: Mathematics Knowledge

Time: 24 Minutes

25 Questions

Directions: Each of the following questions has four possible answer choices. Choose the best answer for each question. No calculators are permitted.

1. The area of a rectangle 25 feet wide and 40 feet long is

   A. 100 ft.^{2}
   B. 130 ft.^{2}
   C. 1,000 ft.^{2}
   D. 1,300 ft.^{2}

2. The marching band finds that if they organize into rows with five members in each row, there is one person left over. If they form rows of six people, there is still one person left over. Which of these could be the number of band members?

   A. 131
   B. 141
   C. 151
   D. 161

3. If triangle *RST* and trapezoid *WXYZ* are cut off the figure shown, what polygon is left?

   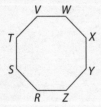

   A. trapezoid
   B. rectangle
   C. pentagon
   D. hexagon

4. Jorge wants to use boards to enclose a triangular section of land as a flower garden. He has chosen boards for two of the sides of the triangle; one is 3 feet long and the other is 5 feet long. He has other boards of different lengths to choose from for the third side. Which length board could *not* make the third side of the triangle?

   A. 2 feet
   B. 3 feet
   C. 5 feet
   D. 7 feet

5. A teacher needs to give each of her students one sheet each of red and of yellow paper for an art project. The red paper comes in packs of 12 sheets, and the yellow paper comes in packs of 15 sheets. The teacher buys the minimum number of packs of each paper that will guarantee equal amounts of each color. How many students can do the project?

   A. 27
   B. 30
   C. 54
   D. 60

6. Alberto saves $12 each week. Dahlia has already saved $270, and each week she spends $15 of that savings. When they both have the same amount in savings, they combine their money. What is the combined amount?

   A. $120
   B. $216
   C. $240
   D. $432

7. If the cost of manufacturing storage containers is $580 plus 18¢ per container, what is the cost of manufacturing 5,000 containers?

   A. $900
   B. $1,480
   C. $29,000
   D. $90,580

8. At the moment that a 35-foot maple tree casts a shadow 7 feet long, how long is the shadow of a 6-foot man, in inches?

   A. 1.2 inches
   B. 5.83 inches
   C. 14.4 inches
   D. 30 inches

9. A worker assembling toy cars must place four wheels on each car body. If there are 432 car bodies and 1,584 wheels available, how many complete toy cars can be assembled?

   A. 396
   B. 432
   C. 1,152
   D. 1,584

10. How many cubic feet of packing foam will fit in a shipping carton 2 feet long, 3 feet wide, and 16 inches high?

    A. 8 ft.^{3}
    B. 9 ft.^{3}
    C. 96 ft.^{3}
    D. 1,152 ft.^{3}

11. If the radius of a circle is doubled, by what percent does the area increase?

    A. 400
    B. 300
    C. 200
    D. 100

12. A bag contains balls and blocks in various colors, and the colors are equally distributed. If $\frac{3}{4}$ of the objects in the bag are balls and $\frac{2}{5}$ of the objects are red, what fraction of the objects in the bag would you expect to be red balls?

    A. $\frac{3}{10}$
    B. $\frac{7}{20}$
    C. $\frac{8}{15}$
    D. $\frac{23}{20}$

13. If 8,974 and 4,905 are rounded to the nearest hundred and then added, what is the sum?

    A. 13,800
    B. 13,879
    C. 13,900
    D. 14,000

14. Temperatures in degrees Celsius can be converted to degrees Fahrenheit by the formula $F = \frac{9}{5}C + 32$. Find the Fahrenheit equivalent of a temperature of 20°C.

    A. 68°F
    B. 93.6°F
    C. 42.4°F
    D. $-6\frac{2}{3}$°F

15. Express the sentence "Six more than three times a number, x, is 27" as an equation.

    A. $6 > 3x + 27$
    B. $3x + 6 = 27$
    C. $6x + 3 = 27$
    D. $x = 27 \cdot 3 + 6$

16. Jack and Matt shop for the same items at the same sale. Jack buys 3 shirts and 2 ties for $88.06. Matt buys 2 shirts and 3 ties for $82.44. What would it cost to buy 1 shirt and 1 tie?

    A. $34.10
    B. $39.72
    C. $71.20
    D. $170.50

17. What is the equation of a line with a slope of -3 that passes through the point $(7, -2)$?

    A. $3x + y = 19$
    B. $3x + y = 23$
    C. $-3x + y = 19$
    D. $3x - y = 21$

18. Which of the following is equal to 3^4?

    A. 12
    B. 27
    C. 64
    D. 81

19. $4(30 - 18) - 4 \times 30 - 18 =$

    A. -90
    B. 0
    C. -96
    D. 528

20. The temperature was recorded each morning at 6 o'clock for 5 consecutive days. The temperatures recorded were $42°$, $37°$, $35°$, $41°$, and $45°$. What was the average temperature for this 5-day period?

    A. $33°$
    B. $35°$
    C. $38°$
    D. $40°$

21. Find the value of $\dfrac{a + b^2}{a^2 - b}$ if $a = 8$ and $b = 3$.

    A. $\dfrac{121}{61}$
    B. $\dfrac{17}{61}$
    C. $\dfrac{3}{8}$
    D. $\dfrac{14}{61}$

22. $(x + y)^2$ is equivalent to all the following except

    A. $x^2 + y^2$
    B. $x^2 + 2xy + y^2$
    C. $x^2 + xy + yx + y^2$
    D. $(x + y)(x + y)$

23. One liter of a 50 percent saline solution is mixed with 1 liter of pure water. What is the concentration of the resulting solution?

    A. 25 percent
    B. 33 percent
    C. 50 percent
    D. 75 percent

24. If $2x - 7 = 17$ then $x =$

    A. 5
    B. 10
    C. 12
    D. 15.5

25. $\dfrac{x^2 - 5x + 6}{x - 2} =$

    A. $\dfrac{x^2 + 1}{-2}$
    B. $x - 3$
    C. $-4x - 3$
    D. $x^2 - \dfrac{1}{2}$

IF YOU FINISH BEFORE TIME IS CALLED, CHECK YOUR WORK ON THIS SECTION ONLY. DO NOT WORK ON ANY OTHER SECTION IN THE TEST.

Answer Key

Section 1: Arithmetic Reasoning

1. D	7. A	13. C	19. C	25. C
2. D	8. C	14. C	20. C	26. B
3. C	9. B	15. C	21. B	27. B
4. B	10. C	16. C	22. B	28. D
5. C	11. C	17. D	23. B	29. A
6. C	12. A	18. D	24. A	30. D

Section 2: Word Knowledge

1. B	8. D	15. B	22. A	29. B
2. D	9. A	16. A	23. B	30. A
3. D	10. B	17. C	24. A	31. B
4. B	11. A	18. D	25. B	32. D
5. A	12. A	19. D	26. A	33. C
6. D	13. C	20. A	27. D	34. A
7. C	14. B	21. C	28. C	35. C

Section 3: Paragraph Comprehension

1. C	4. B	7. B	10. B	13. D
2. B	5. C	8. D	11. C	14. D
3. D	6. C	9. D	12. D	15. B

Section 4: Mathematics Knowledge

1. C	6. C	11. B	16. A	21. B
2. C	7. B	12. A	17. A	22. A
3. C	8. C	13. C	18. D	23. A
4. A	9. A	14. A	19. A	24. C
5. D	10. A	15. B	20. D	25. B

Answer Explanations

Section 1: Arithmetic Reasoning

1. **D.** Multiply the price of an ad by the number of ads sold: $400 \times \$7.50 = \$3,000$. *(See Chapter 6, Section D.)*

2. **D.** Divide the amount of popcorn by the size of the bag to find the number of bags needed: $48 \div \dfrac{3}{4} = \dfrac{\overset{16}{\cancel{48}}}{1} \times \dfrac{4}{\cancel{3}} = 64$. You can eliminate answer choices using estimation: If the bags held 1 pound, 48 bags would be needed. Smaller bags mean more than 48 bags are needed. *(See Chapter 7, Section E.)*

3. **C.** Four times the speed of sound is four times 900 ft./sec.: $900 \times 4 = 3,600$ ft./sec. *(See Chapter 6, Section D.)*

4. **B.** Subtract to find the margin of victory: $15,412 - 9,962 = 5,450$ votes. *(See Chapter 6, Section C.)*

5. **C.** There are 12 cookies in a dozen, so 3 dozen = 36 cookies. A dozen eggs ÷ 2 eggs = $12 \div 2 = 6$ batches. 36 cookies per batch × 6 batches = 216 cookies. *(See Chapter 6, Sections D and E; Chapter 7, Section F.)*

6. **C.** 3 rows × 8 bulbs per row = 24 bulbs. 24 bulbs ÷ 4 bulbs for \$3 = 6 groups of bulbs. $6 \times \$3 = \$18$. *(See Chapter 7, Section F.)*

7. **A.** 2 washer loads × \$1.50 = \$3 to do the wash. 45 minutes needed for the dryer ÷ 6 minutes for each quarter = 7.5 quarters, which rounds up to 8 quarters. $8 \times 25 = \$2$ for the dryer. \$3 for the washers + \$2 for the dryer = \$5 to wash and dry. \$10 worth of quarters − \$5 to do the laundry = \$5 left. *(See Chapter 7, Section F.)*

8. **C.** $\dfrac{7}{\cancel{8}} \times \cancel{3,600}^{\,450} = 3,150$ of the union members voted. $\dfrac{2}{\cancel{3}} \times \cancel{3,150}^{\,1,050} = 2,100$ voted to approve the contract. *(See Chapter 7, Section D.)*

9. **B.** $\dfrac{\overset{5}{\cancel{60}} \text{ miles}}{\underset{6}{\cancel{72}} \text{ minutes}} \times \dfrac{\cancel{60}^{\,10} \text{ minutes}}{1 \text{ hour}} = 50$ miles per hour. *(See Chapter 7, Section D.)*

10. **C.** $600 \div \dfrac{3}{5} = \dfrac{\cancel{600}^{\,200}}{1} \times \dfrac{5}{\cancel{3}} = 1,000$ people in the town. *(See Chapter 7, Section E.)*

11. **C.** $\dfrac{1,10\cancel{0}}{22\cancel{0}} = \dfrac{110 \div 11}{22 \div 11} = \dfrac{10}{2} = 5$ planes. *(See Chapter 7, Sections A and E.)*

12. **A.** 20 people ÷ 4 people per package = 5 packages. *(See Chapter 6, Section E.)*

13. **C.** $\dfrac{65 \text{ beats}}{1 \text{ minute}} \times \dfrac{60 \text{ minutes}}{1 \text{ hour}} = \dfrac{3,900 \text{ beats}}{1 \text{ hour}}$. *(See Chapter 5, Section C; Chapter 6, Section D.)*

14. **C.** 17 percent = 0.17, so the part of the value lost in the first year is $\$20,000 \times 0.17 = \$3,400$. The value of the car after 1 year is $\$20,000 - \$3,400 = \$16,600$. *(See Chapter 5, Section E.)*

    Alternately, you could consider that if the car loses 17 percent of its value, it holds 83 percent of its value ($100 - 17 = 83$), and 83 percent of \$20,000 is $\$20,000 \times 0.83 = \$16,600$.

15. **C.** The dimensions of the room are given in feet, but carpeting is sold by the square *yard,* so you need to convert. There are 3 feet in a yard, so 12 feet are equal to 4 yards and 18 feet are equal to 6 yards. Multiplying 4 yards times 6 yards gives you 24 square yards. Multiply 24 square yards times $15 per square yard to get $360. (*See Chapter 5, Sections C and G.*)

Alternately, you could multiply 12 feet times 18 feet and then divide by 9 square feet per square yard to get the number of square yards, but many people forget there are 9 square feet in each square yard.

16. **C.** $4\dfrac{2}{3} - 3\dfrac{1}{2} = 4\dfrac{4}{6} - 3\dfrac{3}{6} = 1\dfrac{1}{6}$ cups of flour needed. (*See Chapter 7, Section C.*)

17. **D.** Multiply $12.30 per hour times 40 hours to get $492. (*See Chapter 6, Section D.*)

18. **D.** Half the cards were from the Brooklyn Dodgers, and one-fourth of the cards were from the New York Giants: $\dfrac{1}{2} + \dfrac{1}{4} = \dfrac{3}{4}$. That means that the remainder of the cards, $\dfrac{1}{4}$, were evenly divided among three teams. $\dfrac{1}{4} \div 3 = \dfrac{1}{4} \times \dfrac{1}{3} = \dfrac{1}{12}$ of the cards, or 15 cards, were from the Browns. If 15 is $\dfrac{1}{12}$ of the collection, there are $15 \times 12 = 180$ cards in the collection. Half were from the Dodgers and half of 180 is 90. (*See Chapter 7, Section F.*)

19. **C.** The original price is $150, and 40 percent of that is $150 \times 0.40 = $60. After the 40 percent discount, the price is $150 − $60 = $90. An additional 10 percent off the $90 price takes an additional $90 \times 0.10 = $9 off, making the final price $90 − $9 = $81. (*See Chapter 5, Section E.*)

20. **C.** 15 percent of $40 is $40 \times 0.15 = $6, so she'll pay $40 − $6 = $34 plus tax. Add 5 percent of $34 to find out what she'll pay: $34 + ($34 \times 0.05) = $34 + $1.70 = $35.70. If she hands the cashier $50, she'll receive $50 − $35.70 = $14.30 change. (*See Chapter 5, Sections D and E.*)

21. **B.** If there are 4,000 residents and it requires 60 percent of them to pass a proposal, it takes $4,000 \times 0.60 = 2,400$ votes to pass. If the proposal did not pass, it did not receive 2,400 votes, so it received at *most* 2,399 votes. That means there were at least $4,000 − 2,399 = 1,601$ votes against. (*See Chapter 6, Sections C and D.*)

22. **B.** $4 + 4 + 5 + 3 + 3 = 19$ boxes packed by the workers in 1 minute. $19 \div 5 = 3.8$ boxes per minute average. (*See Chapter 7, Section F.*)

23. **B.** If 360 students can be transported on eight school buses, there are $360 \div 8 = 45$ students on each bus. Therefore, three buses will hold $3 \times 45 = 135$ students. (*See Chapter 7, Section F.*)

24. **A.** If women make up $\dfrac{2}{3}$ of the workforce, men are $\dfrac{1}{3}$, so the 67 men times 3 will be the total number of employees: $3 \times 67 = 201$ employees. (*See Chapter 7, Section F.*)

25. **C.** Jamal's purchase totals $9 + $23 = $32. If he hands the cashier two $20 bills, he will receive $40 − $32 = $8 in change. (*See Chapter 6, Sections B and C.*)

26. **B.** The sales tax is $520 \times 0.06 = $31.20, so add $520 + $31.20 + $50 = $601.20. (*See Chapter 5, Section D.*)

27. **B.** To find the interest earned, multiply $8,000 \times 0.04 \times 5$ years $= $1,600 interest. Add this to the original investment and the value is $8,000 + $1,600 = $9,600. (*See Chapter 5, Section D.*)

28. **D.** Doing 3 minutes of aerobics for every 5 minutes of weight training means that he's spending 5 out of every 8 minutes, or $\frac{5}{8}$ of his time, weight training. Two hours is 120 minutes and $\frac{5}{_1\cancel{8}} \times \cancel{120}^{15} = 75$ minutes. (*See Chapter 5, Section C, and Chapter 7, Section D.*)

29. **A.** To change from two eggs to a dozen eggs, multiply everything in the recipe by 6: $6 \times 2\frac{3}{4} = {}^3\cancel{6} \times \frac{11}{\cancel{4}_2} = \frac{33}{2} = 16\frac{1}{2}$ cups of oatmeal. (*See Chapter 7, Section D.*)

30. **D.** If there are five Democrats for every four Republicans, there are five Democrats out of every nine residents. If $\frac{5}{9}$ of 18,000 people are Democrats, then $\frac{5}{_1\cancel{9}} \times \frac{\cancel{18,000}^{2,000}}{1} = 10,000$ Democrats. (*See Chapter 7, Section D.*)

Section 2: Word Knowledge

Note: Many words can be used as different parts of speech, depending on their function in a sentence. Because many of the words in this section are not used in a sentence, the part of speech given is the same as the parts of speech of the words in the answer choices.

1. **B.** *Trivial* (adjective) means unimportant or insignificant. (*See Chapter 9, Section A.*)

2. **D.** *Irksome* (adjective) means irritating or annoying. (*Chapter 9, Section A.*)

3. **D.** *Laudable* (adjective) means praiseworthy or admirable. (*See Chapter 9, Section B.*)

4. **B.** *Serene* (adjective) means calm or unbothered. (*See Chapter 9, Section B.*)

5. **A.** A *triumph* (noun) is a victory. (*See Chapter 9, Section A.*)

6. **D.** *Conflagration* (noun) means a great or large fire. (*See Chapter 9, Section B.*)

7. **C.** *Spurious* (adjective) means false. (*See Chapter 9, Section A.*)

8. **D.** *Incessant* (adjective) means without stopping or unrelenting. (*See Chapter 9, Section A.*)

9. **A.** *Gargantuan* (adjective) means huge. (*See Chapter 9, Section A.*)

10. **B.** *Incredulous* (adjective) means skeptical or disbelieving. (*See Chapter 8, Section B; Chapter 9, Section B.*)

11. **A.** *Impassioned* (adjective) means passionate or fervent. (*See Chapter 9, Section B.*)

12. **A.** *Melancholy* (adjective) means sad or depressed. (*See Chapter 9, Section B.*)

13. **C.** *Vacillate* (verb) means to be indecisive or to waver. (*See Chapter 9, Section A.*)

14. **B.** A *hedonist* (noun) is a pleasure-seeker. (*See Chapter 9, Section A.*)

15. **B.** *Torpid* (adjective) means slow or lazy. (*See Chapter 9, Section A.*)

16. **A.** *Extrinsic* (adjective) means external. (*See Chapter 9, Section A.*)

17. **C.** *Dubious* (adjective) means doubtful or uncertain. (*See Chapter 9, Section B.*)

18. **D.** *Exacerbate* (verb) means to aggravate or worsen. (*See Chapter 9, Section B.*)

19. **D.** *Lucrative* (adjective) means profitable or money-making. (*See Chapter 9, Section A.*)

20. **A.** *Malignant* (adjective) means spiteful or hateful. *(See Chapter 8, Section B; Chapter 9, Section A.)*

21. **C.** *Inept* (adjective) means clumsy or incompetent. *(See Chapter 9, Section B.)*

22. **A.** *Benevolent* (adjective) means kindly or compassionate. *(See Chapter 8, Section B; Chapter 9, Section A.)*

23. **B.** *Bellicose* (adjective) means warlike or combative. *(See Chapter 9, Section A.)*

24. **A.** *Revered* (adjective) means highly respected. *(See Chapter 9, Section A.)*

25. **B.** *Enigmatic* (adjective) means mysterious or puzzling. *(See Chapter 9, Section B.)*

26. **A.** *Apprehensive* (adjective) means worried or fearful. *(See Chapter 9, Section B.)*

27. **D.** *Succinct* (adjective) means concise or brief. *(See Chapter 9, Section A.)*

28. **C.** *Groundbreaking* (adjective) means innovative or revolutionary. *(See Chapter 9, Section A.)*

29. **B.** *Diligent* (adjective) means hard-working. *(See Chapter 9, Section B.)*

30. **A.** *Terse* (adjective) means brief. *(See Chapter 9, Section B.)*

31. **B.** *Laconic* (adjective) means not talkative or terse. *(See Chapter 9, Section B.)*

32. **D.** *Diffident* (adjective) means shy or lacking self-confidence. *(See Chapter 9, Section A.)*

33. **C.** *Awe* (noun) means wonder or admiration. *(See Chapter 9, Section A.)*

34. **A.** *Meticulous* (adjective) means extremely neat or careful. *(See Chapter 9, Section A.)*

35. **C.** A *hypothesis* (noun) is a theory. *(See Chapter 9, Section A.)*

Section 3: Paragraph Comprehension

1. **C.** The passage addresses only the physical differences between the leopard and the cheetah, choice C. Information about their mating habits (choice A), preferred prey (choice B), and habitat (choice D) is not included in the passage. *(See Chapter 10, Sections A and B; Chapter 11, Section B.)*

2. **B.** The information in the passage indicates "human-made barriers, such as dams and culverts" (underground ducts or coverings of ducts) are the most significant obstacles to the fish on their spawning journeys, choice B. Choice A may be true, but it isn't the *major* obstacle the fish face. There is no evidence in the passage to support choice C or D. *(See Chapter 10, Sections A and B; Chapter 11, Section B.)*

3. **D.** According to the passage, tornadoes are often accompanied by thunderstorms that cause heavy rains and flash flooding and hail, choice D. The passage states that tornadoes occur in very state, which contradicts choice A. There is no evidence in the passage to support choice B; in fact, most tornadoes occur west of the Rocky Mountains. Choice C is contradicted by the passage: tornadoes hit the United States about 1,200 times a year. *(See Chapter 10, Sections A and B; Chapter 11, Section B.)*

4. **B.** An appropriate title should reflect the main topic of the passage. Because the passage mentions that penguins are currently very popular and that they're quite playful, choice B is an appropriate title. The passage doesn't cover the lifestyle of the penguins, so choice A is incorrect. Choice C is too vague to be a good title for this passage. Choice D is too specific; while the passage mentions movies, they aren't the focus of the passage; in addition, this title doesn't specifically refer to penguins. *(See Chapter 10, Sections A and B; Chapter 11, Section B.)*

5. **C.** The tone of the passage is conveyed by the language and images the author chooses. In this passage, the language is gloomy, choice C, and the images are rather sad and dull. There are no elements of optimism in the passage (choice A). Although the tone is sad, it isn't very angry or irate (choice B). There aren't any frantic images in the passage, so choice D is also incorrect. (*See Chapter 10, Sections A and B; Chapter 11, Section B.*)

6. **C.** The passage includes information on converting the solar energy that creates wind into mechanical energy and subsequently into electricity, choice C. Choice A is incorrect because the heating of the atmosphere is not invariable. Choice B reverses the process of conversion. Choice D is not supported by evidence in the passage. (*See Chapter 10, Sections A and B; Chapter 11, Section B.*)

7. **B.** Although not directly stated in the passage, the correct answer can be inferred from the information given. Wind is virtually unlimited, choice B. Although choice A may be true, there is no information in the passage to support it. Choice C is incorrect because the cost of mechanical generators is not discussed in the passage. Choice D is a generalization that is not supported by the passage. (*See Chapter 10, Sections A and B; Chapter 11, Section B.*)

8. **D.** The passage suggests that warfare led to communication between cultures, which, in turn, led to an increase in knowledge, choice D. Choice A reverses the order of the process. Choices B and C are not supported by evidence in the passage. (*See Chapter 10, Sections A and B; Chapter 11, Section B.*)

9. **D.** The author suggests that when a conqueror defeats and occupies another country, he absorbs the knowledge that has been accumulated in the vanquished nation. Thus, knowledge is increased and progress follows, choice D. Choice A suggests that science is a motivation for exploration equal to warfare, but this is not supported by the passage. Choice B is the opposite of the author's point. Choice C is incorrect based on the information in the passage. (*See Chapter 10, Sections A and B; Chapter 11, Section B.*)

10. **B.** The repetition of *every* emphasizes the pervasiveness of computers in the workplace. Choice A is incorrect because the passage doesn't suggest that technology is too overpowering. Choice C may be a true statement, but it isn't the purpose of repeating *every*. Choice D is not addressed in the passage. (*See Chapter 10, Sections A and B; Chapter 11, Section B.*)

  C. The author implies that Amory Blaine inherited most of his characteristics from his mother, but he inherited his tendency to "waver at crucial moments" from his father, choice C. There is no evidence in the passage to support choice A. Choice B is incorrect because Stephen Blaine inherited his fortune rather than earned it himself. Choice D is contradicted by the description of Stephen Blaine as "ineffectual"; in fact, he went to Bar Harbor "in the first flush of feeling that the world was his," the implication being that he never had this thought before. (*See Chapter 10, Sections A and B; Chapter 11, Section B.*)

11. **D.** The passage makes the point that applying students' familiarity with the model of the solar system to the structure of the atom helps them understand the atom's structure, choice D. Choice A may be a true statement, but it isn't supported by any evidence in the passage. (Don't be fooled by answer choices that are true but are not supported by the passage.) Choice B is incorrect because the nucleus is surrounded by orbiting electrons. Choice C is incorrect because Bohr didn't create a model of the solar system; he created a model of the atom. (*See Chapter 10, Sections A and B; Chapter 11, Section B.*)

13. **D.** Choice D makes a true statement that can be supported by the last sentence of the passage. The passage indicates that new and effective anti-poaching laws are in effect in many African nations, so choice A is incorrect. Choice B is incorrect because the passage states that some elephants live 70 years. Choice C is inaccurate; the passage doesn't state that elephants are preyed on by lions. (*See Chapter 10, Sections A and B; Chapter 11, Section B.*)

14. **D.** The passage mentions several reasons why people yawn; sleepiness is not the only reason, choice D. Choices A, B, and C can't be supported by evidence from the passage. *(See Chapter 10, Sections A and B; Chapter 11, Section B.)*

15. **B.** Choice B fits the stated qualifications for president. Choice A is incorrect because the man was born in England. Choice C is incorrect because this man *would* be eligible to be president. Choice D is incorrect because a president can't serve for 9 years. *(See Chapter 10, Sections A and B; Chapter 11, Section B.)*

Section 4: Mathematics Knowledge

1. **C.** The area of a rectangle is the product of the length and the width: $A = 25 \times 40 = 1,000$ ft.². *(See Chapter 13, Section E.)*

2. **C.** The number of people in the band must be one more than a multiple of 5 but also one more than a multiple of 6. Subtract one from each of the answer choices and consider their divisors. All are multiples of 5. A number is divisible by 6 if it is divisible by both 2 and 3. All the choices are divisible by 2, so test for divisibility by 3 by adding the digits. If the sum of the digits is divisible by 3, the number is divisible by 3: $1 + 3 + 0 = 4$, $1 + 4 + 0 = 5$, $1 + 5 + 0 = 6$, and $1 + 6 + 0 = 7$. Only 150 is divisible by 5 and 6, so there are 151 band members. *(See Chapter 12, Section A.)*

3. **C.** Eliminate triangle *RST* and trapezoid *WXYZ* and count the sides of the remaining polygon. A polygon with five sides is a pentagon. *(See Chapter 13, Section F.)*

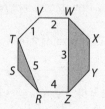

4. **A.** The third side of a triangle must be less than the sum of the other two sides. All the answer choices fit that criterion. In order for that relationship to hold all the way around the triangle, however, the third side plus 3 feet must be more than 5 feet. A 2-foot board will not do the job. *(See Chapter 13, Section C.)*

5. **D.** You're looking for the least common multiple of 12 and 15. You could look at the prime factorization of each number to determine the least common multiple, but a quick list of multiples is probably faster. Multiples of 12 include 24, 36, 48, 60, 72, and so on. Multiples of 15 include 30, 45, 60, and so on. The first multiple on both lists, 60, is the number of sheets of each color paper the teacher will buy; therefore, 60 students will be able to do the project. *(See Chapter 12, Section A.)*

6. **C.** You can tackle this algebraically. Let x be the number of weeks until Alberto and Dahlia have the same amount of money. $12x = 270 - 15x$ means that $27x = 270$ and $x = 10$. They will have the same amount in 10 weeks, when they will each have $120. If they pool their money, they'll have $240. *(See Chapter 12, Section D.)*

7. **B.** The cost is $580 + $0.18 \times $5,000 = $580 + $900 = $1,480$. *(See Chapter 12, Section C.)*

8. **C.** If a 35-foot maple tree casts a shadow 7 feet long, the length of the shadow is one-fifth of the height of the tree. A 6-foot man is $6 \times 12 = 72$ inches tall. One-fifth of 72 inches is 14.4 inches. *(See Chapter 14, Section B.)*

9. **A.** The worker certainly can't make more than 432 cars, but the real question is whether there are an adequate number of wheels to build all those cars. There are 1,584 wheels available, which, when divided by 4 (because each car needs four wheels), gives you 396 sets of wheels and, therefore, 396 cars. (*See Chapter 12, Section D.*)

10. **A.** Be sure to convert the 16 inches to feet before multiplying to find the volume. 16 inches are equivalent to $\frac{16}{12} = \frac{4}{3} = 1\frac{1}{3}$ feet. The carton can hold $2 \times 3 \times 1\frac{1}{3} = 2 \times \cancel{3} \times \frac{4}{\cancel{3}} = 8$ ft.^{3}. (*See Chapter 13, Section I.*)

11. **B.** If the radius of a circle is doubled, $A = \pi r^2$ becomes $A = \pi(2r)^2 = 4\pi r^2$. Don't be seduced by the 400 percent. The question is "by what percent does the area increase?" The increase is $4\pi r^2 - \pi r^2 = 3\pi r^2$. The percent increase is $\frac{\text{increase}}{\text{original}} = \frac{3\pi r^2}{\pi r^2} = 300$ percent. (*See Chapter 13, Section H.*)

12. **A.** We would expect that if $\frac{3}{4}$ of the objects are balls and $\frac{2}{5}$ are red, $\frac{3}{\underset{2}{\cancel{4}}} \times \frac{\cancel{2}}{5} = \frac{3}{10}$ will be red balls. Note that we can't be certain that this is the case. A bag with 15 balls and 5 blocks could have 5 red blocks and 3 red balls. It contains $\frac{3}{4}$ balls, and $\frac{2}{5}$ of the objects are red, but only $\frac{3}{20}$ are red balls. The expectation, however, would be that the red objects are proportionally spread over blocks and balls, so we expect that $\frac{2}{5}$ of the balls, or $\frac{2}{5}$ of $\frac{3}{4}$ of the objects, are red balls. (*See Chapter 15, Sections A and B.*)

13. **C.** Rounded to the nearest hundred, 8,974 becomes 9,000 and 4,905 becomes 4,900. Adding them gives you 13,900. (*See Chapter 12, Section A.*)

14. **A.** $F = \frac{9}{5}C + 32 = \frac{9}{\cancel{5}}(\cancel{20}^4) + 32 = 36 + 32 = 68$. (*See Chapter 12, Section C.*)

15. **B.** Don't be misled by "more than"; the question asks for an equation, not an inequality. "Six more than" translates to adding 6 to "three times a number" or $3x$. The verb *is* translates to the equal sign, giving you $3x + 6 = 27$. (*See Chapter 5, Section B.*)

16. **A.** Let S = the price of 1 shirt and T = the price of 1 tie. Then Jack's purchase is $3S + 2T = \$88.06$ and Matt's is $2S + 3T = \$82.44$. Solve the system $\begin{cases} 3S + 2T = 88.06 \\ 2S + 3T = 82.44 \end{cases}$ by multiplying and then subtracting to find the price of a tie, T.

$$
\begin{array}{llll}
3S + 2T = 88.06 & \rightarrow & 2(3S + 2T) = 2(88.06) & \rightarrow & 6S + 4T = 176.12 \\
2S + 3T = 82.44 & & 3(2S + 3T) = 3(82.44) & & \underline{6S + 9T = 247.32} \\
& & & & -5T = -71.20 \\
& & & & T = \dfrac{-71.20}{-5} \\
& & & & T = 14.24
\end{array}
$$

Once you know the price of a tie, substitute it into one of the original equations to find the price of a shirt.

$$3S + 2(14.24) = 88.06$$
$$3S + 28.48 = 88.06$$
$$3S = 59.58$$
$$S = 19.86$$

A shirt costs $19.86 and a tie costs $14.24. One shirt and one tie will cost $19.86 + $14.24 = $34.10. (*See Chapter 12, Section E.*)

17. **A.** Use point-slope form $y - y_1 = m(x - x_1)$ and replace m with -3, x_1 with 7, and y_1 with -2:

$$y - y_1 = m(x - x_1)$$
$$y - -2 = -3(x - 7)$$
$$y + 2 = -3x + 21$$
$$y = -3x + 19$$

Since all of the answer choices are in standard form, add $3x$ to both sides to get $3x + y = 19$. (*See Chapter 12, Section K.*)

18. **D.** $3^4 = 3 \times 3 \times 3 \times 3 = 9 \times 9 = 81$. (*See Chapter 12, Section C.*)

19. **A.** Remember to follow the order of operations:

$$4(30 - 18) - 4 \times 30 - 18 = 4(12) - 4 \times 30 - 18$$
$$= 48 - 120 - 18$$
$$= -90$$

(*See Chapter 12, Section A.*)

20. **D.** The average refers to the mean, so add the five temperature readings and divide by 5: $42° + 37° + 35° + 41° + 45° = 200°$. The average temperature for the 5-day period is $200 \div 5 = 40°$.

You can also find the average by starting with the middle value (the median) and averaging the pull of the higher and lower values. The median here is $41°$. Express the difference between $41°$ and each of the values as a positive or negative number: $42°$ is $+1$, $37°$ is -4, $35°$ is -6, $41°$ is 0, and $45°$ is $+4$. Add the positive and negative numbers: $+1 + (-4) + (-6) + 0 + 4 = -5$. Divide -5 by 5 to get -1, and the mean is one unit lower than the median. So, $41 - 1 = 40°$. (*See Chapter 15, Section C.*)

21. **B.** If $a = 8$ and $b = 3$, $\dfrac{a + b^2}{a^2 - b} = \dfrac{8 + 3^2}{8^2 - 3} = \dfrac{8 + 9}{64 - 3} = \dfrac{17}{61}$. (*See Chapter 12, Section H.*)

22. **A.** $(x + y)^2 = (x + y)(x + y) = x^2 + xy + yx + y^2 = x^2 + 2xy + y^2$. Therefore, choice A, $x^2 + y^2$, is the answer choice that is not equivalent to $(x + y)^2$. (*See Chapter 12, Section F.*)

23. **A.** The 50 percent saline solution contains half a liter of salt and half a liter of water. When it's mixed with 1 liter of pure water, the result is $\frac{1}{2}$ liter of salt with $1\frac{1}{2}$ liters of water. Each of the 2 liters of the new solution is 25 percent salt. (*See Chapter 12, Section J.*)

24. **C.** If $2x - 7 = 17$, adding 7 to both sides tells you that $2x = 24$ and dividing by 2 gives $x = 12$. (*See Chapter 12, Section D.*)

25. **B.** Factor the numerator before trying to cancel. $\dfrac{x^2 - 5x + 6}{x - 2} = \dfrac{(x - 2)(x - 3)}{x - 2} = x - 3$. (*See Chapter 12, Section H.*)

Chapter 5

Arithmetic Reasoning: Word Problems

The questions of the Arithmetic Reasoning section of the ASVAB are presented almost exclusively as "word problems." That's a funny term if you think about it, because even if only numbers were written on the page, you would read them using words. Words are how we communicate. If I type 2 + 2, you read "two plus two." The challenge in word problems is translating from words of your native language to the symbols of mathematical language.

A. Parts of Speech

Translating the words of a problem to the symbols of arithmetic or algebra means that you need to know what symbols are equivalent to the words of the problem. There are far more words than symbols, but fortunately word problems are often very patterned, so the vocabulary is limited. It's possible to identify words typically used and the symbols to which they translate.

Numbers and Placeholders

The easiest part of translating a word problem is writing the numbers. They may already be written using digits, like 194 or 14.2, or they may be written in words, like thirty-seven or two and seven tenths. Some tips when writing numbers include the following:

Place Value

- Use commas to divide groups of three digits in large numbers. Example:

"three hundred twenty-two million, four hundred ninety-two thousand, one hundred seventy-four"	322,492,174

- Use zeros to keep things in the proper places. Example:

"three hundred million twenty-two"	300,000,022

- Remember that the word "and" signals a decimal point. Examples:

"three hundred seven"	307
"three hundred and seven tenths"	300.7
"three and seven hundredths"	3.07

- Places to the right of the decimal point have names that end in "th": tenths, hundredths, thousandths, etc. Places to the left do not: tens, hundreds, thousands, etc.

Variables

Of course, each problem usually has a missing number, the number you need to find. That number is represented by a variable. Variables are often letters, like x or y, but could be a blank space or an empty box to fill in. If you're asked "what number should be added to 27 to make 43?" you could write $27 + x = 43$ or $27 + \_\_\_ = 43$. The idea is the same, but blank spaces are easy to lose track of, so letters are more common. Here are a few tips for using variables:

- Most problems only need one variable. If you think you have more than one unknown, check to see if they're related before using a second variable. For example, "the sum of two numbers is 26" could be $x + y = 26$, but you can probably get by with one number is x and the other is $26 - x$.

- If you can choose your own variable, use one that will help you remember what it stands for. If you just think of x as just "some number," it could be 12 or 3.5 or -2 and still seem reasonable. If you remind yourself that p is the number of people at a concert, you'll know immediately that 3.5 or -2 can't be correct.

Connections

In most problems, numbers and variables work together under one or more of the operations of arithmetic. If numbers are combined or increased, you're probably adding, while decreasing or spending might signal subtraction. Multiplication is about repeated addition or duplication, and division is about sharing or comparing.

Addition, subtraction, multiplication, and division are all technically binary operations, meaning they turn two numbers into one number. For addition and multiplication, we have strategies for working with more than two numbers, but you don't actually multiply $3 \times 7 \times 5 \times 2$ all at once. You multiply two of them, then that answer times another and so on. For addition and multiplication, the order of the numbers won't matter: $5 + 4 = 4 + 5$ and $6 \times 3 = 3 \times 6$. For subtraction and division, however, changing the order makes a very different problem. $100 - 3 = 97$, but $3 - 100$ is a negative number, -97. $100 \div 5 = 20$, but $5 \div 100$ is less than 1, $\frac{1}{20}$ or 0.05.

Most problems will make the order of the numbers clear, but there is one phrase that is sometimes confusing, especially when variables are involved. If "23 is 7 less than some number," you can probably figure out that 23 is 7 less than 30, so you know 23 is 7 less than x. It can sound as though this might be written $23 = 7 - x$ or $23 = 7 < x$. If you put 30 in place of x, however, $23 = 7 - 30$ is not correct, and $23 = 7 < 30$ doesn't even make sense. The correct arrangement, using numbers, is $23 = 30 - 7$ or using the variable, $23 = x - 7$. The phrase "7 less than a number" translates to $x - 7$.

Symbols show up in problems in a variety of phrases:

	Common Phrases	Translate to:
Addition	17 increased by 5	$17 + 5$
	the sum of 16 and 32	$16 + 32$
	the total of 42 and 93	$42 + 93$
	11 more than 83	$83 + 11$
	86 and 22	$86 + 22$
Subtraction	108 decreased by 12	$108 - 12$
	79 reduced by 18	$79 - 18$
	the difference of 51 and 29	$51 - 29$
	7 less than 23	$23 - 7$
Multiplication	14 times 29	14×29
	$\frac{1}{3}$ of 42	$\frac{1}{3} \times 42$
	the product of 5 and 7.3	5×7.3

	Common Phrases	Translate to:
Division	128 divided by 9	128 ÷ 9
	the quotient of 51 and 17	51 ÷ 17

Practice

Directions: For each phrase, choose the correct symbolic representation.

1. Four more than a number

   A. $4 \div x$
   B. $4 - x$
   C. $x - 4$
   D. $x + 4$

2. Seventeen decreased by 11

   A. $17 \div 11$
   B. $17 + 11$
   C. $17 - 11$
   D. $11 - 17$

3. The product of 8 and 7

   A. $8 \div 7$
   B. 8×7
   C. $8 + 7$
   D. $8 - 7$

4. The quotient of 42 and 6

   A. 42×6
   B. $42 - 6$
   C. $42 + 6$
   D. $42 \div 6$

5. One hundred twenty reduced by 14

   A. $120 \div 14$
   B. $120 - 14$
   C. $120 + 14$
   D. 120×14

6. The total of 6, 8, and 10

   A. $6 \times 8 + 10$
   B. $6 \times 8 \times 10$
   C. $6 + 8 \times 10$
   D. $6 + 8 + 10$

7. Four more than 8

   A. $4 - 8$
   B. $8 - 4$
   C. $4 + 8$
   D. 4×8

8. Seventy-three decreased by 14

   A. $73 - 14$
   B. $73 + 14$
   C. $73 \div 14$
   D. $14 + 73$

9. Nineteen less than 22

   A. $19 - 22$
   B. $22 - 19$
   C. $19 \div 22$
   D. $22 \div 19$

10. The sum of 14 and 38

    A. $14 - 38$
    B. $38 - 14$
    C. $14 + 38$
    D. $38 \div 14$

Answers

1. **D.** Four more than a number is a signal to add: 4 + a number or a number + 4. The choices use x for "a number," so $x + 4$.

2. **C.** Seventeen decreased by 11 is a subtraction: $17 - 11$.

3. **B.** The *product* is the result of multiplication. The product of 8 and 7 is 8×7.

4. **D.** The *quotient* is the result of division. The quotient of 42 and 6 is $42 \div 6$.

5. **B.** *Reduced by* is a signal to subtract. One hundred twenty reduced by 14 is $120 - 14$.

6. **D.** You get a *total* by adding. The total of 6, 8, and 10 translates to $6 + 8 + 10$.

7. **C.** Four more than 8 is another addition problem: $4 + 8$, but because addition is commutative, $8 + 4$ is equivalent.

8. **A.** Seventy-three decreased by 14 translates to a subtraction: $73 - 14$.

9. **B.** Nineteen less than 22 signals subtraction, but in the opposite order of how it's stated: $22 - 19$.

10. **C.** The *sum* is the result of addition. The sum of 14 and 38 is $14 + 38$.

B. Translation

Putting words together into the sentences that form problems requires nouns, like numbers, and variables, but also verbs. As detailed in the last section, operations of addition, subtraction, multiplication, and division are connectors, so contrary to what people sometimes think, they are not verbs.

Verbs

The verbs of math are the symbols that tell *how* numbers relate to one another. The most common verb is = , or *is equal to*. In a problem, it generally appears just as *is*, although you may find variations such as *equals, makes,* or *results in.*

The following chart shows some common verbs.

Symbol	Read as ...	Appears in Problems as Phrases Such as ...
=	Is equal to	Equals, makes, results in
>	Is greater than	Is more than, exceeds
<	Is less than	Is less than
≥	Is greater than or equal to	Is at least, is no less than
≤	Is less than or equal to	Is at most, is no more than

The negation, or opposite, of = is ≠, or *is not equal to*. The negation of > is ≤, and the negation of < is ≥.

Practice

Directions: For each sentence, choose the correct symbolic representation.

1. The sum of 7 and 19 is no more than 30.

   A. $7 \times 19 \leq 30$
   B. $7 + 19 < 30$
   C. $7 + 19 \leq 30$
   D. $7 + 19 \geq 30$

2. The quotient of 43 and 7 is at least 6.

   A. $43 \div 7 < 6$
   B. $43 \div 7 \geq 6$
   C. $43 \div 7 > 6$
   D. $7 \div 43 > 6$

3. The product of 90 and 70 is not equal to 630.

   A. $90 \times 70 = 630$
   B. $90 \div 70 > 630$
   C. $90 \times 70 \neq 630$
   D. $90 + 70 \neq 630$

4. Thirty-eight increased by 9 is 47.

   A. $38 + 9 > 47$
   B. $38 \times 9 = 47$
   C. $38 \times 9 < 47$
   D. $38 + 9 = 47$

5. The sum of a number and 18 is 39.

   A. $n + 18 = 39$
   B. $n - 18 = 39$
   C. $n = 18 + 39$
   D. $n \div 18 = 39$

6. A number decreased by 8 is less than 12.

   A. $x = 12 - 8$
   B. $x < 12 - 8$
   C. $x - 8 = 12$
   D. $x - 8 < 12$

7. The quotient of 72 and 6 exceeds 9.

   A. $72 - 6 < 9$
   B. $72 \div 6 > 9$
   C. $72 \div 6 \leq 9$
   D. $72 + 6 \leq 9$

8. The product of 14 and a number is at least 70.

   A. $n \cdot 14 > 70$
   B. $n \div 14 > 70$
   C. $14 \cdot n \geq 70$
   D. $14 \div n \geq 70$

9. Four less than the product of 9 and 8 is 68.

   A. $4 - 9 \times 8 = 68$
   B. $9 \times 8 - 4 = 68$
   C. $4 < 9 \times 8 + 68$
   D. $9 \times 8 - 4 < 68$

10. Nineteen decreased by 7 is no more than 12.

   A. $19 - 7 \leq 12$
   B. $19 - 7 < 12$
   C. $19 - 7 > 12$
   D. $19 - 7 \geq 12$

Answers

1. **C.** *The sum of 7 and 19* translates as 7 + 19, and *is no more than* becomes a ≤ sign, so the sentence is 7 + 19 ≤ 30.

2. **B.** The quotient is the result of division and *is at least* becomes a ≥ sign. *The quotient of 43 and 7 is at least 6* translates to 43 ÷ 7 ≥ 6.

3. **C.** Use the symbol ≠ for *is not equal to.* The product of 90 and 70 is not equal to 630 becomes 90 × 70 ≠ 630.

4. **D.** *Increased by* signals addition and the verb *is* becomes an equal sign. *Thirty-eight increased by 9 is 47* translates as 38 + 9 = 47.

5. **A.** This one is an equation, and *sum* denotes addition. *The sum of a number and 18 is 39* becomes $n + 18 = 39$.

6. **D.** To decrease a number, you subtract, so this one is $x - 8$, and the verb *is less than* translates to <. *A number decreased by 8 is less than 12* becomes $x - 8 < 12$.

7. **B.** You produce a quotient by dividing, and the verb *exceeds* translates into >. *The quotient of 72 and 6 exceeds 9* becomes 72 ÷ 6 > 9.

8. **C.** The verb *is at least* translates to ≥. *The product of 14 and a number is at least 70* can be written as $14 \cdot n ≥ 70$.

9. **B.** This sentence is more complex. The word *product* tells you to multiply and the *four less than* tells you to subtract 4 from the product. *Four less than the product of 9 and 8 is 68* translates to 9 × 8 − 4 = 68.

10. **A.** If some number is no more than 12, it's less than or equal to 12. *Nineteen decreased by 7 is no more than 12* is represented by 19 − 7 ≤ 12.

C. Word Problems

Repetition of something you have learned strengthens your understanding until the information is so familiar that you can begin to combine ideas in new ways. In the world of word problems, there are problem types that you encounter again and again. Practicing with them not only increases your speed and comfort in solving that type of problem but also helps you solve a variety of word problems built on that model.

Before looking at some of the common problem types, let's take a few minutes to talk about units, one of the things that distinguish word problems from simple calculations. A calculation, like 7 + 12, talks only about numbers. Problems talk about counting things, like people or oranges or boxes of paper clips, or about measuring things, like distance or weight or time. You would not add 7 people to 12 oranges or subtract 50 feet from 300 pounds. Like with like has to be the rule, and that means that sometimes you will have to convert units of measurement given in a problem to be certain you have compatible units.

Unit Conversion

Some unit conversion is just making a substitution, replacing 1 minute with 60 seconds, or 1 yard with 3 feet. It might require a little multiplication: 1 minute = 60 seconds, so 5 minutes = 300 seconds. Converting a rate is a little more complicated because each rate involves two measurements. You may need to change one or the other or both to different units.

Converting One Measurement in a Rate

To change 15 feet per second to feet per minute, take the following steps:

1. Write the rate as a fraction: $\dfrac{15 \text{ feet}}{1 \text{ second}}$. Notice whether the measurement that needs to change is in the numerator or in the denominator.

2. Create another fraction that expresses the conversion: $\dfrac{60 \text{ seconds}}{1 \text{ minute}}$. 60 seconds goes in the numerator because the 1 second in the original denominator needs to change.

3. Multiply the fractions: $\dfrac{15 \text{ feet}}{1 \text{ \sout{second}}} \times \dfrac{60 \text{ \sout{seconds}}}{1 \text{ minute}} = \dfrac{900 \text{ feet}}{1 \text{ minute}}$. Numbers may or may not cancel, but if you set up properly, the units you don't want will cancel out, and the units you want will remain.

Converting Both Measurements in a Rate

To convert both measurements in a rate, for example, to convert meters per second to kilometers per hour, you could convert meters to kilometers and then convert seconds to hours. It is possible, however, to do it in one pass if you set up carefully.

1. Write the rate: $\dfrac{16 \text{ meters}}{1 \text{ second}}$.

2. Write the conversion for the numerator as a rate: $\dfrac{1 \text{ kilometer}}{1,000 \text{ meters}}$.

Tip: If you don't know the conversion factor to go directly from one unit to another, you can do it in steps, like seconds to minutes and then minutes to hours.

3. Write the conversion for the denominator as a rate: $\dfrac{60 \text{ seconds}}{1 \text{ minute}} \times \dfrac{60 \text{ minutes}}{1 \text{ hour}}$.

4. Multiply to convert the rate:

$$\frac{16 \text{ \sout{meters}}}{1 \text{ \sout{second}}} \times \frac{1 \text{ kilometer}}{1,000 \text{ \sout{meters}}} \times \frac{60 \text{ \sout{seconds}}}{1 \text{ \sout{minute}}} \times \frac{60 \text{ \sout{minutes}}}{1 \text{ hour}} = \frac{16 \times 60 \times 60 \text{ kilometers}}{1,000 \text{ hours}}$$

$$= \frac{57,600 \text{ kilometers}}{1,000 \text{ hours}}$$

$$= 57.6 \frac{\text{km}}{\text{hr}}$$

Practice

Directions: Choose the answer that represents the correct conversion.

1. 180 feet per minute to feet per second

    A.   180 feet per second
    B.   18 feet per second
    C.   3 feet per second
    D.   0.3 feet per second

2. 50 meters per second to kilometers per hour

    A.   1,800 kilometers per hour
    B.   180 kilometers per hour
    C.   50 kilometers per hour
    D.   3.6 kilometers per hour

3. 425 grams per centimeter to kilograms per meter

    A.   42.5 kilograms per meter
    B.   425 kilograms per meter
    C.   4.25 kilograms per meter
    D.   42,500 kilograms per meter

4. 144 ounces per day to ounces per hour

    A.   144 ounces per hour
    B.   6 ounces per hour
    C.   1.44 ounces per hour
    D.   0.16 ounces per hour

5. 90 pounds per foot to ounces per inch

    A.   1,440 ounces per inch
    B.   7.5 ounces per inch
    C.   90 ounces per inch
    D.   120 ounces per inch

6. 8 kilograms per meter to grams per centimeter

    A.   8 grams per centimeter
    B.   12.5 grams per centimeter
    C.   80 grams per centimeter
    D.   8,000 grams per centimeter

7. 480 calories per pound to calories per ounce

    A.   7,680 calories per ounce
    B.   30 calories per ounce
    C.   480 calories per ounce
    D.   330 calories per ounce

8. 90 inches per hour to feet per hour

    A.   7.5 feet per hour
    B.   90 feet per hour
    C.   450 feet per hour
    D.   1,080 feet per hour

9. 4 teaspoons per cup to teaspoons per ounce

    A.   0.5 teaspoons per ounce
    B.   2 teaspoons per ounce
    C.   4 teaspoons per ounce
    D.   32 teaspoons per ounce

10. 39 grams per meter to kilograms per kilometer

    A.   3.9 kilograms per kilometer
    B.   39 kilograms per kilometer
    C.   390 kilograms per kilometer
    D.   3,900 kilograms per kilometer

Answers

1. **C.** $\dfrac{\overset{3}{\cancel{180}} \text{ feet}}{\cancel{\text{minute}}} \times \dfrac{1 \cancel{\text{ minute}}}{\cancel{60} \text{ seconds}} = \dfrac{3 \text{ feet}}{\text{second}}$

2. **B.** $\dfrac{\overset{1}{\cancel{50}} \text{ meters}}{\cancel{\text{second}}} \times \dfrac{\text{kilometer}}{\underset{1\ 20}{\cancel{1,000}} \text{ meters}} \times \dfrac{\overset{3}{\cancel{60}} \text{ seconds}}{1 \cancel{\text{ minute}}} \times \dfrac{60 \cancel{\text{ minutes}}}{1 \text{ hour}} = \dfrac{180 \text{ kilometers}}{\text{hour}}$

3. **A.** $\dfrac{425 \text{ grams}}{\cancel{\text{centimeter}}} \times \dfrac{\text{kilogram}}{\underset{10}{\cancel{1,000}} \text{ grams}} \times \dfrac{\cancel{100} \text{ centimeters}}{1 \text{ meter}} = \dfrac{425 \text{ kilograms}}{10 \text{ meters}} = \dfrac{42.5 \text{ kilograms}}{\text{meter}}$

4. **B.** $\dfrac{\overset{6}{\cancel{144}} \text{ ounces}}{\cancel{\text{day}}} \times \dfrac{1 \cancel{\text{ day}}}{24 \text{ hours}} = \dfrac{6 \text{ ounces}}{\text{hour}}$

5. **D.** $\dfrac{\overset{15}{\cancel{90}} \text{ pounds}}{\cancel{\text{foot}}} \times \dfrac{\overset{8}{\cancel{16}} \text{ ounces}}{1 \cancel{\text{ pound}}} \times \dfrac{1 \cancel{\text{ foot}}}{\underset{z}{\cancel{12}} \text{ inches}} = \dfrac{120 \text{ ounces}}{\text{inch}}$

6. **C.** $\dfrac{8 \text{ kilograms}}{\cancel{\text{meter}}} \times \dfrac{\overset{10}{\cancel{1,000}} \text{ grams}}{1 \cancel{\text{ kilogram}}} \times \dfrac{1 \cancel{\text{ meter}}}{\cancel{100} \text{ centimeters}} = \dfrac{80 \text{ grams}}{\text{centimeter}}$

7. **B.** $\dfrac{\overset{30}{\cancel{480}} \text{ calories}}{\cancel{\text{pound}}} \times \dfrac{1 \cancel{\text{ pound}}}{\cancel{16} \text{ ounces}} = \dfrac{30 \text{ calories}}{\text{ounce}}$

8. **A.** $\dfrac{\overset{7.5}{\cancel{90}} \cancel{\text{ inches}}}{\text{hour}} \times \dfrac{1 \text{ foot}}{\cancel{12} \cancel{\text{ inches}}} = \dfrac{7.5 \text{ feet}}{\text{hour}}$

9. **A.** $\dfrac{\overset{0.5}{\cancel{4}} \text{ teaspoons}}{\cancel{\text{cup}}} \times \dfrac{1 \cancel{\text{ cup}}}{\cancel{8} \text{ ounces}} = \dfrac{0.5 \text{ teaspoons}}{\text{ounce}}$

10. **B.** $\dfrac{39 \text{ grams}}{\cancel{\text{meter}}} \times \dfrac{1 \cancel{\text{ kilogram}}}{\cancel{1,000} \text{ grams}} \times \dfrac{\cancel{1,000} \cancel{\text{ meters}}}{1 \text{ kilometer}} = \dfrac{39 \text{ kilograms}}{\text{kilometer}}$

Distance Problems

Problems involving travel of some kind are common. The basic rule that covers these problems tells you that the distance traveled is equal to the rate of speed at which you travel multiplied by the time spent traveling. Breaking that down:

distance traveled is equal to the rate of speed at which you travel multiplied by the time spent traveling

distance is equal to rate multiplied by time

distance = rate × time

$d = rt$

If you're asked to find a distance, multiply speed and time, and check the units to make sure you're doing things correctly. Miles per hour times hours will give you miles, and feet per second times seconds will give you feet.

$$\frac{\text{miles}}{\text{hour}} \times \frac{\text{hours}}{1} = \frac{\text{miles}}{1} \qquad\qquad \frac{\text{feet}}{\text{seconds}} \times \frac{\text{seconds}}{1} = \frac{\text{feet}}{1}$$

If you find you're multiplying units that don't simplify nicely, that's a signal that you need to convert some units. If you realize that you're multiplying feet per second by minutes, you'll need to change the minutes to seconds, and if you've got miles per hour and minutes, you need to changes minutes to hours or the hours to minutes.

EXAMPLE:

Mr. Smith drove for $4\frac{1}{2}$ hours at 60 mph. How far did he travel?

A. $13\frac{1}{3}$ miles

B. 75 miles

C. 240.5 miles

D. 270 miles

Distance equals rate times time, so the distance Mr. Smith traveled is equal to 60 mph times $4\frac{1}{2}$ hours, or $60 \times 4\frac{1}{2} = (60 \times 4) + \left(60 \times \frac{1}{2}\right) = 240 + 30 = 270$ miles. Choice D is correct.

EXAMPLE:

A new robot can move forward at 15 feet per second. How far can it travel in 30 minutes?

A. 2 feet

B. 7.5 feet

C. 450 feet

D. 27,000 feet

The distance traveled is the rate of 15 feet per second times the time of 30 minutes, but the units are not compatible. Change 30 minutes to seconds.

$$\frac{30 \text{ minutes}}{1} \times \frac{60 \text{ seconds}}{1 \text{ minute}} = \frac{1,800 \text{ seconds}}{1}$$

Then find the distance traveled by multiplying 15 feet per second by 1,800 seconds: $15 \times 1,800 = (10 \times 1,800) + (5 \times 1,800) = 18,000 + 9,000 = 27,000$ feet. Choice D is correct.

Not all distance problems ask for the distance, of course. If you're asked for a rate of speed, divide the distance by the time. Check the units again. Miles divided by hours gives you miles per hour, and feet divided by seconds gives you feet per second. Check that the answer choices are in units that match what your division is producing. If they're not, you need to do a conversion.

If you know the distance and the time and need to find the rate of speed, divide the distance by the time.

$$d = r \times t$$
$$\frac{d}{t} = r$$

If you're asked for the time, divide distance by the speed. Checking the units for these is a little more complicated because you're dividing by miles per hour or feet per second or some other "distance per time" unit. Think of the calculation as dividing by a fraction.

$$\text{miles} \div \frac{\text{miles}}{\text{hour}} = \text{miles} \times \frac{\text{hour}}{\text{miles}} = \text{hour}$$

If you know the distance and the rate of speed and need to find the time, divide the distance by the rate of speed.

$$d = r \times t$$
$$\frac{d}{r} = t$$

EXAMPLE:

If you drive 135 miles in 90 minutes, what is your speed in miles per hour?

    A.   202.5 mph
    B.   90 mph
    C.   66 mph
    D.   1.5 mph

First change 90 minutes to hours by dividing 90 minutes by 60 minutes per hour. That gives you $1\frac{1}{2}$ hours.

Then divide the distance, 135 miles, by the time, $1\frac{1}{2}$ hours, to find the speed:

$$135 \div 1\frac{1}{2} = \frac{135}{1} \div \frac{3}{2} = \frac{\overset{45}{\cancel{135}}}{1} \times \frac{2}{\cancel{3}} = 90 \text{ mph}$$

Choice B is correct.

EXAMPLE:

How long will it take to run 400 meters at 8 meters per second?

    A.   3,200 seconds
    B.   53 seconds
    C.   50 seconds
    D.   20 seconds

There's no need to adjust the units here, so divide 400 meters by 8 meters per second to find the time of 50 seconds. Choice C is correct.

Practice

Directions: Choose the best answer for each question.

1. How far can a train travel in 7 hours at an average speed of 85 miles per hour?

    A. 595 miles
    B. 92 miles
    C. 78 miles
    D. 12 miles

2. If a runner completes a 100-meter dash in 16 seconds, what is his speed in meters per second?

    A. 1,600 m/sec.
    B. 116 m/sec.
    C. 84 m/sec.
    D. 6.25 m/sec.

3. A trip of 840 miles requires a total of 14 hours of driving. What is the average rate of speed?

    A. $16\frac{2}{3}$ mph
    B. 60 mph
    C. 66 mph
    D. $166\frac{2}{3}$ mph

4. If you walk at 3.5 mph, how far can you walk in 2 hours?

    A. 1.5 miles
    B. 1.75 miles
    C. 5.5 miles
    D. 7 miles

5. If a hike of 10 miles takes you 4 hours, what is your average hiking speed?

    A. 2.5 mph
    B. 4 mph
    C. 6 mph
    D. 10 mph

6. A train travels at an average speed of 72 miles per hour. How far will it travel in 45 minutes?

    A. 16 miles
    B. 54 miles
    C. 96 miles
    D. 324 miles

7. The kudzu vine is reputed to grow half an inch per hour. If this claim is true, how far will it grow in a day? (This isn't a typical distance problem, but you handle it the same way.)

    A. 12 inches
    B. 24 inches
    C. 30 inches
    D. 48 inches

8. The driving distance between New York and Los Angeles is estimated to be 2,451 miles. If you can make the drive at an average speed of 50 miles per hour, approximately how long will the trip take?

    A. 5 hours
    B. 12 hours
    C. 49 hours
    D. 123 hours

9. If a runner completes the 10,000 meters in 40 minutes, what is his speed in meters per hour?

    A.   250 m/hr.
    B.   1,500 m/hr.
    C.   2,500 m/hr.
    D.   15,000 m/hr.

10. The International Space Station orbits the earth every 90 minutes. If the orbital speed is 26,720 kilometers per hour, what is the length of its orbit?

    A.   2,404,800 km
    B.   40,080 km
    C. $17,813\frac{1}{3}$ km
    D. $296\frac{8}{9}$ km

Answers

1. **A.** 85 mph × 7 hours = 595 miles

2. **D.** 100 meters ÷ 16 seconds = 6.25 m/sec.

3. **B.** 840 miles ÷ 14 hours is 60 mph

4. **D.** 3.5 mph × 2 hours = 7 miles

5. **A.** 10 miles ÷ 4 hours = 2.5 mph

6. **B.** Change 45 minutes to $\frac{3}{4}$ hour. 72 mph × $\frac{3}{4}$ hour = 54 miles

7. **A.** $\frac{1}{2}$ inch per hour × 24 hours = 12 inches or 1 foot, which is why kudzu is nicknamed the foot-a-day plant.

8. **C.** 2,451 miles ÷ 50 mph = 49.02 hours, so round to 49 hours.

9. **D.** Change 40 minutes to $\frac{2}{3}$ hour. 10,000 meters ÷ $\frac{2}{3}$ hour = 15,000 m/hr.

10. **B.** Change 90 minutes to 1.5 hours. 26,720 kilometers per hour × 1.5 hours = 40,080 km

D. Tax, Tip, and Interest

When shopping, you often pay a sales tax, and you frequently leave a tip for service. You may pay interest on a loan or receive interest on your savings or investment. What all these have in common is the way in which they're calculated. Each of them is generally calculated as a percentage of some other quantity. Sales tax is the percentage of the amount purchased; the tip is usually a percentage of the total bill; and interest is a percentage of the amount borrowed, saved, or invested.

Change percents to decimals or fractions before doing any calculations. *Percent* literally means out of 100, so 6 percent is $\frac{6}{100}$ and 15 percent is $\frac{15}{100}$. If you prefer to work with decimals, drop the percent sign (or the word *percent*) and move the decimal point two places left: $\frac{15}{100}$ = 15 percent = 0.15.

To calculate the tax (or tip or interest), multiply the fraction or decimal version of the percent by the amount of the purchase (or the price of the service or the amount of the loan or investment).

EXAMPLE:

> If Jason bought a circular saw for $99 and the sales tax is 6 percent, how much tax did he pay?
>
> **A.** $5.94
> **B.** $59.40
> **C.** $99.06
> **D.** $104.94

Change 6 percent to 0.06 and multiply by $99. (Expect your answer to be just a little less than $6.) So, 0.06 × $99 = $5.94. Choice A is correct.

EXAMPLE:

> If you believe in leaving a 15 percent tip for service, how much of a tip should you leave on a check of $48?
>
> **A.** $3.20
> **B.** $7.20
> **C.** $15
> **D.** $63

Change 15 percent to $\frac{15}{100}$ and reduce to $\frac{3}{20}$. Now, multiply: $\frac{3}{\cancel{20}_5} \times \$\cancel{48}^{12} = \frac{36}{5} = 7\frac{1}{5} = \$7.20$. Choice B is correct.

EXAMPLE:

> You establish a certificate of deposit that pays 3.5 percent interest per year. If you deposit $2,000, how much interest will you receive after 1 year?
>
> **A.** $7
> **B.** $21.50
> **C.** $70
> **D.** $571

Change 3.5 percent to a decimal by dropping the word *percent* and moving the decimal point two places to the left: 3.5 percent = 0.035. Multiply: 0.035 × $2,000 = $70. Choice C is correct.

To find the total bill including tax or tip or the new balance including interest, calculate the tax (or tip or interest) and add it to the original amount. In the first example above, the total bill would be $99 plus $5.94 tax, or $104.94. In the second example, adding the $7.20 tip to the $48 check will bring the total to $55.20. In the third example, your CD will be worth $2,000 + $70 or $2,070 after 1 year.

All in One

The total bill including tax or tip, or the total value including interest, is equal to 100 percent of the original amount plus a percentage for tax, tip, or interest. For example, if the question from the circular-saw example were revised to say "If Jason bought a circular saw for $99 plus 6 percent sales tax, how much did he pay?" you would be looking for 100 percent of $99 plus 6 percent of $99. Since 100 percent, when changed to a decimal, is simply 1, that calculation becomes $(1 \times \$99) + (0.06 \times \$99) = 1.06 \times \$99$. You can get to the total amount in one step by adding 1 to the percent and multiplying.

EXAMPLE:

> If Mr. Johnson wants to leave a 20 percent tip on a restaurant bill of $58.60, what is the total amount he will pay?

You could find 20 percent of $58.60 and then add that amount to $58.60, but you can accomplish the same thing by adding 1 (for 100 percent of the bill) to 0.20 (for 20 percent) and multiplying $1.2 \times \$58.60$.

$$\begin{array}{r} 58.60 \\ \times\ 1.2 \\ \hline 11720 \\ 58\,600 \\ \hline 70.320 \end{array}$$

Mr. Johnson will pay $70.32.

The Long Run

Interest is paid at an annual rate—4 percent per year, for example. For 1 year, finding the interest is simply a matter of finding a percent of the principal in the account. When you look at an investment that earns interest for more than a year, however, you need to involve that length of time in your calculation. The formula for simple interest is interest = principal (the amount of money invested) times the annual percentage rate times the number of years, or $I = prt$. **Remember:** That's only calculating the interest though, not the total amount.

EXAMPLE:

> If you invest $2,500 for one year at an annual interest rate of 4.5 percent, how much interest will you earn the first year? What will the total value of your investment be at the end of the year?

The principal is $2,500. The interest rate is 4.5 percent or 0.045. The time is 1 year. $I = prt = 2,500 \times 0.045 \times 1 = 112.5$.

$$\begin{array}{r} 2500 \\ \times\,0.045 \\ \hline 12\,500 \\ 100\,000 \\ \hline 112.500 \end{array}$$

In the first year, you earn $112.50 interest, so your investment is worth $2,500 + $112.50 = $2612.50.

Practice

Directions: Choose the best answer for each question.

1. Marianne buys a new television for $450 plus 8 percent tax. What is the total cost?

   A. $360
   B. $414
   C. $486
   D. $810

2. Jerry invested $5,000 at 4.5 percent interest per year. How much interest did he earn for the first year?

   A. $22.50
   B. $225
   C. $4,775
   D. $5,225

3. A restaurant adds an 18 percent tip to the bill for parties of eight or more. How much is the tip if the bill is $220 for a party of 10?

   A. $1.44
   B. $14.40
   C. $26
   D. $39.60

4. If you deposit $8,000 in an account that pays 4 percent per year interest, how much will the account be worth after 1 year?

   A. $320
   B. $3,200
   C. $8,320
   D. $11,200

5. Find the total cost of a new car that lists for $24,000 if sales tax of 5 percent is added.

   A. $25,200
   B. $27,400
   C. $28,600
   D. $36,000

6. If you invest $10,000 at 4 percent per year for 3 years, how much interest will you earn?

   A. $300
   B. $400
   C. $700
   D. $1,200

7. What is the total bill if a tip of 17 percent is added to a restaurant check of $80?

   A. $13.60
   B. $93.60
   C. $97
   D. $136

8. Frank buys a DVD player for $130 plus 8 percent sales tax. What is the total cost?

   A. $10.40
   B. $104
   C. $140.40
   D. $234

9. If you borrow $300 at 6 percent interest per year for 5 years, how much interest will you pay?

   A. $18
   B. $90
   C. $318
   D. $390

10. What is the total bill if you add a 15 percent tip to a restaurant bill of $120?

    A. $18
    B. $135
    C. $138
    D. $180

Answers

1. **C.** You want the total amount, so multiply $1.08 \times \$450 = \$486$.

2. **B.** You're looking just for the interest, so multiply the interest rate, as a decimal, by the amount invested: $0.045 \times \$5,000 = \$225$.

3. **D.** You were only asked to find the tip, not the total bill, so multiply $0.18 \times \$220 = \$39.60$.

4. **C.** At 4 percent per year, $8,000 will grow to $1.04 \times \$8,000 = \$8,320$.

5. **A.** Five percent of $24,000 plus the full $24,000 is $1.05 \times \$24,000 = \$25,200$.

6. **D.** To find the interest on $10,000 at 4 percent per year for 3 years, use the $I = prt$ formula: $I = 10,000 \times 0.04 \times 3 = \$1,200$.

7. **B.** The total bill, including a 17 percent tip, is $1.17 \times \$80 = \$93.60$.

8. **C.** To find the total cost, multiply 1.08 times the price of the DVD player: $1.08 \times \$130 = \$140.40$.

9. **B.** $I = prt$, so multiply $\$300 \times 0.06 \times 5 = \$90$.

10. **C.** If you add 15 percent to the bill, you'll leave 115 percent of the bill. So, 115 percent of $120 is $1.15 \times \$120 = \$138$.

E. Discount and Depreciation

Problems involving discount and depreciation can be worked in a fashion similar to tax, tip, and interest problems. Unlike tax and tips that are added to the bill, discounts are amounts subtracted from the price of a purchase. While interest adds to the value of an investment, depreciation reduces the value.

Change percents to decimals or fractions and multiply by the original amount of the purchase or investment to find the amount of the discount or depreciation, just as you did with tax. But to find the final price or the final value of the investment, subtract the discount or depreciation from the original amount.

EXAMPLE:

Rachel buys a new coat that lists for $180, but she receives a 20 percent discount. What is the price of the coat after the discount?

    A. $144
    B. $160
    C. $200
    D. $216

Change 20 percent to 0.20 and multiply by $180. Then $0.20 \times \$180 = \$36$ is the discount, so the price of the coat after the discount is $\$180 - \$36 = \$144$. Choice A is correct.

EXAMPLE:

The value of a new car depreciates 12 percent after the first year. If the car sells for $20,000, how much does the value decrease after the first year?

    A. $17,600
    B. $12,000
    C. $8,000
    D. $2,400

Change 12 percent to 0.12 and multiply by $20,000. The decrease in the value of the car is $0.12 \times \$20,000 =$ $2,400. Choice D is correct.

A Shortcut

Do you want to find the final value quickly? You can, but instead of adding 1 to the percent, as you did for tax, subtract the percent from 1, which you can usually do in your head, and then multiply this percentage by the original amount.

EXAMPLE:

The value of a new car depreciates 12 percent in the first year. If the car sells for $20,000, what is its value after 1 year?

    A. $17,600
    B. $12,000
    C. $8,000
    D. $2,400

You could calculate the amount of depreciation as in the earlier example, and then subtract, but to get directly to the value of the car, subtract $1 - 0.12 = 0.88$. The car is worth 88 percent of its original value. $0.88 \times \$20,000 = \$17,600$. Choice A is correct.

Practice

Directions: Choose the best answer for each question.

1. If a $540 refrigerator is on sale at a 20 percent discount, how much will you save on the purchase?

    A. $54
    B. $108
    C. $432
    D. $648

2. Machinery purchased for a factory depreciates at a rate of 8 percent per year. If the factory owner installs $50,000 in new equipment, what will it be worth at the end of the first year?

    A. $4,000
    B. $40,000
    C. $46,000
    D. $54,000

3. If you purchase a sweater that lists for $60 at a 15 percent discount, what is the price of the sweater after the discount?

   A. $9
   B. $15
   C. $45
   D. $51

4. Equipment valued at $120,000 depreciates at 7 percent per year. How much of its value does it lose after the first year?

   A. $8,400
   B. $36,000
   C. $84,000
   D. $111,600

5. What is the final price of a washer that lists for $590 if it's on sale at a 15 percent discount?

   A. $88.50
   B. $501.50
   C. $505
   D. $575

Answers

1. **B.** You can quickly calculate this in your head as follows: Ten percent of $540 is $54, so 20 percent is $108. You save $108. Or you can multiply to solve: $0.20 \times \$540 = \$108$.

2. **C.** If the equipment depreciates at a rate of 8 percent, multiply by 0.92 to find its value after 1 year: $0.92 \times \$50,000 = \$46,000$.

3. **D.** If the sweater is 15 percent off, multiply by 0.85 to find the sale price: $0.85 \times \$60 = \$51$.

4. **A.** The equipment loses 7 percent of its value, and $0.07 \times \$120,000 = \$8,400$.

5. **B.** If the washer is discounted by 15 percent, you pay 85 percent of the price. So, $0.85 \times \$590 = \$501.50$.

F. Commission

Commission is also calculated as a percentage, in this case, a percentage of sales. Problems involving commission are a little different in that a worker generally receives a salary as well as commission, so the two amounts must be calculated separately and then added together.

EXAMPLE:

Mr. Ellison earns $18 per hour plus a 2 percent commission on his sales. How much does he earn in a week when he works 40 hours and sells $80,000?

   A. $720
   B. $1,600
   C. $1,614
   D. $2,320

His hourly salary amounts to $18 × 40 hours = $720. His commission is 0.02 × $80,000 = $1,600. Add salary plus commission to find that he earns $720 + $1,600 = $2,320 for the week. Choice D is correct.

Practice

Directions: Choose the best answer for each question.

1. Mrs. Anderson earns $12.50 per hour plus 3 percent commission on her sales. Find her total earning for a week in which she works 30 hours and sells $800 worth of merchandise.

    A. $240
    B. $375
    C. $377.40
    D. $399

2. Roger earns $7.50 per hour plus 4 percent commission on sales. How much does he earn in a week during which he works 20 hours and sells $1,800 worth of merchandise?

    A. $870
    B. $222
    C. $150
    D. $72

3. Find Raul's total earning for a week in which he works 40 hours and makes sales totaling $20,000, if he earns $12 per hour and 1.5 percent commission.

    A. $300
    B. $480
    C. $780
    D. $3,480

4. Roger earns $14.25 per hour plus 2 percent commission on sales. How much does he earn in a week during which he works 34 hours and sells $600 worth of merchandise?

    A. $264.50
    B. $462.50
    C. $484.50
    D. $496.50

5. Tonya earns $11 per hour plus 2.5 percent commission on her sales. Find her total earning for a week in which she works 40 hours and sells $1,200 worth of merchandise.

    A. $440
    B. $443
    C. $470
    D. $740

Answers

1. **D.** ($12.50 per hour × 30 hours) + (0.03 × $800) = $375 + $24 = $399

2. **B.** ($7.50 per hour × 20 hours) + (0.04 × $1,800) = $150 + $72 = $222

3. **C.** (40 hours × $12 per hour) + ($20,000 × 0.015) = $480 + $300 = $780

4. **D.** ($14.25 per hour × 34 hours) + (0.02 × $600) = $484.50 + $12 = $496.50

5. **C.** ($11 per hour × 40 hours) + (0.025 × $1,200) = $440 + $30 = $470

G. Perimeter and Area

Other common problems—and these don't involve percents—come from geometry. Calculating perimeter and area are common challenges.

Perimeter is simply the distance around the outside of a figure, so it can be found by adding the lengths of the sides. Perimeter is measured in linear units like feet, inches, meters, or centimeters.

EXAMPLE:

> Find the perimeter of a rectangle that is 2 feet wide and 3 feet long.
>
>   A.   6 feet
>   B.   10 feet
>   C.   12 feet
>   D.   36 feet

The perimeter is the sum of the lengths of the sides, so $P = 2 + 3 + 2 + 3 = 10$ feet. Choice B is correct.

The area of rectangles and squares can be found by multiplying length by width, and the area of a triangle is half of its base times its height. Area is always measured in square units.

EXAMPLE:

> Find the area of a triangle with a base of 12 inches and a height of 9 inches.
>
>   A.   108 in.^{2}
>   B.   54 in.^{2}
>   C.   42 in.^{2}
>   D.   27 in.^{2}

The area of a triangle is half the product of the base and the height, so $A = \frac{1}{2} \times 12 \times 9 = 6 \times 9 = 54$ in.^{2}. Choice B is correct.

If the area and one dimension of a rectangle are given, you can find the other dimension by dividing.

EXAMPLE:

> Find the length of a rectangle that is 11 cm wide if the area is 231 cm^2.
>
>   A.   10.5 cm
>   B.   21 cm
>   C.   104.5 cm
>   D.   110 cm

The area is 231 cm^2 and the width is 11 cm, so $231 \div 11 = 21$ cm in length. Choice B is correct.

If the perimeter of a rectangle is known and one dimension is given, you can calculate the other dimension. The perimeter is twice the sum of the length and the width, so divide the perimeter by 2 and subtract the known dimension to find the other.

EXAMPLE:

Find the width of a rectangle 8 inches long if its perimeter is 46 inches.

   A.   30 inches
   B.   19 inches
   C.   15 inches
   D.   5.75 inches

The perimeter of 46 inches is equal to twice the sum of the length and the width, so the length plus the width will equal 23 inches. Since the width is 8 inches, the length will be 23 − 8 = 15 inches. Choice C is correct.

Practice

Directions: Choose the best answer for each question.

1. Find the perimeter of a triangle whose sides measure 8 cm, 12 cm, and 17 cm.

   A.   37 cm
   B.   45 cm
   C.   96 cm
   D.   126 cm

2. Find the area of a rectangle 25 inches wide and 30 inches long.

   A.   75 in.^{2}
   B.   110 in.^{2}
   C.   375 in.^{2}
   D.   750 in.^{2}

3. Find the area of a triangle with a base of 18 feet and a height of 9 feet.

   A.   45 ft.^{2}
   B.   54 ft.^{2}
   C.   81 ft.^{2}
   D.   162 ft.^{2}

4. Find the width of a rectangle 7 feet long, if the area is 84 square feet.

   A.   12 feet
   B.   77 feet
   C.   91 feet
   D.   588 feet

5. Find the perimeter of a rectangle 13 m long and 6 m wide.

   A.   19 m
   B.   38 m
   C.   39 m
   D.   78 m

6. Find the area of a triangle with a base of 4 inches and a height of 3 inches.

   A.   6 in.^{2}
   B.   12 in.^{2}
   C.   14 in.^{2}
   D.   48 in.^{2}

7. Find the length of a rectangle 3.2 m wide if the area of the rectangle is 64 m².

   A. 57.6 m
   B. 32 m
   C. 30.4 m
   D. 20 m

8. Find the width of a rectangle with length 19 inches if the perimeter is 80 inches.

   A. 61 inches
   B. 30.5 inches
   C. 21 inches
   D. 4.2 inches

9. Find the perimeter of a square whose side is 8 cm long.

   A. 64 cm
   B. 32 cm
   C. 20 cm
   D. 16 cm

10. Find the area of a square 12 inches on each side.

   A. 144 in.²
   B. 120 in.²
   C. 48 in.²
   D. 24 in.²

Answers

1. **A.** To find perimeter, add the lengths of the sides: 8 + 12 + 17 = 37 cm.

2. **D.** The area of a rectangle is the product of the length and the width, so 25 inches × 30 inches = 750 in.².

3. **C.** The area of a triangle is half the product of the base and the height, so multiply $\frac{1}{2} \times 18$ feet $\times 9$ feet $= 9 \times 9 = 81$ ft.².

4. **A.** To find the width, divide the area by the length: 84 ÷ 7 = 12 feet.

5. **B.** Find the perimeter by adding the lengths of the sides. In a rectangle, opposite sides are the same lengths, so the perimeter is twice the length plus twice the width. The perimeter is (2 × 13) + (2 × 6) = 26 + 12 = 38 m.

6. **A.** The area of a triangle is half the base times the height, so multiply $\frac{1}{2} \times 4 \times 3 = 2 \times 3 = 6$ in.².

7. **D.** Divide to find the width: 64 ÷ 3.2 = 20 m.

8. **C.** The perimeter is twice the length plus twice the width, or twice the sum of the length and the width, so divide the perimeter by 2 to find that the length plus width is 80 ÷ 2 = 40 inches. Since the length is 19 inches, subtract to find the width: 40 − 19 = 21 inches.

9. **B.** All four sides of the square measure 8 cm, so the perimeter is 4 × 8 = 32 cm.

10. **A.** The area of a square equals length times width, but because length and width are the same, the area is the length of the side, squared: $12^2 = 12 \times 12 = 144$ in.².

Chapter 6

Arithmetic Reasoning: Whole Numbers and Decimals

The questions on the Arithmetic Reasoning section of the AFQT use the four basic operations of arithmetic: addition, subtraction, multiplication, and division. They ask you to perform those operations, singly or in combination, on whole numbers, fractions, and decimals. Fractions will be the focus of the next chapter, but here we'll look at whole numbers and decimals. It makes sense to do these together because the rules are basically the same. There's an invisible decimal point at the end of each whole number, and if you make it visible and annex a zero (or several zeros), the whole number suddenly looks like a decimal. There's a little more to think about for multiplication and division when the digits after the decimal point are not all zeros, but you'll see it's not a big difference.

Reviewing the basic rules for each operation and lots of practice will both be helpful because your time is limited; anything you can do to get the arithmetic done more quickly will improve your score. So, for each operation, we'll look at shortcuts that may speed your work.

A. Place Value

Fractions and decimals often get lumped together because what we call decimals are actually decimal fractions. Fractions and decimals both express part of a whole, but decimals are a type of fraction that extends the decimal place value system. Common fractions (the full name for fractions) have their own rules. Decimal fractions fit into the place value system of whole numbers.

Whole numbers have an invisible decimal point after the last digit, the ones digit. We don't show the decimal point in whole numbers because we don't need it to separate the whole from the fraction, but we could choose to show it. Then the digit to the immediate left of the decimal point indicates how many ones are in the number, and the next to the left shows how many tens. As you move to the left, each digit is worth ten times as much.

$$5 \underset{\text{millions}}{5} , \underset{\substack{\text{hundred-}\\\text{thousands}}}{2} \underset{\substack{\text{ten-}\\\text{thousands}}}{8} \underset{\text{thousands}}{1} , \underset{\text{hundreds}}{7} \underset{\text{tens}}{3} \underset{\text{ones}}{9.}$$

To the other side of the decimal point, the places for decimal fractions begin with tenths $\left(\dfrac{1}{10}\right)$ and get smaller as you move right.

$$\underset{\text{millions}}{5} , \underset{\substack{\text{hundred-}\\\text{thousands}}}{2} \underset{\substack{\text{ten-}\\\text{thousands}}}{8} \underset{\text{thousands}}{1} , \underset{\text{hundreds}}{7} \underset{\text{tens}}{3} \underset{\text{ones}}{9} . \underset{\text{tenths}}{4} \underset{\text{hundredths}}{0} \underset{\text{thousandths}}{6} \underset{\substack{\text{ten-}\\\text{thousandths}}}{5}$$

For many addition and subtraction problems, as long as you align decimal points and therefore keep digits with the same place value under one another, there is no other concern about the decimals.

B. Addition

Addition is about putting together, combining, and, unless you're working with negative numbers, getting bigger. In the last chapter, we reviewed some of the keywords that signal addition when you come across them in a problem. Now you need to work on the addition itself.

Whole Numbers

Whole numbers include all the numbers you use to count—1, 2, 3, 4, 5, and on and on—as well as 0. It's easier to describe whole numbers by what they *don't* include: fractions, decimals, and negative numbers. When you add whole numbers, you stack them up one under the other with the right side aligned so that the invisible decimal points are lined up and add the right-hand column—the ones digits—first. If that total has more than one digit, you place the ones digit of the total in the ones column of the answer and carry the other digits over to the tens column. Repeat in this manner, moving left to the tens, hundreds, and higher-valued places.

EXAMPLE:

Add ones column:	Add tens column:	Add hundreds column:	Add thousands column:
$8 + 3 + 7 = 18$	$7 + 5 + 9 + 1 \text{ (carried)} = 22$	$3 + 1 + 4 + 2 \text{ (carried)} = 10$	$1 \text{ (carried)} = 1$
Place 8 in the answer.	Place 2 in the answer.	Place 0 in the answer.	Place 1 in the answer.
Place 1 in tens column.	Place 2 in hundreds column.	Place 1 in thousands column.	

$$
\begin{array}{r}
3\ 7\ 8 \\
1\ 5\ 3 \\
4\ 9\ 7 \\
\end{array}
\quad \rightarrow \quad
\begin{array}{r}
3\ \overset{1}{7}\ 8 \\
1\ 5\ 3 \\
4\ 9\ 7 \\
\hline
8
\end{array}
\quad \rightarrow \quad
\begin{array}{r}
\overset{2}{3}\ \overset{1}{7}\ 8 \\
1\ 5\ 3 \\
4\ 9\ 7 \\
\hline
2\ 8
\end{array}
\quad \rightarrow \quad
\begin{array}{r}
{}^{1}\ \overset{2}{3}\ \overset{1}{7}\ 8 \\
1\ 5\ 3 \\
4\ 9\ 7 \\
\hline
1,\ 0\ 2\ 8
\end{array}
$$

Compatible Numbers

If the numbers you're adding are small, you may just keep the addition in a line. Called upon to add $4 + 2 + 5$, you probably wouldn't bother to rewrite them one under another. When you're adding a group of numbers, especially if they're in a line, look for compatible numbers. The term *compatible numbers* usually refers to pairs that add to 10, but you can extend the concept to make it more useful.

To add $5 + 4 + 9 + 2 + 1 + 6 + 8$, look for pairs that add to 10, and rearrange the problem.

$$5 + 4 + 9 + 2 + 1 + 6 + 8 = (4 + 6) + (2 + 8) + (9 + 1) + 5 = 10 + 10 + 10 + 5 = 35$$

It's easy to add up the 10s and then add on the little bit extra, so looking for pairs that make 10 can speed up the calculation. But if the numbers don't conveniently give you pairs that make 10, you can use the same idea with a different repeating sum. You can look for groups that add to 5 or to 9 or to your favorite number. Just keep it to one goal per problem so you don't confuse yourself.

$$8 + 3 + 7 + 1 + 6 + 2 + 3 = (8 + 1) + (7 + 2) + (6 + 3) + 3 = 9 + 9 + 9 + 3 = 27 + 3 = 30$$

Minor Adjustments

Another strategy that can help speed up addition is to add numbers that are close to the ones in your problem, and then adjust. To add 39 and 47, for example, round up. Since 39 is close to 40 and 47 is close to 50, think about 40 + 50. That answer of 90 puts you in the right neighborhood. Your actual answer is a little less than 90. Look at your answer choices. Sometimes that's enough to rule out all but one answer choice. If you need the exact answer, take the 90 and adjust. Since 39 is one less than 40 and 47 is three less than 50, the exact total is 1 + 3 or 4 units less than 90. So, 39 + 47 = 90 − 4 = 86. Even rounding one of the numbers can speed up the work. 39 + 47 is close to 40 + 47 = 87. 39 is one less than 40, so your answer is one less than 87.

Practice

Directions: Choose the best answer for each question.

1. Josh ran 4 miles on Monday, 3 miles on Tuesday, and 6 miles on Wednesday. How far has he run this week?

   A. 7 miles
   B. 9 miles
   C. 13 miles
   D. 23 miles

2. The weather service recorded 12 inches of snow in January, 18 inches in February, and 6 inches in March. What is the total snowfall for the first quarter of the year?

   A. 26 inches
   B. 30 inches
   C. 34 inches
   D. 36 inches

3. If Jane packs a mixer that weighs 22 pounds and a blender that weighs 9 pounds into a shipping box, how much will the contents of the box weigh?

   A. 30 pounds
   B. 31 pounds
   C. 32 pounds
   D. 33 pounds

4. A fruit basket contains 8 apples, 7 oranges, 3 pears, and 4 bananas. How many pieces of fruit are in the basket?

   A. 14
   B. 18
   C. 22
   D. 25

5. A recipe for party punch calls for 46 ounces of pineapple juice, 12 ounces of lemon juice, 12 ounces of orange juice, 112 ounces of sparkling water, and 32 ounces of ginger ale. How many ounces of punch will the recipe make?

   A. 102
   B. 190
   C. 202
   D. 214

6. Jason lifts weights and is increasing the amount he can lift. Right now, he is lifting a bar that weighs 54 pounds with a 50-pound plate on each end. If he adds a 20-pound plate to each end, how much will he be lifting?

   A. 124 pounds
   B. 144 pounds
   C. 174 pounds
   D. 194 pounds

7. Lydia has a collection of 53 teapots. If she receives 12 more teapots as gifts, how many teapots will she have?

   A. 55
   B. 63
   C. 65
   D. 75

8. If you have $327 in your checking account and you deposit $415, how much will you have in your account?

   A. $842
   B. $742
   C. $732
   D. $715

9. An aquarium contains 117 fish. If 37 new fish are introduced and all of them survive, what is the population of the aquarium?

   A. 165 fish
   B. 160 fish
   C. 157 fish
   D. 154 fish

10. At 8 a.m., there were 7 cars in the parking lot. If 13 more cars entered over the next hour and none left, how many cars were in the lot at 9 a.m.?

   A. 21
   B. 20
   C. 16
   D. 15

Answers

1. **C.** Four and six are a compatible pair. So, $4 + 3 + 6 = (4 + 6) + 3 = 10 + 3 = 13$.

2. **D.** Take the 2 from the 12 and the 8 from 18 to make a 10. So, $12 + 18 + 6 = (10 + 2) + (10 + 8) + 6 = 10 + 10 + (2 + 8) + 6 = 36$.

3. **B.** Adding 10 is easy. Adding 9 is one less. So, $22 + 9 = 22 + (10 - 1) = 32 - 1 = 31$.

4. **C.** The 7 and 3 make 10. So, $8 + 7 + 3 + 4 = (7 + 3) + (8 + 4) = 10 + 12 = 22$. You could also notice that the 3 and the 4 are 7, so you have two 7s and an 8. So, $8 + 7 + (3 + 4) = 8 + 7 + 7 = 8 + 14 = 22$.

5. **D.** You might want to stack these to add, but the two 12s make 24, which adds nicely with the 46. So, $46 + (12 + 12) + 112 + 32 = 46 + 24 + 112 + 32 = 70 + 32 + 112 = 102 + 112 = 214$.

6. **D.** Add the 50s and the 20s, and save the 54 for last. So, $54 + (50 + 50) + (20 + 20) = 54 + 100 + 40 = 194$.

7. **C.** Fifty and 10 are 60, and 3 and 2 are 5. So, $53 + 12 = 65$.

8. **B.** Round 327 to 330 and adjust back down at the end. So, $\$327 + \$415 \approx \$330 + \$415 \approx \$745$. Adjust: $\$745 - \$3 = \$742$.

9. **D.** Round up both numbers. So, $117 + 37 \approx 120 + 40 \approx 160$. Each number was rounded up three, so adjust the total down by six: $160 - 6 = 154$.

10. **B.** $7 + 13 = 20$.

Decimals

When adding whole numbers, you lined up the rightmost digits of the numbers and that aligned the invisible decimal points and guaranteed that each column held digits with the same place value: ones under ones, tens under tens, and so on.

To add decimals correctly, you also want to line up the decimal points. Different? Not really, but in this case, the decimal point will be visible. If it makes your work easier, once the decimal points are aligned, you can add zeros to the end of any number so that each number has the same number of digits after the decimal point. This will fill out the columns of digits. Once you've lined up the decimal points, you can add the numbers just as if they were whole numbers.

EXAMPLE:

$$128.37 + 42.9 + 1{,}602.539 =$$

$$
\begin{array}{r}
128.37 \\
42.9 \\
1{,}602.539 \\
\hline
\end{array}
=
\begin{array}{r}
128.370 \\
42.900 \\
1{,}602.539 \\
\hline
\end{array}
=
\begin{array}{r}
\overset{1\ 1\ \ 1}{128.370} \\
42.900 \\
1{,}602.539 \\
\hline
1{,}773.809
\end{array}
$$

Practice

Directions: Choose the best answer for each question.

1. Jason bought a circular saw for $269.97, a set of wrenches for $54.96, and a pair of safety goggles for $11.47. What is his total bill?

    A. $334
    B. $336.91
    C. $336.40
    D. $337

2. Mallory combined 2.1 grams of sugar with 8.9 grams of cinnamon. What was the weight, in grams, of the mixture?

    A. 11.1 g
    B. 11 g
    C. 10.1 g
    D. 10 g

3. Kevin bought a pen for $1.25, a notebook for $2.87, and computer software for $31. What was his total bill?

    A. $44.30
    B. $35.12
    C. $34.43
    D. $4.43

4. Elias needed to cut three wires, one 4.85 cm long, one 5.2 cm, and one 12.385 cm. What is the shortest length of wire he can use to cut these pieces?

    A. 12.922 cm
    B. 21.472 cm
    C. 22 cm
    D. 22.435 cm

5. Mrs. Williamson bought four items on her shopping list that cost $40.49, $11.98, $29.99, and $22.20. How much did she spend?

   A. $104.66
   B. $104.48
   C. $104.45
   D. $103.66

6. If the airfare to your vacation spot is $125.10 and the return flight costs $193.60, what is the price of a round-trip ticket?

   A. $387.20
   B. $320
   C. $318.70
   D. $250.20

7. A runner records the distance she has run for each of 3 days as 22.5 km, 22.63 km, and 25 km. What is the total distance run over the 3 days?

   A.   25.13 km
   B.   27.38 km
   C.   45.38 km
   D.   70.13 km

8. Arthur the Alien is taking his new space ship out on a sightseeing trip. He travels from Uranus to Jupiter, a distance of 13.94 AU (astronomical units), and then from Jupiter to Earth, a distance of 4.2 AU. Foolishly, Arthur plans to make the final leg of the trip the 1 AU from Earth to the Sun. What is the total distance Arthur would have traveled if he could survive the trip to the Sun?

   A.   19.14 AU
   B.   18.96 AU
   C.   15.36 AU
   D.   14.37 AU

9. One cup of lima beans contains 0.303 mg of vitamin B_1; a medium wedge of watermelon, 0.094 mg; and an average avocado, 0.135 mg. If you ate all these foods, how much vitamin B_1 would you consume?

   A.   5.32 mg
   B.   4.105 mg
   C.   0.532 mg
   D.   0.262 mg

10. A survey of restaurants looked at how they cooked hamburgers. If 0.005 of the restaurants cooked the hamburgers until they were red, 0.087 of them until they were pink, and 0.208 of them until they were light brown, what part of the restaurants cooked the hamburgers pink, red, or light brown?

   A.   0.3
   B.   0.345
   C.   0.372
   D.   0.7

Answers

1. **C.** Round to get an estimate. So, $270 + 55 + 11 \approx 270 + 66 \approx 336$. Adjust down 3¢, down 4¢, and up 47¢, for a net change of 40¢ up. So, $269.97 + $54.96 + $11.47 = $336.40.

2. **B.** Add the whole number parts to get 10 and the decimal parts for another 1. So, $2.1 + 8.9 = (2 + 8) + (0.1 + 0.9) = 10 + 1 = 11$.

3. **B.** Add the smaller dollar and cents amounts first, and break them up to use mental math. So, $1.25 + $2.87 = 1 + 2 + (0.20 + 0.80) + (0.05 + 0.07) = 3 + 1 + 0.12 = 4.12. Add the $31 to the $4.12 to get $35.12.

4. **D.** Make sure the decimal points are lined up, and add zeros if it helps you keep places aligned:

$$
\begin{array}{r}
\overset{1\,1\ \ 1}{4.850} \\
5.200 \\
12.385 \\
\hline
22.435
\end{array}
$$

5. **A.** Round for a quick estimate: $40.49 + $11.98 + $29.99 + $22.20 ≈ 40 + 12 + 30 + 22 ≈ 70 + 34 ≈ 104. Make the adjustment: up 49¢, down 2¢, down 1¢, and up 20¢. So, 104 + 0.49 − 0.02 − 0.01 + 0.20 = $104.66.

6. **C.** If you estimate this as 125 + 200, two answer choices seem unreasonable: Choice A ($387.20) because it seems too big, and Choice D ($250.20) because it seems too small. You rounded $193.60 up several dollars and $125.10 down only a few cents, so your actual answer should be a few dollars less than the estimate of $325. So, $125.10 + $193.60 = $318.70.

7. **D.** A good estimate will help here: 22.5 + 22.63 + 25 ≈ 22 + 22 + 25 ≈ 69. The decimals account for slightly more than another 1, making 70.13 km the only reasonable answer. The various wrong answers are the result of failing to align the decimal points before adding.

8. **A.** Align the decimal points and add two 0s to 1 and a 0 to 4.2 if that helps you. You can save the 1 AU from the Sun to Earth to add on at the end, but don't forget about it.

$$
\begin{array}{r}
\overset{1}{1.00} \\
4.20 \\
13.94 \\
\hline
19.14
\end{array}
$$

9. **C.** 0.303 + 0.094 + 0.135 ≈ 0.300 + 0.100 + 0.100 ≈ 0.500, so expect an answer close to that number. So, 0.303 + 0.094 + 0.135 = 0.397 + 0.135 = 0.532.

10. **A.** Don't be tempted to ignore leading zeros. They keep the places aligned.

$$
\begin{array}{r}
\overset{1\ 2}{0.005} \\
0.087 \\
0.208 \\
\hline
0.300
\end{array}
$$

C. Subtraction

Subtraction is often seen as taking away, removing something, and looking at what's left. Mathematically, it's an undoing, an inverse or opposite operation; specifically, it's the opposite of addition. Because addition and subtraction are related operations, they share some rules about things like lining up the decimal points.

Whole Numbers

When subtracting whole numbers, line up the rightmost digits (and the unseen decimal point). You won't have to worry about a whole stack of numbers, because you'll only subtract one number at a time. The actual process of subtracting does require some backward thinking, since 8 – 5 means "what would I add to 5 to get 8?", but luckily you only deal with single digits most times. Subtraction also sometimes demands a regrouping commonly called *borrowing*.

EXAMPLE:

$$382 - 275 =$$

Start from the right side. It's impossible to subtract 5 from 2 (unless we can use negative numbers, and we can't in this situation). Instead, borrow a ten from the 8 tens and regroup it with the 2 ones. That leaves 7 tens in the middle column, and gives us 12 ones. Subtract 5 from 12 to get 7:

$$
\begin{array}{r}
3\,{}^{7}\!\!\not{8}\,{}^{1}2 \\
-2\ 7\ 5 \\
\hline
7
\end{array}
$$

Moving to the middle column, where there are 7 tens left on the top, 7 minus 7 is 0, and on the left, 3 minus 2 is 1:

$$
\begin{array}{r}
3\,{}^{7}\!\!\not{8}\,{}^{1}2 \\
-2\ 7\ 5 \\
\hline
1\ 0\ 7
\end{array}
$$

Making Change

One technique you can use to help with mental math subtractions is the adding back technique often used by cashiers when giving change. If you make a $12.49 purchase and give the cashier a $20 bill, you may be given your change with an explanation something like "1 makes 50 (handing you a penny), and 50 makes $13 (giving you another 50 cents), and 7 makes $20 (handing you 7 dollars)." Taking your $12.49 and adding $0.01 makes $12.50, and adding $0.50 to that makes exactly $13. Subtracting $13 from $20 is easier, and gives $7. So your change is $7 + $0.50 + $0.01 = $7.51. You can often use this adding-back technique to perform a subtraction mentally.

Practice

Directions: Choose the best answer for each question.

1. If you're making a trip of 810 miles and the trip odometer reads 623 miles, how many more miles do you have to drive?

    A. 213 miles
    B. 187 miles
    C. 97 miles
    D. 93 miles

2. Cole collected 842 baseball cards and Andy collected 927. How many more cards does Andy have?

    A. 95
    B. 89
    C. 85
    D. 82

3. If you must earn 15,000 points to move to the next level in a video game, and you're 1,439 points short of the next level, how many points have you earned?

   A. 14,651
   B. 13,561
   C. 661
   D. 610

4. According to the mission schedule, astronauts planned to work outside the shuttle for 390 minutes. If they've been outside for 158 minutes, how much longer do they plan to work?

   A. 248 minutes
   B. 232 minutes
   C. 148 minutes
   D. 132 minutes

5. When John purchased a used car, it showed that it had been driven 48,391 miles. Today, it shows 87,294 miles. How far has John driven the car?

   A. 39,903 miles
   B. 39,197 miles
   C. 38,903 miles
   D. 38,197 miles

6. A factory produced 78,493 widgets last month and 92,312 this month. How many more widgets were produced this month?

   A. 14,819
   B. 13,981
   C. 13,919
   D. 13,819

7. Elise has read 287 pages of a 421-page book. How many pages does she have left to read?

   A. 134
   B. 166
   C. 234
   D. 266

8. In the most recent census, the population of a town was recorded as 13,472. In the prior census, it had been 11,398. By how much did the population increase?

   A. 2,174
   B. 2,074
   C. 2,070
   D. 2,026

9. Phil is saving for a flat-screen TV that costs $839. If he has saved $407 so far, how much more does he need to save?

   A. $446
   B. $442
   C. $432
   D. $426

10. If the Eagles have scored 48 points and the Giants have scored 32 points, how many points must the Giants score to tie the game?

    A. 70
    B. 25
    C. 21
    D. 16

Answers

1. **B.** Make change to do this mentally. Start with 623. Seven will make 630. Seventy more puts you at 700. Another hundred makes 800. Then you need 10 more. So, 7 + 70 + 100 + 10 = 187.

2. **C.** 920 – 840 = 80, and 7 – 2 = 5. So, 927 – 842 = 85.

3. **B.** You can subtract 1,439 from 15,000 a bit at a time if that's easier. 15,000 – 1,000 = 14,000. Then 14,000 – 400 = 13,600. Then 13,600 – 30 = 13,570. Minus 9 more is 13,561.

4. **B.** They're at 158 now; 2 more minutes will make 160, and 30 more is 190. Another 200 minutes will make 390. Add: 2 + 30 + 200 = 232.

5. **C.** The numbers are large, but you can make change. Start with 48,391, and you need 3 to make 48,394. Nine hundred will put you at 49,294, another thousand is 50,294, and 37,000 gets you to 87,294. Add up 3 + 900 + 1,000 + 37,000 = 38,903.

6. **D.** This one is probably best done by stacking the numbers.

$$
\begin{array}{r}
{\scriptstyle 8\ {}^1 1\ {}^1 2\ {}^1 0}\\
\cancel{9\,2,\!3\,1}\,{}^1 2\\
-7\,8,\ 4\,9\,3\\
\hline
1\,3,\ 8\,1\,9
\end{array}
$$

7. **A.** You can make change here. 287 + 3 = 290. Then 290 + 10 = 300, and another hundred makes 400. You need another 21 to make 421. So, 3 + 10 + 100 + 21 = 134.

8. **B.** A quick estimate says that 13,000 – 11,000 = 2,000. Look at the other digits and notice that 472 – 398 is about 472 – 400, or approximately 72. Therefore, 13,472 – 11,398 ≈ 2,072, but you rounded 398 up to 400, so give back 2: 13,472 – 11,398 = 2,074.

9. **C.** If Phil had saved $400, he'd need another $439. Because he saved $407, he's $7 closer to his goal, so he needs $432.

10. **D.** Recognize these from your eights multiplication facts? (6 × 8) – (4 × 8) = 2 × 8. So, 48 – 32 = 16.

Decimals

Subtracting decimals, like adding decimals, is very similar to working with whole numbers, except that you need to align the decimal points. There will be no big stacks of numbers here, since you'll only subtract one number at a time.

Even Them Out

When you add decimals, once the decimal points are aligned, you may choose to add zeros so that all the addends have the same number of places. When you're subtracting decimals, adding those zeros is not just recommended—it's almost required.

EXAMPLE:

$$
\begin{array}{r}
45.927\\
-23.48\\
\hline
\end{array}
\quad\rightarrow\quad
\begin{array}{r}
45.927\\
-23.480\\
\hline
22.447
\end{array}
$$

This subtraction could be completed without adding a zero, if you remember to bring down the 7. Why do you bring down the 7? Because 7 minus the unseen zero at the end of 23.480 is 7. The next example really wants the added zeros.

EXAMPLE:

$$
\begin{array}{r}
839.5\\
-371.934\\
\hline
\end{array}
$$

If you don't add the two extras zeros to 839.5, it's easy to "bring down" the 3 and the 4 from 371.934, which would be incorrect. Those digits need to be subtracted from something; you need the zeros so there's something to subtract them from.

$$\begin{array}{r} 839.500 \\ -371.934 \\ \hline \end{array}$$

Since you can't subtract 4 from zero, you try to borrow from the digit to the left, but that's a zero as well. Keep moving left. Borrow a 1 from the 5 in the tenths place.

$$\begin{array}{r} 839.\overset{4}{\cancel{5}}{}^{1}0\ 0 \\ -371.9\ 3\ 4 \\ \hline \end{array}$$

That one-tenth becomes ten-hundredths, and then you borrow 1 from the 10 in the hundredths place, leaving 9, and regroup it as 10 in the thousandths place. In the thousandths column, subtract 4 from 10 to get 6. In the hundredths column, subtract 3 from 9 to get 6.

$$\begin{array}{r} 839.\overset{4}{\cancel{5}}\overset{9}{\cancel{0}}{}^{1}0 \\ -371.9\ 3\ 4 \\ \hline 6\ 6 \end{array}$$

When you get to the tenths place, you'll need to borrow again. Borrow a 1 from the 9 ones, and regroup it as 10 tenths. Those 10 tenths added to the 4 tenths already in the tenths place gives you 14 tenths. Subtract 9 from 14 to get 5 in the tenths place and 1 from the remaining 8 ones to get 7 in the ones place.

$$\begin{array}{r} 83\overset{8}{\cancel{9}}.\overset{14}{\cancel{5}}\overset{9}{\cancel{0}}{}^{1}0 \\ -371.9\ 3\ 4 \\ \hline 7.5\ 6\ 6 \end{array}$$

One more borrowing will let you complete the subtraction. Borrowing 1 hundred from the 8 hundreds leaves 7 hundreds and gives you 13 tens. Those 13 tens minus 7 tens leaves 6 tens, and finally, 3 hundreds subtracted from the remaining 7 hundreds leaves 4 hundreds.

$$\begin{array}{r} \overset{7}{\cancel{8}}{}^{1}3\overset{8}{\cancel{9}}.\overset{14}{\cancel{5}}\overset{9}{\cancel{0}}{}^{1}0 \\ -371.9\ 3\ 4 \\ \hline 467.5\ 6\ 6 \end{array}$$

Practice

Directions: Choose the best answer for each question.

1. If a pen measures 4.2 cm and a pencil measures 6.9 cm, how much longer is the pencil than the pen?

   A. 11.1 cm
   B. 10.7 cm
   C. 2.7 cm
   D. 2.3 cm

2. A company produced 428.5 million transistors last year and 649.75 million transistors this year. How many more transistors did they produce this year?

   A. 220.75 million
   B. 221.25 million
   C. 606.90 million
   D. 1,078.25 million

3. In 2001, a tree was 14.86 meters tall. By 2006, it was 18.75 meters. How much did the tree grow in those 5 years?

   A. 4.89 m
   B. 4.11 m
   C. 3.89 m
   D. 3.11 m

4. The perimeter of a triangle is 94.27 cm. If two of the sides total 73.8 cm, what is the length of the third side?

   A. 20.47 cm
   B. 20.53 cm
   C. 21.47 cm
   D. 21.53 cm

5. The distance from the barracks to the mess hall is 85.3 meters, and along the path connecting them there is a bench. If the bench is 23.7 meters from the mess hall, how far is it from the barracks?

   A. 42.65 m
   B. 61.6 m
   C. 64.5 m
   D. 109 m

6. Susan is knitting a scarf and wants it to be 250 cm long. If it is currently 183.9 cm, how much more does she need to knit?

   A. 15.89 cm
   B. 67 cm
   C. 66.1 cm
   D. 158.9 cm

7. You earn $478.29 a week, but $86.09 of federal tax is withheld. How much do you actually take home?

   A. $392.20
   B. $392.38
   C. $391.80
   D. $400.39

8. A baby who was 21.7 cm long at birth is 30.5 cm long at his 6-month checkup. How much did he grow?

   A. 9.2 cm
   B. 9.1 cm
   C. 8.8 cm
   D. 8.2 cm

9. If you've saved $372.39 and want to buy a computer that costs $693.89, how much more do you need to save?

   A. $322.38
   B. $321.59
   C. $321.50
   D. $320.96

10. If you purchase a jacket for $89.95 and give the cashier a $100 bill, how much change will you receive?

    A. $11.95
    B. $11.05
    C. $10.95
    D. $10.05

Answers

1. **C.** Since both measurements have the same number of decimal places, alignment is easy:

$$
\begin{array}{r}
6.9 \\
-4.2 \\
\hline
2.7
\end{array}
$$

2. **B.** The "million" just tags along and has no effect on your calculation. Annexing a zero on 428.5 is optional.

$$
\begin{array}{r}
649.75 \\
-428.50 \\
\hline
221.25
\end{array}
$$

3. **C.** You're taking a little less than 15 away from 18.75. Expect an answer a bit bigger than 3.75.

$$
\begin{array}{r}
1\,\overset{7}{\cancel{8}}.\overset{16}{\cancel{7}}\,{}^{1}5 \\
-\,1\,4.\,8\,\,6 \\
\hline
3.\,8\,\,9
\end{array}
$$

4. **A.** Annexing a zero on 73.8 is optional, but be sure to line up the decimal points.

$$
\begin{array}{r}
9\,\overset{3}{\cancel{4}}.{}^{1}2\,7 \\
-\,7\,3.\,8\,0 \\
\hline
2\,0.\,4\,7
\end{array}
$$

5. **B.** Estimate this as 85 – 24 and expect an answer around 61.

$$
\begin{array}{r}
8\,\overset{4}{\cancel{5}}.{}^{1}3 \\
-\,2\,3.\,7 \\
\hline
6\,1.\,6
\end{array}
$$

6. **C.** Place the decimal at the end of 250 and add a zero.

$$
\begin{array}{r}
\overset{1}{\cancel{2}}\,\overset{14}{\cancel{5}}\,\overset{9}{\cancel{0}}.{}^{1}0 \\
-\,1\,8\,3.\,9 \\
\hline
6\,6.\,1
\end{array}
$$

7. **A.** Estimation may help. The $86 withheld takes away the $78 plus another $8, so expect an answer around $392. The 9 cents then comes off the 29 cents.

$$
\begin{array}{r}
\overset{3}{\cancel{4}}\,{}^{1}7\,8.2\,9 \\
-\,\,\,\,\,\,8\,6.0\,9 \\
\hline
3\,9\,2.2\,0
\end{array}
$$

8. **C.** You can make change here, even if the larger number is a decimal. From 21.7, 0.3 will make 22, 8 more will make 30, and then you need another 0.5.

$$
\begin{array}{r}
\overset{2}{\cancel{3}}\,\overset{9}{\cancel{0}}.{}^{1}5 \\
-\,2\,1.\,7 \\
\hline
8.\,8
\end{array}
$$

9. **C.** No borrowing needed:

$$
\begin{array}{r}
693.89 \\
-372.39 \\
\hline
321.50
\end{array}
$$

10. **D.** Make change. A nickel will make it $90, and then you'll get another 10 dollars. So, $100 – $89.95 = $10.05.

$$
\begin{array}{r}
\cancel{1}\,\overset{9}{\cancel{0}}\,\overset{9}{\cancel{0}}.\overset{9}{\cancel{0}}\,{}^{1}0 \\
-\,8\,9.\,9\,5 \\
\hline
1\,0.\,0\,5
\end{array}
$$

D. Multiplication

Multiplication is repeated addition. The phrase *3 times 12* tells you to add three 12s, as in 12 + 12 + 12 (or twelve 3s, but we won't write that out). That's easy enough to think about when one or both of the *factors* (the numbers being multiplied) are small numbers, but when both factors are decimals or when working with larger numbers, you'll want to rely on the algorithm—the step-by-step processes—to get the job done.

Whole Numbers

All whole number multiplication actually happens by multiplying one digit times one digit, as many times as necessary. The traditional method of multiplication arranges the numbers one under the other and multiplies each of the digits in the bottom number, starting from the right, by each of the digits in the upper number, moving right to left. If any product has two digits, we write the ones digit and "carry" the tens digit to add to the next multiplication.

EXAMPLE:

$$
\begin{array}{r}
492 \\
\times\, 23 \\
\hline
\end{array}
$$

First, multiply the 3 from 23 by the 2 in 492 and write the 6 below the 3. Continue multiplying by 3. Three times 9 is 27, so write the 7 in the tens place and carry the 2 to add to the next product. Three times 4 is 12; add the 2 you carried, and that makes 14. That fills the hundreds place and spills over into the thousands place.

$$
\begin{array}{r}
\overset{2}{4}92 \\
\times\, 23 \\
\hline
1476 \\
????? \\
\hline
?????
\end{array}
$$

Next, you want to multiply 492 by the 2 in 23, but because that 2 represents two tens, you're actually multiplying by 20. Multiplying by 20 amounts to multiplying by 2 and annexing a 0, so you take care of the 0 first by placing a zero in the ones place under the 6, and then multiply by 2. Two times 2 is 4, so put 4 in the tens place. Two times 9 is 18, so place the 8 in the hundreds place and carry the 1. Two times 4 is 8, plus the 1 you carried makes it 9.

$$
\begin{array}{r}
\overset{1}{4}92 \\
\times\, 23 \\
\hline
1476 \\
9840
\end{array}
$$

Finally, add the results of the individual multiplications:

$$
\begin{array}{r}
492 \\
\times 23 \\
\hline
\overset{1}{1},\overset{1}{4}76 \\
9,840 \\
\hline
11,316
\end{array}
$$

Lattice Multiplication

There is another style of multiplication that some people find faster and others prefer because it's not as demanding when it comes to things being done in a specific order. Lattice multiplication makes a grid of squares, with a row for each digit in one of the factors and a column for each digit in the other. Each square has a diagonal drawn from lower left to upper right. The factors are written across the top and down the right side.

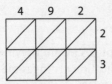

Each digit on the top is multiplied by each digit on the right, and the result is placed in the square at the intersection of that row and column. A single-digit product is placed in the lower triangle. If the product has two digits, the ones digit is placed below the diagonal and the tens digit is placed above it.

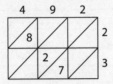

The order in which the multiplications are done is insignificant. Complete the multiplications for each pair of digits.

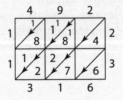

Finally, add along each diagonal. If a sum has two digits, place the ones digit and carry the tens digit to the next diagonal. The final product appears down the left side and across the bottom.

Distribute

When you need to perform mental multiplication, you can ease the process by using the *distributive property,* which tells you that the result of adding two numbers and then multiplying the sum by another number is the same as multiplying each of the addends by the multiplier and adding the results. In easier-to-understand terms, that means that $5 \times 12 = (5 \times 10) + (5 \times 2) = 50 + 10 = 60$; therefore, $5 \times 12 = 60$.

EXAMPLE:

$12 \times 53 = (12 \times 50) + (12 \times 3) = 600 + 36 = 636$

Quick Tips

Need to multiply by 5? Add a 0 and divide by 2. You're actually multiplying by 10 and dividing by 2, but the result is the same as multiplying by 5, and often easier.

EXAMPLE:

$$48 \times 5 = 480 \div 2 = 240$$

EXAMPLE:

$$67 \times 5 = 670 \div 2 = 335$$

Eleven times a single-digit number is an easy multiplication: $7 \times 11 = 77$ and $4 \times 11 = 44$. But there's also a shortcut for multiplying a two-digit number by 11: Separate the two digits, making space for one digit between them. Add the digits and place the sum in the empty space. If the sum is two digits, put the ones digit in the space and add the tens digit to the leftmost digit.

EXAMPLE:

$$27 \times 11 \rightarrow 2\_\_7 \rightarrow (2 + 7 = 9) \rightarrow 2\underline{9}7$$

EXAMPLE:

$$85 \times 11 \rightarrow 8\_\_\_5 \rightarrow (8 + 5 = 13) \rightarrow \overset{1}{8}\_\underline{3}\_5 = 935$$

Practice

Directions: Choose the best answer for each question.

1. There are 47 volunteers at campaign headquarters, and each volunteer gives 9 hours of time to the campaign. How many hours did volunteers work?

    A.   367
    B.   393
    C.   423
    D.   463

2. If your daily commute is 28 miles and you work 5 days a week, how many miles do you commute each week?

    A.   180
    B.   140
    C.   104
    D.   33

3. Genevieve can quilt one square of a quilt in 2 hours. How long will it take her to finish a quilt that has 84 squares?

    A.   42 hours
    B.   86 hours
    C.   164 hours
    D.   168 hours

4. If each box contains 24 cookies and you buy 8 boxes, how many cookies do you have?

    A.   192
    B.   184
    C.   164
    D.   104

5. If there are 365 days in a year and 24 hours in a day, how many hours are in a year?

    A. 1,582
    B. 2,190
    C. 7,446
    D. 8,760

6. If a charter company has 138 buses and each bus can hold 45 people, what is the largest number of passengers they can transport?

    A. 6,210
    B. 5,565
    C. 5,525
    D. 1,242

7. A school has 42 classrooms with 35 desks in each room. How many desks are in the school?

    A. 77
    B. 210
    C. 336
    D. 1,470

8. Jim needs to move 22 cinder blocks. If each block weighs 42 pounds, how much will the entire load weigh?

    A. 964 pounds
    B. 924 pounds
    C. 804 pounds
    D. 168 pounds

9. An auto factory can produce 147 cars per hour. How many cars can it produce during an 8-hour shift?

    A. 896
    B. 905
    C. 1,176
    D. 1,185

10. If you packed ornaments into boxes that hold 12 ornaments each, and you filled seven boxes, how many ornaments did you pack?

    A. 84
    B. 74
    C. 72
    D. 64

Answers

1. **C.** Estimate this as $47 \times 10 = 470$. You rounded the 9 up 1, so subtract 47 from 470 to get 423. Using the step-by-step algorithm:

$$\begin{array}{r} \overset{6}{4}7 \\ \times\,9 \\ \hline 423 \end{array}$$

2. **B.** To multiply by 5, tack on a 0 and divide by 2: $280 \div 2 = 140$. Here's the multiplication shown step by step:

$$\begin{array}{r} \overset{4}{2}8 \\ \times\,5 \\ \hline 140 \end{array}$$

3. **D.** You can choose to go back to the definition if the numbers are small, adding $84 + 84$ if you find that easier. Using the algorithm:

$$\begin{array}{r} 84 \\ \times\,2 \\ \hline 168 \end{array}$$

4. **A.** You can distribute when you multiply a single digit by a two-digit number. So, $24 \times 8 = (20 \times 8) + (4 \times 8) = 160 + 32 = 192$. Here's the multiplication shown step by step:

$$\begin{array}{r} \overset{3}{2}4 \\ \times\,8 \\ \hline 192 \end{array}$$

5. **D.** You can do $(365 \times 20) + (365 \times 4)$ if you don't want to use the standard algorithm. It's a little bit too much to hold in your head, so you'll need to jot down the partial products: $(365 \times 20) + (365 \times 4)$ $= ([300 \times 20] + [60 \times 20] + [5 \times 20]) + ([300 \times 4] + [60 \times 4] + [5 \times 4]) = (6,000 + 1,200 + 100) + (1,200 + 240 + 20) = 7,300 + 1,460 = 8,760$. So, $365 \times 24 = 8,760$. Using the step-by-step algorithm:

$$
\begin{array}{r}
\scriptstyle 1\ 1 \\
\scriptstyle 2\ 2 \\
365 \\
\times 24 \\
\hline
\scriptstyle 1 \\
1,460 \\
7,300 \\
\hline
8,760
\end{array}
$$

6. **A.** Factor and rearrange to make the multiplying easier: $138 \times 45 = (69 \times 2) \times (5 \times 9) = (69 \times 9) \times (2 \times 5) = (540 + 81) \times 10 = 6,210$. So, $138 \times 45 = 6,210$. Using the algorithm:

$$
\begin{array}{r}
\scriptstyle 1\ 3 \\
\scriptstyle 1\ 4 \\
138 \\
\times 45 \\
\hline
\scriptstyle 1\ 1 \\
690 \\
5,520 \\
\hline
6,210
\end{array}
$$

7. **D.** $42 \times 35 = (6 \times 7) \times (7 \times 5) = (7 \times 7) \times (6 \times 5) = 49 \times 30 = 1,470$. Here's the multiplication shown step by step:

$$
\begin{array}{r}
\scriptstyle 1 \\
42 \\
\times 35 \\
\hline
210 \\
1,260 \\
\hline
1,470
\end{array}
$$

8. **B.** There's a multiple of 11, so think about it this way: $22 \times 42 = 11 \times 2 \times 42 = 11 \times 84$. Eight plus 4 is 12. Separate the 8 and the 4, like this: $8\_\_4$; then put down the 2 from the 12 and add the 1 from the 12 to the 8: $84 \times 11 \rightarrow 8\_\_\_4 \rightarrow (8 + 4 = 12) \rightarrow 8\,\underset{}{\overset{1}{\_2\_}}4 = 924$. So, $22 \times 42 = 11 \times 84 = 924$. Using the step-by-step algorithm:

$$
\begin{array}{r}
42 \\
\times 22 \\
\hline
84 \\
\scriptstyle 1 \\
840 \\
\hline
924
\end{array}
$$

9. **C.** Estimate first: $150 \times 8 = 1,200$. The estimate rounds 147 up 3, so subtract three 8s or 24: $1,200 - 24 = 1,176$. Here's the multiplication shown step by step:

$$
\begin{array}{r}
\scriptstyle 3\ 5 \\
147 \\
\times\ \ \ 8 \\
\hline
1,176
\end{array}
$$

10. **A.** Distribute $7 \times 12 = (7 \times 10) + (7 \times 2) = 70 + 14 = 84$. Using the algorithm:

$$\begin{array}{r} \overset{1}{12} \\ \underline{\times 7} \\ 84 \end{array}$$

Decimals

It can seem as though multiplication of decimals is a different operation from multiplication of whole numbers because it has rules to place the decimal point correctly. It actually follows the same patterns as multiplication of whole numbers, and estimation will help you place the decimal point correctly. The common rule says to count the number of digits after the decimal point in each of the factors, add those counts, and place the decimal point in the product so that there are that many places after the decimal point.

EXAMPLE:

The basic arithmetic of multiplying 4.83×2.1 is the same basic arithmetic as multiplying 483×21.

$$\begin{array}{r} 483 \\ \underline{\times 21} \\ 483 \\ \underline{9660} \\ 10143 \end{array}$$

If the problem had actually been 483×21, you'd be done except for a comma to separate 10 thousand from 143. But the problem was 4.83×2.1, so you need to place a decimal point. Count digits to the right of the decimal points.

$$4.83 \times 2.1 = 4.\underset{\text{2 digits}}{\underbrace{83}} \times 2.\underset{\text{1 digit}}{\underbrace{1}} = 10.\underset{\text{3 digits}}{\underbrace{143}}$$

Estimation can help you place the decimal point as well. In the example above, 4.83 rounds to 5 and 2.1 rounds to 2, so you should expect an answer around 10. The rule for counting digits gave you a number a little larger than 10, just as expected.

EXAMPLE:

Each of these multiplications has the same basic arithmetic as the example above, but must have the decimal point placed differently.

$$48.3 \times 2.1 \approx 50 \times 2 \approx 100, \text{ so } 48.3 \times 2.1 = 101.43$$

$$4.83 \times 0.21 \approx 5 \times 0.2 \text{ or } 5 \times \frac{1}{5} \approx 1, \text{ so } 4.83 \times 0.21 = 1.0143$$

This last one is harder to estimate, and you may find the digit counting easier. Either way, you'll need to insert some zeros before the 10143.

$$0.483 \times 0.0021 \approx \frac{1}{2} \times 0.002 \approx 0.001, \text{ so } 0.483 \times 0.0021 = 0.0010143$$

Round About

If you're asked to round a number to a particular decimal place, the process of rounding is the same as you would use when rounding whole numbers. Just remember the place value system for decimals.

$$0.62345 = \quad 0. \quad \underset{\text{tenths}}{6} \quad \underset{\text{hundredths}}{2} \quad \underset{\text{thousandths}}{3} \quad \underset{\text{ten-thousandths}}{4} \quad \underset{\text{hundred-thousandths}}{5}$$

To round:

1. Look at the digit to the right of your desired place.

2. If the digit is 5 or higher, add 1 to the digit in your desired place and drop all following digits.

3. If the digit in that next place is 4 or lower, leave the digit in your desired place as is and drop all following digits.

Practice

Directions: Choose the best answer for each question.

1. Find the area of a rectangle 4.5 feet long and 1.75 feet wide.

   A. 7.875 ft.²
   B. 7.5 ft.²
   C. 4.375 ft.²
   D. 3.375 ft.²

2. If a boat travels 19.1 km per hour, how far will it travel in 6.25 hours?

   A. 1,193.75 km
   B. 119.375 km
   C. 114.25 km
   D. 114.025 km

3. Erin bought a coat for $149.95 and paid sales tax equal to 0.06 of the cost of the coat. How much tax did she pay, to the nearest penny?

   A. $0.90
   B. $9
   C. $150.01
   D. $158.95

4. Jason uses 1.6 packages of chocolate. If each package contains 4.9 grams of chocolate, how much chocolate did he use?

   A. 2.94 g
   B. 4.54 g
   C. 7.84 g
   D. 9.4 g

5. Find the area of a field 34.5 km long and 18.3 km wide.

   A. 612.15 km²
   B. 613.5 km²
   C. 631.35 km²
   D. 6,313.5 km²

6. Jenny ordered 4.75 kg of cheese that sold for $7.99 per kg. What is the cost of her order to the nearest penny?

   A. $28.75
   B. $32.01
   C. $33.25
   D. $37.95

7. A company sells 3.6 million widgets for $2.50 per widget. What is its revenue from the sale?

A. $1.44 million
B. $6.3 million
C. $8.1 million
D. $9 million

8. A fertilizer manufacturer recommends using 6.25 pounds of fertilizer per 1,000 square feet. How much fertilizer will you need for 2,100 square feet?

A. 13.125 pounds
B. 131.25 pounds
C. 1,312.5 pounds
D. 13,125 pounds

9. The speed of light is approximately 300 million meters per second. How far does light travel in 1.5 minutes?

A. 45 billion meters
B. 27 billion meters
C. 18 billion meters
D. 450 million meters

10. The speed of sound is approximately 761.2 miles per hour. How far does sound travel in 0.2 hours?

A. 15.224 miles
B. 150.224 miles
C. 152.24 miles
D. 152.4 miles

Answers

1. **A.** Break this up to make it easier to handle: 4.5×1.75 is 4×1.75 and 0.5×1.75 (or half of 1.75). So, $(4 \times 1.75) + (0.5 \times 1.75) = 7 + 0.875 = 7.875$ ft.^{2}. Using the step-by-step algorithm:

$$
\begin{array}{r}
\overset{3}{3}\,\overset{2}{2} \\
1.75 \\
\times\, 4.5 \\
\hline
875 \\
7000 \\
\hline
7.875
\end{array}
$$

2. **B.** In 6.25 hours, it will travel 6×19.1 plus 0.25×19.1 (or a quarter of 19.1). Estimate 6×19.1 is close to 120 and a quarter of 19.1 is close to 5, so expect an answer close to 125. Then $6 \times 19.1 = 114.6$ and $0.25 \times 19.1 = 4.775$. Adding, you get 119.375. Using the algorithm:

$$
\begin{array}{r}
\overset{5}{\underset{4}{1}} \\
19.1 \\
\times\, 6.25 \\
\hline
955 \\
\overset{2}{3820} \\
114600 \\
\hline
119.375
\end{array}
$$

3. **B.** Just multiply $149.95 by 6 and don't worry about the decimal places yet. Six times 150 is 900, so 6 times 149.95 is 900 minus 30¢, or 899.70. Nearly $900 in tax on a $150 purchase is clearly unreasonable, so think now about where the decimal point belongs. The 0.06 means 6 hundredths, or $6 tax on every hundred dollars of a purchase. That makes 8.9970 sound much more reasonable. Two decimal places in 149.95 and two in 0.06 confirm four decimal places in the answer. $8.9970 rounds to $9. Going step-by-step:

$$
\begin{array}{r}
\overset{2}{}\,\overset{5}{}\,\overset{5}{}\,\overset{3}{} \\
149.95 \\
\times\quad .06 \\
\hline
8.9970
\end{array}
$$

4. **C.** 1.6 times 5 would be 8, so 1.6 × 4.9 should be close to that. 1.6 × 4.9 = (1 × 4.9) + (0.6 × 4.9) = 4.9 + 2.94 = 7.84 grams. Using the step-by-step algorithm:

$$
\begin{array}{r}
\overset{2}{}\overset{5}{} \\
1.6 \\
\times\,4.9 \\
\hline
144 \\
640 \\
\hline
7.84
\end{array}
$$

5. **C.** The basic algorithm makes sense here. You could break it up, but it wouldn't really be faster.

$$
\begin{array}{r}
\overset{3}{}\overset{4}{} \\
\overset{1}{}\overset{1}{} \\
34.5 \\
\times 18.3 \\
\hline
\overset{1}{}\overset{1}{} \\
1035 \\
27600 \\
34500 \\
\hline
631.35
\end{array}
$$

6. **D.** Estimate first: 4.75 times $8 would be (4 × 8) + (0.75 × 8) = 32 + 6 = 38. That rounded the price up a penny, so take off 4.75 pennies, to get $37.9525, which rounds to $37.95. Then 4.75 × $7.99 = $37.9525. Using the algorithm:

$$
\begin{array}{r}
\overset{3}{}\,\,\overset{3}{} \\
\overset{6}{}\,\,\overset{6}{} \\
\overset{4}{}\,\,\overset{4}{} \\
7.99 \\
\times 4.75 \\
\hline
\overset{1}{}\overset{2}{}\overset{1}{} \\
3995 \\
55930 \\
319600 \\
\hline
37.9525
\end{array}
$$

7. **D.** Just carry the million along. Do a little regrouping and this one gets easier: 3.6 million × $2.50 = 1.8 million × 2 × 2.50 = 1.8 million × 5 = $9 million.

8. **A.** 2,100 square feet is 2.1 thousands (2,100 ÷ 1,000), so multiply 2.1 × 6.25 = (2 × 6.25) + (0.1 × 6.25) = 12.5 + 0.625 = 13.125. Using the step-by-step algorithm:

$$
\begin{array}{r}
6.25 \\
\times 2.1 \\
\hline
\overset{1}{} \\
625 \\
12\,500 \\
\hline
13.125
\end{array}
$$

9. **B.** 300 million meters per second × 60 seconds = 18,000 million meters per minute or 18 billion meters per minute. 18 billion meters per minute × 1.5 minutes = 27 billion meters in 1.5 minutes.

10. **C.** Multiply by 2, and place the decimal point:

$$
\begin{array}{r}
\overset{1}{} \\
761.2 \\
\times 0.2 \\
\hline
152.24
\end{array}
$$

E. Division

Just as subtraction is the opposite of addition, division is the opposite of multiplication. When you ask what $18 \div 6$ equals, you're actually asking what you would multiply by 6 to produce a product of 18. Division brings a bit of new vocabulary. If you divide 18 by 6, 18 is the *dividend* and 6 is the *divisor*. The answer is the *quotient,* but if the dividend is not a multiple of the divisor, there may be a *remainder,* a little bit left over.

Whole Numbers

The common algorithm for long division using the front-end digits of the divisor and dividend to estimate a digit in the quotient, multiplies, subtracts, brings down digits, and repeats the process.

EXAMPLE:

$$23\overline{)8,735}$$

Estimate $87 \div 23$ and place the estimate of 3 above the 7.

$$
\begin{array}{r}
3 \\
23\overline{)8735}
\end{array}
$$

Multiply $3 \times 23 = 69$ and place the product under the 87. Subtract 69 from 87.

$$
\begin{array}{r}
3 \\
23\overline{)8735} \\
69 \\
\hline
18
\end{array}
$$

Bring down the next digit and begin the process again. You're dividing 183 by 23.

$$
\begin{array}{r}
37 \\
23\overline{)8735} \\
69 \\
\hline
183 \\
161 \\
\hline
225
\end{array}
$$

Repeat until there are no digits left to bring down.

$$
\begin{array}{r}
379 \\
23\overline{)8735} \\
69 \\
\hline
183 \\
161 \\
\hline
225 \\
207 \\
\hline
18
\end{array}
$$

Remainders, Mixed Numbers, and Decimals

Notice that when you reached the end of the division in the previous example, you still had a remainder of 18. There are 379 copies of 23 in 8,735 and 18 units left over. The remainder will always be smaller than the divisor. If it's not, check for an error.

Sometimes you'll be content to just have a remainder. Other times, you may want to place the remainder over the divisor to express the quotient as a mixed number, or place a decimal point and zeros at the end of the dividend so you can keep dividing and have a decimal.

Short Division

Most of the division you'll encounter on the test will not demand long or complicated calculations. They'll often be problems you can handle with short division. Short division—as opposed to long division—doesn't draw down all the multiplications and subtractions.

EXAMPLE:

$$13\overline{)40339}$$

Estimate that 13 goes into 40 three times.

$$\overset{3}{13\overline{)40339}}$$

Three times 13 is 39, which leaves a remainder of 1.

Place the remainder of 1 in front of the next digit, making it look like 13, and the divisor of 13 goes into this new 13 once, with no remainder.

$$\overset{3\ 1}{13\overline{)40^139}}$$

The next digit is 3. Thirteen does not go into 3, so place a 0 in the quotient, and there is 3 left over. Write that in front of the 9.

$$\overset{3\ 10}{13\overline{)40^1339}}$$

Finally 13 into 39 goes three times.

$$\overset{3\ 10\ 3}{13\overline{)40^133^39}}$$

40,339 divided by 13 is 3,103.

What's in There?

For mental math, it can be helpful to phrase a division like $42 \div 6$ as "How many 6s are in 42?" Even if the question refers to numbers larger than those in basic math facts, looking for repetitions of a number can help you take the problem apart.

EXAMPLE:

$143 \div 13 =$

How many 13s are in 143? Well, ten 13s would be 130, and that would leave another 13, so $143 \div 13 = 11$.

Practice

Directions: Choose the best answer for each question.

1. If 196 grapefruit are packed into bags holding 7 grapefruit each, how many bags will be needed?
   A. 26
   B. 27
   C. 28
   D. 29

2. If you have 216 pieces of fruit to distribute into 12 baskets, how many pieces of fruit should you place in each basket?
   A. 10
   B. 14
   C. 18
   D. 22

3. A project requires 1,480 hours of work and must be completed in a week. Each worker who can be assigned to the project works 40 hours a week. How many workers must be assigned to complete the project in one week?
   A. 37
   B. 18
   C. 8
   D. 6

4. If 272 goldfish are to be evenly divided among 16 tanks, how many goldfish should be placed in each tank?
   A. 14
   B. 15
   C. 16
   D. 17

5. An office purchases shipments of 576 reams of paper at a time. If they use 9 reams of paper per day, how many days will the shipment last?
   A. 66
   B. 64
   C. 62
   D. 60

6. A troop of 59 Girl Scouts sells 6,136 boxes of cookies. If each girl sold the same number of boxes, how many boxes did each girl sell?
   A. 1,004
   B. 144
   C. 140
   D. 104

7. A widget factory produced 3,624 widgets during an 8-hour shift. How many widgets did it produce per hour?
   A. 453
   B. 493
   C. 853
   D. 906

8. Katrina is moving and has 456 books to pack. She can fit 24 books into each carton. How many cartons will she need for the books?
   A. 25
   B. 17
   C. 19
   D. 21

9. If 1,260 people need to be transported on buses, each of which can hold 45 people, how many buses will be needed?

   A. 26
   B. 28
   C. 30
   D. 32

10. The mess hall used 1,147 pounds of potatoes in 31 days. How many pounds of potatoes did it use each day?

   A. 34
   B. 35
   C. 36
   D. 37

Answers

1. **C.** Use short division to find $196 \div 7 = 28$.

$$7\overline{)19\,^56}\quad\begin{array}{c}2\ 8\end{array}$$

2. **C.** Short division will do: $216 \div 12 = 18$.

$$12\overline{)21\,^96}\quad\begin{array}{c}1\ 8\end{array}$$

3. **A.** $1,480 \div 40$ can become $148 \div 4 = 37$. Using short division:

$$40\overline{)148\,^{28}0}\quad\begin{array}{c}3\ 7\end{array}$$

4. **D.** Short division runs into a snag here. You can estimate that 16 goes into 27 once, but most of us wouldn't recognize how many times 16 goes into 112. Instead, realize that 272 is more than 10×16, or 160, but less than 20×16, or 320. Subtract $320 - 272 = 48$. Sixteen goes into 48 three times, so 272 is three 16s less than 320. Then $272 \div 16 = 17$. Using long division:

$$
\begin{array}{r}
17 \\
16\overline{)272} \\
\underline{16} \\
112 \\
\underline{112}
\end{array}
$$

5. **B.** Short division should do the job: $576 \div 9 = 64$.

$$9\overline{)57\,^36}\quad\begin{array}{c}6\ 4\end{array}$$

6. **D.** A quick estimate of $6,000 \div 60$ will tell you to expect an answer around 100. The actual division may be challenging because once you get past 59 goes into 61 once, and then place a 0 for 59 into 23, you're faced with 59 into 236. Use the context clue: No one sold a fraction of a box of cookies, so 236 must be a multiple of 59. To end in 6, it will have to be 59×4. So, $6,136 \div 59 = 104$. Using long division:

$$
\begin{array}{r}
104 \\
59\overline{)6136} \\
\underline{59} \\
23 \\
\underline{0} \\
236 \\
\underline{236}
\end{array}
$$

7. **A.** Short division should handle it: $3,624 \div 8 = 453$.

$$8)\overline{36^{4}2^{2}4}$$
$$4\ 5\ 3$$

8. **C.** To divide 456 by 24, try $456 \div (2 \times 12) = (456 \div 2) \div 12 = 228 \div 12 = 19$. Using long division:

$$
\begin{array}{r}
19 \\
24\overline{)456} \\
\underline{24} \\
216 \\
\underline{216}
\end{array}
$$

9. **B.** $1,260 \div 45 = 1,260 \div (5 \times 9) = (1,260 \div 9) \div 5 = 140 \div 5 = 28$. Using long division:

$$
\begin{array}{r}
28 \\
45\overline{)1260} \\
\underline{90} \\
360 \\
\underline{360}
\end{array}
$$

10. **D.** Estimate $1,147 \div 31$ as $1,200 \div 30 = 40$. Check that $40 \times 31 = 1,240$ and $1,240 - 1,147 = 93$. Since 93 is 3×31, you know that $1,147 \div 31 = 40 - 3 = 37$. Using long division:

$$
\begin{array}{r}
37 \\
31\overline{)1147} \\
\underline{93} \\
217 \\
\underline{217}
\end{array}
$$

Decimals

To divide a decimal by a whole number, place the decimal dividend under the division "house" and place a decimal point in the quotient directly above the decimal point in the dividend. Place the whole number divisor in the divisor space on the left, and then divide normally.

$$17)\overline{258.362}$$

The decimal point is where it belongs.

$$
\begin{array}{r}
15.197 \\
17\overline{)258.362} \\
\underline{17} \\
88 \\
\underline{85} \\
33 \\
\underline{17} \\
166 \\
\underline{153} \\
132 \\
\underline{119} \\
13
\end{array}
$$

The rule for dividing by a decimal is simple: don't. Instead, find an equivalent problem in which the divisor is a whole number. That may sound challenging, but it's actually quite simple. You can quickly verify that

$40 \div 2$ has the same quotient as $400 \div 20$ or $4,000 \div 200$. Adding those extra zeros has no effect as long you add the same number of zeros to the dividend and the divisor.

Adding those zeros is actually multiplying both the dividend and the divisor by a power of ten—10 or 100 or 1,000 or some other power of ten. If you have a decimal division problem like $5.48 \div 0.004$, you can multiply the dividend and divisor by 1,000, and you have $5,480 \div 4$. That has the same quotient as $5.48 \div 0.004$, but it has a whole number divisor.

Why did we pick 1,000 as the multiplier? Because the last digit in the divisor 0.004 is in the thousandths place. If we had $2.97 \div 0.6$, we'd only need to multiply by 10 because the divisor ends in the tenths place. We'd change the question to $29.7 \div 6$. The effect is to move the decimal point to the end of the divisor and the same number of places in the dividend. This makes your divisor a whole number. Divide, and place the decimal point in the quotient directly above the decimal point in the dividend.

EXAMPLE:

$5.48 \div 0.004 =$

$$0.004\overline{)5.480} \rightarrow 4\overline{)5480.} \quad \text{(quotient } 1370.\text{)}$$

EXAMPLE:

$2.94 \div 0.6 =$

$$0.6\overline{)2.94} \rightarrow 6\overline{)29.4} \quad \text{(quotient } 4.9\text{)}$$

Practice

Directions: Choose the best answer for each question.

1. If four people share a raffle prize of $533.60, how much will each person receive?

   A. $133.40
   B. $133.15
   C. $131.60
   D. $131.40

2. If 8.25 pounds of mixed nuts are packed into bags each containing 0.75 pound, how many bags will be filled?

   A. 5
   B. 7
   C. 9
   D. 11

3. The area of a rectangle is 42.9 square inches. If the length of the rectangle is 7.15 inches, find the width.

   A. 5.8 inches
   B. 6 inches
   C. 6.1 inches
   D. 6.8 inches

4. The sales tax on the purchase of a refrigerator is $35.88. If the local tax rate is 0.06, what was the price of the refrigerator before tax?

   A. $215.28
   B. $598
   C. $1,672
   D. $2,152.80

5. A spool that contains 25.5 feet of ribbon is cut into streamers, each measuring 1.5 feet. How many streamers were cut?

   A. 13
   B. 15
   C. 17
   D. 19

6. Kurt has $903.44 in his savings account. If he withdraws $112.93 each month to pay his student loan, how many payments can he make?

   A. 8
   B. 7
   C. 6
   D. 5

7. The yards gained by a running back totaled 238.5. If he carried the football 18 times, what was his average gain per carry?

   A. 13.5 yards
   B. 13.45 yards
   C. 13.25 yards
   D. 13.2 yards

8. A defensive lineman was credited with 16.5 sacks in 11 games. What was his average number of sacks per game?

   A. 1.5
   B. 1.55
   C. 1.6
   D. 1.65

9. If the total bill for 15 tacos is $17.85, what is the price of one taco?

   A. $1.17
   B. $1.19
   C. $1.23
   D. $1.25

10. The distance from the pitcher's mound to home plate in Major League Baseball is 60.5 feet. Nolan Ryan once threw a fastball that traveled 147.9 feet per second. How long did it take that ball to travel from the pitcher's mound to home plate to the nearest hundredth of a second?

    A. 0.40 seconds
    B. 0.41 seconds
    C. 0.45 seconds
    D. 0.49 seconds

Answers

1. **A.** You're dividing by 4, a whole number, so it's not necessary to move any decimal points. A rough estimate will help confirm the placement of the decimal point. $533.60 divided by 4 should be more than $100, but less than $200. Use short division.

$$\frac{133.40}{4\overline{)5^13^13.^160}}$$

2. **D.** Move the decimal point two places to make 0.75 into a whole number, and move it two places in 8.25 as well. Now you're dividing 825 by 75. Think of it as a fraction and reduce to lowest terms.

$$\frac{825}{75} = \frac{\cancel{25} \cdot 33}{\cancel{25} \cdot 3} = \frac{33}{3} = 11$$

3. **B.** The number of places you move the decimal point is determined by the divisor. In this case, that's 7.15, so move the decimal point two places. Your problem becomes 4,290 divided by 715. Since 4,200 divided by 700 is 6, you should expect an answer around 6. You can use the distributive property to check: $6 \times 715 = (6 \times 700) + (6 \times 15) = 4,200 + 90 = 4,290$. The answer is exactly 6.

4. **B.** Move the decimal point and this problem becomes $3588 \div 6$. Use short division:

$$6\overline{)35^5 8^4 8} \quad \begin{array}{c} 5\ 9\ 8 \end{array}$$

5. **C.** Move the decimal point one place in each number and think of this division as a fraction.

$$\frac{25.5}{1.5} = \frac{255}{15} = \frac{\cancel{5} \times 51}{\cancel{5} \times 3} = \frac{51}{3} = 17$$

6. **A.** A quick estimate $(900 \div 100)$ tells you this can't be more than 9. Move the decimal point two places in each number and divide.

$$11293\overline{)90344} \quad \begin{array}{c} 8 \end{array}$$
$$\underline{90344}$$

7. **C.** You're dividing by a whole number, so the decimal point stays put. Estimate $(200 \div 20)$, and you'll expect an answer around 10. It's worthwhile to add a zero or two and keep dividing to see if this quotient will terminate—that is, if you'll get to a 0 remainder. Here, you do.

$$18\overline{)23^5 8.^4 5^9 0} \quad \begin{array}{c} 1\ 3.\ 2\ 5 \end{array}$$

If you didn't get to a 0 remainder after a couple of decimal places, you'd want to round your answer.

8. **A.** Remember the trick for multiplying by 11? You can work it backward, too. Then 16.5 divided by 11 looks like 1 point something, and the 5 on the end makes you guess it is 1.5. Then, 15 times 11 is 165, so $16.5 \div 11 = 1.5$.

9. **B.** Those tacos cost more than a dollar each, so use short division to find the total for the midnight munchies.

$$15\overline{)17.^2 8^{13} 5} \quad \begin{array}{c} 1.\ 1\ 9 \end{array}$$

Was that last $135 \div 15$ troublesome? Take it apart. Do you know that 15×4 is 60? So $15 \times 8 = 120$, and you'll need one more 15 to make the 135.

10. **B.** There's no way around this except serious division. You have a distance (60.5) and a speed (147.9) and you're looking for a time, so distance divided by speed will give you time. You were asked for your answer to the nearest hundredth of a second, so you know you have to carry the division out for three decimal places and then round your answer to 0.41.

$$147.9\overline{)60.5,000} \quad \begin{array}{c} 0.409 \end{array}$$
$$\begin{array}{r} 59\,16 \\ \hline 134\,0 \\ 0 \\ \hline 134\,00 \\ 133\,11 \\ \hline 89 \end{array}$$

Chapter 7

Arithmetic Reasoning: Fractions and Mixed Operations

The Arithmetic Reasoning section of the AFQT also includes questions involving fractions that, like the whole number and decimal questions, focus on addition, subtraction, multiplication, and division. This chapter will examine the arithmetic of fractions. The techniques for these basic operations with fractions are different enough that it makes sense to look at them on their own.

A. Simplifying

A fraction is in *simplest form*—also known as *lowest terms*—when the numerator and denominator have no common divisors. The value of the fraction is the same whether it's in simplest form or not, so if you're in the midst of work, you can choose whether to simplify. The advantage to having fractions in simplest form is that it's easier to work with smaller numbers. When you're looking at your answer choices, remember that the choices are probably in simplest form, so make sure your answer is, too.

To simplify a fraction, divide the numerator and the denominator by the same number. To reach simplest form quickly, divide by the *greatest common factor,* the largest number that is a factor of both the numerator and the denominator. If you're not sure what the greatest common factor is, just use numbers you're sure divide evenly into both the numerator and the denominator, and repeat until there are no more common factors.

EXAMPLES:

Write $\dfrac{32}{36}$ in simplest form.

$$\frac{32}{36} = \frac{32 \div 4}{36 \div 4} = \frac{8}{9}$$

Write $\dfrac{12}{18}$ in simplest form.

$$\frac{12}{18} = \frac{12 \div 2}{18 \div 2} = \frac{6}{9} = \frac{6 \div 3}{9 \div 3} = \frac{2}{3}$$

Mixed Numbers and Improper Fractions

A *mixed number* is one that has a whole number part and a fraction part. Examples of mixed numbers include $3\dfrac{1}{2}$, $14\dfrac{2}{3}$, and $47\dfrac{51}{68}$. An *improper fraction* is a fraction whose value is more than 1. This occurs when the numerator is larger than the denominator. A fraction like $\dfrac{13}{12}$ is called an improper fraction because its value is greater than 1. You'll often want to turn it into a mixed number. The fraction $\dfrac{13}{12}$ can become the mixed number $1\dfrac{1}{12}$ because $\dfrac{13}{12} = \dfrac{12}{12} + \dfrac{1}{12}$ and $\dfrac{12}{12}$ is equal to 1.

An improper fraction can be converted to a mixed number by dividing the numerator by the denominator. The quotient will be the whole number part of the mixed number, and writing the remainder over the divisor (the original denominator) creates the fraction part of the mixed number.

EXAMPLE:

Convert $\dfrac{36}{5}$ to a mixed number.

Divide the numerator by the denominator: $36 \div 5 = 7$ with a remainder of 1. 7 is the whole number part. Place 1 over 5 to make the fraction part, $\dfrac{1}{5}$. Therefore, $\dfrac{36}{5} = 7\dfrac{1}{5}$.

You can convert a mixed number to an improper fraction in one of two ways. To convert $5\dfrac{3}{4}$ to an improper fraction, you can think of 1 as $\dfrac{4}{4}$, and therefore 5 as $\dfrac{20}{4}$.

$$5\frac{3}{4} = 5 + \frac{3}{4} = \frac{20}{4} + \frac{3}{4} = \frac{23}{4}$$

The alternate is to multiply the denominator times the whole number part, add the numerator, and place the result over the original denominator: $5\dfrac{3}{4} = \dfrac{4 \times 5 + 3}{4} = \dfrac{23}{4}$.

EXAMPLE:

Convert $8\dfrac{2}{3}$ to an improper fraction.

Multiply the denominator, 3, times the whole number, 8, to get 24. Add on the numerator of the fraction, 2, to get 26. Put 26 over the original denominator. $8\dfrac{2}{3} = \dfrac{3 \times 8 + 2}{3} = \dfrac{26}{3}$.

To simplify a mixed number, you generally only need to simplify the fraction part, but if the fraction part should happen to be an improper fraction, you'll have to deal with that. It's uncommon, but we'll look at an example.

EXAMPLE:

Simplify $13\dfrac{21}{35}$.

The fraction is a proper fraction, so you only need to simplify the fraction and just let 13 come along.

$$13\frac{21}{35} = 13\frac{3 \times 7}{5 \times 7} = 13\frac{3}{5}$$

EXAMPLE:

Simplify $8\frac{21}{12}$.

In this case the fraction part is an improper fraction, so focus on that and just let the 8 sit off to the side for a bit: $8\frac{21}{12} = 8 + \frac{21}{12}$. Convert the improper fraction to a mixed number: $\frac{21}{12} = 1\frac{9}{12}$. Add the whole number parts and simplify the fraction part: $8 + 1\frac{9}{12} = 9\frac{9}{12} = 9\frac{3}{4}$.

Don't be too quick to change improper fractions into mixed numbers, however. Working with the improper fraction is often easier. Don't change until you're ready to look at your answer choices, and then only if the answer choices are mixed numbers.

Practice

Directions: Choose the best answer for each question.

1. The simplest form of $\frac{18}{45}$ is

A. $\frac{1}{5}$

B. $\frac{2}{5}$

C. $\frac{2}{9}$

D. $\frac{6}{15}$

2. The simplest form of $\frac{125}{625}$ is

A. $\frac{1}{500}$

B. $\frac{5}{25}$

C. $\frac{1}{25}$

D. $\frac{1}{5}$

3. The simplest form of $\frac{51}{153}$ is

A. $\frac{1}{3}$

B. $\frac{3}{17}$

C. $\frac{4}{13}$

D. $\frac{17}{51}$

4. The simplest form of $\frac{234}{351}$ is

A. $\frac{2}{3}$

B. $\frac{2}{13}$

C. $\frac{26}{39}$

D. $\frac{78}{117}$

5. The simplest form of $\dfrac{396}{495}$ is

   A. $\dfrac{44}{55}$

   B. $\dfrac{36}{45}$

   C. $\dfrac{4}{5}$

   D. $\dfrac{1}{11}$

6. Convert $\dfrac{106}{12}$ to a mixed number in simplest form.

   A. $9\dfrac{2}{12}$

   B. $8\dfrac{10}{12}$

   C. $8\dfrac{5}{6}$

   D. $4\dfrac{5}{6}$

7. Convert $\dfrac{89}{17}$ to a mixed number in simplest form.

   A. 7

   B. $7\dfrac{4}{17}$

   C. $5\dfrac{4}{17}$

   D. $5\dfrac{12}{17}$

8. Convert $6\dfrac{2}{7}$ to an improper fraction in simplest form.

   A. $\dfrac{19}{7}$

   B. $\dfrac{20}{7}$

   C. $\dfrac{42}{7}$

   D. $\dfrac{44}{7}$

9. Convert $9\dfrac{8}{15}$ to an improper fraction in simplest form.

   A. $\dfrac{17}{15}$

   B. $\dfrac{129}{15}$

   C. $\dfrac{135}{15}$

   D. $\dfrac{143}{15}$

10. The simplest form of $7\dfrac{79}{12}$ is

    A. $1\dfrac{7}{12}$

    B. $6\dfrac{7}{12}$

    C. $8\dfrac{7}{12}$

    D. $13\dfrac{7}{12}$

Answers

1. **B.** Divide the numerator and denominator by 9: $\dfrac{18}{45} = \dfrac{2 \times \cancel{9}}{5 \times \cancel{9}} = \dfrac{2}{5}$.

2. **D.** The numerator and denominator are both multiples of 125, but if you don't spot that, you can start by dividing both by 25 or even by 5: $\dfrac{125}{625} = \dfrac{5 \times \cancel{25}}{25 \times \cancel{25}} = \dfrac{5}{25} = \dfrac{\overset{1}{\cancel{5}}}{5 \times \cancel{5}} = \dfrac{1}{5}$.

3. **A.** Divide the numerator and denominator by 3 and you'll see you can also divide both by 17:
$\frac{51}{153} = \frac{3 \times 17}{3 \times 51} = \frac{\cancel{3} \times \cancel{17}}{3 \times \cancel{3} \times \cancel{17}} = \frac{1}{3}$.

4. **A.** If the greatest common divisor is not obvious, just start with any common divisor. Divide the numerator and denominator by 3 and by 3 again, and then by 13:
$\frac{234}{351} = \frac{3 \times 78}{3 \times 117} = \frac{3 \times 3 \times 26}{3 \times 3 \times 39} = \frac{\cancel{3} \times \cancel{3} \times 2 \times \cancel{13}}{\cancel{3} \times \cancel{3} \times 3 \times \cancel{13}} = \frac{2}{3}$.

5. **C.** Divide the numerator and denominator by 9 and then by 11: $\frac{396}{495} = \frac{9 \times 44}{9 \times 55} = \frac{\cancel{9} \times 4 \times \cancel{11}}{\cancel{9} \times 5 \times \cancel{11}} = \frac{4}{5}$.

6. **C.** Divide 106 by 12. The quotient of 8 is the whole number part, and the remainder of 10 goes over the denominator of 12. Simplify the fraction: $\frac{106}{12} = 8\frac{10}{12} = 8\frac{5}{6}$.

7. **C.** Divide 89 by 17 to get 5 with a remainder of 4. Place the remainder over the denominator of 17:
$\frac{89}{17} = 5\frac{4}{17}$.

8. **D.** Multiply the denominator, 7, by the whole number, 6, to get 42, and then add the numerator, 2. The total of 44 goes over the denominator of 7: $6\frac{2}{7} = \frac{7 \times 6 + 2}{7} = \frac{42 + 2}{7} = \frac{44}{7}$.

9. **D.** Multiply the denominator, 15, by the whole number, 9, and add on the numerator, 8. The result, 143, is the numerator over a denominator of 15: $9\frac{8}{15} = \frac{15 \times 9 + 8}{15} = \frac{135 + 8}{15} = \frac{143}{15}$.

10. **D.** Separate the whole number, 7, from the improper fraction. Change the improper fraction to a mixed number by dividing 79 by 12 to get a whole number part of 6 and a remainder of 7, which goes over the denominator, 12, to make the fraction. Don't forget to add the 7 back in. Therefore, $7\frac{79}{12} = 7 + \frac{79}{12} = 7 + 6\frac{7}{12} = 13\frac{7}{12}$.

B. Addition

Sometimes addition of fractions is as simple as addition of whole numbers. Five tables plus four tables is nine tables. Six cars plus two cars is eight cars. Five-twelfths plus four-twelfths is nine-twelfths, and $\frac{6}{17} + \frac{2}{17} = \frac{8}{17}$. The bottom number in a fraction is the *denominator;* it tells you what denomination or kind of fraction you have. The top number is the *numerator;* it tells you the number of those things you have. If your fractions are the same kind of things—if they have the same denominator—all you have to do is add up the numerators to know how many of those things you have. Tables plus tables gives you tables, cars plus cars gives you cars, twelfths plus twelfths gives you twelfths, and so on.

The problem comes in when you start to add different kinds of things, different denominators. Seven apples plus 9 apples are 16 apples, and 4 oranges plus 8 oranges are 12 oranges, but 7 apples plus 8 oranges are neither 15 apples nor 15 oranges. Seven apples plus 8 oranges are 15 fruits. Just as we need to find a category into which both apples and oranges fit, when we add fractions with different denominators, we have to find a denominator to which both fractions can be converted.

The denominator that fits both fractions is the *common denominator*. The common denominator is a number divisible by both denominators. Generally, you try to find the least common multiple of the two denominators to keep the numbers as small as possible, but any common denominator will do the job.

To add $\frac{1}{3} + \frac{1}{2}$, you'd probably want to use a common denominator of 6 because 6 is a multiple of 3 and a multiple of 2. You could still get the addition done, however, if you used a larger common denominator, like 12, because both 2 and 3 are divisors of 12. If you use the larger denominator, you'll need to simplify after adding.

Once you've chosen your common denominator, change each fraction by multiplying it by a disguised version of the number 1. Multiplying a number by 1 leaves its value unchanged: $4 \times 1 = 4$, $\frac{2}{5} \times 1 = \frac{2}{5}$. The disguise comes from writing the 1 as a number over itself, as in $\frac{2}{2}$ or $\frac{11}{11}$. When you multiply by a disguised 1, you change the way the fraction looks, but you don't change its value. So, $\frac{1}{2} \times \frac{4}{4} = \frac{4}{8}$ and $\frac{1}{2} \times \frac{13}{13} = \frac{13}{26}$. Now, $\frac{1}{2}$, $\frac{4}{8}$, and $\frac{13}{26}$ look different, but they're all worth $\frac{1}{2}$.

EXAMPLE:

Add $\frac{3}{5} + \frac{1}{8}$.

Use a common denominator of 40 because 40 is divisible by both 5 and 8. Multiply $\frac{3}{5}$ by $\frac{8}{8}$, and multiply $\frac{1}{8}$ by $\frac{5}{5}$:

$$\frac{3}{5} + \frac{1}{8} = \left(\frac{3}{5} \times \frac{8}{8}\right) + \left(\frac{1}{8} \times \frac{5}{5}\right) = \frac{24}{40} + \frac{5}{40}$$

Then add the numerators:

$$\frac{24}{40} + \frac{5}{40} = \frac{29}{40}$$

The Bowtie

A quick shortcut for adding two fractions with different denominators is nicknamed the bowtie because of the shape the arrows make. First, multiply diagonally from the lower right to the upper left and write the number over the fraction on the left. Next, multiply diagonally from the lower left to the upper right and write the number above the right fraction. Then, multiply the two denominators and write that product as the denominator for both new fractions. Finally, add the two new numerators to get your answer.

$$\frac{3}{4} + \frac{1}{3} = \overset{3 \times 3 = 9 \quad 4 \times 1 = 4}{\frac{3}{4} * \frac{1}{3}} = \frac{9}{12} + \frac{4}{12} = \frac{13}{12}$$
$$4 \times 3 = 12$$

Practice

Directions: Choose the best answer for each question.

1. Melanie eats $\frac{1}{4}$ of a pizza and Marc eats $\frac{1}{3}$ of a pizza. What fraction of the pizza do they eat together?

   A. $\frac{1}{12}$

   B. $\frac{1}{6}$

   C. $\frac{2}{7}$

   D. $\frac{7}{12}$

2. Elise mixed $\frac{5}{6}$ of a quart of red paint with $\frac{5}{8}$ of a quart of yellow paint. How much orange paint did she make?

   A. $1\frac{11}{24}$ quarts

   B. $\frac{5}{7}$ quart

   C. $\frac{25}{48}$ quart

   D. $\frac{5}{24}$ quart

3. Olivia painted $8\frac{1}{2}$ feet of fence, and Omar painted $6\frac{2}{3}$ feet of fence. How many feet of fence did they paint in all?

   A. $14\frac{1}{6}$

   B. $14\frac{1}{3}$

   C. $14\frac{1}{2}$

   D. $15\frac{1}{6}$

4. A recipe calls for $\frac{1}{3}$ cup of milk and $\frac{3}{4}$ cup of water. How much liquid is this?

   A. $\frac{1}{4}$ cup

   B. $\frac{3}{7}$ cup

   C. $1\frac{1}{12}$ cups

   D. $1\frac{6}{7}$ cups

5. Yesterday, the rain gauge recorded $\frac{5}{8}$ inch of rain, and today it showed $1\frac{1}{4}$ inches. How much rain fell over the 2 days?

   A. $1\frac{7}{8}$ inches

   B. $1\frac{3}{4}$ inches

   C. $1\frac{5}{8}$ inches

   D. $1\frac{3}{8}$ inches

6. Jeff glues together two boards. One is $\frac{3}{4}$ inch thick and the other is $\frac{1}{2}$ inch thick. What is the thickness of the resulting board?

   A. $\frac{7}{8}$ inch

   B. $1\frac{1}{8}$ inches

   C. $1\frac{1}{4}$ inches

   D. $1\frac{3}{8}$ inches

7. John bought $\frac{1}{2}$ pound of roast beef, $\frac{3}{4}$ pound of ham, $1\frac{1}{4}$ pounds of turkey, $2\frac{1}{2}$ pounds of American cheese, and $1\frac{3}{4}$ pounds of Swiss cheese. How many pounds of food did he buy?

A. $6\frac{3}{4}$

B. $6\frac{1}{4}$

C. $5\frac{3}{4}$

D. $5\frac{1}{4}$

8. Hector worked on Mr. Collins's car for $4\frac{1}{2}$ hours on Tuesday and finished the job in $6\frac{3}{4}$ hours on Wednesday. How many hours did Hector work on the car?

A. $10\frac{3}{4}$

B. $11\frac{1}{4}$

C. $11\frac{1}{2}$

D. $11\frac{3}{4}$

9. Susan walked from her home to the supermarket, a distance of $1\frac{1}{2}$ miles, and then walked $2\frac{2}{3}$ miles from the supermarket to her grandmother's house. How far did she walk in all?

A. $4\frac{1}{3}$ miles

B. $4\frac{1}{6}$ miles

C. $3\frac{5}{6}$ miles

D. $3\frac{2}{3}$ miles

10. Charlotte used $5\frac{1}{2}$ cups of flour to make bread and $3\frac{3}{4}$ cups of flour in a cookie recipe, and then added $\frac{3}{8}$ cup of flour to gravy. How much flour did she use in all?

A. $9\frac{5}{8}$ cups

B. $9\frac{1}{2}$ cups

C. $9\frac{3}{8}$ cups

D. $8\frac{5}{8}$ cups

Answers

1. **D.** Use the bowtie to add: $\frac{1}{4}+\frac{1}{3}=\frac{(1\times3)+(1\times4)}{4\times3}=\frac{3+4}{12}=\frac{7}{12}$.

2. **A.** You can use the bowtie, but you'll have to reduce your answer to lowest terms:

   $\frac{5}{6}+\frac{5}{8}=\frac{(5\times8)+(5\times6)}{6\times8}=\frac{40+30}{48}=\frac{70}{48}=1\frac{22}{48}=1\frac{11}{24}$.

   Alternatively, you can just change both fractions to a denominator of 24:

   $\frac{5}{6}+\frac{5}{8}=\left(\frac{5}{6}\times\frac{4}{4}\right)+\left(\frac{5}{8}\times\frac{3}{3}\right)=\frac{20}{24}+\frac{15}{24}=\frac{35}{24}=1\frac{11}{24}$.

3. **D.** When adding mixed numbers, add the whole number parts and then add the fractions:

   $8\frac{1}{2}+6\frac{2}{3}=8+6+\frac{1}{2}+\frac{2}{3}=14+\frac{1}{2}+\frac{2}{3}$.

   Now, you can use the bowtie on the fractions: $14+\frac{1}{2}+\frac{2}{3}=14+\frac{(1\times3)+(2\times2)}{2\times3}=14\frac{3+4}{6}=14\frac{7}{6}$.

   If you end up with an improper fraction, as above, convert it to a mixed number and add the whole

   number part of that mixed number to the whole number that you already have: $14\frac{7}{6}=14+1\frac{1}{6}=15\frac{1}{6}$.

4. **C.** The bowtie works here, but you'll need to change the improper fraction answer to a mixed number:

   $\frac{1}{3}+\frac{3}{4}=\frac{(1\times4)+(3\times3)}{3\times4}=\frac{4+9}{12}=\frac{13}{12}=1\frac{1}{12}$.

5. **A.** Add the fractions, and the 1 will just go along for the ride:

   $\frac{5}{8}+1\frac{1}{4}=1+\frac{5}{8}+\frac{1}{4}=1+\frac{5}{8}+\left(\frac{1}{4}\times\frac{2}{2}\right)=1+\frac{5}{8}+\frac{2}{8}=1\frac{7}{8}$.

6. **C.** Change the $\frac{1}{2}$ to $\frac{2}{4}$, add, and then change to a mixed number: $\frac{3}{4}+\frac{1}{2}=\frac{3}{4}+\left(\frac{1}{2}\times\frac{2}{2}\right)=\frac{3}{4}+\frac{2}{4}=\frac{5}{4}=1\frac{1}{4}$.

7. **A.** The idea of compatible numbers can work for fractions, too. Here, group the halves and the

   quarters: $\frac{1}{2}+\frac{3}{4}+1\frac{1}{4}+2\frac{1}{2}+1\frac{3}{4}=\left(\frac{1}{2}+2\frac{1}{2}\right)+\left(\frac{3}{4}+1\frac{1}{4}\right)+1\frac{3}{4}$. Then $\frac{1}{2}+2\frac{1}{2}=3$ and $\frac{3}{4}+1\frac{1}{4}=2$, so you

   have $3+2+1\frac{3}{4}=6\frac{3}{4}$.

8. **B.** First, add whole numbers: $4\frac{1}{2}+6\frac{3}{4}=4+6+\frac{1}{2}+\frac{3}{4}=10+\frac{1}{2}+\frac{3}{4}$. Change the $\frac{1}{2}$ to $\frac{2}{4}$ and add the

   fractions: $10+\frac{2}{4}+\frac{3}{4}=10+\frac{5}{4}$. Change the improper fraction to a mixed number: $10+\frac{5}{4}=10+1\frac{1}{4}=11\frac{1}{4}$.

9. **B.** Add the whole numbers: $1\frac{1}{2}+2\frac{2}{3}=1+2+\frac{1}{2}+\frac{2}{3}=3+\frac{1}{2}+\frac{2}{3}$. Then use the bowtie for the fractions:

   $3+\frac{(1\times3)+(2\times2)}{2\times3}=3+\frac{3+4}{6}=3\frac{7}{6}=4\frac{1}{6}$.

10. **A.** Add the whole numbers: $5\frac{1}{2}+3\frac{3}{4}+\frac{3}{8}=5+3+\frac{1}{2}+\frac{3}{4}+\frac{3}{8}=8+\frac{1}{2}+\frac{3}{4}+\frac{3}{8}$. Change all the fractions to a

    denominator of 8: $8+\left(\frac{1}{2}\times\frac{4}{4}\right)+\left(\frac{3}{4}\times\frac{2}{2}\right)+\frac{3}{8}=8+\frac{4}{8}+\frac{6}{8}+\frac{3}{8}$. Add the fractions and change the improper

    fraction to a mixed number: $8+\frac{4}{8}+\frac{6}{8}+\frac{3}{8}=8+\frac{13}{8}=8+1\frac{5}{8}=9\frac{5}{8}$.

C. Subtraction

Subtraction is often seen as taking away, removing something, and looking at what's left. Mathematically, it's an undoing, an inverse or opposite operation, the opposite, specifically, of addition. Subtracting fractions is just like adding fractions, except you subtract. Yes, that's a silly statement, but you must have a common denominator to subtract fractions; when you have fractions with a common denominator, you subtract the numerators.

The Bowtie

You can use the bowtie method to subtract fractions with different denominators, as long as you're careful to put each product in the correct position:

$$\frac{5}{8} - \frac{1}{5} = \frac{(5 \times 5) - (8 \times 1)}{8 \times 5} = \frac{25 - 8}{40} = \frac{17}{40}$$

Borrow Properly or Avoid It Improperly

Subtracting mixed numbers can present you with situations that need the same kind of borrowing and regrouping you did with whole number subtraction. When you add mixed numbers, you add the whole numbers and add the fractions. When you subtract mixed numbers, you generally subtract the whole numbers and subtract the fractions, as in $6\frac{3}{4} - 2\frac{1}{4} = (6-2) + \left(\frac{3}{4} - \frac{1}{4}\right) = 4\frac{2}{4} = 4\frac{1}{2}$. If you try to subtract $6\frac{1}{4} - 2\frac{3}{4}$ by the same method, however, you bump into a problem when you try to subtract $\frac{3}{4}$ from $\frac{1}{4}$.

You have two choices for dealing with the problem. One is a borrowing and regrouping strategy. Borrow 1 from the 6 and regroup it as $\frac{4}{4}$:

$$6\frac{1}{4} - 2\frac{3}{4} = 5 + 1 + \frac{1}{4} - 2\frac{3}{4} = 5 + \frac{4}{4} + \frac{1}{4} - 2\frac{3}{4} = 5\frac{5}{4} - 2\frac{3}{4}$$

Now you can subtract $5\frac{5}{4} - 2\frac{3}{4} = (5-2) + \left(\frac{5}{4} - \frac{3}{4}\right) = 3\frac{2}{4} = 3\frac{1}{2}$.

The other possibility is to change both mixed numbers to improper fractions, subtract, and then convert back: $6\frac{1}{4} - 2\frac{3}{4} = \frac{25}{4} - \frac{11}{4} = \frac{14}{4} = 3\frac{2}{4} = 3\frac{1}{2}$.

Either method will do the job, but the improper-fraction method can be tedious if the numbers are large.

Practice

Directions: Choose the best answer for each question.

1. If $2\frac{3}{8}$ inches are cut off a board that is $14\frac{1}{2}$ inches long, how much is left?

   A. $11\frac{1}{8}$ inches

   B. $11\frac{1}{2}$ inches

   C. $12\frac{1}{8}$ inches

   D. $12\frac{1}{4}$ inches

2. If you're making a trip that takes $8\frac{1}{2}$ hours and you've been traveling for $5\frac{3}{4}$ hours, how much longer do you need to travel?

   A. $3\frac{3}{4}$ hours

   B. $3\frac{1}{4}$ hours

   C. $2\frac{3}{4}$ hours

   D. $2\frac{1}{4}$ hours

3. A fencepost $8\frac{3}{4}$ feet long is driven $1\frac{1}{8}$ feet into the ground. How much of the fencepost remains above ground?

   A. $7\frac{5}{8}$ feet

   B. $7\frac{1}{2}$ feet

   C. $7\frac{1}{4}$ feet

   D. $6\frac{5}{8}$ feet

4. Elizabeth practiced piano for $7\frac{3}{5}$ hours last week and $11\frac{1}{3}$ hours this week. How much longer did she practice this week?

   A. $4\frac{2}{5}$ hours

   B. $3\frac{11}{15}$ hours

   C. $3\frac{2}{3}$ hours

   D. $3\frac{2}{5}$ hours

5. If Steve ran $3\frac{1}{2}$ miles and Mike ran $4\frac{3}{5}$ miles, how much farther did Mike run?

   A. $\frac{9}{10}$ mile

   B. $\frac{19}{20}$ mile

   C. $1\frac{1}{10}$ miles

   D. $1\frac{1}{5}$ miles

6. Hector worked on Mr. Collins's car for $4\frac{1}{2}$ hours on Tuesday and finished the job in $6\frac{3}{4}$ hours on Wednesday. How much longer did he work on the car on Wednesday?

   A. $1\frac{1}{4}$ hours

   B. $1\frac{1}{2}$ hours

   C. $1\frac{3}{4}$ hours

   D. $2\frac{1}{4}$ hours

7. Yesterday, the rain gauge recorded $\frac{5}{8}$ inch of rain, and today it showed $1\frac{1}{4}$ inches. How much more rain fell today than yesterday?

   A. $\frac{1}{8}$ inch

   B. $\frac{1}{2}$ inch

   C. $\frac{5}{8}$ inch

   D. $\frac{7}{8}$ inch

8. Olivia painted $8\frac{1}{2}$ feet of fence and Omar painted $6\frac{2}{3}$ feet of fence. How much more did Olivia paint?

   A. $1\frac{5}{6}$ feet

   B. $1\frac{11}{12}$ feet

   C. $2\frac{1}{6}$ feet

   D. $2\frac{5}{6}$ feet

9. Working together, Pete and Beatrice processed $34\frac{1}{6}$ dozen eggs. If Beatrice processed $18\frac{2}{3}$ dozen, how many did Pete process?

   A. $16\frac{1}{2}$ dozen

   B. $15\frac{5}{6}$ dozen

   C. $15\frac{2}{3}$ dozen

   D. $15\frac{1}{2}$ dozen

10. Your trip to work is made on a train and on foot. If the trip takes $1\frac{1}{12}$ hours and you spend $\frac{3}{4}$ hour on the train, how long do you walk?

    A. $\frac{1}{3}$ hour

    B. $\frac{1}{4}$ hour

    C. $\frac{1}{6}$ hour

    D. $\frac{1}{12}$ hour

Answers

1. **C.** Change to a common denominator of 8. So, $14\frac{1}{2} - 2\frac{3}{8} = 14\frac{4}{8} - 2\frac{3}{8} = 12\frac{1}{8}$.

2. **C.** Borrow 1 from the 8, and change to a common denominator of 4:

   $8\frac{1}{2} - 5\frac{3}{4} = 7 + 1 + \frac{1}{2} - 5\frac{3}{4} = 7\frac{3}{2} - 5\frac{3}{4} = 7\frac{6}{4} - 5\frac{3}{4} = 2\frac{3}{4}$.

3. **A.** Change to a denominator of 8, and there's no need to borrow: $8\frac{3}{4} - 1\frac{1}{8} = 8\frac{6}{8} - 1\frac{1}{8} = 7\frac{5}{8}$.

4. **B.** Change to a common denominator of 15: $11\frac{1}{3} - 7\frac{3}{5} = 11\frac{5}{15} - 7\frac{9}{15}$. You'll need to borrow 1 from the

   11: $10 + 1 + \frac{5}{15} - 7\frac{9}{15} = 10 + \frac{15}{15} + \frac{5}{15} - 7\frac{9}{15} = 10\frac{20}{15} - 7\frac{9}{15} = 3\frac{11}{15}$.

5. **C.** Just change to a common denominator of 10: $4\frac{3}{5} - 3\frac{1}{2} = 4\frac{6}{10} - 3\frac{5}{10} = 1\frac{1}{10}$.

6. **D.** Convert $\frac{1}{2}$ to $\frac{2}{4}$, and then simply subtract: $6\frac{3}{4} - 4\frac{1}{2} = 6\frac{3}{4} - 4\frac{2}{4} = 2\frac{1}{4}$.

7. **C.** Try changing $1\frac{1}{4}$ to an improper fraction, and then change to a denominator of 8:

   $1\frac{1}{4} - \frac{5}{8} = \frac{5}{4} - \frac{5}{8} = \frac{10}{8} - \frac{5}{8} = \frac{5}{8}$.

8. **A.** Your common denominator is 6, and you'll need to borrow 1 from the 8:

   $8\frac{1}{2} - 6\frac{2}{3} = 8\frac{3}{6} - 6\frac{4}{6} = 7 + 1 + \frac{3}{6} - 6\frac{4}{6} = 7 + \frac{6}{6} + \frac{3}{6} - 6\frac{4}{6} = 7\frac{9}{6} - 6\frac{4}{6} = 1\frac{5}{6}$.

9. **D.** Borrow instead of using improper fractions, because 6 times 34 will be too big:

   $34\frac{1}{6} - 18\frac{2}{3} = 34\frac{1}{6} - 18\frac{4}{6} = 33 + 1 + \frac{1}{6} - 18\frac{4}{6} = 33 + \frac{6}{6} + \frac{1}{6} - 18\frac{4}{6} = 33\frac{7}{6} - 18\frac{4}{6} = 15\frac{3}{6} = 15\frac{1}{2}$.

10. **A.** An easy way to solve is to take the $\frac{3}{4}$ away from the 1, leaving $\frac{1}{4}$. Then add the $\frac{1}{12}$ to the $\frac{1}{4}$ using a

    common denominator of 12. So, $\frac{1}{12} + \frac{3}{12} = \frac{4}{12} = \frac{1}{3}$.

    Alternately, you can use a common denominator of 12 and change $1\frac{1}{12}$ to an improper fraction and

    then subtract: $1\frac{1}{12} - \frac{3}{4} = \frac{13}{12} - \frac{9}{12} = \frac{4}{12} = \frac{1}{3}$.

D. Multiplication

The basic rule for multiplication of fractions is very simple: Multiply numerator times numerator and denominator times denominator. If you follow that rule faithfully, however, you'll find yourself working with much larger numbers than necessary and doing a lot of simplifying answers.

The better way to proceed is to get your simplifying done early. Always make sure that the fractions you're multiplying are in simplest form. Once you've written the multiplication, you can cancel any numerator with any denominator.

EXAMPLE:

$$\frac{6}{49} \times \frac{14}{15} = \frac{\overset{2}{\cancel{6}}}{\underset{7}{\cancel{49}}} \times \frac{\overset{2}{\cancel{14}}}{\underset{5}{\cancel{15}}} = \frac{2 \times 2}{7 \times 5} = \frac{4}{35}$$

Mixed Numbers

When you need to multiply mixed numbers, your best strategy is to change the mixed numbers to improper fractions first. Multiply the improper fractions and then convert back to a mixed number, if necessary.

EXAMPLE:

$$5\frac{4}{7} \times 4\frac{2}{3} = \frac{(7 \times 5) + 4}{7} \times \frac{(3 \times 4) + 2}{3} = \frac{39}{7} \times \frac{14}{3} = \frac{\overset{13}{\cancel{39}}}{\underset{1}{\cancel{7}}} \times \frac{\overset{2}{\cancel{14}}}{\underset{1}{\cancel{3}}} = 26$$

Avoid the temptation to multiply the whole number by the whole number and the fraction by the fraction. That strategy of separation works for addition, but not for multiplication.

Bottom Up

For mental math, listen to the problem and deal with what the denominator is telling you first. "One-sixth of 24" is just $24 \div 6 = 4$, and "one-fifth of 20" is $20 \div 5 = 4$. Multiplication by a *unit fraction* (a fraction with a numerator of 1) can be handled by division, but so can other fractions. To find three-fifths of 20, first find one-fifth of 20, which is 4, and then multiply by 3. Three-fifths of 20 is 12. Five-sixths of 24 is 5 times one-sixth of 24, or 5 times 4.

Practice

Directions: Choose the best answer for each question.

1. Joanne had $2\frac{1}{2}$ yards of ribbon. She used $\frac{3}{5}$ of it to trim a dress. How much ribbon did she use?

   A. $4\frac{1}{6}$ yards

   B. 3 yards

   C. $1\frac{9}{10}$ yards

   D. $1\frac{1}{2}$ yards

2. If you've driven $\frac{3}{4}$ of the way to work and you work $\frac{5}{6}$ mile from home, how far have you driven?

   A. $\frac{5}{8}$ mile

   B. $\frac{1}{2}$ mile

   C. $\frac{2}{5}$ mile

   D. $\frac{1}{12}$ mile

3. If you purchased a $\frac{1}{2}$ gallon of milk and the container is now $\frac{1}{3}$ full, how much milk do you have?

   A. $\frac{5}{6}$ gallon

   B. $\frac{3}{8}$ gallon

   C. $\frac{1}{6}$ gallon

   D. $\frac{1}{8}$ gallon

4. Henry ate $\frac{1}{5}$ of the turkey in the refrigerator. If the package contained $1\frac{1}{4}$ pounds, how much turkey did Henry eat?

   A. $\frac{4}{25}$ pound

   B. $\frac{1}{4}$ pound

   C. $\frac{4}{5}$ pound

   D. $\frac{1}{20}$ pound

5. Jesse and Clarissa painted $\frac{3}{4}$ of the living room. If Jesse did $\frac{2}{3}$ of the painting, what part of the room did he paint?

   A. $\frac{1}{12}$

   B. $\frac{1}{4}$

   C. $\frac{1}{2}$

   D. $\frac{8}{9}$

6. A radio-controlled airplane uses $\frac{3}{8}$ gallon of fuel each hour. How much fuel will it use in a $\frac{1}{4}$ hour?

   A. $\frac{1}{8}$

   B. $\frac{3}{32}$

   C. $\frac{1}{4}$

   D. $\frac{3}{8}$

7. The gravity on the moon is approximately $\frac{1}{6}$ of that on Earth. If an astronaut weighs 189 pounds on Earth, what will he weigh on the moon?

   A. $31\frac{1}{2}$ pounds

   B. 33 pounds

   C. 133 pounds

   D. 1,134 pounds

8. The gravity on Venus is about $\frac{7}{8}$ of that on Earth. What would a 184-pound astronaut weigh on Venus (if he could actually survive the atmosphere of Venus)?

   A. 216 pounds

   B. 210 pounds

   C. 165 pounds

   D. 161 pounds

9. If Jackie can run at an average speed of $11\frac{1}{3}$ km per hour, how far can she run in $\frac{3}{4}$ hour?

   A. $15\frac{1}{9}$ km

   B. $11\frac{1}{3}$ km

   C. $10\frac{7}{12}$ km

   D. $8\frac{1}{2}$ km

10. What is the area of a room that measures $10\frac{2}{3}$ feet by $12\frac{3}{4}$ feet?

    A. 136 ft.^{2}

    B. $128\frac{1}{2}$ ft.^{2}

    C. 128 ft.^{2}

    D. $120\frac{1}{2}$ ft.^{2}

Answers

1. **D.** She used $\frac{3}{5}$ of $2\frac{1}{2}$ yards. Convert $2\frac{1}{2}$ to an improper fraction and then multiply: $\frac{3}{\cancel{5}}\times\frac{\cancel{5}}{2}=\frac{3}{2}=1\frac{1}{2}$.

2. **A.** You've driven $\frac{3}{4}$ of $\frac{5}{6}$ mile, which is $\frac{\cancel{3}}{4}\times\frac{5}{\cancel{6}_2}=\frac{5}{8}$.

3. **C.** You have $\frac{1}{3}$ of $\frac{1}{2}$ gallon, or $\frac{1}{3}\times\frac{1}{2}=\frac{1}{6}$.

4. **B.** Henry ate $\frac{1}{5}$ of $1\frac{1}{4}$ pounds. Convert $1\frac{1}{4}$ to an improper fraction and then multiply: $\frac{1}{\cancel{5}}\times\frac{\cancel{5}}{4}=\frac{1}{4}$.

5. **C.** Jesse did $\frac{2}{3}$ of $\frac{3}{4}$ or $\frac{\cancel{2}}{\cancel{3}}\times\frac{\cancel{3}}{\cancel{4}_2}=\frac{1}{2}$ of the painting.

6. **B.** It will use $\frac{1}{4}$ of $\frac{3}{8}$ gallon, which is $\frac{1}{4}\times\frac{3}{8}=\frac{3}{32}$ gallon of fuel each hour. Resist the temptation to cancel two denominators. You may only cancel a numerator with a denominator.

7. **A.** Gravity acting on mass determines weight, so $\frac{1}{6}$ the gravity means $\frac{1}{6}$ of the weight. So, $\frac{1}{6}\times 189=189\div 6=31\frac{3}{6}=31\frac{1}{2}$.

8. **D.** First, find $\frac{1}{8}$ of 184, which is 23, then multiply by 7: $7 \times 23 = (7 \times 20) + (7 \times 3) = 140 + 21 = 161$. So $\frac{7}{\cancel{8}}\times\cancel{184}^{23}=161$.

9. **D.** Her speed of $11\frac{1}{3}$ km per hour times the time of $\frac{3}{4}$ hour gives the distance. Convert $11\frac{1}{3}$ to an improper fraction and then multiply: $11\frac{1}{3}\times\frac{3}{4}=\frac{\cancel{34}^{17}}{\cancel{3}}\times\frac{\cancel{3}}{\cancel{4}_2}=\frac{17}{2}=8\frac{1}{2}$.

10. **A.** Area is $10\frac{2}{3}$ feet times $12\frac{3}{4}$ feet. Convert both mixed numbers to improper fractions and then multiply: $10\frac{2}{3}\times 12\frac{3}{4}=\frac{\cancel{32}^{8}}{\cancel{3}}\times\frac{\cancel{51}^{17}}{\cancel{4}}=136$.

E. Division

The rule for dividing by fractions is simple: Don't. You never actually divide by a fraction. Instead, you *multiply* by the reciprocal of the divisor. Two numbers are *reciprocals* if they multiply to equal 1. The simplest way to find the reciprocal of a fraction is just to invert it—swap the numerator and denominator. To find the reciprocal of a whole number or a mixed number, first write it as a fraction and then invert it. Once you've rewritten the problem as a multiplication problem, simply follow the rules for multiplying fractions.

Picturing the Pie

The use of pictures of pies to illustrate fraction problems has become a cliché, but for division, it could be useful. Just as you can hear the problem $12 \div 4$ as "How many fours are there in a group of 12?", so you can imagine the question $8\frac{1}{2} \div \frac{1}{4}$ as a picture of eight and a half pies, each cut into pieces equal to a quarter of a pie. How many quarters are there? The eight whole pies account for 32 quarters and half a pie accounts for two more, so $8\frac{1}{2} \div \frac{1}{4} = \left(8 \div \frac{1}{4}\right) + \left(\frac{1}{2} \div \frac{1}{4}\right) = \left(\frac{8}{1} \times \frac{4}{1}\right) + \left(\frac{1}{2} \times \frac{4}{1}\right) = 32 + 2 = 34$.

Practice

Directions: Choose the best answer for each question.

1. If Alex can run at $17\frac{3}{5}$ feet per second, how long will it take him to run 880 feet?

   A. $40\frac{8}{13}$ seconds

   B. 47 seconds

   C. 50 seconds

   D. $51\frac{13}{17}$ seconds

2. How many strands of ribbon, each $2\frac{1}{2}$ feet long, can be cut from a roll 100 feet long?

   A. 35

   B. 40

   C. 45

   D. 50

3. If the area of a rectangle is $60\frac{1}{2}$ square feet and the length is $14\frac{2}{3}$ feet, find the width.

   A. $3\frac{5}{8}$ feet

   B. $3\frac{7}{8}$ feet

   C. 4 feet

   D. $4\frac{1}{8}$ feet

4. If you divide $44\frac{1}{3}$ pounds of ground beef into packages of $3\frac{1}{6}$ pounds each, how many packages will you have?

   A. 12

   B. 14

   C. 16

   D. 18

5. Marisa used $1\frac{1}{2}$ cups of flour in a recipe. If this was $\frac{2}{5}$ of the flour in the canister, how much flour was originally in the canister?

A. $3\frac{3}{4}$ cups

B. 3 cups

C. $1\frac{1}{5}$ cups

D. $\frac{4}{15}$ cup

6. If Jack hiked $39\frac{3}{8}$ miles in $5\frac{1}{4}$ hours, what was his average speed?

A. $7\frac{3}{7}$ mph

B. $7\frac{1}{2}$ mph

C. $9\frac{3}{10}$ mph

D. 15 mph

7. If $59\frac{1}{4}$ cups of popcorn are packed into bags containing $\frac{3}{4}$ cup each, how many bags will be filled?

A. 75

B. 77

C. 79

D. 81

8. The area of a triangle is half the product of the base and the height. Find the height of a triangle with an area of $66\frac{2}{3}$ square inches if the base measures $12\frac{1}{2}$ inches.

A. $5\frac{1}{3}$ inches

B. $5\frac{5}{6}$ inches

C. $10\frac{2}{3}$ inches

D. $21\frac{1}{3}$ inches

9. If Andrew wants to lose $16\frac{1}{2}$ pounds at a rate of $1\frac{1}{2}$ pounds a week, how long will the process take?

A. 9 weeks

B. 11 weeks

C. 13 weeks

D. 15 weeks

10. Find the width of a rectangle $4\frac{3}{4}$ feet long if the area of the rectangle is $15\frac{7}{16}$ square feet.

A. $5\frac{1}{2}$ feet

B. $4\frac{1}{3}$ feet

C. $3\frac{3}{4}$ feet

D. $3\frac{1}{4}$ feet

Answers

1. **C.** Divide the distance by the speed to get the time: $880 \div 17\frac{3}{5} = \frac{880}{1} \div \frac{88}{5} = \frac{\overset{10}{\cancel{880}}}{1} \times \frac{5}{\cancel{88}} = 50.$

2. **B.** Divide the total length of ribbon available by the desired length of each strand to get the number of strands: $100 \div 2\frac{1}{2} = \frac{100}{1} \div \frac{5}{2} = \frac{\overset{20}{\cancel{100}}}{1} \times \frac{2}{\cancel{5}} = 40.$

3. **D.** Divide the area by the known dimension: $60\frac{1}{2} \div 14\frac{2}{3} = \frac{121}{2} \div \frac{44}{3} = \frac{\overset{11}{\cancel{121}}}{2} \times \frac{3}{\cancel{44}_4} = \frac{33}{8} = 4\frac{1}{8}.$

4. **B.** Divide the total weight by the weight of each package to get the total number of packages:
$44\frac{1}{3} \div 3\frac{1}{6} = \frac{133}{3} \div \frac{19}{6} = \frac{133}{\cancel{3}} \times \frac{\overset{2}{\cancel{6}}}{19} = \frac{266}{19} = 14.$

5. **A.** One and one-half is two-fifths of the total. Divide $1\frac{1}{2}$ by $\frac{2}{5}$ to find the total amount of flour:
$1\frac{1}{2} \div \frac{2}{5} = \frac{3}{2} \div \frac{2}{5} = \frac{3}{2} \times \frac{5}{2} = \frac{15}{4} = 3\frac{3}{4}.$

6. **B.** Distance divided by time will give you speed: $39\frac{3}{8} \div 5\frac{1}{4} = \frac{315}{8} \div \frac{21}{4} = \frac{\overset{45}{\cancel{315}}}{\cancel{8}_2} \times \frac{\cancel{4}}{\cancel{21}_3} = \frac{45}{6} = 7\frac{3}{6} = 7\frac{1}{2}.$

7. **C.** Divide the total amount by the amount in each bag to find the number of bags needed:
$59\frac{1}{4} \div \frac{3}{4} = \frac{237}{4} \div \frac{3}{4} = \frac{\overset{79}{\cancel{237}}}{\cancel{4}} \times \frac{\cancel{4}}{\cancel{3}} = 79.$

8. **C.** The area of a triangle is half the product of the base and the height. The area is $66\frac{2}{3}$, so base times height is $2 \times 66\frac{2}{3} = 132\frac{4}{3} = 133\frac{1}{3}$. Divide that by the base of $12\frac{1}{2}$, and you have
$133\frac{1}{3} \div 12\frac{1}{2} = \frac{400}{3} \div \frac{25}{2} = \frac{\overset{16}{\cancel{400}}}{3} \times \frac{2}{\cancel{25}} = \frac{32}{3} = 10\frac{2}{3}.$

9. **B.** Divide the total desired loss by the loss per week to find the number of weeks:
$16\frac{1}{2} \div 1\frac{1}{2} = \frac{33}{2} \div \frac{3}{2} = \frac{\overset{11}{\cancel{33}}}{\cancel{2}} \times \frac{\cancel{2}}{\cancel{3}} = 11.$

10. **D.** Divide the area of the rectangle by the known dimension:
$15\frac{7}{16} \div 4\frac{3}{4} = \frac{247}{16} \div \frac{19}{4} = \frac{\overset{13}{\cancel{247}}}{\cancel{16}_4} \times \frac{\cancel{4}}{\cancel{19}} = \frac{13}{4} = 3\frac{1}{4}.$

F. Mixed Operations

The Arithmetic Reasoning test will involve addition, subtraction, multiplication, and division of whole numbers, fractions, and decimals. Most often, however, questions will combine two or more operations and possibly more than one type of number, so it's a good idea to practice some problems that combine different operations and numbers. These may sound familiar at first, but each has a little twist from its first appearance.

Practice

Directions: Choose the best answer for each question.

1. Josh ran 4 miles on Monday, 5 miles on Tuesday, and 6 miles on Wednesday. If he wants to run 26 miles a week, how much farther must he run this week?

   A. 11 miles
   B. 15 miles
   C. 20 miles
   D. 21 miles

2. The National Weather Service recorded 11 inches of snow in January, 18 inches in February, and 7 inches in March. What is the average monthly snowfall for the first quarter of the year?

   A. 11 inches
   B. 12 inches
   C. 18 inches
   D. 36 inches

3. Jane packs a mixer that weighs 22 pounds and a blender that weighs 9 pounds into a shipping box. The shipping company charges $5.95 for any box up to 25 pounds and an additional $1.25 for each additional 3 pounds. What will Jane have to pay to ship the box?

   A. $7.20
   B. $8.45
   C. $12.92
   D. $13.45

4. A fruit basket contains 8 apples, 7 oranges, 3 pears, and 4 bananas. If 20 people each take one piece of fruit, how many pieces of fruit are left in the basket?

   A. 1
   B. 2
   C. 3
   D. 4

5. A recipe for a party punch calls for 46 ounces of pineapple juice, 12 ounces of lemon juice, 12 ounces of orange juice, 112 ounces of sparkling water, and 32 ounces of ginger ale. One cup is 8 ounces. How many cups of punch will you have?

   A. $25\dfrac{1}{4}$
   B. 26
   C. $26\dfrac{3}{4}$
   D. 27

6. Jason lifts weights and is increasing the amount he can lift. Right now, he is lifting a bar that weighs 54 pounds with a 50-pound plate on each end. If he increases the weight by 10 pounds per week, how much will he lift in 8 weeks?

   A. 134 pounds
   B. 180 pounds
   C. 184 pounds
   D. 234 pounds

7. Lydia had a collection of 53 teapots and received 12 more teapots as gifts. She then divided her collection equally among her three daughters, keeping the teapots that were left over after each daughter had received an equal number. How many teapots does Lydia have left?

   A. 1
   B. 2
   C. 3
   D. 4

8. If you have $327 in your checking account, you deposit $415, and then you write checks for $38 and $105, how much will you have left in your account?

    A. $272
    B. $599
    C. $742
    D. $885

9. An aquarium contains 117 fish, and 35 new fish are introduced. All of them survive. If the volume of the tank is 76 ft.³, what is the number of fish per cubic foot of space?

    A. 1
    B. 2
    C. 3
    D. 4

10. At 8 a.m., there were 7 cars in the parking lot. If 13 more cars entered over the next hour and 3 left, how many cars were in the lot at 9 a.m.?

    A. 4
    B. 6
    C. 10
    D. 17

11. Melanie eats $\frac{1}{4}$ of a pizza and Marc eats $\frac{1}{3}$ of a pizza. What fraction of the pizza is left?

    A. $\frac{5}{12}$
    B. $\frac{2}{7}$
    C. $\frac{7}{12}$
    D. $\frac{5}{7}$

12. Olivia painted $8\frac{1}{2}$ feet of fence and Omar painted $6\frac{2}{3}$ feet of fence. If the fence is 20 feet long, how many feet of fence are left to paint?

    A. $5\frac{5}{6}$ feet
    B. $5\frac{1}{6}$ feet
    C. $4\frac{5}{6}$ feet
    D. $4\frac{1}{6}$ feet

13. Yesterday the rain gauge recorded $\frac{5}{8}$ inch of rain, and today it showed $1\frac{1}{4}$ inches. What was the average rainfall over the 2 days?

    A. $\frac{7}{8}$ inch
    B. $\frac{15}{16}$ inch
    C. $1\frac{3}{8}$ inches
    D. $1\frac{7}{8}$ inches

14. Hector worked on Mr. Collins's car for $4\frac{1}{2}$ hours on Tuesday and finished the job in $6\frac{3}{4}$ hours on Wednesday. If he bills Mr. Collins $60 for parts and $80 per hour for labor, what is the total bill for the repairs on the car?

    A. $675
    B. $880
    C. $900
    D. $960

15. Susan walked from her home to the supermarket, a distance of $1\frac{1}{2}$ miles, and then walked $2\frac{2}{3}$ miles from the supermarket to her grandmother's house. If she walks at an average speed of $2\frac{1}{2}$ mph, how long did the trip take?

   A. $1\frac{1}{15}$ hours

   B. $1\frac{2}{3}$ hours

   C. $2\frac{1}{12}$ hours

   D. $2\frac{1}{2}$ hours

16. Charlotte used $5\frac{1}{2}$ cups of flour to make bread and $3\frac{3}{4}$ cups of flour in a cookie recipe, and then added $\frac{3}{8}$ of a cup of flour to gravy. If she began with 12 cups of flour, how much did she have left?

   A. $2\frac{3}{8}$ cups

   B. $2\frac{5}{8}$ cups

   C. $3\frac{3}{8}$ cups

   D. $3\frac{5}{8}$ cups

17. Jason bought a circular saw for $269.97, a set of wrenches for $54.96, and a pair of safety goggles for $11.47. A 6 percent sales tax was added to his bill. What is his total bill to the nearest penny?

   A. $201.84

   B. $336.40

   C. $356.58

   D. $538.24

18. Mallory combined 8.9 grams of sugar with 3.1 grams of cinnamon, and sprinkled the mixture over three dozen cookies. How much cinnamon sugar was on each cookie?

   A. $\frac{1}{3}$ gram

   B. $\frac{1}{4}$ gram

   C. 3 grams

   D. 4 grams

19. Kevin bought a pen for $1.25, a notebook for $2.87, and computer software for $31. If he gave the cashier a $50 bill, how much change did he receive?

   A. $5.70

   B. $14.88

   C. $26.88

   D. $45.57

20. Mrs. Williamson bought four items on her shopping list that cost $40.49, $11.98, $29.99, and $22.20. If she has a coupon giving her 15 percent off her total bill, how much will she pay?

   A. $15.70

   B. $88.96

   C. $89.66

   D. $99.43

Answers

1. **A.** Add the miles run over the three given days: $4 + 5 + 6 = 15$ miles. Then subtract that total from the desired 26 miles: $26 - 15 = 11$.

2. **B.** To average, add the readings and divide by the number of readings: $11 + 18 + 7 = 36$ inches of snow over three months. There are three readings, so $36 \div 3 = 12$ inches per month on average.

3. **B.** The total weight of the box is $22 + 9 = 31$ pounds. So, \$5.95 will cover the first 25 pounds, but the additional $31 - 25 = 6$ pounds will be billed at an additional \$1.25 for every 3 pounds. That means there will be two charges of \$1.25 each added to the \$5.95. So, $\$5.95 + 2(\$1.25) = 5.95 + 2.50 = \$8.45$.

4. **B.** There are a total of $8 + 7 + 3 + 4 = 22$ pieces of fruit in the basket. If 20 people each take one piece, there will be $22 - 20 = 2$ pieces remaining.

5. **C.** Find the total number of ounces: $46 + 12 + 12 + 112 + 32 = 214$ ounces. Divide the total ounces by the 8 ounces in 1 cup to get the number of cups: $214 \div 8 = 26.75 = 26\frac{3}{4}$.

6. **D.** Currently, Jason is lifting $54 + 2(50) = 154$ pounds. If he increases that by 10 pounds per week for 8 weeks, he will increase the weight from 154 to $154 + 10(8) = 154 + 80 = 234$.

7. **B.** Lydia starts with 53 teapots and receives 12 more for a total of $53 + 12 = 65$ teapots. She divides them among her three daughters, so that's $65 \div 3 = 21$ with a remainder of 2. Each daughter receives 21 teapots, and Lydia keeps the remaining 2 teapots.

8. **B.** You begin with \$327 and deposit \$415, bringing the total in your account to $\$327 + \$415 = \$742$. You then write checks for \$38 and \$105, a total of $38 + 105 = \$143$. That \$143 is deducted from the \$742. So, $\$742 - \$143 = \$599$.

9. **B.** Add $117 + 35 = 152$ to find the number of fish in the tank. Read the question carefully. "Fish per cubic foot" tells you to divide 152 fish by 76 ft.³ So, $152 \div 76 = 2$ fish per cubic foot.

10. **D.** The hour starts with 7 cars, then 13 are added and 3 subtracted: $7 + 13 = 20$ and $20 - 3 = 17$.

11. **A.** Together Melanie and Marc eat $\frac{1}{4} + \frac{1}{3} = \frac{(1 \times 3) + (1 \times 4)}{4 \times 3} = \frac{7}{12}$ of the pizza. Subtract that from 1, for one whole pizza: $1 - \frac{7}{12} = \frac{12}{12} - \frac{7}{12} = \frac{5}{12}$.

12. **C.** Together, Olivia and Omar painted $8\frac{1}{2} + 6\frac{2}{3} = 8\frac{3}{6} + 6\frac{4}{6}$ feet of fence.

    So, $8\frac{3}{6} + 6\frac{4}{6} = 8 + 6 + \frac{3}{6} + \frac{4}{6} = 14 + \frac{7}{6} = 14 + 1\frac{1}{6} = 15\frac{1}{6}$. Use estimation to avoid mistakes. They painted a little more than 15 of the 20 feet, so there should be a little less than 5 feet left.

    So, $20 - 15\frac{1}{6} = 19\frac{6}{6} - 15\frac{1}{6} = 4\frac{5}{6}$ feet are left to paint.

13. **B.** To find the average, add the readings and divide by the number of readings. In this case, it will be easier to change $1\frac{1}{4}$ to an improper fraction. Then, $\frac{5}{8} + 1\frac{1}{4} = \frac{5}{8} + \frac{5}{4} = \frac{5}{8} + \frac{10}{8} = \frac{15}{8}$, so the total rainfall is $\frac{15}{8}$ inches. Don't rush to change that to a mixed number because you still need to divide by 2.

    So, $\frac{15}{8} \div 2 = \frac{15}{8} \times \frac{1}{2} = \frac{15}{16}$ inch average rainfall.

14. **D.** First, find the total time Hector worked on the car: $4\frac{1}{2}+6\frac{3}{4}=4+6+\frac{2}{4}+\frac{3}{4}=10+\frac{5}{4}=11\frac{1}{4}$ hours. Multiply that time by \$80 to find the cost of labor. The distributive property will help here. Eleven times 80 is 880 and $\frac{1}{4}$ of 80 is 20 so $11\frac{1}{4}\times80=880+20=900$. Don't forget to add on the \$60 for parts to get \$960.

15. **B.** You'll need to add the distances, and then divide the total by Susan's walking speed, so it may be easier to work with improper fractions. She walked $1\frac{1}{2}+2\frac{2}{3}=\frac{3}{2}+\frac{8}{3}=\frac{9+16}{6}=\frac{25}{6}$ miles. Divide that by $2\frac{1}{2}=\frac{5}{2}$ mph: $\frac{25}{6}\div\frac{5}{2}=\frac{\overset{5}{\cancel{25}}}{\underset{3}{\cancel{6}}}\times\frac{\cancel{2}}{\cancel{5}}=\frac{5}{3}=1\frac{2}{3}$.

16. **A.** The flour used totaled $5\frac{1}{2}+3\frac{3}{4}+\frac{3}{8}=5+3+\frac{4}{8}+\frac{6}{8}+\frac{3}{8}=8+\frac{13}{8}=8+1\frac{5}{8}=9\frac{5}{8}$ cups. Subtract that from 12 cups to find out how much flour is left: $12-9\frac{5}{8}=11\frac{8}{8}-9\frac{5}{8}=2\frac{3}{8}$.

17. **C.** Add the costs of the items purchased: \$269.97 + \$54.96 + \$11.47 = \$336.40. To find the total bill, multiply \$336.40 by 1.06 (1 for 100 percent of the original bill plus 0.06 for the 6 percent tax). Then \$336.40 × 1.06 = \$356.584, which rounds to \$356.58.

18. **A.** The mixture of 8.9 grams of sugar and 3.1 grams of cinnamon makes 8.9 + 3.1 = 12 grams of cinnamon sugar. Those 12 grams are divided among 3 dozen, or 36, cookies. So, $12\div36=\frac{1}{3}$ gram per cookie.

19. **B.** The items purchased total \$1.25 + \$2.87 + \$31 = \$35.12. Subtract from \$50 to find the change: \$50 – \$35.12 = \$14.88.

20. **B.** The original bill is \$40.49 + \$11.98 + \$29.99 + \$22.20 = \$104.66. Since she gets 15 percent off, she will pay 100 percent – 15 percent = 85 percent of that total. So, 0.85 × \$104.66 = \$88.961, which rounds to \$88.96.

Chapter 8

Word Knowledge: Building Word Power

Both verbal subtests of the AFQT—Word Knowledge and Paragraph Comprehension—will test your understanding of vocabulary words. The test-makers know that the ability to understand and use appropriate language is important in all aspects of life: in the military, in the business world, in school, and in daily life. In other words, you'll always need the ability to understand terms and expressions in standard written and spoken English. Of course, the best way to accomplish this successfully is to read, read, read! The more you read, the better you get at it. And the more widely and deeply you read, the more varied the vocabulary you'll encounter. So, for the next few days, weeks, or months, plan to read as much as you can in a variety of subject areas.

A. Five Steps to Better Vocabulary

Step 1: Read

Reading is the best tool to increase your command of the English language. So, what should you read and how should you read?

If you read nothing other than what is required for day-to-day living, you're cheating yourself out of a whole world of experiences. A wealth of print and online materials is available on every topic you can possibly conceive of. Want to know more about cars? Read a car magazine, take a book out of the library, buy a book about cars in your local bookstore, or go online to one of the thousands of websites dedicated to car enthusiasts. Interested in African tree frogs? The possibility of extraterrestrial life? Same routine. Just motivate yourself to find out what someone else has written about the topic, and you'll open up new worlds. And if you're reading about a topic that fascinates you, you won't find reading painful or time-consuming.

If you begin to read an article or a book with your own set of preconceived ideas about the topic, you may miss something new or important. Try to open your mind to the writer and follow her ideas. This process may require you to consider the subject matter in a new light, but that's the right idea. Learning is a life-long process—don't miss an opportunity to educate yourself.

Step 2: Be Curious

Intellectual curiosity is the sign of a good mind at work. Sometimes a comment by a writer will cause you to wonder or question his point. Don't doubt yourself. Seek out ways to satisfy your need to know. Do some research—go online or to the library.

Don't stop your reading: If you find you aren't enjoying a particular book or article, find another one that's written more to your taste or is more relevant to your interests. Try sharing your knowledge or interests with someone—a family member, a friend, a teacher, a co-worker, or an online chatroom.

Step 3: Write It Down

In the course of your reading, you may come across words you've never seen or heard before. Try to figure out the meanings of these unfamiliar words from the context of your reading. Jot down any strange words that you come across in your reading, or ideas that are new and exciting to you. You don't have to stop reading and grab a dictionary. If the words are in your notes, you can look them up later at your leisure.

The classroom is a great place to learn, but it's not the only one available to you. When you're reading, it's easy to jot down unfamiliar vocabulary, but don't ignore other chances to learn. If you're listening to a song or to talk radio, and you hear an unfamiliar word, jot it down and look it up when you have a free minute or two. The same goes for TV shows or movies. If you hear someone speaking at work or in a social setting, take note of any unfamiliar words and try to remember to look them up later.

Step 4: Study and Review

Once you've embarked on this path to a better vocabulary, apply yourself to the task. Write each word down on the front of index cards and write the definition on the back. Now you have a personal set of flash cards.

Try to look over the words you've collected for a few minutes every day. Add new words to your study routine as you commit the old words to memory.

As you prepare for the AFQT, you'll want to improve your vocabulary as quickly as possible. To help you, this chapter will suggest ways to learn as many words as possible in a short period of time.

Step 5: Use the Words

A great educator once said, once you've used a new vocabulary word three times, it's yours for life! Incorporate the words into your speaking and writing whenever possible. As a side benefit to an increased vocabulary, you'll impress your friends and relatives with your word power.

B. Building a Power Vocabulary

Prefixes, Roots, and Suffixes

Many English words consist of three parts: the prefix, the root word, and the suffix. The *prefix* is added on at the beginning of a word (or a root), while the *suffix* is added to the end. Each part contributes to the meaning of a word. The *root* may be a complete word that is familiar to you, or it may be part of a word.

Look at the word *ungovernable* and examine its parts:

un-   a prefix meaning not

govern   a word that means to control or rule

-able   a suffix meaning able or capable

Put the parts together, and you can figure out that *ungovernable* means not able to be controlled or governed.

Let's look at a slightly more complicated word, *irrevocable,* and examine its parts:

ir-	a prefix meaning not
re-	a prefix meaning again or back
voc	a root that means to call
-able	a suffix meaning able or capable

Put the parts together and you can figure out that *irrevocable* means permanent or irreversible—not able to be called back again.

Most words in the English language were borrowed from other languages, usually Latin or Greek. It will be useful for you to learn some of the common origins, or *roots,* of words. Knowing the meanings of the root, the prefix, and the suffix can help you figure out the meanings of unfamiliar words.

Following are tables of some common prefixes, roots, and suffixes you should familiarize yourself with.

Common Prefixes		
Prefix	**Meaning**	**Examples**
a-	not, without	*atypical* (not typical), *amoral* (without morals)
ab-	away from	*abnormal* (not normal), *abstain* (to refrain from)
ambi-	both	*ambidextrous* (skillful with both hands), *ambivalent* (seeing both sides)
auto-	self	*autonomy* (self-rule), *automobile* (self-propelled)
bene-	good	*benefit* (promotes well-being), *beneficent* (performing acts of kindness)
circum-	around	*circumnavigate* (travel around), *circumscribe* (to draw a circle around or to restrict within bounds)
con-, com-	with, together	*congregate* (gather together), *congruent* (in agreement), *community* (a group of people living together)
contra-	against	*contradict* (to speak against), *contrary* (opposed to)
de-	down, away; also reverses the meaning of the root word	*descend* (to go down), *decelerate* (to decrease speed); *destabilize* (to make unstable)
dys-	bad, ill	*dysfunction* (impaired function), *dyslectic* or *dyslexic* (impairment of the ability to read)
eu-	good	*euphoria* (a feeling of happiness), *euphony* (pleasant sounds)
ex-	away from, out of	*expatriate* (one who lives away from his or her native land), *exonerate* (take away blame)
hetero-	different	*heterogeneous* (differing in kind)
homo-	same	*homogeneous* (of the same kind)
il-, im-, in-, ir-	not	*illogical* (not logical), *illicit* (not lawful), *improbable* (not likely), *indefensible* (unable to be defended), *irreducible* (not able to be reduced)
inter-	between	*intervene* (to come between)
intra-	within	*intrastate* (within the state)
mal-	bad	*malign* (to speak badly of), *malignant* (evil, harmful)
micro-	small	*microcosm* (miniature world)
mis-	bad, wrong	*misconduct* (bad conduct), *misaligned* (wrongly aligned)
mono-	one	*monopoly* (exclusive control by one group), *monotheism* (belief in one god)

Prefix	Meaning	Examples
multi-	many	*multifaceted* (many sided), *multifarious* (varied, diverse)
neo-	new	*neologism* (new word), *neophyte* (beginner)
ob-	against	*object* (to express opposition), *obdurate* (hardened in feelings)
philo-	lover	*philanthropist* (lover of mankind)
poly-	many	*polygon* (a many-sided figure), *polyglot* (composed of several languages)
pre-	before	*presage* (to know beforehand), *precedent* (what has previously occurred and may be used as an example)
pro-	forward, in favor of	*proponent* (one who is in favor of), *progress* (to go forward)
pseudo-	false	*pseudonym* (a false name)
re-	again	*renovate* (to make new again), *recapitulate* (to repeat in brief form)
retro-	back	*retrospect* (to look at the past)
sub-	below, under	*subordinate* (belonging to a lower class), *submission* (being under the power of another)
super-	above, beyond	*superfluous* (beyond what is needed; extra), *superlative* (of the highest order)
sym-, syn-	with, together	*symmetry* (an even relationship of parts), *synchronize* (to occur at the same time)
trans-	across	*transmit* (to send from one person or place to another), *transplant* (to move from one place to another)
un-	not	*uneventful* (without incident), *unfruitful* (not productive)

Common Roots

Root	Meaning	Examples
ami, amic	friend	*amiable* (friendly), *amicable* (friendly)
anthropo	mankind	*anthropology* (the study of humans and their works), *misanthrope* (one who dislikes people)
aud	hearing	*audible* (able to be heard)
bell, belli	war	*belligerence* (warlike or aggressive behavior), *bellicose* (eager to fight)
bio	life	*biography* (the story of someone's life), *antibiotic* (a chemical substance that kills bacteria)
brev	brief, short	*abbreviation* (a shortened version), *brevity* (briefness)
cap	take, seize	*capture* (to take prisoner or to seize), *captivate* (to hold the attention of)
ced	to go, yield	*accede* (to give consent), *secede* (to withdraw from)
chron	time	*chronological* (in time order), *anachronism* (something out of place in time)
cogn	know	*cognition* (the process of knowing)
cred	believe	*incredulous* (disbelieving), *credulous* (gullible)
culp	guilt, fault, blame	*culprit* (a guilty person), *exculpate* (free from guilt)
cur, curs	to run	*concurrent* (running at the same time)
demo	people	*democracy* (rule by the people), *epidemic* (a disease that affects many people)
dic	speak, say	*dictate* (a command), *dictum* (an authoritative pronouncement)
epi	upon, following, among	*epidemic* (spreading among the people)
equ	uniform, balanced, equal	*equilibrium* (in an evenly balanced state)

continued

Root	Meaning	Examples
fac, fec, fic	to make or do	*effective* (to make useful), *malefactor* (one who makes evil)
gen	birth, origin	*generate* (to create or breed), *progeny* (offspring)
graph	writing	*autobiography* (the life story of the writer)
greg	group	*gregarious* (sociable; likes to be in a group), *aggregate* (to cluster together)
gress	to step or move	*regress* (to move backward)
laud	praise	*plaudit* (an expression of praise or approval)
logos	word, study	*biology* (the study of life), *monologue* (a long speech by one speaker)
loqu, locu	speak	*loquacious* (very talkative), *eloquent* (speaking beautifully)
luc	light	*elucidate* (to clarify), *lucid* (clear or comprehensible)
magna/ magni	great, large	*magnanimous* (generous), *magnify* (to make larger)
min	small	*minute* (very small)
mort	death	*moratorium* (an official halt in an activity), *immortal* (not subject to death)
mut	change	*mutation* (a change in form), *transmute* (to change from one form to another)
nov	new	*novice* (a beginner), *novelty* (something new)
nym, nom	name	*pseudonym* (false name), *nominal* (in name only; insignificantly small)
pac	peace	*pacifist* (one who is peace-loving)
path	feeling	*sympathy* (compassion; understanding), *apathy* (without feelings)
phon	sound	*euphony* (pleasant sounds), *cacophony* (unpleasant sounds)
pugn, pug	fight	*pugnacious* (tending to fight), *pugilist* (a fighter or a boxer)
quer, quis	ask	*query* (question), *inquisitive* (curious or inquiring)
sci	to know	*science* (knowledge of the material or physical world)
scrib, scrip	to write	*prescription* (a written direction)
sens, sent	to feel	*sensitive* (have feelings for others), *sentient* (having sensation or consciousness)
simil	same	*similitude* (similarity)
son	sound	*sonar* (a method of locating objects using sound waves)
soph	wisdom	*philosopher* (one who investigates profound questions of life)
spec	to look	*circumspect* (caution; looking around carefully)
sta, stat	stay in position	*stagnant* (lack of movement or development), *stationary* (unmoving)
temp	time	*temporary* (lasting only for a specific time period; not permanent), *temporal* (pertaining to time)
terra	earth	*terrestrial* (living on land), *terrain* (an area of land or ground)
theo	god	*theocracy* (government in which God is supreme ruler), *atheist* (one who denies the existence of God)
vac	empty	*vacuum* (a space empty of matter), *vacuity* (absence of thought or intelligence)
ver	truth	*verify* (to prove true), *verity* (truth)
vert	to turn	*convert* (to change in form or purpose), *invert* (to turn upside down)
vit	life	*vital* (essential to life), *vivacity* (liveliness)
voc	call	*vocal* (spoken aloud), *revoke* (to call back)

Common Suffixes		
Suffix	**Meaning**	**Example**
-able, -ible	able, can do	*portable* (able to be carried)
-agogue	leader	*demagogue* (one who gains power by false promises)
-cide	to kill	*patricide* (the killing of the father), *homicide* (the killing of a person)
-er, -or, -eur	one who	*saboteur* (one who sabotages)
-ish	resembling	*foolish* (resembling a fool)
-ism	belief in	*socialism* (a system of government based on community ownership)
-ly	like	*innocuously* (in a harmless manner)
-ness	state of	*credulousness* (a state of believing everything), *happiness* (state of being happy)
-ology	study of	*psychology* (the study of the human mind)
-philo	lover	*bibliophile* (lover of books)
-phobia	fear of	*arachnophobia* (fear of spiders)
-tude	state of	*certitude* (certainty), *rectitude* (rightness)

Synonym Clusters

You can also build your vocabulary by studying *synonym clusters,* or words that are similar in meaning. Try using index cards to help you study. Begin by writing a heading at the top of the card with the meaning of the words in the synonym cluster. Then list all the words that are similar in meaning to the word in the heading.

In the following table, we list some synonym clusters you should familiarize yourself with.

Synonym Clusters	
Afraid	**Arrogant**
Adjectives: *aghast, alarmed, apprehensive, cowardly, cowed, craven, distressed, frightened, horrified, petrified, shocked, terrified, timid*	**Adjectives:** *bombastic, conceited, egotistical, haughty, imperious, overbearing, peremptory, presumptuous, pretentious, pompous, proud, snobbish, supercilious, vainglorious*
Bold or Courageous	**Noisy**
Adjectives: *adventurous, audacious, courageous, daring, dauntless, fearless, forceful, intrepid, resolute, valiant, valorous*	**Adjectives:** *blatant, boisterous, clamorous, deafening, obstreperous, raucous, rowdy, strident, vociferous*
Words of Praise	**Words of Criticism**
Nouns: *accolade, acclaim, adulation, approbation, commendation, encomium, eulogy, kudos, laudation, panegyric, reverence* **Verbs:** *celebrate, commemorate, exalt, extol, laud, revere, worship*	**Nouns:** *censure, disapprobation, disapproval, disparagement, obloquy, opprobrium, shame* **Verbs:** *abuse, assail, bash, belittle, berate, blame, carp, castigate, censure, chastise, chide, condemn, denounce, disparage, excoriate, fulminate, impugn, malign, reprehend, reprimand, reprobate, revile, scathe, vilify*
Stubborn	**Changeable**
Adjectives: *adamant, inflexible, intractable, intransigent, obdurate, obstinate, recalcitrant*	**Adjectives:** *arbitrary, capricious, erratic, fickle, fluctuating, inconsistent, irresolute, mercurial, mutable, random, vacillating, variable, volatile, whimsical*
Wordy or Talkative	**Quiet or Reserved**
Adjectives: *effusive, garrulous, loquacious, prolix, redundant, voluble*	**Adjectives:** *brief, brusque, concise, curt, laconic, pithy, reticent, succinct, taciturn, terse, uncommunicative*

Harmful	Short-Lived
Adjectives: *baleful, baneful, deleterious, detrimental, inimical, injurious, lethal, malicious, nocuous, noxious, pernicious, sinister, virulent*	**Adjectives:** *ephemeral, evanescent, fleeting, fugitive, impermanent, transient, transitory*
Hatred	**Hard-Working**
Nouns: *anathema, animosity, animus, antipathy, aversion, malevolence, odium, repugnance, repulsion* **Verbs:** *abhor, abominate, deprecate, despise, detest, execrate, loathe*	**Adjectives:** *assiduous, conscientious, diligent, indefatigable, industrious, persistent, sedulous, unflagging, unrelenting*

Practice

Directions: Circle the TWO words that are most similar in meaning to the keyword.

1. Arbitrary
   - A. concise
   - B. diligent
   - C. random
   - D. capricious

2. Snobby
   - A. arrogant
   - B. ephemeral
   - C. haughty
   - D. terse

3. Diligent
   - A. hard-working
   - B. voluble
   - C. humorous
   - D. industrious

4. Fleeting
   - A. unflagging
   - B. ephemeral
   - C. transitory
   - D. arrogant

5. Pragmatic
   - A. reticent
   - B. practical
   - C. sensible
   - D. craven

6. Berate
   - A. castigate
   - B. laud
   - C. extol
   - D. reprimand

7. Praise
   - A. censure
   - B. encomium
   - C. adulation
   - D. repulsion

8. Antipathy
   - A. eulogy
   - B. acclaim
   - C. malevolence
   - D. hatred

9. Explicit
   - A. supercilious
   - B. aghast
   - C. clear
   - D. unambiguous

10. Obstinate
    - A. capricious
    - B. whimsical
    - C. obdurate
    - D. intractable

Directions: Based on the tables of prefixes, roots, and suffixes earlier in this chapter, find the best definition of the words in the questions.

11. Extraterrestrial

   A. lover of earth
   B. small earth
   C. inside the land
   D. not from earth

12. Immutable

   A. belief in change
   B. easy to change
   C. sensitive to change
   D. unable to be changed

13. Culpable

   A. self-guilt
   B. false guilt
   C. guilty
   D. without guilt

14. Philosopher

   A. hater of mankind
   B. lover of wisdom
   C. lover of words
   D. believer in many religions

15. Polytheism

   A. having many names
   B. in support of life
   C. belief in many gods
   D. empty of wisdom

16. Loquacious

   A. talkative
   B. gloomy
   C. lacking
   D. passive

17. Demographics

   A. historical study of government
   B. statistical data about a population
   C. cultural biases
   D. freedom of thought

Directions: For each word in the left-hand column, find the letter of the best definition in the right-hand column.

18. _____ illicit		A warlike
19. _____ ambivalent		B liveliness
20. _____ euphoria		C kind
21. _____ moribund		D reprimand
22. _____ beneficent		E varied
23. _____ vivacity		F illegal
24. _____ eschew		G hatred
25. _____ mercurial		H dying
26. _____ animosity		I surrender
27. _____ ardor		J free from blame
28. _____ multifarious		K passion
29. _____ chastise		L pleasant feelings
30. _____ bellicose		M avoid
31. _____ capitulate		N capricious
32. _____ exonerate		O seeing both sides

Answers

1. **C, D.** *Arbitrary* means based on random choice or personal whim and is most similar in meaning to *random* and *capricious*.

2. **A, C.** *Snobby* means overly proud and is most similar in meaning to *arrogant* and *haughty*.

3. **A, D.** *Diligent* means having care and conscientiousness in one's work or duties and is most similar in meaning to *hard-working* and *industrious*.

4. **B, C.** *Fleeting* means passing by quickly and is most similar in meaning to *ephemeral* and *transitory*.

5. **B, C.** *Pragmatic* means dealing with things sensibly and realistically (in a practical way) and is most similar in meaning to *practical* and *sensible*.

6. **A, D.** *Berate* means to scold or criticize and is most similar in meaning to *castigate* and *reprimand*.

7. **B, C.** *Praise* means words that speak highly of and is most similar in meaning to *encomium* and *adulation.*

8. **C, D.** *Antipathy* means hatred (*anti* = against and *path* = feelings) and is most similar in meaning to *malevolence* and *hatred.*

9. **C, D.** *Explicit* means stated clearly and in detail and is most similar in meaning to *clear* and *unambiguous.*

10. **C, D.** *Obstinate* means stubborn and is most similar in meaning to *obdurate* and *intractable.*

11. **D.** *Ex-* is a prefix that means outside of or away from, and *terra* is a root that means earth. An *extraterrestrial* (think E.T.) is an alien or something not from earth.

12. **D.** *Im-* is a prefix that means not, *mut* is a root that means change, and *-able* is a suffix that means having ability. *Immutable* means not able to be changed.

13. **C.** *Culp* is a root that means guilt, and *-able* is a suffix that means having ability. *Culpable* means guilty.

14. **B.** *Philo-* is a prefix that means lover, and *soph* is a root that means wisdom. A *philosopher* is one who loves (or seeks) wisdom.

15. **C.** *Poly-* is a prefix that means many, and *theo* is a root that means god. *Polytheism* is the belief in many gods.

16. **A.** *Loqu* is a root that means speak. The suffix *-cious* means characterized by or possessing. A *loquacious* person is one who speaks a lot.

17. **B.** *Demo* is a root that means people, and *graph* is a root that means writing. *Demographics* is the data (quantifiable characteristics) of a population (a specific group of people).

18. **F.** *Illicit* means not legal or licit. *Il-* is a prefix that means not.

19. **O.** *Ambivalent* means seeing both sides of an issue. *Ambi-* is a prefix that means both.

20. **L.** *Euphoria* means pleasant feelings. *Eu-* is a prefix that means good.

21. **H.** *Moribund* means dying. *Mor* is a root that means death.

22. **C.** *Beneficent* means kind and generous. *Bene-* is a prefix that means good; *fic* is a root that means to make.

23. **B.** *Vivacity* means liveliness. *Vi* is a root that means life.

24. **M.** *Eschew* means to avoid.

25. **N.** *Mercurial* means changeable.

26. **G.** *Animosity* means hatred.

27. **K.** *Ardor* means passion.

28. **E.** *Multifarious* means diverse or varied. *Multi-* is a prefix that means many.

29. **D.** *Chastise* means to reprimand.

30. **A.** *Bellicose* means warlike. *Belli* is a root that means war.

31. **I.** *Capitulate* means to surrender.

32. **J.** *Exonerate* means to free from blame or to find innocent. *Ex-* is a prefix that means away from.

Chapter 9

Word Knowledge: Testing Your Vocabulary

Words are the most valuable tools human beings have for spoken and written communication, so a test of your vocabulary knowledge will reveal much about your ability to communicate. Without a good vocabulary, you may have problems understanding spoken and written exchanges, which is why the Word Knowledge subtest is an important part of the AFQT. To serve effectively in the military, you must be able to understand written and spoken information and to communicate your own thoughts and ideas clearly and effectively.

The Word Knowledge subtest tests your ability to understand the meaning of words. You may be presented with a highlighted word and asked to find the *synonym* (a word that has the same or nearly the same meaning as the word in the question). Or, you may be presented with a highlighted word in a sentence and asked what it means. Either way, your task is to find the best answer—the one that has the same or nearly the same meaning as the highlighted word in the question.

Here are some strategies for scoring well on the Word Knowledge subtest:

- Relax and focus. Don't assume the words will be too hard for you, even if many of them look unfamiliar.
- Read the word or the sentence carefully. Sound out the word and pronounce it in your head. This may help you remember a situation in which you might have heard or read the word before.
- If the word is familiar to you, think of the definition and check through the choices to find the answer closest in meaning to the word.
- If the word is not familiar, ask yourself the following questions: Does the word sound like a positive word or a negative word? Have I heard it used in a specific context? Can I connect it to any experience in my life?
- Use your knowledge of prefixes, roots, and suffixes. Take apart the word and try to figure out the meaning of each part. Then put the parts together and try to make sense of the word.
- If the word is in a sentence, use the clues in the context of the sentence to help you figure out the meaning of the word.
- Look through the choices and try to eliminate those that you think are wrong. You can usually narrow the choices down to two.
- If you're unsure of the answer, take an educated guess. Trust your gut feeling and go with the answer that seems most correct.
- Keep moving and don't spend too much time on any one question. Each question is worth the same number of points, so choose an answer and keep going.

A. Word Knowledge: Synonym Questions

Some Word Knowledge questions present you with a highlighted word and ask you to find the answer that is closest in meaning to the word in the question. For these questions, you won't have any *context clues* (clues in the sentence) to help you figure out the meaning.

Form a First Impression

Look at the word carefully, and try to get a general impression of the word. Is it familiar to you? If you've studied the word or it's part of your *sight vocabulary* (the words you understand immediately upon seeing them), then think of the definition. Look at the four answer choices, and begin to eliminate those that you know are wrong. Very often, you'll be able to eliminate two choices and be left with two possible answers.

The test-makers frequently include a *distracter,* a word that you may associate with the word in the question. It might sound like or look similar to the word in the question, but the distracter is not the best definition for the word in the question. Be careful not to be thrown off by the distracters.

Pronounce the Word in Your Head

Sometimes the sound of the word can help you figure out the meaning. Some words such as *sinister* or *malignant* just sound like they have negative meanings. Saying the word to yourself can also jog your memory. You may have heard someone you know use the word, or you may have heard it on a TV show or in a movie. If you sound out the word and hear it in your head, you're using your sense of hearing as well as your sense of sight to help you figure out the definition.

EXAMPLE:

> *Demeaning* most nearly means
>
>   **A.**   genuine
>   **B.**   spiteful
>   **C.**   humorous
>   **D.**   humiliating

First impression: This is a negative word—the prefix *de-* sounds like something bad. Eliminate the two positive answer choices: *genuine* and *humorous.* You're left with two negative words: *spiteful* and *humiliating.* Choice B is the distracter. The *mean* part of *demeaning* sounds like something mean or spiteful. But, *demeaning* means to diminish worth or lower self-confidence. Thus, choice D, *humiliating,* is the closest synonym to *demeaning.*

Think Broadly

You may have heard the word in the question used in context. For example, if you watch political debates on TV or news commentary shows, you may have heard someone say, "I can refute that argument." You may not know the exact definition of the word *refute,* but you can gather from the context that the speaker is going to argue against a position. Now you have a very good sense of what *refute* (to disprove) means. This technique will work for many words that are commonly used in the media.

A word on the Word Knowledge subtest may be in a form that is unfamiliar to you, but if you think broadly and try to recall other forms of the word, you may figure out its meaning. For example, you may see the word *certitude* on the test. This is not a particularly common word, so it may be unfamiliar to you. But, if you think broadly, you might realize that you know the words *certain* and *certainly.* Now look at the answer choices.

EXAMPLE:

Certitude most nearly means

    A. sophistication
    B. attitude
    C. rebellion
    D. sureness

If you think about the meaning of the words you know, *certain* and *certainly,* you understand they have something to do with being sure. Reading through the choices, you can reject choice A because sophistication doesn't have much to do with sureness. Choice B is a little tricky; it's the distracter because it looks a lot like the word in the question. Don't fall into this trap: Eliminate choice B. Choice C also doesn't have much to do with being sure; cross it out. Now you see that choice D is the best answer for you to select. Because you know that the meaning of *certitude* probably is related to being sure, sureness is a very good educated guess.

Analyze the Word

Analysis is the process of taking something apart and examining it carefully. Just as you might take apart a car engine to examine its parts, sometimes you can take apart a word and figure out its meaning. Look at the unfamiliar word in the question, and see if you can break it down. Refer to the prefixes, roots, and suffixes charts in Chapter 8 to refresh your memory.

EXAMPLE:

Interminable most nearly means

    A. frustrating
    B. unending
    C. monotonous
    D. confusing

First impression: You think this is a word you can analyze. You notice the prefix *in-* and remember that this prefix often means *not.* The root *termin* might remind you of the word *terminate* or the movie *The Terminator.* You think terminate means end, and you recall the Terminator was an expert at finishing the job. The suffix *-able* means capable of, so now you can put the parts back together: not able to be ended. This should lead you to the correct answer, choice B, unending.

EXAMPLE:

Plaudits most nearly means

    A. endings
    B. noises
    C. praises
    D. metals

First impression: Clearly, this word refers to "things" as all the choices are plural nouns. Think positive or negative: Does the word give off a positive or negative vibe? Notice that none of the answer choices is particularly negative, so you won't be able to eliminate any choices based on your first sense of the word. Let's try analysis: If you studied the roots chart in Chapter 8, you might recall the root *laud* means praise. That's all you need to encourage you to select the correct answer, choice C. Plaudits are praises or cheers of approval. (Think *applaud*.)

Practice

Directions: Select the word or phrase that is nearest in meaning to the italicized word.

1. *Flexible* most nearly means

   A. greedy
   B. obedient
   C. rigid
   D. pliant

2. *Versatile* most nearly means

   A. having the appearance of truth
   B. able to do many different things
   C. incapable of movement
   D. having a poetic quality

3. *Humble* most nearly means

   A. meek
   B. freakish
   C. horrid
   D. quiet

4. A synonym for *dubious* is

   A. brave
   B. cooperative
   C. doubtful
   D. strong

5. A synonym for *frugal* is

   A. risky
   B. endangered
   C. lifelike
   D. thrifty

6. A synonym for *baffling* is

   A. confusing
   B. shrewd
   C. dirty
   D. persuasive

7. *Effervescent* most nearly means

   A. skillful
   B. bubbly
   C. necessary
   D. noisy

8. *Laudable* most nearly means

   A. deserving blame
   B. underappreciated
   C. worthy of praise
   D. exceedingly loud

9. A synonym for *magnanimous* is

   A. rude
   B. bulky
   C. imaginary
   D. generous

10. *Exculpate* most nearly means

    A. to free from blame
    B. to include in punishment
    C. to resemble a crime
    D. to stand in judgment

11. *Apathetic* most nearly means

    A. uncaring
    B. tempting
    C. restless
    D. alert

12. *Credible* most nearly means

    A. explicit
    B. believable
    C. murky
    D. creamy

13. *Belligerent* most nearly means

    A. lucid
    B. ringing
    C. hostile
    D. rancid

14. *Inadvertent* most nearly means

    A. jumpy
    B. foolish
    C. alive
    D. accidental

15. *Precursor* most nearly means

    A. forerunner
    B. looter
    C. follower
    D. mentor

Answers

1. **D.** *Flexible* is an adjective that means bendable or pliant. Think "able to be flexed or bent."

2. **B.** *Versatile* is an adjective that means able to do many different things.

3. **A.** *Humble* is an adjective that means meek.

4. **C.** *Dubious* is an adjective that means doubtful.

5. **D.** *Frugal* is an adjective that means careful with money or thrifty.

6. **A.** *Baffling* is an adjective that means confusing.

7. **B.** *Effervescent* is an adjective that means bubbly or enthusiastic.

8. **C.** *Laudable* is an adjective that means worthy of praise (notice the root *laud*).

9. **D.** *Magnanimous* is an adjective that means generous. (The root *magna* means great or large; a magnanimous person has a big heart.)

10. **A.** *Exculpate* is a verb that means to free from blame. (The prefix *ex-* means away from; the root *culp* means guilt.)

11. **A.** *Apathetic* is an adjective that means uncaring. (The prefix *a-* means without; the root *path* means feeling.)

12. **B.** *Credible* is an adjective that means believable. (The root *cred* means belief; the suffix *-ible* means able.)

13. **C.** *Belligerent* is an adjective that means hostile. (The root *belli* means war.)

14. **D.** *Inadvertent* is an adjective that means accidental or unintentional.

15. **A.** *Precursor* is a noun that means forerunner or one who is out in the front. (The prefix *pre-* means before; the root *cur* means to run; the suffix *-or* means one who.)

B. Word Knowledge: Words in Sentences

Some of the vocabulary words on the Word Knowledge subtest of the AFQT appear in sentences. When the word is used in a sentence, you will have a context to help you find the best definition.

Use the Clues

Carefully read the sentence in which the word appears to see if the sentence itself contains any hints or clues to the meaning of the highlighted word. Not every sentence will give you an obvious clue to the meaning of the highlighted word, but many times the context will help.

EXAMPLE:

> The officers chose an *inconspicuous* location from which to spy on the enemy.
>
>   **A.** highly public
>   **B.** inappropriate
>   **C.** not easily seen
>   **D.** difficult to understand

Examine the logic of the clues in the sentence: If the officers wanted to spy on the enemy, they would choose a location that is somewhat hidden. They certainly wouldn't choose a highly public location, so eliminate choice A. They also wouldn't choose an inappropriate location because that would be counterproductive; eliminate choice B. Based on the context clues in the sentence, choice C makes sense. If you're spying, you wouldn't want to be easily seen. Choice D doesn't make sense in this sentence (why would a location be hard to understand?), so choice C is the best answer.

Substitution

Sometimes the sentence in the question doesn't offer much in the way of a context clue. In these cases, try the substitution method. Take out the highlighted word, and replace it with the words in the choices. Try to use your ears to hear the logic of the sentence, and select the answer choice that sounds most logical to you.

EXAMPLE:

> The state dinner was *lavish*.
>
>   **A.** tasteless
>   **B.** ignored
>   **C.** brief
>   **D.** elaborate

Use the substitution method: Take out the word *lavish,* and substitute each of the words in the answer choices. Because the sentence contains very little in the way of context clues, any of the words could conceivably fit. But, does one word sound better or more logical than the others? Look at choice A. Sure, the dinner could be tasteless, but it is a state dinner, so that's unlikely. Now, examine choice B. A dinner can certainly be ignored, but again, that seems like a bit of a stretch and not a very logical choice. Choice C is a distinct possibility. A dinner can be brief (although probably not a state dinner). When you move on to choice D, it should sound the most logical to you. A state dinner is likely to be elaborate (opulent, sumptuous, rich). You may not be sure you're correct, but choice D is the best educated guess.

Practice

Directions: Select the word or phrase that is nearest in meaning to the italicized word.

1. Hoping to *mitigate* the situation, Matt offered several good reasons for his lateness.

   A. support
   B. ease
   C. reject
   D. find

2. Alicia got *maudlin* last night and spent the evening in tears.

   A. magnificent
   B. overly sentimental
   C. boring
   D. energetic

3. The thief *furtively* entered the house.

   A. obviously
   B. traditionally
   C. sneakily
   D. regretfully

4. The rising flood *imperiled* the livestock.

   A. overcame
   B. endangered
   C. signaled
   D. coerced

5. The lieutenant was called in to help the soldiers resolve the *dilemma*.

   A. predicament
   B. convention
   C. intervention
   D. treatment

6. Jenny was pleased to find that her bunkmates were *amiable*.

   A. strange
   B. careful
   C. strong
   D. friendly

7. We left the beach as *ominous*, dark clouds blew in from the north.

   A. threatening
   B. clear
   C. offensive
   D. inexplicable

8. The invaders used *subterfuge* to remain undetected as they entered the armed compound.

   A. violence
   B. deceitfulness
   C. weaponry
   D. boisterousness

9. Several witnesses were called in to *corroborate* the testimony of the accused man.

   A. question
   B. contradict
   C. confirm
   D. defuse

10. Both sides of the political issue hoped the truce would *eradicate* the threat of open conflict.

   A. revise
   B. reform
   C. recede
   D. remove

11. Many students are surprised to learn that Mark Twain is the *pseudonym* of Samuel Langhorne Clemens.

    A. arch enemy
    B. well-known acquaintance
    C. false name
    D. vocation

12. The children wanted to extend their thanks to the *benefactor* who donated funds for a new library.

    A. saboteur
    B. genius
    C. derelict
    D. sponsor

13. The *sparse* vegetation offered the troops little protection.

    A. thin
    B. dangerous
    C. lush
    D. fertile

14. Many neophytes were *cowed* by the harsh commands of their overbearing leader.

    A. demoted
    B. smitten
    C. enraged
    D. frightened

15. Surprisingly, the soldiers did not feel the *animosity* they expected to feel toward their enemies.

    A. unfamiliarity
    B. hatred
    C. ignorance
    D. domination

Answers

1. **B.** *Mitigate* is a verb that means to ease or to make less severe. Use the context clue in the sentence. Matt would want to ease the situation by offering excuses.

2. **B.** *Maudlin* is an adjective that means overly sentimental. Alicia cried all night because she was feeling very sentimental. (There may have been other reasons for her tears, but the other answer choices don't make sense with the context clue.)

3. **C.** *Furtively* is an adverb that means sneakily. A thief would most likely enter a house in a sneaky manner.

4. **B.** *Imperiled* is an adjective that means put in danger. (*Peril* means danger.) A flood would put livestock in danger.

5. **A.** *Dilemma* is a noun that means a predicament or a difficult situation. When you need to call someone in to resolve a situation, it is usually a predicament or a difficult situation.

6. **D.** *Amiable* is an adjective that means friendly. (The root *ami* means friend.) Having friendly bunkmates would be pleasing.

7. **A.** *Ominous* is an adjective that means threatening. Dark clouds indicate the threat of rain.

8. **B.** *Subterfuge* is a noun that means using trickery or deceit to achieve one's goals. It would likely take trickery or deceit to enter an armed compound without being detected.

9. **C.** *Corroborate* is a verb that means to confirm or to back up. Witnesses are often called to confirm the testimony of another person.

10. **D.** *Eradicate* is a verb that means to eliminate or remove. A truce would (you hope) remove the threat of an open conflict.

11. **C.** *Pseudonym* is a noun that means false name. (*Pseudo-* is a prefix that means false and *nym* is a root that means name.) Samuel Langhorne Clemens took the pen name (or false name) Mark Twain from the cry of a riverboat pilot; *mark twain* means the water is two fathoms (about 4 yards) deep.

12. **D.** *Benefactor* is a noun that means a supporter or sponsor. *Bene-* is a prefix that means good, and *-or* is a suffix that means one who. One who donates money to a library is one who does kind acts.

13. **A.** *Sparse* is an adjective that means thinly dispersed or scattered. Thin vegetation would offer the troops little protection.

14. **D.** *Cowed* is an adjective that means frightened (think coward). Neophytes (*neo-* is a prefix that means new) are beginners who would be frightened by an overbearing leader.

15. **B.** *Animosity* is a noun that means hatred. The soldiers expected to feel hatred for an enemy; thus, they were surprised when they didn't.

C. Glossary of Vocabulary Words

Try to familiarize yourself with as many of these vocabulary words as possible. The best technique is to put each word on an index card, and write the definition on the back. Then divide them into small groups, and learn one group of words at a time. As you study, say the words out loud. That way, you're using your ears and your eyes to help you retain the definition in your memory. Try to use the words; sprinkle them into your conversations and dazzle your friends and family.

aberration: An abnormality

abet: To aid in the commission (usually of a crime)

abrasive: Rough; coarse

abscond: To depart suddenly and secretly

abstemious: Characterized by self-denial or abstinence

abstruse: Difficult to understand

acquiesce: To comply; to agree; to submit

acrid: Bitter; pungent

acrimonious: Bitter; spiteful

acumen: Quickness of intellectual insight

admonition: Gentle scolding or warning

affable: Good-natured; easy to approach

affluence: Wealth

agile: Able to move quickly, either physically or mentally

alacrity: Cheerful willingness or promptness

alleviate: To relieve; to make less hard to bear

ally: Friend; associate (n); to side with or support (v)

aloof: Reserved; distant

altruism: Unselfishness; charitableness

amalgamate: To mix or blend together

ambiguous: Having a double meaning

ambivalent: Having mixed feelings or contradictory ideas

ameliorate: To relieve; to make better

amiable: Friendly

animosity: Hatred

annihilate: To destroy; to obliterate

antipathy: Deep dislike or hatred

apathetic: Showing no feeling or interest

apocryphal: Of doubtful authority or authenticity

apparition: Ghostly sight

appease: To soothe

approbation: Approval

arboreal: Pertaining to trees

arcane: Difficult to understand; known to only a few

ardor: Passion

articulate: Eloquent; able to express oneself well

ascetic: One who practices self-denial and excessive abstinence

ascribe: To assign as a quality or attribute

asperity: Harshness or roughness

assess: Evaluate or estimate the quality of

assiduous: Unceasing; persistent

assuage: To relieve

astute: Keenly perceptive and insightful

audacious: Bold; fearless

auspicious: Favorable

austere: Severely simple; strict; harsh

authoritarian: Demanding; despotic

avarice: Greed

awe: Wonder; amazement

baffling: Confusing

baleful: Malignant

banal: Commonplace; trite

banish: Send someone away; get rid of

barrier: An obstacle or fence

bellicose: Warlike

belligerent: Displaying a warlike spirit

benefactor: One who does kindly and charitable acts

beneficent: Generous or charitable

benevolence: An act of kindness or generosity

benign: Good and kind

berate: To scold severely

bewilder: To confuse

blithe: Carefree; joyous

bog: Swampy wetland

boisterous: Lively; rowdy; overexcited

bolster: To support

bombast: Pompous or inflated language

boorish: Rude

brevity: Briefness

burnish: To make brilliant or shining

cacophony: A disagreeable or discordant sound

cajole: To convince by flattering speech

callow: Young and inexperienced

calumny: Slander

candid: Straightforward; honest

cantankerous: Grouchy; irritable

capacious: Roomy

capitulate: To surrender

castigate: To punish

caustic: Sarcastic and severe

censure: To criticize severely

certitude: Certainty; sureness

chagrin: Embarrassment or dismay

chastise: Scold; reprimand

chicanery: The use of trickery to deceive

clamorous: Noisy, loud, and rowdy

circumstantial: Based on inference rather than conclusive proof

cloying: Excessively sweet

coerce: To force

cogent: Strongly persuasive

collusion: A secret agreement for a wrongful purpose

comedic: Amusing

compendious: Concise

compound: To combine; to intensify

comprehensive: All-inclusive; broad in scope

compromise: Meet halfway; expose to danger or disgrace

compunction: Uneasiness caused by guilt or remorse

conciliatory: Tending to reconcile

concord: Harmony

confidential: Intended to be kept secret

conflagration: A great fire

congeal: To coagulate

congenial: Agreeable; friendly

connoisseur: An expert judge of art, especially one with thorough knowledge and sound judgment

console: To comfort

conspicuous: Clearly visible

constrict: To bind

contemplative: Calm and thoughtful

contrite: Remorseful

copious: Plentiful

corroboration: Confirmation

cowed: Intimidated; frightened

credible: Convincing; able to be believed

credulous: Easily deceived

culpable: Guilty

cupidity: Greed

curtail: To cut off or cut short

dearth: Scarcity

decipher: Decode; unscramble

deleterious: Hurtful

demeaning: Degrading; humiliating

denounce: To condemn; to criticize harshly

deplete: To reduce or lessen

depraved: Wicked; morally corrupt

deride: To ridicule

derivative: Taken from some other source; not original

desiccant: A drying agent

deter: To frighten away

detrimental: Harmful

diatribe: A bitter or malicious criticism

didactic: Pertaining to teaching

diffidence: Shyness; lack of self-confidence

dilatory: Tending to cause delay

dilemma: A difficult situation or problem

diligent: Hard-working; industrious

discern: To distinguish; to see clearly

disconsolate: Hopelessly sad

dissemble: To hide by putting on a false appearance

disseminate: To scatter; to distribute

dissent: Disagreement

divulge: To tell something previously private or secret

dogmatic: Stubbornly opinionated; making statements without argument or evidence

draconian: Very harsh or severe

dubious: Doubtful; skeptical; questionable

duplicity: Deceitfulness; dishonesty

ebullient: Showing enthusiasm

eclectic: Coming from a variety of sources

effervescent: Bubbly; enthusiastic

effrontery: Boldness; audacity

egalitarian: Believing in equality

elucidate: To clarify

elude: To avoid capture

elusive: Tending to escape

embellish: To add decoration

embezzle: To misappropriate secretly

emulate: To try to equal or surpass

encroach: To infringe on another's territory

encumbrance: A burdensome and troublesome load

enervate: To weaken

engender: To produce

enigma: A riddle or puzzle

enmity: Hatred

equable: Equal; serene

equanimity: Calmness; composure

equivocate: To be deliberately vague or misleading

eradicate: To destroy thoroughly

erratic: Irregular

erroneous: Incorrect

erudite: Scholarly; very learned

eschew: To avoid

euphonious: Pleasant sounding

euphoria: State of intense happiness; bliss

evanescent: Existing briefly; ephemeral; fleeting

evoke: To call or summon forth

exacerbate: To make worse

exculpate: To free from blame

execrate: To detest

exonerate: To free from blame

exotic: Unusual; nonnative; striking

expedient: Useful and advantageous

explicate: To explain; to clarify

explicit: Clear; unambiguous

expropriate: To deprive of possession

expunge: To erase; to remove from a record

extant: Still existing and known

extenuate: To make less severe

extinct: No longer in existence

extirpation: Complete removal

extol: To praise in the highest terms

extraneous: Irrelevant

extraterrestrial: Of or from outside the earth

extrinsic: Inessential; from outside

facetious: Amusing

facile: Easy

fallacious: Illogical; misleading

fatuous: Idiotic; stupid

fervid: Intense; passionate

flamboyant: Flashy; showy

flaunt: To show off

fleeting: Lasting only briefly

flexible: Capable of bending without breaking; pliable

flippant: Frivolous; inappropriately lacking seriousness

flout: To treat with contempt

fray: A fight (n); to unravel (v)

fretful: Irritated; distressed

frivolity: Silly and trivial behavior or activities

frugal: Economical

furtive: Secretive; sneaky

gargantuan: Enormous; huge

garrulous: Talkative; chatty

gentility: Refinement; courtesy

germane: Relevant

grate: To irritate; to shred

gregarious: Sociable; outgoing

guile: Duplicity

gullible: Credulous

harangue: A tirade

harbinger: First sign; messenger

hedonism: Pursuit of pleasure

heed: Pay attention to

heinous: Shockingly evil

heresy: An opinion or doctrine that opposes accepted beliefs or principles

humble: Modest; meek; of low social rank

hybrid: Crossbreed; mixture

hypocrisy: Extreme insincerity; pretending to have a virtue or admirable belief

hypothesis: Theory

iconoclasm: A challenge to or overturning of traditional beliefs, customs, or values

idiosyncrasy: A habit peculiar to an individual; a quirk

ignoble: Low in character or purpose

ignominious: Shameful

illicit: Unlawful

illusory: Deceptive; misleading

immaculate: Clean; without spot or blemish

imminent: Close at hand

immutable: Unchangeable

impassioned: Filled with passion; fervent

impassive: Unmoved by or not exhibiting feeling

impecunious: Having no money

impede: To block; to obstruct

imperil: To endanger

imperious: Insisting on obedience; arrogant

imperturbable: Calm

impervious: Impenetrable

impetuous: Impulsive

implacable: Incapable of being pacified or appeased

implicate: To hint or suggest involvement

implicit: Implied

impromptu: Anything done or said on the spur of the moment

improvident: Lacking foresight or thrift

impugn: To oppose or attack

impulsive: Tending to act quickly without thinking

impute: To attribute

inadvertent: Accidental; unintentional

inane: Silly

incessant: Unceasing

inchoate: In the early stages; unformed

incipient: Initial; beginning of development

incite: To rouse to a particular action

incisive: Sharp; perceptive

incongruous: Unsuitable for the time, place, or occasion

inconspicuous: Not easily seen

incredulous: Skeptical; disbelieving

inculcate: To teach by frequent repetitions

indelible: Permanent; unable to be removed

indigence: Poverty

indigenous: Native

indignant: Angry at unfairness

indolence: Laziness

indomitable: Unconquerable

indulgent: Yielding to the desires of oneself or those under one's care; lenient; permissive

ineffable: Unable to be expressed in words

ineluctable: Impossible to avoid

inept: Not competent or suitable

inevitable: Unavoidable

inexorable: Unrelenting

ingenuity: Cleverness; originality; inventiveness

ingenuous: Candid, frank, or open in character

inimical: Adverse; harmful

innocuous: Harmless

inscrutable: Impenetrably mysterious or profound

insinuate: To imply

insipid: Tasteless; dull; uninteresting

instigate: To start; to cause trouble

insurrection: Active resistance to authority

interminable: Without end

intransigent: Unyielding

intrepid: Fearless and bold

introspection: The act of observing and analyzing one's own thoughts and feelings

inundate: To flood

inure: To harden or toughen by use or exposure

inveterate: Habitual

invidious: Showing or feeling envy

invincible: Unable to be conquered, subdued, or overcome

iota: Small or insignificant amount

irascible: Prone to anger

irate: Moved to anger

ire: Anger

irksome: Annoying

irrefutable: Certain; undeniable

irresolution: Indecisiveness

itinerant: Wandering

jeopardy: Danger of loss or harm

jocular: Inclined to joke

jovial: Merry

judicious: Prudent

lackadaisical: Listless

laconic: Brief; concise

languid: Relaxed

lascivious: Lustful

lassitude: Lack of vitality or energy

laudable: Praiseworthy

lavish: Sumptuous; elaborately rich

legacy: A bequest; something handed down from the past

lethal: Deadly

licentious: Immoral

listless: Inattentive; lacking energy or enthusiasm

lithe: Supple

loquacious: Talkative

lucrative: Profitable

lugubrious: Indicating sorrow; mournful

lustrous: Shining

magnanimous: Generous and forgiving

malevolence: Ill will

malign: To speak evil of; to slander

malignant: Evil; harmful

malleable: Pliant

manipulate: To handle or control

maudlin: Foolishly and tearfully sentimental

meager: Inadequate; insufficient

meander: To wander aimlessly

melancholy: Sad

mendacious: Untrue

mendicant: A beggar

mercurial: Changeable; fickle

mesmerize: To hypnotize

meticulous: Careful; painstaking; fussy

mettle: Courage

microcosm: The world or universe on a small scale

mien: The external appearance or manner of a person

mirth: Laughter; happiness

misanthrope: One who hates mankind

miser: A stingy person

misnomer: A name wrongly or mistakenly applied

mitigate: To make less severe

mobilize: To prepare for active service; to marshal; to muster

modicum: A small amount

mollify: To soothe

momentous: Highly significant

mordant: Sarcastically biting

moribund: On the point of dying

morose: Gloomy

multifarious: Having great diversity or variety

mundane: Worldly; ordinary

munificent: Extraordinarily generous

myriad: A large indefinite number

mystical: Spiritual; magical

nadir: The lowest point

nefarious: Wicked or evil

negligent: Careless

neophyte: A beginner

noisome: Very offensive, particularly to the sense of smell

nondescript: Having no distinguishing characteristics

noxious: Hurtful; harmful; poisonous

obfuscate: To confuse; to make unnecessarily complicated

oblivious: Unaware

obscure: Hard to understand; indistinct; not known

obsequious: Showing a servile readiness; slavish obedience

obstinate: Stubborn

obstreperous: Boisterous

obtrude: To push oneself on others

obviate: To prevent or make unnecessary

odious: Hateful

officious: Meddling in what is not one's concern

ominous: Threatening

onerous: Burdensome or oppressive

onus: A burden or responsibility

opportunist: One who takes advantage of something, especially in a devious way

opprobrium: Shame; disgrace

ostentation: A showy display

ostracism: Exclusion from society

palatial: Magnificent; palace-like

panacea: A cure-all

paragon: A model of excellence

pariah: A social outcast

parsimonious: Cheap; stingy

partisan: Showing devotion to a party or one side of an issue

pathos: The quality that arouses emotion or sympathy

paucity: Scarcity; lack

pedantic: Too concerned with correct rules and accuracy; plodding

pedestrian: Dull; ordinary; humdrum

penchant: A strong liking

penurious: Excessively cheap or stingy

peremptory: Authoritative; dictatorial

perfidy: Treachery; traitorousness

perfunctory: Just going through the motions; mechanical

peripheral: Tangential; unimportant; minor

perjury: Lying under oath

permeate: To pervade

pernicious: Harmful; poisonous

perspicacity: Sharp insightfulness or discernment

perturbation: Mental excitement or confusion

pervasive: Widespread

petulant: Childish irritability

philanthropy: Generosity; humanitarianism

philosopher: A thinker about the nature of knowledge and existence

phlegmatic: Sluggish; lacking energy

pious: Religious

placate: To calm or appease

platitude: A written or spoken statement that is dull, or commonplace

plaudits: Praises; acclaim

plethora: Excess; abundance

pluralism: Different groups with different beliefs existing within one society

poignant: Emotionally painful

polytheism: Belief in the existence of more than one god

ponderous: Unusually weighty; clumsy; labored

portent: Anything that indicates what is to happen; an omen or sign

pragmatic: Practical

precarious: Perilous; risky; unstable

preclude: To prevent

precocious: Advanced for one's age

precursor: Forerunner; ancestor

predominate: To be chief in importance

premature: Occurring too soon

presage: To foretell

prescience: Knowledge of events before they take place

prevalent: Widespread

prevaricate: To avoid giving an honest answer; to be deliberately misleading

primordial: Existing at the beginning of time

pristine: Pure; unspoiled

probity: Virtue or integrity

proclivity: A natural inclination

procrastination: Delay

prodigal: Wasteful or extravagant

prodigious: Immense

profligacy: Extremely wasteful; having low moral standards

profound: Showing great perception; having deep meaning

profuse: Produced or displayed in overabundance

prolix: Wordy

prominence: Fame; celebrity

prosaic: Unimaginative

provident: Providing for the future

prudence: Caution

pseudonym: False name

puerile: Childish

pugnacious: Quarrelsome

punctilious: Strictly observant of the rules prescribed by law or custom

quandary: A puzzling predicament

quibble: A trivial objection

quiescence: Being quiet, still, or at rest; inactive

quixotic: Chivalrous or romantic to a ridiculous or extravagant degree

quotidian: Of an everyday character; ordinary

ramify: To divide or subdivide into branches or subdivisions; to have complicating consequences

recalcitrant: Stubbornly resistant

recant: To withdraw formally one's belief (in something previously believed or maintained)

recidivism: The tendency to relapse into crime

recluse: One who lives in retirement or seclusion

recondite: Understood by only a select few; arcane; esoteric

recuperate: To recover

regeneration: Rebirth; renewal

relegate: To demote

relentless: Persistent; unyielding

renovate: To restore

repast: A meal

repudiate: To refuse to have anything to do with; to reject

repulsive: Grossly offensive

resilience: The ability to bounce back, cope, or adapt

respite: Interval of rest

retaliate: Strike back; get even

reticent: Reserved; unwilling to communicate

retrench: To cut back; to economize

revelatory: Revealing an emotion or quality

revere: To respect highly; to worship

ritual: Established pattern of behavior, often ceremonial

ruse: Trick; hoax

sagacious: Wise and perceptive

salutary: Beneficial

sanction: To approve authoritatively

sanguine: Cheerfully confident; optimistic

sardonic: Scornfully or bitterly sarcastic

satiate: To satisfy fully the appetite or desire of

scintillating: Dazzling; sparkling

scrupulous: Precise; having moral integrity

secede: To separate from; to withdraw

secular: Nonreligious

seclusion: Isolation

sedulous: Diligent; persistent

self-effacing: Modest; humble

serene: Calm

shrewd: Characterized by skill at understanding and profiting from circumstances

sluggard: A person habitually lazy or idle

snobby: Arrogant

solace: Comfort

solvent: Having sufficient funds

somnolent: Sleepy

sophomoric: Immature

soporific: Causing sleep

sordid: Filthy; morally degraded

sparse: Thinly spread

specious: Something that has the appearance of truth but is actually false

spontaneous: impulsive; natural; spur-of-the-moment

spurious: Not genuine

squalid: Dirty and/or poverty-stricken

stalemate: Deadlock

stanch: To stop the flowing of; to check

static: Motionless; unchanging

stealthy: Sneaky; sly

stingy: Cheap; unwilling to spend money

streamline: To make more efficient

subsume: To include in something larger

subterfuge: A deceitful maneuver

subterranean: Underground

subtle: Slight; understated

succinct: Concise

sumptuous: Rich and costly

supercilious: Haughty and arrogant

superfluous: More than is needed

suppress: To prevent from being disclosed or published

sustenance: Nourishment

sybarite: One who loves luxuries

sycophant: A servile flatterer

taciturn: Quiet; untalkative

tedious: Boring; monotonous

temerity: Boldness; nerve

terse: Brief; concise

timid: Fearful; shy

timorous: Lacking courage

torpid: Dull; sluggish

tractable: Easily led or controlled

tranquil: Calm; peaceful

transitory: Existing for a short time only

trepidation: Fear

trite: Made commonplace by frequent repetition

triumph: Victory

trivial: Minor; unimportant

truculence: Ferocity

turbid: In a state of turmoil; muddled

turbulent: Moving violently

turgid: Swollen; excessively ornamented

ubiquitous: Being present everywhere

unctuous: Insincerely earnest

undermine: To subvert in an underhand way; to weaken

undulate: To move like a wave or in waves

upbraid: To scold

vacillate: To waver between choices

vapid: Dull; uninteresting

vehement: Very eager or urgent

venal: Mercenary; corrupt

venial: Forgivable; pardonable

veracity: Truthfulness

verbose: Wordy

versatile: Adaptable; with many uses

vestige: A remaining trace of something gone

vigilant: Alert and watchful

vindictive: Vengeful

vital: Essential for life; energetic

vitiate: To corrupt

vivacity: Liveliness

vociferous: Forcefully loud

volatile: Unstable; explosive

voluble: Talkative

voluminous: Large; long; prolific

whimsical: Fanciful; lighthearted; quirky

Practice

Note: Study the words in Chapter 8 and earlier in this chapter before you attempt to answer the following practice questions. These 30 questions follow the same format as the questions on the Word Knowledge subtest of the AFQT.

Directions: Select the word or phrase that is nearest in meaning to the italicized word.

1. There was no *paucity* of food at the family reunion.

    A. variety
    B. abundance
    C. scarcity
    D. freshness

2. The *indolent* cat slept on the porch, basking in the sun all day.

    A. hairy
    B. lazy
    C. sneaky
    D. powerful

3. The new edition of the book eliminated all *superfluous* material.

    A. terse
    B. excellent
    C. relevant
    D. unnecessary

4. *Obscure* most nearly means

    A. obstinate
    B. explosive
    C. indistinct
    D. burning

5. *Penurious* most nearly means

    A. cheap
    B. energetic
    C. golden
    D. depressed

6. The best synonym for *plethora* is

    A. brevity
    B. precursor
    C. pain
    D. excess

7. The best synonym for *divulge* is

    A. disappear
    B. reveal
    C. improve
    D. eradicate

8. *Nefarious* most nearly means

    A. amiable
    B. edible
    C. dreary
    D. evil

9. After the huge holiday meal, Grandpa felt *somnolent.*

    A. refreshed
    B. sleepy
    C. dissatisfied
    D. cheerful

10. It is important to be *vigilant* when walking in unlit areas of the city.

    A. tough
    B. watchful
    C. frightened
    D. silent

11. Before returning to work after an illness, it is important to *recuperate* fully.

    A. communicate
    B. recover
    C. diagnose
    D. prescribe

12. *Undermine* most nearly means

    A. weaken
    B. emphasize
    C. underscore
    D. underline

13. *Modicum* most nearly means

    A. iota
    B. extravagance
    C. style
    D. moderation

14. *Squalid* most nearly means

    A. dirty
    B. unstable
    C. innocent
    D. evil

15. *Turbulent* most nearly means

    A. without emotion
    B. overflowing with water
    C. standing at attention
    D. moving violently

16. *Tranquil* most nearly means

    A. harmful
    B. painful
    C. peaceful
    D. annoying

17. *Procrastination* most nearly means

    A. delay
    B. prediction
    C. indication
    D. endorsement

18. *Vindictive* most nearly means

    A. curious
    B. vengeful
    C. clever
    D. violent

19. The best synonym for *affluence* is

    A. passion
    B. influence
    C. wealth
    D. satisfaction

20. The *acrid* odor from the chemistry lab spread throughout the building.

    A. heavy
    B. bitter
    C. pleasant
    D. mild

21. The best synonym for *trepidation* is

    A. difficulty
    B. immorality
    C. fear
    D. communication

22. The confident young man was *sanguine* as he waited for his AFQT scores.

    A. disappointed
    B. meek
    C. inferior
    D. cheerfully optimistic

23. The audience was shocked by the *acrimonious* tone of the presidential debate.

    A. apologetic
    B. calm
    C. spiteful
    D. dignified

24. The best synonym for *lethal* is

    A. late
    B. miserable
    C. brilliant
    D. deadly

25. We avoided the new restaurant because of its *insipid* food.

   A. cold
   B. overpriced
   C. tasteless
   D. filthy

26. The residents fled the building as *noxious* fumes spread rapidly.

   A. fragrant
   B. poisonous
   C. innocuous
   D. salutary

27. *Grate* most nearly means

   A. irritate
   B. return
   C. hope
   D. cook

28. The best synonym for *annihilate* is

   A. surround
   B. release
   C. capture
   D. destroy

29. *Regeneration* most nearly means

   A. rebuttal
   B. reinforcement
   C. rebirth
   D. reinstatement

30. After winning the lottery, the woman became famous for her *philanthropy*.

   A. parsimony
   B. quiescence
   C. duplicity
   D. generosity

Answers

1. **C.** *Paucity* is a noun that means scarcity. A family reunion is usually characterized by lots of food, so there would be no scarcity.

2. **B.** *Indolent* is an adjective that means lazy. A sleeping cat is the picture of laziness.

3. **D.** *Superfluous* is an adjective that means unnecessary. *Super-* is a prefix that means above or beyond. Something superfluous is beyond what is needed.

4. **C.** *Obscure* means indistinct or little known. Don't be fooled by the distracter in choice A. *Obstinate* looks similar to *obscure,* but *obstinate* means stubborn.

5. **A.** *Penurious* is an adjective that means cheap or stingy.

6. **D.** *Plethora* is a noun that means an excess or abundance of something.

7. **B.** *Divulge* is a verb that means to tell a secret or reveal some information.

8. **D.** *Nefarious* is an adjective that means evil or wicked.

9. **B.** *Somnolent* is an adjective that means sleepy. Eating a big meal often makes people feel sleepy.

10. **B.** *Vigilant* is an adjective that means watchful, alert, or cautious. The clues in the sentence—an unlit area of the city—should signal the need for watchfulness.

11. **B.** *Recuperate* is a verb that means to recover from an illness. The logic of the sentence is a clue that one should recover completely from a sickness before returning to work.

12. **A.** *Undermine* is a verb that means to weaken.

13. **A.** *Modicum* is a noun that means a very little bit or an iota.

14. **A.** *Squalid* is an adjective that means dirty.

15. **D.** *Turbulent* is an adjective that means in turmoil or moving violently.

16. **C.** *Tranquil* is an adjective that means peaceful.

17. **A.** *Procrastination* is a noun that means delay.

18. **B.** *Vindictive* is an adjective that means vengeful (desiring revenge).

19. **C.** *Affluence* is a noun that means wealth.

20. **B.** *Acrid* is an adjective that means bitter. Chemical smells are often bitter smells.

21. **C.** *Trepidation* is a noun that means fear.

22. **D.** *Sanguine* is an adjective that means cheerfully optimistic.

23. **C.** *Acrimonious* is an adjective that means bitter or spiteful. A spiteful tone is likely to shock an audience, especially in a presidential debate.

24. **D.** *Lethal* is an adjective that means deadly. Think of the movie *Lethal Weapon*.

25. **C.** *Insipid* is an adjective that means tasteless. All the answer choices in this question are negative words, so it's difficult to get help from the context. However, insipid is one of the words in the glossary. Study the words carefully, and you'll increase your chances of knowing the definitions on your AFQT.

26. **B.** *Noxious* is an adjective that means poisonous. Fumes that cause residents to flee would most likely be harmful. All three of the other answer choices are positive words, so you can eliminate all but choice B.

27. **A.** *Grate* is a verb that means to irritate. Think of the action of a grater: When you rub cheese against the rough surface of a grater, it shreds the cheese. In the same way, if something grates on you, it rubs you the wrong way and irritates you.

28. **D.** *Annihilate* is a verb that means to completely wipe out or to destroy.

29. **C.** *Regeneration* is a noun that means rejuvenation or rebirth. (*Re-* is a prefix that means again; *gen* is a root that means birth.)

30. **D.** *Philanthropy* is a noun that means generosity. (*Philo-* is a prefix that means lover; *anthro* is a root that means mankind.) A person who loves mankind is a humanitarian, one who is generous and charitable.

Chapter 10
Paragraph Comprehension: Improving Your Reading Skills

Although many Americans watch a lot of television and movies, most of the information we get comes from reading. Every day, in almost any activity or job, you're confronted by the written word. Effective reading is the key to success in many arenas. This chapter helps you prepare for the Paragraph Comprehension subtest of the AFQT and also for all the reading you'll be doing at different stages in your life.

A. How to Be a Good Reader

Whether you're reading a newspaper, a popular magazine, or a website you need to read effectively in order to understand the written word. In the military, you'll have to read orders, instructions, regulations, technical material for your job, or even the post newspaper. Here are some techniques to assist you in your quest to become a better reader.

Understand the Structure of Paragraphs

As you read, take note of the structure of the paragraph. A good writer will have a clear beginning, middle, and end to his paragraphs. Often, but not always, the main idea will be stated in a sentence at the beginning called the *topic sentence* (or sometimes called the *thesis*). Look for this sentence as you read the paragraph.

EXAMPLE:

> More and more often, baseball fans allow their enthusiasm to carry them over the line of acceptable behavior. They engage in name calling and harass the umpires unmercifully. Some rowdy spectators even get into fights with fans from the opposing team. It is not unusual to see fists fly and some unrepentant fans get ejected by ballpark security. Perhaps the time has come to teach a mandatory course in spectator etiquette.

The topic sentence of this paragraph is the first sentence. It states the main idea of the passage: *baseball fans allow their enthusiasm to carry them over the line of acceptable behavior.*

The middle of the paragraph contains the supporting evidence or specific details that prove the topic sentence: *They engage in name calling and harass the umpires unmercifully. Some rowdy spectators even get into fights with fans from the opposing team. It is not unusual to see fists fly and some unrepentant fans get ejected by ballpark security.*

The last sentence of the paragraph is the conclusion. It usually sums up the main idea or extends and broadens the main idea. In this passage, the writer has concluded by summing up with a humorous idea: *Perhaps the time has come to teach a mandatory course in spectator etiquette.*

Once you understand the structure of the paragraph, you'll be more skillful in following the development of the writer's ideas.

For this passage, you might find a question like this on the Paragraph Comprehension subtest:

> According to the passage, rowdy baseball fans engage in all of the following behaviors *except*
>
> **A.** throwing beers at opposing fans
> **B.** shouting inappropriate comments at the referees
> **C.** fighting with other spectators
> **D.** getting thrown out of the stadium

Choice A is the correct answer. To answer this question correctly, you have to look at the middle section of the paragraph, the supporting evidence the writer uses to prove his point. After you've read the passage and read the question, you know you have to look back into the passage to find the specific details the author lists. Skim over the paragraph to identify the behaviors listed in the answer choices. Check them off as you find them in the paragraph. You won't find choice A. The author doesn't mention beer throwing in this passage. It is possible that you've witnessed this beer-throwing behavior in a stadium, but if it isn't included in the passage, then that is the correct choice, the exception.

Build a Good Vocabulary

In order to comprehend what you're reading, you need a good vocabulary. If you don't understand some key words or phrases in a passage, you'll most likely have difficulty understanding the author's meaning. If you have completed the vocabulary study in Chapters 8 and 9, your vocabulary should be much improved. But don't stop there. Continue to learn new words through your reading. Use the context of a passage to help you figure out what a word means; if you can't get a sense of the meaning from the context, be sure to look the word up online or in a dictionary.

EXAMPLE:

> The earth was not, in its natural condition, completely adapted to the use of man, but only to the sustenance of wild animals and wild vegetation. These live, multiply their kind in just proportion, and attain their perfect measure of strength and beauty, without producing or requiring any change in the natural arrangements of surface, or in each other's spontaneous tendencies. However, at times, a natural and mutual limit on growth is necessary to prevent the extirpation of one species by the encroachment of another.

If you know all the vocabulary words in the passage, Wow! Great! If not, you may have found a few words that are unfamiliar to you, such as *sustenance, spontaneous, extirpation,* and *encroachment.*

Let's use the context to figure out what *sustenance* means: According to the first sentence, the earth was adapted to the sustenance of animals and vegetation. Thinking logically, you can figure out that the earth supports wildlife and plant life, so *sustenance* means support for life or nourishment.

Now let's look at *spontaneous.* The second sentence states that animals and plants live naturally, without requiring any change in their natural states. Thus, *spontaneous* means natural or unrestrained (sometimes impulsive).

The third sentence includes two challenging vocabulary words: *extirpation* and *encroachment.* Again, logic is your best guide to meanings of the words. A limit on growth will prevent one species from *encroachment* (infringing on another's territory) that might lead to the *extirpation* (complete removal) of one or the other species.

For this passage, you might find a question like this on the Paragraph Comprehension subtest:

As it is used in the passage, the word *sustenance* most nearly means

A. destruction
B. starvation
C. support
D. captivity

Choice C is correct. The best way to approach a vocabulary-in-context question is to replace the word in the question one at a time with the words in the choices. See which word best fits the context of the sentence. In this case, neither destruction (choice A) nor starvation (choice B) fits the context. The earth, in its natural condition, would not cause destruction and starvation for animals and plants; if so, no plants or animals would have existed before mankind entered the scene. Choice D (captivity) also contradicts the context. Without mankind, who would put animals (and plants) into captivity? Therefore, choice D doesn't make sense. If you plug in *support,* however, the sense of the sentence is far more logical. Choice C is the best answer.

Read Between the Lines

Good readers understand more than just the obvious points that the writer is making. They detect the subtle and complex ideas that are sometimes embedded in the passage. They know how to "read between the lines," an essential skill for all astute (remember that word from Chapter 9?) readers.

Reading between the lines means drawing conclusions from information that is implied, rather than directly stated. What you gather from this process is called an *inference.*

EXAMPLE:

The psychological growth of a child is not influenced by days and years, but by the impressions passing events make on his mind. What may prove a sudden awakening to one, giving an impulse in a certain direction that may last for years, may make no impression on another. People wonder why children of the same family differ so widely, though they have had the same domestic discipline, have had the same school and church teaching, and have grown up under the same influences and in the same environment.

You may draw several inferences from this passage. For example, you can infer that children from the same family may grow up to be very different. Or you can infer that *nurture,* the act of rearing a child, can have as profound an effect on a child as *nature,* the inborn characteristics of the child.

For this passage, you might find a question like this on the Paragraph Comprehension subtest:

> Which of the following statements can be inferred from the paragraph?
>
> **A.** All children from the same family will share psychological characteristics.
> **B.** Siblings may exhibit very different behaviors.
> **C.** The influence of family and school has been greatly exaggerated by some social scientists.
> **D.** An impulse that affects one member of a family will ultimately affect all members of that family.

Choice B is correct. After you read the passage and read the question, look back in the passage for evidence to support one of the four choices. Choices A and D are contradicted by the second sentence in the passage: *What may prove a sudden awakening to one, giving an impulse in a certain direction that may last for years, may make no impression on another.* Choice C may be a true statement, but it isn't supported by evidence in this passage. Choice B is the best answer. This can be inferred from the author's assertion: *People wonder why children of the same family differ so widely.*

Be an Active Reader

Good readers aren't passive. If you're a good reader, you don't allow your eyes to move through a passage while your brain is engaged elsewhere. You read actively and think about what you're reading as you're reading it.

Make Predictions

As you're reading, you should generate questions in your mind, almost as if you're having a dialogue with the writer. You should also think ahead and make predictions about what the author's next idea will be. This keeps your mind on the author's development and reinforces your understanding of the passage. You're ready for the next idea even before it comes.

Visualize

Often, visualization techniques can help you comprehend a passage. Create a mental image in your mind as you read. If the passage is fiction, see it unfold like a movie in your brain. If the passage explains a process, picture yourself following the steps. Tap into your prior knowledge, make connections, and pay attention to details.

EXAMPLE:

> Mrs. Rachel, before she had fairly closed the door, had taken a mental note of everything that was on that table. There were three plates laid, so that Marilla must be expecting some one home with Matthew to tea; but the dishes were everyday dishes and there was only crab-apple preserves and one kind of cake, so that the expected company could not be any particular company. Yet what of Matthew's white collar and the sorrel mare? Mrs. Rachel was getting fairly dizzy with this unusual mystery about quiet, unmysterious Green Gables.

Since this is a narrative passage, one that tells a story, you should visualize the events. Picture Mrs. Rachel entering the house and immediately noticing that the table is set for three people. Imagine that she is puzzled. She can't reconcile the idea of company with the ordinary manner in which the table is set. Then the author indicates that this is a mystery. Now you can make a prediction. Think of some reasons why the company that is expected is not "particular company." You'll expect to find out further on in the story just who is expected for tea.

If you're doing this thinking process, then you're reading actively and engaging all your powers of reasoning and logic. You're becoming a much more effective reader.

For this passage, you might find a question like this on the Paragraph Comprehension subtest:

> According to the passage, it is most likely that Mrs. Rachel was "fairly dizzy" because
>
> **A.** She had walked briskly from her home to Marilla's house.
> **B.** Marilla was serving only one kind of cake.
> **C.** She had closed the door too quickly.
> **D.** Things are not as they usually are in Marilla's house.

Choice D is correct. You don't know if Mrs. Rachel had walked briskly or if she had closed the door too quickly, so you should eliminate choices A and C. Choice B, that Marilla is serving only one kind of cake, is confusing to Mrs. Rachel, but it is just one of many confusing events in the passage. As you read the passage, you should take note of Mrs. Rachel's response to the whole series of unusual happenings in Marilla's house. It can be inferred that Mrs. Rachel is both observant and nosy. Not knowing exactly what is going on in her neighbor's house makes her uncomfortable—so uncomfortable that she is "fairly dizzy" over all the mysterious goings on. Choice D is the best answer because the accumulation of all the unusual events is what has upset Mrs. Rachel.

Stay Focused

Good readers don't allow their minds to drift away from the passage. You can't be in the middle of a paragraph and start to think about how many questions you have left or what you're going to do when the test is over. Concentrate and keep your brain totally focused on the passage you're reading.

EXAMPLE:

> Bacteria are often divided up into aerobic bacteria, which require oxygen to live, and anaerobic bacteria, which die when exposed to oxygen. Bacterial infections are often caused by toxins released by bacteria. Antibiotics have been used to fight bacterial infections, but some disease-causing organisms have become resistant to drug therapy. Because they are adaptable, bacteria have developed ways to resist the effects of antibiotics. Adding to the problem, the public has a tendency to overuse these drugs and pressure physicians into over-prescribing them.

This paragraph contains a lot of information. In order to comprehend it all, you must concentrate on each sentence. When you finish reading the passage, you should be able to understand the following:

- The two kinds of bacteria
- How bacteria cause infections

- Why some bacteria are immune to antibiotics
- Why some physicians hesitate to prescribe antibiotics

That is a lot of information packed into one passage, but you don't have to rely on your memory to answer the questions. Since you'll have the passage right in front of you, you can look back into the passage and find the information you need to answer the questions.

For example, suppose the question on the AFQT is:

According to the passage, why do some previously effective antibiotics stop working?

   A.   Some antibiotics require oxygen to work.
   B.   Some bacteria are killed by toxins.
   C.   Some doctors hesitate to prescribe antibiotics.
   D.   The bacteria develop a resistance to the drug.

Choice D is correct. To answer this question correctly, you have to be careful of the *true-but-incorrect* answer choices—those answer choices that are true statements but that don't answer the question that is being asked. For example, choices A and C are factual statements that can be supported by the passage; however, neither choice answers the question *why* some previously effective antibiotics stop working. Choice B is inaccurate based on the information in the passage. The passage states: *Bacterial infections are often caused by toxins released by bacteria.* It doesn't state that *bacteria are killed by toxins.* Choice D is the correct answer; the passage states that the development of drug-resistant bacteria is the reason that some medicines stop working.

Read Widely and Deeply

The reading passages on the AFQT are taken from many subject areas. If you read only the sports section of your local newspaper, you're limiting your exposure to a particular content and style. Also, because you have prior knowledge of this subject and a strong interest in it, the reading is probably easy for you. Try to broaden your reading to include fiction as well as nonfiction. Try some science reading or even some short stories or novels. If novels are your favorite reading materials, then switch to some history or biography. The point is, don't limit yourself to what is easy and appealing. You must stretch your reading ability if you want to become a better reader.

EXAMPLE:

Velocardiofacial Syndrome (VCFS), also called 22Q Syndrome, affects 1 in 2,000 live births. It is caused by a partial deletion of chromosome 22. Included in its effects are 180 possible symptoms involving every system in the body. Among the most common symptoms are cardiac abnormalities, distinctive facial structure, and palate deformities. The National VCFS Organization is lobbying to include the syndrome in routine prenatal screening.

This passage is about a little-known medical condition. You may find that you have to concentrate a bit harder on material that is unfamiliar to you, but that is good preparation for your military career. In the service, you may find you have to read highly technical material on different topics, some of which may be totally unknown to you.

For this passage, you might find a question like this on the Paragraph Comprehension subtest:

It can be inferred from the passage that

    A.   Including VCFS in prenatal screening will eliminate the occurrence of this syndrome.

    B.   All cardiac abnormalities can be related to VCFS.

    C.   An incomplete chromosome can cause widespread physical abnormalities.

    D.   This syndrome is also called 22Q because there are 22 symptoms of VCFS.

Choice C is correct. Choices A and B are broad, sweeping generalities that aren't supported by the passage. Screening won't eliminate the disease; it will just identify it. Clearly, it is illogical that *all* cardiac abnormalities are caused by VCFS. Choice D is incorrect because the passage states that there are 180 symptoms of VCFS. Choice C is correct because the passage lists some of the many physical abnormalities that are symptoms of VCFS.

Monitor and Adjust to the Material

You may have to adjust your speed and concentration level as you read. Fiction reading generally goes faster than nonfiction. Highly technical material may require you to slow down even more to be sure you comprehend processes, relationships, and results. Good readers constantly monitor their reading speed and focus and adjust as the content demands.

EXAMPLE:

    When steam engines were first invented, a need arose to compare the output of the new machines to a known power, the power of workhorses. James Watt first coined the term *horsepower;* he calculated that a horse can lift 330 pounds of coal 100 feet in one minute. Thus, one horsepower is defined as 33,000 foot pounds per minute. One horsepower for rating electric motors is equal to an output of 746 watts.

The passage begins in a straightforward manner, but then it becomes rather technical. You should adjust your reading speed and concentration to the level of difficulty of the passage. For this passage, you should slow down as it gets more technical.

For this passage, you might find a question like this on the Paragraph Comprehension subtest:

According to the passage, if a coal worker used a cart pulled by two horses, he could expect it to be able to lift

    A.   330 pounds of coal 50 feet in 2 minutes

    B.   330 pounds of coal 200 feet in 1 minute

    C.   660 pounds of coal 200 feet in 2 minutes

    D.   746 pounds of coal 100 feet in 1 minute

Choice B is the correct answer. This question requires careful reading and a little bit of arithmetic. The passage states that one horsepower is equal to 33,000 foot pounds per minute or the energy needed to lift 330 pounds of coal 100 feet in one minute. From this statement, you can conclude that two horsepower would be 66,000 foot pounds. To arrive at that figure, only choice B, lifting 330 pounds of coal 200 feet in 1 minute, will work. Choice A reduces the horsepower by lowering the number of feet. Choice C doubles all the figures, which results in a much higher output than 66,000 foot pounds. Choice D uses the incorrect figure of 746 (which is the wattage of one horsepower).

Scan for Answers

On most reading comprehension tests, you have to look back into a passage to find the answer to a specific question. If the test is an open-book test like the Paragraph Comprehension subtest, you don't have to rely on your memory to get the right answer. You can scan through the paragraph to find it.

Scanning is a quick movement of the eyes through the material. You skim through the passage to pinpoint the information needed to obtain the correct answer.

Here are some useful techniques for scanning:

- **Know what you're looking for.** Read the question after the paragraph and rephrase it in your mind so you know exactly what the question is asking.
- **Don't reread the entire paragraph.** Look for the key words that will lead you to the pertinent information.
- **Know the organization of the passage.** Section A of this chapter discussed the importance of understanding the structure of paragraphs. So, if you're scanning for the main idea, look at the topic sentence. If you're looking for a detail, scan the middle. If you're trying to find the conclusion or solution, scan the end.

Let's practice scanning. Read the following passage and answer the question that follows it by scanning the paragraph and looking for key words.

EXAMPLE:

> The nerves of the human body translate, or enable the mind to translate, the impressions of the world into facts of consciousness and thought. Different nerves are suited to the perception of different impressions. We do not see with the ear, nor hear with the eye. Each nerve, or group of nerves, selects and responds to those for the perception of which it is specially organized. The optic nerve passes from the brain to the back of the eyeball and there spreads out, to form the retina, a web of nerve filaments, on which the images of external objects are projected by the optical portion of the eye. This nerve is limited to visual perception and is oblivious to other stimuli.
>
> According to the passage, the retina is best defined as
>
> A.   an impression of the world
> B.   a part of the brain
> C.   a web of perception
> D.   a meshwork of nerve filaments

The correct answer is D. Use the scanning technique: First, know exactly what you're looking for—in this case, a detail or definition within the passage. Now, skim through the paragraph looking for key words. You should see the word *retina* in the fifth sentence of the paragraph. Following the word *retina,* you'll find an explanation: *a web of nerve filaments.* Now evaluate the four answer choices. Choice A is incorrect because *an impression of the world* is not *a web of nerve filaments.* A retina is also not *a part of the brain,* so eliminate choice B. Choice C is a little tricky because it contains the word *web,* but the definition in the paragraph is not *a web of perception.* Choice D is correct, but it is a bit challenging because you have to understand that a *meshwork* is the same as a *web.*

B. Reading in Different Content Areas

The ability to use effective reading strategies is important to understanding texts in any subject area. However, good readers know that different content areas require different skills. In order to perform well on reading comprehension tests, you have to adjust your reading and thinking to the content of the material.

Fiction

Most readers are familiar with fiction, which includes narratives like short stories, plays, or novels. In fact, when you first learned to read, your teacher probably used high-interest stories to motivate you to read because storytelling is a universal form of communication. Most readers can quickly become interested in characters and plots. Although the passages on the AFQT are brief, you should be thinking about the characters, their motivations, their actions, and their interactions with other characters. In addition, try to determine the setting (time and place) and the mood (atmosphere) of the story.

EXAMPLE:

> I had been sent up by my employers on a job connected with the big power-house at Corbury Junction, and a long-drawn carpenters' strike had so delayed the work that I found myself anchored at Starkfield—the nearest habitable spot—for the best part of the winter. I chafed at first, and then, under the hypnotising effect of routine, gradually began to find a grim satisfaction in the life. During the early part of my stay I had been struck by the contrast between the vitality of the climate and the deadness of the community. Day by day, after the December snows were over, a blazing blue sky poured down torrents of light and air on the white landscape, which gave them back in an intenser glitter. One would have supposed that such an atmosphere must quicken the emotions as well as the blood; but it seemed to produce no change except that of retarding still more the sluggish pulse of Starkfield. When I had been there a little longer, and had seen this phase of crystal clearness followed by long stretches of sunless cold; when the storms of February had pitched their white tents about the devoted village and the wild cavalry of March winds had charged down to their support; I began to understand why Starkfield emerged from its six months' siege like a starved garrison capitulating without quarter.
>
> It can be inferred from the passage that the narrator
>
> A. enjoyed the vitality of the community of Starkfield
> B. found himself drawn into in a battle with a neighboring town
> C. looked forward to the coming of spring with dread
> D. fell under the influence of the depressing climate

Choice D is the correct answer. To answer this question correctly, you have to read carefully and think about the narrator's perceptions of the climate of Starkfield and its effect on the townspeople. He is surprised that the "blazing blue sky" doesn't invigorate the people; instead, it has a deadening effect. He feels the "hypnotising" effect of the "deadness of the community." Choice A is incorrect because he doesn't observe the vitality of the community. Choice B is incorrect because no battle takes place: The narrator speaks metaphorically of a "six months' siege," referring to the six months of winter weather. Choice C is incorrect because the narrator suggests that spring will bring an end to the siege, an eagerly awaited change.

Science

Scientific passages test your ability to read and understand science-related topics. The questions require you to understand the sequence of events, recall facts, and draw conclusions. These passages are often quite dense, jam-packed with information. You should monitor and adjust your speed and concentration as you read, and carefully look for *signal words* that show relationships or sequences of events.

EXAMPLE:

> When Leeuwenhoek in 1675 first discovered bacteria, he thought they were animals. Indeed, under a microscope, many of them bear a close resemblance to those minute worms found in vinegar that are known as "vinegar-eels." The idea that they belonged to the animal kingdom continued to hold ground until after the middle of the 19th century; but with the improvement in microscopes, a more thorough study became possible, and they were classified as vegetable. Now scientists classify them as neither plant nor animal, but as prokaryotes, single-cell organisms with no internal structures.

The signal words in this passage are *when, indeed, continued, more thorough,* and *now.* These words connect and signal the relationships between ideas. The word *when* tells you this event occurred at the beginning of Leeuwenhoek's investigation. The word *indeed* emphasizes the similarity in appearance between bacteria and vinegar eels. The word *continued* indicates this theory was popular until the word *but* indicates a change in thinking. The words *more thorough* explain how and why the change came about, and the word *now* introduces the current thinking about the classification of bacteria.

A list of signal words can be found in Chapter 11.

Now you're ready to try a reading comprehension question based on the preceding science passage.

> Which of the following statements is true according to information in the passage?
> - **A.** Vinegar eels are bacteria.
> - **B.** Bacteria are classified as prokaryotes.
> - **C.** Prokaryotes are vegetables that are composed of a single cell.
> - **D.** Bacteria are currently classified as both animals and plants.

Choice B is correct. According to the passage, bacteria were once thought to be animals, then vegetables, and, finally, prokaryotes. Choice A is incorrect because vinegar eels are small worms. Choice C is incorrect because prokaryotes aren't vegetables. Choice D is incorrect; scientists have created a specific category called prokaryotes for single-cell organisms.

Social Science

Readings in social science usually are informative presentations of material that has been gathered by research. These passages are similar to what is presented in social studies textbooks. To answer the questions, you will often have to follow the chronology of the events in the passage, understand the ramifications of political actions, or make conclusions about a series of events.

EXAMPLE:

> Queen Elizabeth knew she could rely on one of England's great heroes, Francis Drake. He was son of a chaplain in the navy and as a boy played in the rigging of the great ships-of-war, as other boys play in the streets. In time, young Drake was apprenticed to the skipper of a small trading vessel. Fortune smiled on the boy early in life. His master died and, out of love for the apprentice who had served him so well, left him the vessel. Francis Drake became, thus, a shipmaster on his own account and, in time, the most popular of Queen Elizabeth's sea captains.
>
> According to the passage, fortune smiled on Francis Drake because
>
> **A.** Queen Elizabeth appointed him to the position of Admiral in her navy.
> **B.** His father was a chaplain in the army.
> **C.** His skipper died and left Drake his ship.
> **D.** Drake played in the streets and met Queen Elizabeth.

The correct answer is choice C. Choice A is wrong because there is no evidence in the paragraph that Queen Elizabeth made Drake an admiral. Choice B is wrong because the passage states that Drake's father was a chaplain in the navy, not the army. Choice D is wrong because the passage states that Drake played in the riggings of war ships, not in the streets, and the passage does not state that he met the queen.

Technical Subjects

As you begin to read more widely, you may come across passages that are highly technical. For example, instruction manuals often contain blueprints, diagrams, tables, and schematics. For many jobs in the military, the ability to read technical material is a highly useful skill; you'll have to read safety manuals, instruction manuals, and regulations.

One technique that you can use is to draw on prior experience. Try to think of some contact you've had that is related to the material you're reading. Drawing on your previous experience can help you comprehend the passage. For example, if you're reading a passage about the environment and polluting emissions, consider what you've seen as you ride along a highway. You've probably noticed trucks belching out clouds of black smoke. Or you may have taken your car for an inspection and discovered that it's over the limit of safe emissions. Now, think about government efforts to control this pollution on a large scale.

Here is an example of a technical paragraph that you might find on the Paragraph Comprehension subtest that you can relate to a prior experience.

EXAMPLE:

In a cap-and-trade system, the governing body places a cap on the total amount of air or water pollution that may be emitted by issuing an equivalent number of allowances, denominated in units of pollution. These allowances may be issued by the government to the business entities that are regulated by the program in amounts similar to their expected production, to lessen the economic impact, or those entities may have to purchase the allowances from the government in an auction.

According to the passage, an allowance is

- **A.** a set amount of money the government puts aside to fix environmental problems
- **B.** a unit of pollution that the government permits a business to emit
- **C.** the economic impact of the war on pollution
- **D.** a system by which a business buys permission to exceed government regulations

The correct answer is B. After you read the paragraph and read the question and answer choices, use your scanning technique to quickly look for the answer. The term *allowances* is defined in the first sentence as a unit of pollution that the government allows a business to emit. It has nothing to do with money, so choices A and C can be eliminated. The passage doesn't state that a business can exceed government regulations, so choice D is incorrect.

A technical paragraph may also contain a process that you must follow in order to comprehend the paragraph. You need to be able to identify sequence words, follow the steps in a process, and recognize transition points.

EXAMPLE:

Acid rain is a term that refers to precipitation that carries higher-than-normal amounts of nitric and sulfuric acids from the atmosphere to the earth. First, power plants and other industries burn fossil fuels and emit sulfur dioxide and nitrogen oxides into the air. Then, these gases mix with water, oxygen, and other chemicals in the atmosphere. Next, these chemicals are blown long distances by wind and are carried down by rain. Finally, they seep into the ground and damage soil and vegetation, and into bodies of water where they harm aquatic life.

Consider the following events and put them in the correct order. Select the answer choice that has the correct order.

- **I.** Gases mix with water, oxygen, and other chemicals in the atmosphere.
- **II.** Power plants burn fossil fuels.
- **III.** Chemicals seep into the ground.
- **IV.** Rain containing contaminating chemicals falls to earth.
- **A.** I, II, IV, III
- **B.** IV, III, II, I
- **C.** II, I, IV, III
- **D.** II, IV, III, I

The correct answer is C. To answer this question, you have to follow the sequence clues in the paragraph. The initial event is introduced by the word *first.* Now you know that II has to be first in your answer, so you can eliminate choices A and B. The next event in the sequence is introduced by *then,* which is I, the gases mixing in the atmosphere. At this point, you can eliminate choice D. But if you want to make sure, you can continue on: The third event is introduced by *next* (IV, the falling rain), and the last event (III, chemicals seeping into the earth) is introduced by *finally.* By following the sequence clues in the paragraph, you should get the correct order of events.

Practice

This is your chance to practice all the enhanced reading techniques you learned in this chapter. As you read each passage, be sure to take note of the structure of the paragraph, use the context to help you figure out unfamiliar vocabulary, make predictions, stay focused, read between the lines, monitor and adjust to the difficulty of the material, and scan for answers. In addition, vary your reading strategies according to the content of the passage.

The following passages are similar to those on the Paragraph Comprehension subtest of the AFQT.

Directions: Read each passage, and then select the best answer from among the four choices.

Question 1 is based on the following passage.

One major advantage of the Internet is the implementation of targeted e-mailing. With a single click of the mouse, a sender can transmit a message to a preset list of recipients, all of whom have in some way been targeted as potential clients. The sender can broadcast new products or services, publicize important information, and set up a system for ordering products. In addition to its advantage of instantaneous speed, e-mail is inexpensive and accessible to most households in the United States.

1. The main idea of this passage is that

   A. Use of the Internet will guarantee an increase in sales for all online products.
   B. The Internet is a valuable tool because it is fast, inexpensive, and available.
   C. An effective marketing tool is cold calling, random phone calls made to potential customers.
   D. Although many older citizens are potential clients, Internet sales are low among senior citizens.

Question 2 is based on the following passage.

As the price of fossil fuels rises in response to increasing demands, ecologically responsible scientists are looking for alternative sources of energy. Wind turbines may be the answer. Currently, wind power provides about 1.9 percent of electricity used in the United States. Unlike generating plants that use fossil fuels and that have consistent output, however, wind turbines are naturally limited by the highly variable properties of wind.

2. According to the passage, one drawback to wind turbines is that

   A. They run on expensive fossil fuels.
   B. They provide very little energy to power machinery.
   C. As a steady source of energy, they're subject to variations in wind velocity.
   D. They aren't used very frequently in the United States.

Question 3 is based on the following passage.

Even though specific platforms will change in the future, the concept of social media is likely to stay. As such it will become more and more important to engage with social media and become 'digitally literate' rather than avoiding or resisting its use at all. There are still many gray areas surrounding social media in society. Unexpected new uses of the medium emerge constantly and carry various opportunities and challenges with them, one good example being citizen live-reporting during recent disasters. While we are starting to establish rules of good practice for some scenarios, society is still trying to evaluate the full impact of others. Understanding social media, and having the knowledge and confidence to use it appropriately and effectively for professional purposes will become essential skills to be included in a scientist's skills tool kit.

3. According to the information in the passage, which of the following is an example of a new and valuable use of social media?

    A.   posting new scientific discoveries on Facebook

    B.   a civilian report of an imminent flood in the area

    C.   teaching children to become 'digitally literate'

    D.   increased knowledge of social platforms

Question 4 is based on the following passage.

For years, scientists who studied the laws of physics depended on two major theories to explain the physical properties of the universe: relativity, which deals with the universe on a large scale, and quantum mechanics, which deals with the smallest particles of the physical world. These theories, however, presented a problem for physicists because they are incompatible: the universe does not consist of only either large parts or small parts; thus, to have two sets of laws makes no sense. The study of physics had reached a roadblock until development of super-string theory resolved the dilemma.

4. According to the passage, the importance of super-string theory is that it

    A.   supports all known laws of chemistry

    B.   deals with the smallest particles in the physical world

    C.   resolves the conflict between relativity and quantum mechanics

    D.   explores the universe on a large scale

Question 5 is based on the following passage.

Blood pressure is the pressure the blood exerts on the walls of the vessels in the body. For each heartbeat, the person's blood pressure varies between the systolic (maximum) and the diastolic (minimum) rhythm. A technician will usually state blood pressure in terms of the systolic pressure first and then the diastolic pressure. For example, normal blood pressure indicating healthy vessels is somewhere around 115/75.

5. From the passage it is reasonable to assume

    A.   A blood pressure of 120/80 means the diastolic pressure is 120 and the systolic pressure is 80.

    B.   Measuring blood pressure is one way to determine the health of the blood vessels.

    C.   Technicians will often use a finger-prick test to determine blood pressure.

    D.   It is not particularly important for a person to have regular blood-pressure checkups.

Question 6 is based on the following passage.

World War I was the first major war that the American military had to fight on foreign soil. On the European front, six destroyers under the command of Admiral William S. Sims set out to aid Britain in the struggle against the submarines that were threatening to cripple the country's food supply. Ultimately, there would be 300 ships of all kinds embroiled in the conflict.

6. From this passage, it is reasonable to assume that

    A. Britain and the United States were allies in World War I.
    B. Submarines were ineffective against the greater power of the United States' destroyers.
    C. Admiral Sims was in charge of a fleet of 300 submarines.
    D. The War of 1812 was the first war that the United States fought on foreign soil.

Question 7 is based on the following passage.

The sundial is one of the oldest of all scientific instruments. In principle, it is simple: the sun shines on the dial, and the protruding piece casts a shadow along the hour lines marked on the flat plate. Yet, its simplicity is deceptive. The dial must be precisely laid out with respect to the equator in order for the instrument to be accurate in showing the correct hour.

7. From this passage, it is reasonable to assume that

    A. The sundial is the oldest scientific instrument known to mankind.
    B. Directional calculations must be made before situating a sundial.
    C. The sundial is too simple to be an accurate instrument for telling time.
    D. A sundial can be placed in any direction in a garden.

Question 8 is based on the following passage.

The continuing evolution of automotive technology aims to deliver even greater safety benefits and Automated Driving Systems (ADS) that—one day—can handle the whole task of driving when we don't want to or can't do it ourselves. Fully automated cars and trucks that drive us, instead of us driving them, will become a reality. These self-driving vehicles ultimately will integrate onto U.S. roadways by progressing through six levels of driver assistance technology advancements in the coming years.

8. Which of the following statements is supported by evidence in the passage?

    A. One drawback to fully automated cars is that they are less safe than human-driven cars.
    B. Continuing technological advances will be implemented before ADS are fully integrated into the U.S. highway system.
    C. ADS will soon replace hybrid and electric cars because ADS are more economical and environmentally safe.
    D. ADS technology is currently available to all those who can't or don't want to handle the task of driving a passenger vehicle.

Question 9 is based on the following passage.

Because of increased federal deficits, some lawmakers are proposing a national tax on every step in the chain of production and distribution of goods and services. Many European nations already have a valued added tax, or VAT. The revenues from this tax could be used to fund healthcare, social services, or reduction of the national debt.

9. According to the passage:

    A. Only consumers purchasing goods and services would pay the VAT.

    B. All the revenue from the VAT would be used to pay down the national debt.

    C. The United States would be the only country to institute a VAT.

    D. With the proposed plan, manufacturers, wholesalers, retailers, and consumers would pay a VAT.

Question 10 is based on the following passage.

Many bacteria are unable to move from place to place; they have, however, a vibrating movement known as the *Brownian motion* that is purely physical. Some other kinds of bacteria are endowed with powers of locomotion. Motion is produced by cilia, fine thread-like organs on the outside of the bacteria cell. By means of the rapid vibration of these organs, the cell can move. These cilia are so delicate that it requires special treatment to demonstrate their presence.

10. The main idea of the passage is that

    A. All bacteria are incapable of movement, although some can vibrate in place.

    B. Bacteria are able to travel rapidly by means of their strong whip-like tails.

    C. Some bacteria can move by vibrating their cilia.

    D. Bacteria were originally categorized as animals, but because of their inability to move, they have been reclassified as plants.

Question 11 is based on the following passage.

In every society, even the most primitive, some form of musical expression exists. From the sounds of prehistoric man beating on a hollow log to the magnificent symphonies of Beethoven, music satisfies a need for artistic expression in human society. The universal appeal of musical expression suggests that it is linked to our psychological makeup. We use music to express feelings of love, despair, fear, and hope. In recent research, the influence of music on human psychological states has revealed the power of sound to create or alter mood. Music has even been used to reduce pain in chronic sufferers. Was William Congreve correct then, when he said, "Music soothes the savage breast"?

11. The author uses the example of William Congreve to

    A. contrast with Beethoven's belief that music is artistic rather than mathematical

    B. support the claim of psychologists that music can cure psychotic episodes

    C. link the primitive forms of music to the magnificent symphonies of the 17th century

    D. support his position that music has mood-altering properties

Question 12 is based on the following passage.

The Tunguska explosion was a powerful explosion that occurred in Central Siberia in 1908 near the Tunguska River. Herds of reindeer within a few miles of the blast were instantaneously incinerated; nomads were thrown from their tents miles away; all vegetation within a 2,000-square-mile radius was destroyed. When observers finally arrived at the site several months later, they found not a huge crater as they had predicted, but thousands of trees knocked outward from the blast center. Today, most scientists attribute the blast to an air burst from a comet or a meteor exploding several miles above the surface of the earth.

12. Which of the following examples is most similar to the effect of the blast on the trees?

    A. falling debris from an imploded building that crashes inward toward the center of the site
    B. a random pattern of falling blocks from a 2-foot tower that is knocked over
    C. the spoke-like arrangement of pick-up sticks when a tightly held bunch is released
    D. the straight parallel lines formed by iron filings when a U-shaped magnet is drawn through them

Questions 13 and 14 are based on the following passage.

Before the Civil War had ended, however, the transformation of the United States from a nation of farmers and small-scale manufacturers to a highly organized industrial state had begun. Probably the most important single influence was the war itself. Those four years of bitter conflict illustrate, perhaps more graphically than any similar event in history, the power that military operations may exercise in stimulating all the productive forces of a people.

13. In this passage, the word *exercise* most nearly means

    A. work out
    B. exert
    C. enjoy
    D. improve

14. According to the passage, the change in the United States from an agricultural nation to an industrial nation began

    A. immediately after the end of the Civil War
    B. during the Revolutionary War
    C. four years after the Revolutionary War
    D. during the Civil War

Question 15 is based on the following passage.

I have strong memories of my grandparents' apartment in the city, although I was 5 years old when they moved to another state. The swirling patterns of red and yellow on the carpet are burned into my brain. The smell of fresh bread baking in my grandmother's kitchen comes back to me whenever I step into a bakery. But sadly, I can't bring their faces into close focus, no matter how hard I try.

15. From this passage, it is reasonable to assume that

    A. The author has no memories of her grandparents before they moved to another state.

    B. The author did not have a close relationship with her grandparents early in her life.

    C. The author intensely disliked the carpet in her grandparents' home.

    D. The author wishes she had more vivid images of her grandparents' faces.

Answers

1. **B.** The passage supports the main idea that the Internet is a valuable tool, choice B. Choice A is not supported by evidence in the passage. The passage doesn't discuss cold calling, so choice C is incorrect. There is no evidence in the passage to support low Internet sales among senior citizens, so choice D is incorrect.

2. **C.** Choice C is correct because the passage states that wind turbines are subject to variations in the winds. Choice A is wrong because wind turbines don't run on fossil fuels. Choice B is inaccurate because wind turbines are able to power machinery. Choice D may be a true statement, but it isn't a drawback to wind turbines.

3. **B.** The correct answer to this detail question is choice B. The passage states that an example of an unexpected new use of social media is *citizen live-reporting during recent disasters.* Choice A is incorrect because the passage doesn't discuss posting new scientific discoveries. Choice C is incorrect because the passage states it is important to become 'digitally literate,' but it doesn't list teaching children this skill as a new and valuable use of social media. Choice D is incorrect because, according to the passage, increased knowledge of social platforms is not a new and valuable use of social media.

4. **C.** Choice C is correct; according to the passage, super-string theory resolved the dilemma between the two other theories. Choice A is incorrect because the passage isn't about the laws of chemistry. Choices B and D are incorrect because super-string theory deals with both small and large elements in the universe.

5. **B.** This inference question requires you to read between the lines to determine that choice B is correct. Blood pressure is a tool to help diagnose blood-vessel health. Choice A has the incorrect order of systolic and diastolic measures. Choice C is incorrect; a finger-prick test can't check blood pressure. Choice D is incorrect; the passage implies that having good blood pressure is important.

6. **A.** Choice A is a reasonable assumption. If the United States sent six destroyers to aid Britain, it's reasonable to assume that the two countries were allies. Choice B isn't supported by evidence in the passage. Choice C is inaccurate according to the passage. Choice D is inaccurate based on the first sentence of the passage, which states that World War I was the first major war fought by the United States on foreign soil.

7. **B.** Choice B is correct because the passage states that the sundial must be positioned correctly in relation to the equator. Choice A is not a reasonable assumption. The passage states that the sundial is *one* of the oldest, not *the* oldest instrument. Choice C is not supported by evidence in the passage. Choice D is inaccurate based on information in the passage.

8. **B.** Choice B is correct based on the information in the last sentence of the passage: technological advances will be implemented before ADS are fully integrated onto U.S. roadways. The evidence in the passage doesn't support choice A; no safety comparison is given between ADS and human-driven cars. There isn't any mention of electric and hybrid cars being replaced by ADS, so choice C is wrong. The passage never states that ADS technology is currently available; in fact, it states "one day," so choice D is incorrect.

9. **D.** Choice D is correct because manufacturers, wholesalers, retailers, and consumers are all steps in the chain of production and distribution. Choice A is inaccurate because the passage states that every step in the chain of production will pay the VAT. Choice B is incorrect; the national debt is only one use of the money from the VAT. Choice C is inaccurate based on the information in the passage. The passage states that several European countries have a VAT.

10. **C.** Choice C is correct because it's stated in the passage. Choice A is incorrect because the passage states that some bacteria can move. Choice B is incorrect because the passage doesn't mention tails. Choice D is incorrect based on the information in the passage.

11. **D.** Choice D is the correct interpretation of the purpose of Congreve's comment. Choice A is incorrect because Congreve's comment doesn't contrast with anything said by Beethoven. In fact, no statement by Beethoven is mentioned in the passage. Choice B goes beyond what is stated about the power of music to create or alter mood. Choice C is not accurate based on the information in the passage.

12. **C.** Choice C is correct because the passage states that the trees fell outward from the blast center. Choice A is incorrect because the buildings implode or fall inward. Choice B is a random pattern, so it isn't correct. Choice D is inaccurate because the pattern isn't two parallel lines.

13. **B.** As it is used in the passage, *exercise* most nearly means exert. Choices A, C, and D don't make sense in the paragraph.

14. **D.** According to the first sentence of the passage, the change in the United States from agricultural society to industrial society occurred before the Civil War had ended, choice D. Choice A is inaccurate. Choice B has the wrong war, as does choice C.

15. **D.** From the information in the passage, it is reasonable to assume that the author wishes she had more vivid images of her grandparents, choice D. You can infer this from her use of the phrase *But sadly*. Choice A is inaccurate based on the information in the passage; the author does have memories of her grandparents. It isn't reasonable to assume that she wasn't close to her grandparents early in life, so choice B is wrong. There is no evidence in the passage to support choice C.

Chapter 11
Paragraph Comprehension: Answering the Reading Questions

The Paragraph Comprehension subtest of the AFQT tests your ability to obtain information from short paragraphs on a variety of topics. You'll have to read different types of passages of varying lengths and styles and respond to questions based on information presented in each passage. There are 15 questions in this section, and you have 13 minutes to complete as many as you can. Concepts include identifying main ideas and primary purpose, locating and comprehending stated and implied facts, figuring out the meaning of a word in context, drawing conclusions, determining a sequence of events, determining the author's tone, and identifying style and technique.

A. Strategies for the Paragraph Comprehension Section

To successfully complete the AFQT reading passages, keep in mind the following strategies:

- **Always read actively.** Focus on what the author is trying to tell you. Think as you read—don't allow your mind to drift away from the paragraph.

- **If you're confused by a sentence, don't reread.** The sentence may become clearer as you read, or there may not be any questions about that part of the passage. If you have to reread, do so as you answer the questions.

- **Stay interested in the passage.** Link the passage to a familiar topic. This strategy will help you stay focused.

- **Watch for key words and phrases that indicate a shift or transition in the passage.** A passage may appear to present a position that the author supports; then the author may begin a sentence with *but* or *however* and negate the previous position.

- **Don't allow your personal feelings or your own knowledge about the topic to influence your answers.** Always go back to what is stated in or implied by the text for support for your answer.

- **Always read *all the answer choices before you select your answer*.** Use process of elimination as you read the choices. If you're sure an answer choice is wrong, eliminate it. After you've read all the choices, look again only at the choices that you haven't eliminated, and evaluate their accuracy. Don't be fooled by an answer choice that makes a correct statement but doesn't answer the specific question. A statement may be true based on the information in the passage, but it may still be the incorrect answer because it doesn't answer the question you're being asked.

- **Don't second-guess questions that appear to be too easy.** The test is constructed with a range of questions, and, especially at the beginning, an answer may simply be more accessible.

- **Be on the lookout for *except or not questions*.** For *except* and *not* questions, three of the answer choices will be true. In these questions, you're looking for the *one* answer choice that is *not* true.

B. Kinds of Paragraph Comprehension Questions

There are several different kinds of questions on the Paragraph Comprehension subtest. Many of the questions fall into the following categories:

- General overview
- Supporting facts or ideas
- Vocabulary in context
- Inference
- Sequence of events
- Structure
- Style and tone

General Overview Questions

Main Purpose

Main purpose questions ask you to determine the author's purpose in writing the passage. In other words, why did the author write this piece? What was he trying to accomplish? To answer these questions, you must think about the passage as a whole. Is the author trying to argue a position? Describe a situation? Propose a new approach? Prove or disprove a theory?

Sometimes, within a paragraph an author will have more than one purpose, but for this question type, you're only looking for the *main* purpose.

EXAMPLE:

> During the first period of feudalism, that is to say from the middle of the 9th to the middle of the 12th centuries, the inhabitants of castles had little time to devote to the pleasures of private life. They had not only to be continually under arms for the endless quarrels of the king and the great chiefs; but they had also to oppose the Normans on one side, and the Saracens on the other, who, being masters of the Spanish peninsula, spread like the rising tide.
>
> The author's main purpose in writing this paragraph is to
>
> A. detail the importance of privacy in feudal castles
> B. argue the merits of feudalism as a way of life
> C. explain the priorities in the feudal society
> D. propose a new way of examining feudal life

Choice C is the correct answer. The author points out that war with neighboring rulers took priority over private concerns in feudal times. Choice A, which emphasizes privacy, contradicts the author's main point. Choice B is far too general an answer; the passage concerns only a small aspect of feudal life. Choice D is inaccurate because the author doesn't propose a new way to look at feudal life. He describes the main concern for those in the castle: protection from enemies.

Central or Main Idea

Central idea questions may be posed in several ways:

- What is the main idea of the passage?
- With which of the following statements would the author most likely agree?
- What is the best title for the passage?
- This passage is primarily concerned with....

To answer a central idea question, ask yourself: If I had to sum up the gist of this passage in one sentence, what would I say? It's often helpful to think about this question as you read each passage.

Try to follow the author's logic as you read, and be alert for the main idea of the passage.

EXAMPLE:

> In the United States, the majority undertakes to supply a multitude of ready-made opinions for the use of individuals, who are thus relieved from the necessity of forming opinions of their own. Everybody there adopts great numbers of theories, on philosophy, morals, and politics, without questioning the opinions of the outspoken majority. The fact that the political laws of the Americans are such that the majority rules the community with sovereign sway materially increases the power which that majority naturally exercises over the mind.
>
> Which of the following best states the central idea of this paragraph?
>
> A. America is a nation founded on the premise that the convictions of the individual are more powerful than the will of the majority.
> B. The foundation of political power in this country rests in the hands of those with superior wisdom.
> C. The beliefs of the majority in America are sovereign and inform the opinions of the individual.
> D. Because it is a country ruled by the majority, the United States is politically omnipotent.

Choice C is correct. The main idea is stated in the first sentence of the passage. Choice A is the opposite of the writer's thesis; choice B is a misreading of his point that the individual believes the majority has superior wisdom; and choice D is not supported by the passage.

Supporting Idea

To answer supporting idea questions, you must first distinguish between main and subordinate ideas. You may be asked about a specific piece of information and how it's used in the passage. You may be asked to assess the value of information that's given as evidence to support the main idea, or to ascertain why the author included a particular piece of information.

Consider the detail in light of the author's purpose. If he's trying to support a theory, the detail may be evidence. On the other hand, he may be using it to argue against the ideas of another. Also, consider why the author chose this particular piece of information to use: Why is it effective or ineffective?

EXAMPLE:

Environmentalists have been arguing for years that more effort is needed to save the planet's forests. They assert that forests play a crucial role in absorbing carbon dioxide (CO_2). Their theory is that as forests are destroyed, the carbon dioxide is released into the atmosphere. The excess of carbon dioxide in the atmosphere then traps the earth's heat and is a major contributor to global warming.

According to the passage, saving forests is important because

> **A.** Forests are important contributors to an increase in global warming.
> **B.** Forests absorb the carbon dioxide that can be a factor in causing global warming.
> **C.** The earth needs forests to provide a haven for plants and animals.
> **D.** Environmentalists have factual evidence that carbon dioxide is harmful to forests.

The correct answer is B. The writer uses the detail about CO_2 to support his main point about the importance of forests. According to the passage, if carbon dioxide, which is absorbed by forests, is released into the atmosphere, it contributes to global warming. Choice A is inaccurate because forests don't increase global warming; an excess of CO_2 does. Choice C may be true, but it isn't supported by any information in the passage. (Watch out for true but incorrect answer choices.) Choice D is incorrect; there is no evidence in the passage to support the "fact" that CO_2 is harmful to forests.

Vocabulary in Context

Vocabulary-in-context questions ask about the meaning of a word as it is used in the passage. Often, words that have multiple meanings are selected. You must find the appropriate choice for the context.

For example, the word *common* has many meanings. It can mean shared equally, like land held in common. It can mean widespread, like common knowledge. It can mean occurring frequently, like a common mistake. It can mean average or ordinary, like a common garter snake. It can mean inferior in manner or vulgar, like behavior that is offensive and common.

The best technique is to go back to the text, circle the word, and reread the whole sentence. Then replace the circled word with the words in the answer choices. Select the answer choice that is most like the original meaning of the sentence.

- **Don't rely on *denotation* (the dictionary meaning of a word) alone.** The correct response often requires you to consider *connotation* (the suggested meaning or implication of a word).

- **Very often, the most common meaning of a word—the one that pops right into your head—is not the correct answer.** Always look at the *context* (the sentences surrounding the word) to help you decide on the best choice.

- **Most of the words will be familiar to you, not like the difficult words from the word knowledge questions.** This is a test of your ability to understand context rather than a test of your vocabulary.

EXAMPLE:

It is certain that the most important facts in the life of Belle Boyd, the Confederate spy, constitute some of the most thrilling adventures in the great conflict between the sections—the Civil War in the United States. She was only a girl when the flag was fired on at Sumter and her father and all the members of her family immediately enlisted in the Confederate army. When the Union troops took possession of Martinsburg, Belle Boyd found herself unwillingly inside the Federal lines. She had no formal commission from any of the Southern officers, but circumstances and her ardent nature made her an intense partisan of what was to be "The Lost Cause."

In this passage, the word *ardent* most nearly means

   A. cloying
   B. inane
   C. passionate
   D. lethal

The correct answer is C. The context gives you a clue to the meaning of the word. The sentence is about Belle's nature: the clue is that she was an intense partisan, which would be expected in one with a passionate nature. Choice A is incorrect because cloying means excessively sweet; it's possible Belle was sweet, but no clue in the passage leads you to that choice. Choice B is incorrect because there is no evidence that Belle was inane (silly), and that choice is incompatible with the content of the passage. Choice D is not a logical choice because there is no evidence that Belle's nature was lethal (deadly).

Inference Questions

These questions ask you to *infer,* to draw conclusions from evidence implied but not directly stated in the passage. You must be able to follow the author's logic as he presents his information and infer the intended meaning from what is suggested. Very often the question will be phrased as follows:

- From the passage, it is reasonable to assume….
- You can infer from the passage that….

Although the answer will not be directly stated in the passage, you can always use textual evidence to support your choice. Be careful not to allow your own opinions to influence your answer to the question.

EXAMPLE:

> The FBI is the lead federal agency for investigating cyber attacks by criminals, overseas adversaries, and terrorists. The threat is incredibly serious—and growing. Cyber intrusions are becoming more commonplace, more dangerous, and more sophisticated. Adversaries target our nation's critical infrastructure, including both private and public sector networks. American companies are targeted for trade secrets and other sensitive corporate data, and universities for their cutting-edge research and development.
>
> From this passage, it is reasonable to assume that
>
> A. Currently, the threat of cyber intrusion has become the focus of all FBI investigations.
> B. Using the latest cutting-edge technology, the FBI has curtailed the increasing threat from cyber intrusions.
> C. Private corporations and major universities are solely responsible for protecting their research and data from cyber attacks.
> D. To respond to cyber threats, the FBI must develop and implement new strategies and new technologies.

The correct answer is D. Choice D is the best answer because the passage implies that as the threat grows more sophisticated, so must the FBI's response. As attacks become more dangerous and sophisticated, the FBI must develop and implement new strategies and technologies. Choice A is incorrect because the passage doesn't indicate that cyber intrusion is the focus of all FBI investigations, only one particularly serious issue. Choice B is incorrect because the passage suggests that cyber intrusions are increasing, so they aren't being curtailed. Choice C is incorrect because the passage discusses the FBI's role, so private corporations and universities aren't solely responsible.

Sequence-of-Events Questions

Sequence-of-events questions test your ability to follow a series of events in the order in which they occurred. The order may be chronological (time) or spatial (large to small, east to west, top to bottom) or specific to general (or general to specific).

EXAMPLE:

> But, one idle and rainy day, it was my fortune to make a discovery of interest. Poking and burrowing into the heaped-up rubbish in the corner, unfolding one and another document, I chanced to lay my hand on a small package, carefully done up in a piece of ancient yellow parchment. There was something about it that quickened an instinctive curiosity and made me undo the faded red tape that tied up the package, with the sense that a treasure would here be brought to light. Unbending the rigid folds of the parchment cover, I found it to be a commission for one long-dead Jonathan Pue. Inside, I found more of his documents, not official, but of a private nature. But the object that most drew my attention to the mysterious package was a piece of fine red cloth, much worn and faded. This rag of scarlet cloth on careful examination, assumed the shape of a letter. It was the capital letter *A*.
>
> What is the correct order of the events in the passage?
>
> **A.** The narrator found the cloth, discovered the commission of Mr. Pue, and poked around the accumulated garbage in the corner of the room.
>
> **B.** The narrator opened the parchment package, did research, and found the scarlet cloth before Mr. Pue died.
>
> **C.** The narrator poked around the rubbish, found and opened the parchment package, discovered Mr. Pue's documents, and found the scarlet cloth.
>
> **D.** After Mr. Pue died, the narrator found the scarlet cloth, undid the faded red tape, and read the documents.

Choice C is correct. Refer to the passage and locate each event. Choice A is incorrect because the narrator found the package when he poked around the rubbish. In choice B, Mr. Pue dies last; since he left the package when he died, the order listed here is incorrect. Choice D reverses the order: the cloth is in the package tied with the red tape.

Structure Questions

The author of a passage clearly had some sense of organization as he wrote the passage. As you read, try to determine the pattern of ideas. You will find clues in the word order, order of the ideas, and signal words to help you understand the structure of the passage.

Here are some common structures utilized in AFQT passages:

- Thesis or theory followed by supporting examples
- Arguments for and against a specific issue, with or without a solution
- A cause-and-effect sequence demonstrating how one aspect is a result of another
- A comparison of several ideas, pointing out similarities and differences among the views
- A chronological survey

Key words can help you determine the structural pattern of a passage. As you read, pay particular attention to *signal words* (introductory or transitional words that establish relationships within the passage).

The following words signal a contrast or contradiction:

- Despite
- However
- In spite of
- Although
- Even though

- Nevertheless
- But
- Yet
- Rather than
- Instead

The following words signal ideas that are similar:

- In addition
- And
- Moreover

- Furthermore
- For example
- Likewise

The following words signal a cause-and-effect relationship:

- Because
- Thus
- As a result
- Therefore

- Consequently
- Hence
- Since

EXAMPLE:

Desert plants generally grow tall and thin rather than wide and full like plants in more temperate climates. To understand the difference in shapes, you must understand that a plant is an organism that must regulate its intake of water and its output of heat. Because the desert offers hours of sunlight and very little rain, the native plants must be thin to expose as little surface to the sun as possible. They must be tall to have a large surface area to allow excessive heat to evaporate. Thus, the design of the desert plant is ideal for its habitat.

Which of the following describes the organization of this passage?

- A. an argument followed by statistics
- B. a defense of a position followed by the counterargument
- C. a statement followed by an explanation
- D. a theory followed by a quote from an expert

The correct answer is C. The author makes a statement: *Desert plants generally grow tall and thin rather than wide and full like plants in more temperate climates.* He then proceeds to explain why—the signal word *because* lets you know an explanation of a reason is coming. There are no statistics in the paragraph so choice A is wrong. There is no counterargument, so choice B is wrong. There is no quote from an expert, so choice D is wrong.

Style and Tone Questions

Some questions on the AFQT ask you to consider the *tone* of a line or of the whole passage. Other questions ask about the author's *attitude* toward someone or something. As you read, consider where you might find this passage: Would it be in a textbook? In a personal response? In a defense? In a scientific journal? Some questions will ask you to figure out the intended audience for a passage or in what type of publication it would most likely be found.

In addition, you should be able to recognize literal versus metaphorical language. *Literal language* is meant to be taken at face value; it denotes what it means. *Metaphorical language* is not meant to be taken literally. For example, the statement "My pockets are empty" may *literally* denote that there is nothing in my pockets; *metaphorically,* it may mean that I'm broke or poor.

Here are key tone/attitude words used on the AFQT, along with their definitions:

- **Indignant:** Angry at unfairness or injustice
- **Objective:** Neutral, impartial
- **Subjective:** Based on personal opinion
- **Detached:** Neutral, not emotionally or personally involved
- **Equivocal:** Deliberately vague or misleading
- **Ambivalent:** Having mixed feelings, seeing both sides of an issue
- **Cynical:** Pessimistic, expecting the worst from others
- **Skeptical, incredulous, dubious:** Disbelieving, doubtful

EXAMPLE:

> For over 80 years, formerly indigenous wolves have been missing from the southwestern United States and Mexico. Hunted to near extinction, the so-called Mexican wolves dwindled to a handful before efforts were made to bring the species back. Nurturing the few remaining animals, the U.S. Fish and Wildlife Service employed state-of-the-art breeding techniques to bring back the population. When efforts were started to reintroduce the wolves, local ranchers protested vigorously. The wolves, they argued, are a natural predator of livestock. Some states have refused to allow the wolves to be released on their lands, arguing that the cost to farmers and ranchers is too great. As the 21st century begins, the future of the Mexican wolf remains uncertain.

> The tone of the passage suggests that the author's attitude toward the reintroduction of the wolves is
>
>   A. indignant because his sympathy clearly lies with the efforts to save this endangered species
>   B. cynical because he does not believe that any effort to save this endangered species has a chance to be successful
>   C. hostile because he has no patience with the efforts of human beings to interfere with the natural world
>   D. ambivalent because he acknowledges that both sides in this issue have valid positions

The correct answer is D. The author understands the differing objectives of both sides of the issue. He is sympathetic to the goal of the U.S. Fish and Wildlife Service to restore an endangered species; he is also sympathetic to the ranchers who lose livestock to the predatory wolves. Choice A is incorrect; the author understands the position of the ranchers as well as that of the U.S. Fish and Wildlife Service. Choice B is incorrect because the author doesn't express cynicism about efforts to save the wolves. Choice C is incorrect because the author doesn't express hostility toward efforts of human beings to address problems in the natural world.

Practice

Directions: Read each passage below and answer the questions based on what is stated in or implied by the information in the passage.

Question 1 is based on the following passage.

As humans travel farther from Earth for longer missions, the systems that keep them alive must be highly reliable while taking up minimal mass and volume. NASA's Orion spacecraft will be equipped with advanced environmental control and life support systems designed for the demands of a deep space mission. A high-tech system already being tested aboard the space station will remove carbon dioxide (CO_2) and humidity from inside Orion. Removal of CO_2 and humidity is important to ensure air remains safe for the crew to breathe. And water condensation on the vehicle hardware is controlled to prevent water intrusion into sensitive equipment or corrosion on the primary pressure structure.

1. According to the passage, which of the following is *not* an essential function of the environmental control and life support systems onboard Orion?

   A. CO_2 removal
   B. humidity control
   C. volume controls for communication networks
   D. prevention of water intrusion

Question 2 is based on the following passage.

It was a grand sight to see the regiment depart at 8:45 p.m. The band was playing; colors were flying at the head of the column—everybody was in high spirits. But there were no civilians to enjoy the spectacle. It was night and but few knew of the departure. The rain had ceased and twilight was deepening into darkness as the regiment excepting Battery A, which was left in camp to follow a few days later, started on the hike.

2. From this passage, it is reasonable to assume that

   A. All the spectators watching the regiment depart are military personnel.
   B. The regiment departed from the camp at dawn.
   C. The regiment is about to be deployed overseas.
   D. Most of the troops are depressed about their departure.

Question 3 is based on the following passage.

Going green can be as simple as making a few changes in your home. The first way to be earth-friendly is to reduce the energy you waste. Begin by checking the old appliances in your home. Replacing an old refrigerator or washing machine can cut energy costs dramatically. You can also turn down the thermostat; keep your house cooler in the winter and warmer in the summer. If everyone does a little bit to help the environment, we can all become better global citizens.

3. The main idea of this passage is

   A. Buying a new refrigerator is the crucial step toward saving the planet.
   B. Air-conditioning and heating units are inefficient energy-consuming appliances.
   C. It is important for people to do what they can to protect the environment.
   D. Small actions can't have a significant impact on the environment; it takes a global initiative to make a difference.

Question 4 is based on the following passage.

Sunday, July 28, found the sea calm in the morning, but a strong gale set in at noon, followed by a heavy rain during the afternoon. A dense fog enveloped the convoy. Foghorns came into play and it was a miserable night aboard for everybody. Standing at the deck rail one could not pierce the fog, although it was known that, within a short radius, all the other ships of the convoy were groping their way through the darkness, each creeping as a black monster through the gloomy night, depending upon the foghorn to keep aloof from their sister convoy ships; a sense of isolation enshrouded the scene.

4. The mood of this paragraph is best described as

   A. lonely
   B. angry
   C. eager
   D. cheerful

Question 5 is based on the following passage.

Everyone yawns, but scientists have yet to discover exactly why we yawn. We know that yawns are involuntary and that they signal sleepiness, tiredness, or boredom, but we don't know for sure what yawning accomplishes. Some theorize that the strong inhaling of air increases the oxygen in the blood and releases the carbon dioxide, but experiments have failed to prove this theory. What we do know is that all human beings yawn and have always done so.

5. From this passage it is reasonable to assume that

   A. Excessive oxygen in the bloodstream leads to increased energy.
   B. Excessive yawning is a sign of chronic fatigue syndrome.
   C. Scientists have successfully proven that yawning is a way for the body to rid itself of impurities.
   D. Scientists are still studying yawns to determine their purpose.

Question 6 is based on the following passage.

Studies have shown that viruses can live on nonporous surfaces like wood, plastic, and metal for one to two days. Some can even live as long as six days. The significance of this in cold and flu season is extraordinary. People touch doorknobs, faucets, and other hard surfaces and then touch their hands to their noses and mouths. The ease with which infection spreads emphasizes the importance of teaching children and adults to wash their hands thoroughly and frequently.

6. The primary purpose of this passage is to

   A. explain how viruses are able to live without food and water
   B. encourage personal hygiene as a way to prevent the spread of disease
   C. discourage people from leaving their homes in cold and flu season
   D. disprove current theories about the longevity of single-cell organisms

Question 7 is based on the following passage.

Mangroves are trees and shrubs that perch on the water with their stilt-like prop roots. Mangroves grow on the coastal margins where land meets water. They are uniquely adapted to low-oxygen soils and brackish waters inundated with salt water during high tides—conditions that would kill other trees. However, since the 80 known species of mangroves cannot tolerate freezing temperatures, they grow only in tropical and sub-tropical regions of the world.

7. Which of the following can be inferred from the passage?

   A. In any area with a tropical climate, mangroves are the most common species to be found.
   B. It would be unlikely to find mangroves growing on the shores of a stream.
   C. The fruit of the mangrove tree can tolerate freezing temperatures.
   D. Mangrove trees have roots that are capable of propelling the trees long distances through brackish waters.

Question 8 is based on the following passage.

Pet therapy, also called animal-assisted therapy, involves using physical contact with animals to help people. Pet therapy can improve a patient's physical, emotional, and intellectual functions. In addition, animals can reduce loneliness and provide opportunities for socialization. Pet therapists have had success with autistic children who sometimes respond better to dogs, cats, and rabbits than to people.

8. According to this passage, one purpose of pet therapy is to

   A. teach people how to care for their pets
   B. cure pets who have physical ailments
   C. establish interactions with autistic children
   D. reduce the number of homeless animals

Question 9 is based on the following passage.

Body fat serves as an energy store, a padding against mechanical impacts, a coating against heat loss, a construction material for tissues and organs, and as a carrier substance for vitamins and other important components of metabolism, just to name a few. Food shortage has been a constant threat throughout human evolution. Without fat as a powerful energy store, humankind would have been extinct long before the Stone Age. A good energy supply is especially important during early childhood, in times of illness and malfunctions of the digestive system, and in old age.

9. According to the passage

    A. For a long and healthy life, it is essential to reduce body fat as much as feasibly possible.

    B. The layer of body fat around internal organs provides a barrier to prevent the invasion of bacteria and harmful microorganisms.

    C. The survival of humankind is directly related to an adequate supply of body fat.

    D. Increasing the amount of body fat will ensure good health during old age.

Question 10 is based on the following passage.

Vampires have become so popular that they dominate best-seller lists, star in several TV series, and delight movie-goers with their superhuman powers. How can we explain this ghoulish obsession? Perhaps the trend owes its birth to the author Bram Stoker, whose 19th-century novel *Dracula* sparked the human fascination with the blood-drinking immortals.

10. The best title for this passage is

    A. Horror Literature of the 19th Century

    B. The Novels of Bram Stoker

    C. How to Kill a Vampire

    D. The Human Passion for Vampires

Question 11 is based on the following passage.

Since scientists now have evidence to prove that the moon is not made of "green cheese" as the old myth suggests, attention has turned from the composition of the lunar body to theories of its origin. One of the early theories proposes that the moon formed at the same time as the earth from the same elements. However, samples collected from the moon's surface by lunar probes show that moon rocks do not contain iron, an element common in earth samples. The model currently in favor says that the moon was formed when a large planetary body struck the earth's surface and broke off a chunk, which spun into orbit. This theory explains the missing iron by theorizing that the iron in the earth had drifted into its core, leaving an iron-free outer layer from which the moon was formed.

11. The primary purpose of this passage is to

    A. criticize a method

    B. present a single position

    C. offer alternative explanations

    D. correct a long-standing factual error

Question 12 is based on the following passage.

The magnificent polar bear, the world's largest terrestrial carnivore, lives most of its life on the ice floes in the Arctic cap and feeds mostly on seals. Recently, the government has listed the polar bear as a "threatened species," a designation that indicates without some form of protection, this species likely faces extinction. The threat to these bears does not come from predators, but from global climate changes. Increased burning of fossil fuels has caused an unprecedented warming, which in turn has caused a loss of sea ice. As their habitat shrinks, the polar bears follow the retreating ice; some bears then find themselves stranded on land.

12. According to the passage, the greatest threat faced by polar bears is the

    A. increased population of large predators that prey on polar bears
    B. human settlements in areas previously inhabited solely by the polar bears
    C. declining herds of seals that provide the major food source to the polar bears
    D. decrease in the size of the ice floes

Question 13 is based on the following passage.

The organization of the militia is indispensable to the liberties of the country. It is only by an effective militia that we can at once enjoy peace and freedom from foreign aggression; it is by the militia that we are constituted an armed nation, standing in perpetual defense in the presence of all the other nations of the earth. To this end it would be necessary, if possible, so to shape its organization as to give it a more united and active energy. There are laws establishing a uniform militia throughout the United States and for arming and equipping its whole body.

13. The main purpose of this passage is to

    A. defend the need for a standing army
    B. argue against the U.S. position on foreign aggression
    C. contrast the U.S. militia with those of other nations
    D. challenge the position that the laws of this country are intended to establish a military presence

Question 14 is based on the following passage.

Throughout history, every civilization has played a game with a stick and a ball. The modern-day game of golf, for example, can trace its history back to Scotland in the Middle Ages. Originally, the game consisted of hitting a ball on the ground from one place to another in the village green. Eventually, the holes were added, and the pastime that has become an obsession for many people evolved into a sport.

14. According to the passage

    A. Golf was originally played only by the wealthy people.
    B. Golf began in the Middle East where it was played in fields.
    C. All the villagers were involved in golf tournaments in the Middle Ages.
    D. Putting the golf ball into a hole was added after the game first began.

Question 15 is based on the following passage.

The digestive system is made up of the digestive tract and other internal organs that help the body break down and absorb food. The food and drink we consume can't be used as nutrition for the body until it is broken down into smaller molecules that can be carried throughout the body. The only voluntary parts of the process of digestion are chewing and swallowing. Once the food moves past the mouth, the involuntary process of digestion begins.

15. According to the passage

    A. Digesting food is a simple process carried out solely in the stomach.

    B. The entire digestive process is involuntary.

    C. Eating is the first step in digestion.

    D. Swallowing is an involuntary response to the stimuli of food in the mouth.

Answers

1. **C.** Choices A, B, and D are all mentioned in the passage as essential functions of Orion's environmental control and life support systems. While choice C is most likely an important feature, it is part of the communications system, not the environmental control and life support systems.

2. **A.** The passage states that no civilians were present to enjoy the departure of the regiment. Therefore, all the spectators must have been military personnel. Choice B is incorrect because the passage states that the regiment departed at 8:45 p.m., not at dawn. Choice C is wrong because the passage states that the regiment was preparing for a hike. Choice D is incorrect because "everybody was in high spirits."

3. **C.** The main idea of this passage is that everyone can contribute to protecting the environment, choice C. Choice A is incorrect because the passage doesn't state that buying a new refrigerator is the single most *crucial* step. Choice B is only alluded to indirectly in the passage; it isn't the main idea. Choice D is contradicted by the information in the passage.

4. **A.** The fog, the isolation of the ship, and the gloomy night all contribute to the lonely mood, choice A. There is no evidence of anger in the passage, so choice B is wrong. Choices C and D are the opposite of the feelings presented by the "sense of isolation" in the description.

5. **D.** The first sentence of the passage implies that scientists are still studying yawns, choice D. The connection described in choice A can't be supported by the information in the passage. There isn't any evidence in the passage to support choices B or C.

6. **B.** The primary purpose of the passage is to encourage people to wash their hands more frequently to stop the spread of viruses, choice B. Choice A is not explained in the passage. Choice C (staying home) is never mentioned in the passage. There is no attempt in the passage to disprove theories about the longevity of viruses, so choice D is wrong.

7. **B.** According to information in the passage, mangroves grow on coastal margins where land meets brackish water: brackish water is very salty as opposed to streams, which are fresh water. Therefore, it would be unlikely to find mangroves growing on the shores of a stream, choice B. Choice A can't be inferred from the passage; although mangroves grow in tropical climates, there is no evidence that they are the most common species. Choice C also can't be inferred from the passage; the fruit of the mangrove is never referenced in the passage. In addition, since the mangrove can't tolerate freezing temperatures, it

is unlikely that the fruit would survive. Choice D is not addressed in the passage; however, the passage does mention the "stilt-like prop roots," suggesting the roots prop up the tree rather than propel it.

8. **C.** According to the passage, pet therapy has been successful in establishing interactions with autistic children, choice C. Choice A is not supported by the evidence in the passage. Choice B is off-topic; the passage doesn't consider curing pets with ailments. Homeless animals (choice D) are not discussed in the passage.

9. **C.** According to the passage, energy storage in the form of body fat is essential for the survival of humankind, choice C. Choice A is incorrect because a reasonable amount of body fat is necessary for health. Choice B is not supported by any evidence in the passage. Choice D is incorrect because while some body fat is essential to good health, no amount of body fat can guarantee good health during old age.

10. **D.** The best title for the passage should reflect the main idea of the passage. Since the passage is about the popularity of vampires, choice D is the best title. Choice A is too general to be the best title. Choice B is too specific to be the best title. Choice C is off-topic; therefore, it isn't the best title.

11. **C.** The primary purpose of the passage is to consider various explanations for the composition of the moon. The passage doesn't criticize a method (choice A) or correct a factual error (choice D). Because the passage offers more than one theory about the moon, choice B is incorrect.

12. **D.** According to the passage, the polar bears face the greatest threat from their shrinking habitat, the ice floes. Choice A is wrong because the passage states, "The threat to these bears does not come from predators…." Choice B is wrong because the passage doesn't list human settlements as a threat, nor does it mention declining herds of seals (choice C).

13. **A.** The main purpose of the passage is to support a militia or a standing army, choice A. It doesn't argue against the U.S. position on foreign aggression (choice B), nor does it contrast the U.S. militia with those of other countries (choice C). The passage doesn't challenge the laws of this country regarding the establishment of a militia (choice D); on the contrary, it supports these laws.

14. **D.** According to the passage, the game of golf originally involved just hitting the ball around a green; putting the ball into a hole came later, choice D. There is no evidence suggesting only wealthy people played golf, so choice A is wrong. The passage states that golf began in Scotland (which is not in the Middle East), so choice B is wrong. There is no evidence in the passage to support choice C, that *all* the villagers participated in golf tournaments.

15. **C.** The passage states that the digestive process begins with putting food in the mouth, chewing, and swallowing; therefore, choice C is correct: eating is the first step in digestion. Choice A is wrong because the passage states that the digestive tract and several organs are included in the digestive process. Choices B and D are wrong because the passage states that chewing and swallowing are voluntary actions.

Chapter 12

Mathematics Knowledge: Algebra

The Mathematics Knowledge subtest of the AFQT presents you with questions based on material you learned in high school math classes. Most people take at least one course that focuses on algebra, so that's a good place to start.

A. Integers

The set of integers includes positive and negative whole numbers and zero. If no sign is shown for a number, it's assumed to be positive, so 7 is +7. Zero is neither positive nor negative.

Absolute Value

The absolute value of a number is the number without its sign, or the positive version of the number. The absolute value of +4 is 4, and the absolute value of −4 is 4. The symbol for the absolute value of a number, n, is $|n|$. So $|-12| = 12$, $|+43| = 43$, and $|0| = 0$.

Addition

To add two integers that have the same sign, add the absolute values and give your answer the same sign:

$$(+5) + (+9) = +(5 + 9) = +14 \qquad (-8) + (-6) = -(8 + 6) = -14$$

If the two numbers to be added have different signs, subtract the absolute values, and take the sign of the number with the larger absolute value:

$$(-13) + (+24) = +(24 - 13) = +11 \qquad (+18) + (-25) = -(25 - 18) = -7$$

Subtraction

The simplest rule for subtracting integers is: Don't. Subtraction is adding the opposite, so change subtraction problems to addition of the first number and the opposite of the second number, and follow the rules for addition:

$$(-29) - (+32) = (-29) + (-32) = -61 \qquad (-171) - (-38) = -171 + 38 = -133$$

Multiplication and Division

Multiplication and division are opposite or inverse operations, but the rules governing signs are the same for both operations. If both numbers have the same sign, the result is positive. If the signs of the two numbers are different, the result is negative:

$$-12 \times (-5) = +60 \qquad +42 \div (-6) = -7$$

Order of Operations

When a problem involves only addition or only multiplication, you can tackle the numbers in any convenient sequence. As soon as you start to mix up operations, you need rules to govern the order in which you perform the operations. Most people remember them by the mnemonic PEMDAS. The letters stand for **P**arentheses, **E**xponents, **M**ultiplication and **D**ivision, **A**ddition and **S**ubtraction.

To simplify $(-7) + (+5) \times (-2) + (-12) \div (-4) - (+3)$, start from the left, move to the right, and do multiplication or division as you meet them:

$$(-7) + (+5) \times (-2) + (-12) \div (-4) - (+3) = (-7) + (-10) + (+3) - (+3)$$

Start from the left again, move to the right, and do addition and subtraction as you meet them. ***Remember:*** Subtraction is adding the opposite.

$$(-7) + (-10) + (+3) - (+3) = (-17) + (+3) - (+3) = (-14) - (+3) = -17$$

When parentheses are present in the expression, first do what is within the parentheses. If there is a multiplier in front of the parentheses, or a minus sign in front of the parentheses, use the distributive property. Once you've cleared parentheses, deal with any exponents that are present.

$$-(2+5\times 3)+6(7-4)^2 \div 2(2^2 -3)$$
$$-(2+15)+6(7-4)^2 \div 2(2^2 -3)$$
$$-17+6(3)^2 \div 2(2^2 -3)$$
$$-17+6\times 9 \div 2(2^2 -3)$$
$$-17+54 \div 2(2^2 -3)$$
$$-17+54 \div 2(4-3)$$
$$-17+54 \div 2(1)$$
$$-17+54 \div 2$$

Continue with multiplication and division. Finally, perform addition and subtraction.

$$-17 + 54 \div 2 = -17 + 27 = 10$$

Practice

Directions: Choose the best answer from the choices provided.

1. Simplify: $(-18) \div (+6) - (-9)$.

    A. -12
    B. $+12$
    C. $+6$
    D. -6

2. Simplify: $(-21) \times (+3) + (+84) \div (-12)$.

    A. -14
    B. $+14$
    C. -70
    D. $+70$

3. Simplify: $(-13) \times (+20) + (-35) + (-15) - (-48) \div (+16)$.

   A. -307
   B. -577
   C. $+583$
   D. $+683$

4. Simplify: $(-17) + (-25) - (+31) + (+48) \times (-2) \div (-8)$.

   A. $+1$
   B. -52
   C. $+61$
   D. -61

5. Simplify: $(-25) - (+18) \div (-6) \times (-21) - (-7)$.

   A. -81
   B. -31
   C. $+45$
   D. $+12$

6. Which of the following expressions has the same value as $-53 - 16$?

   A. $53 + 16$
   B. $53 - 16$
   C. $-53 + (-16)$
   D. $16 - 53$

7. Which of the following expressions has the same value as $42 - 19 + (-8)$?

   A. $42 - 27$
   B. $42 - 11$
   C. $42 + 11$
   D. $42 + 27$

8. Which of these is a correct first step to simplify $15 \div 3 + 7 \times 2 - 5$?

   A. $15 \div 10 \times 2 - 5$
   B. $5 + 7 \times 2 - 5$
   C. $15 \div 3 + 7 \times (-3)$
   D. $10 \div 3 + 7 \times 2$

9. If $5 - 3 + 7 \times 4$ is meant to equal -35, which of the following shows the correct placement of parentheses?

   A. $5 - 3 + (7 \times 4)$
   B. $5(-3 + 7) \times 4$
   C. $(5 - 3) + 7 \times 4$
   D. $5 - (3 + 7) \times 4$

10. If $P = 6(9 + 3) - 2$ and $Q = 6 \times 9 + 3 - 2$, what is the value of $Q - P$?

    A. 15
    B. -15
    C. 5
    D. -5

Answers

1. **C.**

$$(-18) \div (+6) - (-9) = -(18 \div 6) - (-9)$$
$$= (-3) - (-9)$$
$$= (-3) + (+9)$$
$$= +(9 - 3)$$
$$= +6$$

2. **C.**

$$(-21) \times (+3) + (+84) \div (-12) = (-63) + (+84) \div (-12)$$
$$= (-63) + (-7)$$
$$= -70$$

3. **A.**

$$(-13) \times (+20) + (-35) + (-15) - (-48) \div (+16) = (-260) + (-35) + (-15) - (-48) \div (+16)$$
$$= (-260) + (-35) + (-15) - (-3)$$
$$= (-310) + (+3)$$
$$= -307$$

4. **D.**

$$(-17) + (-25) - (+31) + (+48) \times (-2) \div (-8) = (-17) + (-25) - (+31) + (-96) \div (-8)$$
$$= (-17) + (-25) - (+31) + (+12)$$
$$= (-73) + (+12)$$
$$= -61$$

5. **A.**

$$(-25) - (+18) \div (-6) \times (-21) - (-7) = (-25) - (-3) \times (-21) - (-7)$$
$$= (-25) - (+63) - (-7)$$
$$= (-88) + (+7)$$
$$= -81$$

6. **C.** Subtraction is adding the opposite, so $-53 - 16 = -53 + (-16) = -69$. The expressions in the other answer choices do not equal -69. Choice A = $+69$, choice B = 37, and choice D = -37.

7. **A.** Rewriting $42 - 19 + (-8)$ as $42 + (-19) + (-8)$ makes it easier to see the expression as addition of three integers and allows for regrouping:

$$42 - 19 + (-8) = 42 + (-19) + (-8)$$
$$= 42 + (-19 + -8)$$
$$= 42 + (-27)$$
$$= 42 - 27, \text{ choice A}$$

8. **B.** Choice B is correct because it looks from left to right for multiplication or division and does the first instance it finds. Choice A violates the order of operations because it puts addition before multiplication. Choice C and choice D both incorrectly subtract before multiplying and dividing.

9. **D.** Choice D is correct:

$$5 - (3 + 7) \times 4 = 5 - 10 \times 4$$
$$= 5 - 40$$
$$= -35$$

Choice A is incorrect: $5 - 3 + (7 \times 4) = 5 - 3 + 28 = 2 + 28 = 30 \neq -35$. Choice B is incorrect: $5(-3 + 7) \times 4 = 5(4) \times 4 = 20 \times 4 = 80 \neq -35$. Choice C is incorrect: $(5 - 3) + 7 \times 4 = 2 + 7 \times 4 = 2 + 28 = 30 \neq -35$.

10. **B.** First, solve for P and solve for Q:

$$P = 6(9+3)-2 \qquad Q = 6\times9+3-2$$
$$= 6(12)-2 \qquad\quad = 54+3-2$$
$$= 72-2 \qquad\qquad = 57-2$$
$$= 70 \qquad\qquad\quad = 55$$

Therefore, $Q - P = 55 - 70 = -15$.

B. Radicals

Rational numbers can be written as a fraction, but irrational numbers can't. If you change a rational number to a decimal, it will be either an integer, like -8, or a decimal that terminates, like 4.85, or a decimal that repeats a pattern, like 0.3333.... Any number whose decimal goes on forever but doesn't show a repeating pattern is an irrational number.

Perfect squares, like 16 or 81, have square roots that are integers. Some rational numbers have square roots that are rational. The square root of $\frac{4}{9}$ is $\frac{2}{3}$. But there are a great many numbers whose square roots are not rational. Since irrational numbers have messy decimals, it's more convenient and more exact to leave the number in radical form. We'd rather have $\sqrt{2}$ than 1.41421356....

Arithmetic with Radicals

When you need to add or subtract radical expressions, you add or subtract like radicals by adding or subtracting the coefficients that tell you how many of that radical you have:

$$5\sqrt{3} + 3\sqrt{3} = 8\sqrt{3} \qquad\qquad 6\sqrt{7} - 2\sqrt{7} = 4\sqrt{7}$$

But you can't add $\sqrt{5}$ to $\sqrt{11}$. They're unlike and can't be combined.

When you multiply or divide expressions involving radicals, multiply or divide numbers under the radical with numbers under the radical, and numbers outside the radical with numbers outside the radical:

$$4\sqrt{3} \cdot 5\sqrt{2} = 4\cdot5\cdot\sqrt{3}\cdot\sqrt{2} = 20\sqrt{3\cdot2} = 20\sqrt{6} \qquad\qquad \frac{10\sqrt{8}}{5\sqrt{2}} = \frac{10}{5}\cdot\frac{\sqrt{8}}{\sqrt{2}} = 2\sqrt{\frac{8}{2}} = 2\sqrt{4}$$

But notice that $\sqrt{4} = 2$, so $2\sqrt{4} = 2\cdot2 = 4$.

Simplifying

Because you can only add or subtract like radicals, it's important to put radicals in simplest form. Look for factors of the number under the radical that are perfect squares:

$$\sqrt{48} = \sqrt{16\cdot3}$$

Give each factor its own radical:

$$\sqrt{16}\cdot\sqrt{3}$$

Then, since you know $\sqrt{16} = 4$,

$$\sqrt{48} = \sqrt{16}\sqrt{3} = 4\sqrt{3}$$

To add $\sqrt{32} + \sqrt{50}$, simplify each radical:

$$\sqrt{32} = \sqrt{16}\sqrt{2} = 4\sqrt{2} \qquad\qquad \sqrt{50} = \sqrt{25}\sqrt{2} = 5\sqrt{2}$$

So, $\sqrt{32} + \sqrt{50} = 4\sqrt{2} + 5\sqrt{2} = 9\sqrt{2}$.

Dealing with Denominators

When you find that you have a radical in the denominator, like $\dfrac{5}{\sqrt{3}}$ or $\dfrac{\sqrt{3}}{\sqrt{5}}$, rationalize the denominator.

Multiply the numerator and denominator by the radical in the denominator:

$$\frac{5}{\sqrt{3}} \cdot \frac{\sqrt{3}}{\sqrt{3}} = \frac{5\sqrt{3}}{\sqrt{9}} = \frac{5\sqrt{3}}{3} \qquad\qquad \frac{\sqrt{3}}{\sqrt{5}} \cdot \frac{\sqrt{5}}{\sqrt{5}} = \frac{\sqrt{15}}{\sqrt{25}} = \frac{\sqrt{15}}{5}$$

The Human Calculator

Most people don't know the square root of 72,900, but if you look for factors of 72,900 that are perfect squares, you can probably figure it out:

$$\sqrt{72,900} = \sqrt{729 \cdot 100} = \sqrt{9 \cdot 81 \cdot 100} = \sqrt{9} \cdot \sqrt{81} \cdot \sqrt{100} = 3 \cdot 9 \cdot 10 = 27 \cdot 10 = 270$$

Practice

Directions: Choose the best answer from the choices provided.

1. Simplify: $\sqrt{27} + \sqrt{75}$.

    A. $\sqrt{102}$

    B. $3\sqrt{8}$

    C. $8\sqrt{3}$

    D. $15\sqrt{3}$

2. Simplify: $\sqrt{63} \cdot \sqrt{44}$.

    A. $6\sqrt{18}$

    B. $18\sqrt{6}$

    C. $77\sqrt{6}$

    D. $6\sqrt{77}$

3. Simplify: $\dfrac{9\sqrt{51}}{3\sqrt{17}}$.

    A. $3\sqrt{3}$

    B. $3\sqrt{34}$

    C. $6\sqrt{34}$

    D. $6\sqrt{3}$

4. Simplify: $\dfrac{5}{\sqrt{15}}$.

    A. $\dfrac{1}{\sqrt{3}}$

    B. $\dfrac{\sqrt{15}}{3}$

    C. $\sqrt{3}$

    D. $\dfrac{15}{\sqrt{3}}$

5. Simplify: $\sqrt{23,716}$.

   A. 154
   B. 176
   C. 298
   D. 539

6. Write $\sqrt{48}\sqrt{27}$ in simplest radical form.

   A. $12\sqrt{3}$
   B. $\sqrt{36}$
   C. $12\sqrt{6}$
   D. 36

7. Rationalize the denominator and simplify $\dfrac{18}{\sqrt{6}}$.

   A. $\sqrt{3}$
   B. $3\sqrt{6}$
   C. $18\sqrt{6}$
   D. 3

8. Write $\dfrac{\sqrt{28}}{\sqrt{98}}$ in simplest radical form.

   A. $\dfrac{\sqrt{14}}{7}$

   B. $\dfrac{2}{\sqrt{7}}$

   C. $\dfrac{2\sqrt{7}}{7}$

   D. $14\sqrt{7}$

9. The reciprocal of a number N is $\dfrac{1}{N}$. Find the reciprocal of $\sqrt{75}$ in simplest radical form.

   A. $\dfrac{\sqrt{75}}{75}$

   B. $\dfrac{\sqrt{3}}{3}$

   C. $\dfrac{\sqrt{3}}{15}$

   D. $5\sqrt{3}$

10. Express $\dfrac{\sqrt{3}}{2}+\dfrac{2}{\sqrt{3}}$ in simplest radical form.

   A. $\dfrac{7\sqrt{3}}{6}$

   B. $\dfrac{3\sqrt{3}}{5}$

   C. $\dfrac{\sqrt{3}}{2}$

   D. 1

Answers

1. **C.** First simplify each radical, and then add the coefficients of the like radicals:

$$\sqrt{27}+\sqrt{75}=\sqrt{9\cdot 3}+\sqrt{25\cdot 3}$$
$$=\sqrt{9}\cdot\sqrt{3}+\sqrt{25}\cdot\sqrt{3}$$
$$=3\sqrt{3}+5\sqrt{3}$$
$$=8\sqrt{3}$$

2. **D.** Again, simplify each radical before trying to multiply:

$$\sqrt{63} \cdot \sqrt{44} = \sqrt{9 \cdot 7} \cdot \sqrt{4 \cdot 11}$$
$$= \sqrt{9}\sqrt{7} \cdot \sqrt{4}\sqrt{11}$$
$$= 3\sqrt{7} \cdot 2\sqrt{11}$$
$$= 6\sqrt{77}$$

3. **A.** Divide the numbers outside the radicals, and then divide the numbers inside the radicals:

$$\frac{9\sqrt{51}}{3\sqrt{17}} = \frac{9}{3} \cdot \frac{\sqrt{51}}{\sqrt{17}}$$
$$= 3\sqrt{\frac{51}{17}}$$
$$= 3\sqrt{3}$$

4. **B.** Rationalize the denominator by multiplying by $\dfrac{\sqrt{15}}{\sqrt{15}}$. Then reduce the fraction:

$$\frac{5}{\sqrt{15}} = \frac{5}{\sqrt{15}} \cdot \frac{\sqrt{15}}{\sqrt{15}}$$
$$= \frac{5\sqrt{15}}{15}$$
$$= \frac{\sqrt{15}}{3}$$

5. **A.** Don't be discouraged by the size of the number; look for perfect square factors:

$$\sqrt{23,716} = \sqrt{4 \cdot 5,929}$$
$$= \sqrt{4 \cdot 7 \cdot 847}$$
$$= \sqrt{4 \cdot 7 \cdot 7 \cdot 121}$$
$$= \sqrt{4 \cdot 49 \cdot 121}$$

Take the square root of each perfect square and multiply:

$$\sqrt{4} \cdot \sqrt{49} \cdot \sqrt{121} = 2 \cdot 7 \cdot 11$$
$$= 154$$

6. **D.** Rather than multiplying 48 and 27 and trying to simplify the large product, express 48 and 27 in factored form.

$$\sqrt{48}\sqrt{27} = \sqrt{16 \times 3}\sqrt{9 \times 3}$$
$$= \sqrt{16 \times 3 \times 9 \times 3}$$
$$= \sqrt{16}\sqrt{3 \times 3}\sqrt{9}$$
$$= 4 \cdot 3 \cdot 3$$
$$= 36$$

7. **B.** Multiply the numerator and denominator by $\sqrt{6}$ to rationalize the denominator and then simplify.

$$\frac{18}{\sqrt{6}} \cdot \frac{\sqrt{6}}{\sqrt{6}} = \frac{18\sqrt{6}}{6}$$
$$= 3\sqrt{6}$$

8. **A.** It's your choice whether to start by simplifying or by rationalizing, but factoring will help keep the numbers small either way.

$$\frac{\sqrt{28}}{\sqrt{98}} = \sqrt{\frac{2 \cdot 2 \cdot 7}{2 \cdot 7 \cdot 7}}$$
$$= \sqrt{\frac{2}{7}}$$
$$= \frac{\sqrt{2}}{\sqrt{7}}$$
$$= \frac{\sqrt{2}}{\sqrt{7}} \cdot \frac{\sqrt{7}}{\sqrt{7}}$$
$$= \frac{\sqrt{14}}{7}$$

9. **C.** Rationalize the denominator, then simplify the radical in the numerator.

$$\frac{1}{\sqrt{75}} \cdot \frac{\sqrt{75}}{\sqrt{75}} = \frac{\sqrt{75}}{75}$$
$$= \frac{\sqrt{25 \cdot 3}}{75}$$
$$= \frac{5\sqrt{3}}{75}$$
$$= \frac{\sqrt{3}}{15}$$

10. **A.** You could find a common denominator involving a radical and rationalize later, but it's probably simpler to get radicals out of the denominator now. $\dfrac{2}{\sqrt{3}} \cdot \dfrac{\sqrt{3}}{\sqrt{3}} = \dfrac{2\sqrt{3}}{3}$ so

$$\frac{\sqrt{3}}{2} + \frac{2}{\sqrt{3}} = \frac{\sqrt{3}}{2} + \frac{2\sqrt{3}}{3}$$
$$= \frac{3\sqrt{3}}{6} + \frac{4\sqrt{3}}{6}$$
$$= \frac{7\sqrt{3}}{6}$$

C. Variable Expressions

An arithmetic expression is a statement involving numbers and one or more operations. An algebraic expression is a similar expression that involves one or more variables. It may be one number, one term, or more than one term. To evaluate an expression is to find the value of the expression when the variable is replaced with a particular number. To evaluate $3x + 5$ when $x = -2$, rewrite it with -2 in place of x, and do the arithmetic. If $x = -2$, then $3x + 5 = 3(-2) + 5 = -6 + 5 = -1$.

To evaluate $3x - y^3 + 2y$ when $x = 4$ and $y = 2$, replace x with 4 and y with 2; $3x - y^3 + 2y$ becomes $3(4) - (2)^3 + 2(2)$. Following the order of operations, tackle $(2)^3$ first, which gives you $3(4) - 8 + 2(2)$. Next do the multiplication: $3(4) - 8 + 2(2) = 12 - 8 + 4$. Don't jump over the subtraction to get to the addition. The correct way to complete the job is $12 - 8 + 4 = 4 + 4 = 8$.

Simplifying with Exponents

Whenever possible, you want to put variable expressions in simplest form. Generally, an expression is in simplest form when it has as few terms as possible and no parentheses.

Exponents are symbols for repeated multiplication, and they often show up in variable expressions. When you write b^n, you say that you want to use b as a factor n times. The expression 5^3, for example, means $5 \times 5 \times 5$. There are two special exponents you should remember:

- $a^0 = 1$ (provided $a \neq 0$)
- $a^1 = a$

When you're working with exponents, there are three basic rules to remember:

- **When you multiply powers of the same base, keep the base and add the exponents.** To simplify $x^7 \cdot y^3 \cdot x^5$, rearrange and multiply the powers of x by keeping the base and adding the exponents: $x^7 \cdot x^5 \cdot y^3 = x^{12} \cdot y^3$. You cannot apply the rule to different bases, so it isn't possible to simplify any further.

- **When you divide powers of the same base, keep the base and subtract the exponents.** The expression $\dfrac{7^{10} \cdot 5^{12}}{7^6 \cdot 5^4}$ can be simplified using the division rule. The rules for exponents only work for powers of the same base, so there is nothing that can be done to $7^{10} \cdot 5^{12}$ or $7^6 \cdot 5^4$. Instead, divide 7^{10} by 7^6, keeping the base of 7 and subtracting the exponent of the denominator from the exponent in the numerator: $7^{10} \div 7^6 = 7^{(10-6)} = 7^4$. Then divide 5^{12} by 5^4, keeping the base of 5 and subtracting the exponents: $5^{12} \div 5^4 = 5^{(12-4)} = 5^8$. The simplest form is $7^4 \cdot 5^8$.

- **When you raise a power to a power, keep the base and multiply the exponents.** So, $(5^{12})^2 = 5^{(12)(2)} = 5^{24}$ and $(25)^{12}$ could be written as $(5^2)^{12}$ and also simplified to $(5^2)^{12} = 5^{24}$.

Practice

Directions: Choose the best answer from the choices provided.

1. Evaluate $x - 7(y + 3z)$ when $x = 4$, $y = 2$, and $z = 3$.

   A. 3
   B. −1
   C. −33
   D. −73

2. Evaluate $(x + z)^2 + 4y$ when $x = 4$, $y = 2$, and $z = 3$.

   A. 57
   B. 48
   C. 21
   D. 20

3. Evaluate $-t^2$ when $t = 5$.

   A. −10
   B. 10
   C. −25
   D. 25

4. Simplify: $(3xy^2)(5x^2y)$.

   A. $8x^2y^2$
   B. $8x^3y^3$
   C. $15x^2y^2$
   D. $15x^3y^3$

5. Simplify: $\dfrac{15x^2y^3z}{5xyz^2}$.

   A. $3x^2y^3z^2$
   B. $10xy^2z$
   C. $\dfrac{10xy^2}{z}$
   D. $\dfrac{3xy^2}{z}$

6. Evaluate $\dfrac{6-5a}{(2-b)^2}$ if $a = -2$ and $b = 4$.

   A. 4
   B. $-\dfrac{1}{2}$
   C. −1
   D. −4

7. Simplify: $(3x - 7) + (2 - 6x) - 5x$.

   A. $-8x - 5$
   B. $-8x - 9$
   C. $-14x - 5$
   D. $-14x + 9$

8. Evaluate $-16t^2 + 40t + 7$ when $t = \dfrac{1}{4}$.

   A. 13
   B. 16
   C. 18
   D. 33

9. If $x = -7$ and $y = -5$, which of the following is true?

   A. $x^2y^3 = x^3y^2$
   B. $x^2y^3 > x^3y^2$
   C. $x^2y^3 < x^3y^2$
   D. $|x^2y^3| = |x^3y^2|$

10. If $\dfrac{\left(a^3b^2\right)^2}{a^4b^3}$ is equal to 20, and $a = -2$, which of these could be the value of b?

   A. −5
   B. $\dfrac{1}{80}$
   C. $\sqrt{5}$
   D. 5

Answers

1. **D.**

$$x - 7(y + 3z) = 4 - 7(2 + 3 \times 3)$$
$$= 4 - 7(2 + 9)$$
$$= 4 - 7(11)$$
$$= 4 - 77$$
$$= -73$$

2. **A.**

$$(x + z)^2 + 4y = (4 + 3)^2 + 4 \times 2$$
$$= (7)^2 + 4 \times 2$$
$$= 49 + 4 \times 2$$
$$= 49 + 8$$
$$= 57$$

3. **C.** The expression -5^2 is the opposite of 5^2. The order of operations says that exponents operate before multiplication, so in -5^2, which can be thought of as -1×5^2, square 5 first: $-5^2 = -(5 \times 5) = -25$.

4. **D.** $(3xy^2)(5x^2y) = 3 \times 5 \cdot x \cdot x^2 \cdot y^2 \cdot y = 15x^3y^3$

5. **D.** $\dfrac{15x^2y^3z}{5xyz^2} = \dfrac{15}{5} \cdot \dfrac{x^2}{x} \cdot \dfrac{y^3}{y} \cdot \dfrac{z}{z^2} = 3 \cdot x \cdot y^2 \cdot \dfrac{1}{z} = \dfrac{3xy^2}{z}$

6. **A.** If $a = -2$ and $b = 4$, then $\dfrac{6 - 5a}{(2 - b)^2} = \dfrac{6 - 5(-2)}{(2 - 4)^2} = \dfrac{6 + 10}{(-2)^2} = \dfrac{16}{4} = 4$.

7. **A.** Rearrange if helpful and combine like terms.

$$(3x - 7) + (2 - 6x) - 5x = 3x - 7 + 2 - 6x - 5x$$
$$= 3x - 6x - 5x - 7 + 2$$
$$= -8x - 5$$

8. **B.** If $t = \dfrac{1}{4}$, then

$$-16t^2 + 40t + 7 = -16\left(\dfrac{1}{4}\right)^2 + 40\left(\dfrac{1}{4}\right) + 7$$
$$= -16\left(\dfrac{1}{16}\right) + 40\left(\dfrac{1}{4}\right) + 7$$
$$= -1 + 10 + 7$$
$$= 16$$

9. **B.** If $x = -7$ and $y = -5$, $x^2y^3 = (-7)^2 \cdot (-5)^3 = 49(-125) = -6{,}125$ and $x^3y^2 = (-7)^3 \cdot (-5)^2 = -343(25) = -8{,}575$. Now that you know the values of x^2y^3 and x^3y^2, test the answer choices, starting with choice A.

Choice A: $-6{,}125 \neq -8{,}575$, so $x^2y^3 = x^3y^2$ is NOT a true statement.

Choice B: $-6{,}125 > -8{,}575$. Because $-6{,}125$ is less negative than $-8{,}575$, $x^2y^3 > x^3y^2$ is the true statement. There is no need to continue checking the other answer choices.

10. **D.** Simplify first: $\dfrac{\left(a^3b^2\right)^2}{a^4b^3} = \dfrac{a^6b^4}{a^4b^3} = a^2b = (-2)^2\,b = 4b$. If $4b = 20$, then $b = 5$.

D. Solving Equations and Inequalities

Linear equations and inequalities are mathematical sentences that contain variables and constants. The verb in an equation is the equal sign, and in an inequality, it's the less than ($<$) or greater than ($>$) symbol. Linear equations and inequalities take their names from the fact that when two variables are involved, as in the equation $y = 3x + 2$, their graphs are lines, but more on that later.

Simplify Before Solving

Before you begin the actual work of solving an equation, you'll want to make the equation as simple as possible. Focus on one side of the equation at a time, and if parentheses or other grouping symbols are present, remove them by simplifying the expression inside the parentheses or by using the distributive property. If the parentheses are not necessary, just remove them. So, $5(x + 3) = 4 - (5 - x)$ becomes $5x + 15 = 4 - 5 + x$.

Once parentheses have been cleared, combine like terms (and *only* like terms) before you begin solving. Never begin solving with more than two terms on either side of the equal sign. So, $5x + 15 = 4 - 5 + x$ becomes $5x + 15 = -1 + x$.

Isolating the Variable

In solving an equation, your job is to undo the arithmetic that has been performed and get the variable isolated on one side of the equation. Since you're undoing, you do the opposite of what has been done. To keep the equation balanced, you perform the same operation on both sides of the equation.

If there are variable terms on both sides of the equation, add or subtract to eliminate one of them. Next, add or subtract to eliminate the constant term that is on the same side as the variable term. You want to have one variable term equal to one constant term. Finally, divide both sides by the coefficient of the variable term.

In the equation $5x + 15 = -1 + x$, there are variables on both sides. To isolate the variable, start by subtracting x from both sides. Next, remove the constant from the side that has a variable by subtracting 15 from both sides. Finally, divide both sides by 4 to isolate the variable and solve for x:

$$5x + 15 = -1 + x$$
$$5x - x + 15 = -1 + x - x \qquad \text{Subtract } x \text{ from both sides.}$$
$$4x + 15 = -1$$
$$4x + 15 - 15 = -1 - 15 \qquad \text{Subtract 15 from both sides.}$$
$$4x = -16$$
$$4x \div 4 = -16 \div 4 \qquad \text{Divide both sides by 4 to solve for } x.$$
$$x = -4$$

Absolute Value Equations

When an equation has a variable inside absolute value bars, the expression in the absolute value bars could have originally been positive or negative. If $|x| = 7$, x could have been 7 or -7. Each absolute value equation will become two equations and will have two solutions. The expression between the absolute value bars may be equal to the number on the other side of the equal sign, or it may be equal to the opposite of that number. To solve $|3x + 9| = 21$, break it into two equations and solve each equation separately to find the two possible values for x:

$$|3x + 9| = 21$$

$$3x + 9 = 21 \quad \text{or} \quad 3x + 9 = -21$$
$$3x = 12 \quad\quad\quad\quad\quad 3x = -30$$
$$x = 4 \quad\quad\quad\quad\quad\quad x = -10$$

Don't be in a rush to break into two equations. Make sure that the equation is just an absolute value equals a number before you look at the two cases. If there is anything added or subtracted outside the absolute value, eliminate it first, and then consider the two cases.

Practice

Directions: Choose the best answer from the choices provided.

1. Solve for x: $3(x - 5) + 4(2x - 1) = 47$.

   A. $x = -13.2$
   B. $x = -5.6$
   C. $x = 1$
   D. $x = 6$

2. Solve for a: $(6 + a) - (5 - 2a) = -2$.

   A. $a = -13$
   B. $a = -3$
   C. $a = -1$
   D. $a = -\dfrac{1}{3}$

3. Solve for x: $|x + 1| = 2$.

   A. $x = 1$ or $x = -1$
   B. $x = 1$ or $x = -3$
   C. $x = 3$ or $x = -1$
   D. $x = 3$ or $x = -3$

4. Solve for x: $|3 - x| = 5$.

   A. $x = 2$ or $x = -2$
   B. $x = 2$ or $x = -8$
   C. $x = -2$ or $x = 8$
   D. $x = 8$ or $x = -8$

5. Solve for x: $|2x + 5| - 4 = 7$.

   A. $x = 4$ or $x = -4$
   B. $x = 3$ or $x = -3$
   C. $x = 3$ or $x = -4$
   D. $x = 3$ or $x = -8$

6. Solve for x: $9 - 2x = 5(x - 1)$.

   A. $x = -4\dfrac{2}{3}$
   B. $x = 1$
   C. $x = 1\dfrac{1}{3}$
   D. $x = 2$

7. Seven less than a certain number is equal to three times the number. Find the number.

   A. $-3\dfrac{1}{2}$
   B. $-1\dfrac{3}{4}$
   C. $1\dfrac{3}{4}$
   D. 28

8. While shopping for 6 notebooks, you notice that the store is offering a multipack of 4 notebooks for $10. If you buy 1 multipack and 2 additional single notebooks at regular price, you will spend $2 less than if you bought 6 single notebooks. What is the regular price of a single notebook?

   A. $2.00
   B. $2.50
   C. $3.00
   D. $7.00

9. In 2017, Mr. Johnson donated $120 to his school's annual fundraiser. He donated again in 2018 and the difference between the two donations was $30. Which of these describes Mr. Johnson's 2018 donation?

   A. He donated either $45 or $75.
   B. He donated $60.
   C. He donated either $90 or $150.
   D. He donated $240.

10. Janelle runs 5 miles every day. Ayanna runs every day, but her distance varies. Yesterday, the difference between Janelle's distance and twice Ayanna's distance was 3 miles less than Ayanna's distance. Which of these describes the distance Ayanna ran yesterday?

   A. $2\frac{2}{3}$ miles or 8 miles
   B. 2 miles or $2\frac{2}{3}$ miles
   C. 4 miles
   D. 8 miles

Answers

1. **D.** Distribute first, then combine like terms and isolate the variable:

$$3(x-5)+4(2x-1)=47$$
$$3x-15+8x-4=47$$
$$11x-19=47$$
$$11x=66$$
$$x=6$$

2. **C.** In $(6 + a) - (5 - 2a) = -2$, notice that $(5 - 2a)$ is preceded by a minus sign, which changes all the signs. The equation becomes $6 + a - 5 + 2a = -2$. Combine like terms and isolate the variable to solve for a:

$$6+a-5+2a=-2$$
$$1+3a=-2$$
$$3a=-3$$
$$a=-1$$

3. **B.** If $x + 1 = 2$, $x = 1$. If $x + 1 = -2$, $x = -3$.

4. **C.** If $3 - x = 5$, $-x = 2$ and $x = -2$. If $3 - x = -5$, $-x = -8$ and $x = 8$.

5. **D.** To solve $|2x + 5| - 4 = 7$, first add 4 to each side so that the absolute value is isolated, then break it into two equations and solve each equation separately to find the two possible values for x:

$$|2x+5|-4=7$$
$$|2x+5|=11$$

$2x+5=11$	or	$2x+5=-11$
$2x=6$		$2x=-16$
$x=3$		$x=-8$

6. **D.** To solve $9 - 2x = 5(x - 1)$, distribute, then isolate the variable and solve for x: Distribute: $9 - 2x = 5(x - 1)$ becomes $9 - 2x = 5x - 5$. Add $2x$ to both sides and add 5 to both sides. If $9 - 2x = 5x - 5$, then $9 = 7x - 5$ and $14 = 7x$. Divide by 7 and $x = 2$.

$$9-2x=5(x-1)$$
$$9-2x=5x-5$$
$$9=7x-5$$
$$14=7x$$
$$2=x$$

7. **A.** Seven less than a certain number is equal to three times the number. Let x = the number. Translate: $x - 7 = 3x$. Isolate the variable and solve:

$$x-7=3x$$
$$-7=2x$$
$$-3\frac{1}{2}=x$$

8. **C.** 1 multipack and 2 additional single notebooks at regular price = \$2 less than 6 single notebooks. Translate: $\$10 + 2x = 6x - \$2$. Isolate the variable and solve for x:

$$10+2x=6x-2$$
$$10=4x-2$$
$$12=4x$$
$$3=x$$

The regular price of a notebook is \$3.

9. **C.** Let x = the 2018 donation. We don't know which donation was larger, so write $|x - 120| = 30$. Break into two equations and solve both for x:

$$|x-120|=30$$

$x-120=30$	or	$x-120=-30$
$x=150$		$x=90$

He donated either \$90 or \$150.

10. **B.** Let x = Ayanna's distance yesterday. Janelle runs 5 miles every day. We do not know which distance is greater, so use absolute value bars around the subtraction when you translate.

The difference between Janelle's distance and twice Ayanna's distance was 3 miles less than Ayanna's distance. The difference between 5 and $2x$ = 3 miles less than x. Translate:

$$|5 - 2x| = x - 3$$

To solve, break into two equations and solve both for x:

$$5 - 2x = x - 3 \quad \text{or} \quad 5 - 2x = -(x - 3)$$
$$5 = 3x - 3 \qquad\qquad 5 - 2x = -x + 3$$
$$8 = 3x \qquad\qquad\qquad 5 = x + 3$$
$$\frac{8}{3} = x \qquad\qquad\qquad\quad 2 = x$$
$$2\frac{2}{3} = x$$

Ayanna ran 2 miles or $2\frac{2}{3}$ miles.

Solving Inequalities

The rules for solving inequalities are the same as those for solving equations, except at the last step. When you divide both sides of an inequality by the coefficient of the variable term, you have to make a decision about the inequality sign. If you multiply or divide both sides of an inequality by a negative number, reverse the direction of the inequality sign. So, if you divide by a negative number, a < sign will become a > sign, and a > sign will become a < sign. If you divide both sides of an inequality by a positive number, leave the inequality sign is as is.

To solve $5t - 9 \le 8t + 15$, subtract $8t$ from both sides. Next, add 9 to both sides to isolate the variable. Divide both sides by -3 to solve for t. Since you're dividing by a negative number, reverse the direction of the inequality sign in your solution:

$$5t - 9 \le 8t + 15$$
$$5t - 8t \le 8t + 15 - 8t \qquad \text{Subtract } 8t \text{ from both sides.}$$
$$-3t - 9 \le 15$$
$$-3t - 9 + 9 \le 15 + 9 \qquad \text{Add 9 to both sides.}$$
$$-3t \le 24$$
$$\frac{-3t}{-3} \le \frac{24}{-3} \qquad\qquad \text{Divide both sides by } -3.$$
$$t \ge -8 \qquad\qquad\qquad \text{Reverse the direction of the inequality sign since you divided by a}$$
$$\text{negative number.}$$

Compound Inequalities

A compound inequality is simply two inequalities compressed into one statement. If you know that the value of x is greater than 3 but less than 9, you could write $x > 3$ and $x < 9$, or you could compress that information into the statement $3 < x < 9$.

If you're asked to solve a compound inequality, simply break it into its two components, and solve each inequality separately. Then, if you want, you can compress the two answers into a compound inequality. To solve $-5 < 2x - 3 < 7$, rewrite the compound inequality as two inequalities and solve:

$$-5 < 2x - 3 < 7$$

$$-5 < 2x - 3 \quad \text{and} \quad 2x - 3 < 7$$
$$-2 < 2x \qquad\qquad 2x < 10$$
$$-1 < x \qquad\qquad x < 5$$
$$-1 < x < 5$$

There is another type of compound inequality, which is two inequalities connected by the word *or*. An example of this style of compound inequality is $3x - 5 < 7$ or $2x + 1 > 9$. This type has no compressed form, so you just solve each inequality and connect the solutions with the word *or*:

$$3x - 5 < 7 \quad \text{or} \quad 2x + 1 > 9$$
$$3x < 12 \qquad\qquad 2x > 8$$
$$x < 4 \qquad\qquad x > 4$$

Absolute Value Inequalities

When you have an equation with a variable inside the absolute value bars, you have to deal with it as two equations: one in which the expression within the absolute value bars is positive and one in which that expression is negative. Faced with an absolute value inequality, you have to use a similar strategy, but the direction of the less-than and greater-than signs can be confusing.

For an inequality in which the absolute value is less than a number, like $|x| < 7$, the expression in the absolute value bars is less than 7 and greater than its opposite. This means $-7 < x < 7$. Applied to a more complicated inequality, this means that $|x + 7| < 3$ is equivalent to $-3 < x + 7 < 3$. You can break that into two inequalities and solve each separately: $-3 < x + 7$ tells you that $-10 < x$ and $x + 7 < 3$ means $x < -4$. So the solution is $-10 < x < -4$.

An inequality in which the absolute value is greater than a number, like $|x| > 5$, also translates to a compound inequality, but in this case the compound inequality is two inequalities joined by *or*. If $|x| > 5$, x may be greater than 5, or it may be less than -5 (like -6, or -13.) The inequality $|x| > 5$ becomes $x > 5$ or $x < -5$.

Practice

Directions: Choose the best answer from the choices provided.

1. Solve for t: $-8 + 9t > 10t - 23$.

    A. $t < -15$
    B. $t > -15$
    C. $t < 15$
    D. $t > 15$

2. Solve for y: $9y - 6 > 2y + 15$.

    A. $y > 3$
    B. $y < -3$
    C. $y > 15$
    D. $y < 15$

3. Solve for b: $-7 < 2b - 11 < 5$.

   A. $-9 < b < 3$
   B. $-9 < b < 8$
   C. $2 < b < 8$
   D. $2 < b < 3$

4. Solve for x: $|15 - 3x| > 6$.

   A. $3 < x < 7$
   B. $x < 3$ or $x > 7$
   C. $-7 < x < -3$
   D. $x < 7$ or $x > 3$

5. Solve for x: $|5x - 3| \le 7$.

   A. $-2 \le x \le 0.8$
   B. $-0.8 \le x \le 0.8$
   C. $-2 \le x \le 2$
   D. $-0.8 \le x \le 2$

6. Mr. Cook went into the doughnut shop with $10. He got 6 doughnuts and left a $1 tip for the counter person, and still left with between $1 and $2 change from the $10 bill. Which of these could be the price of one doughnut?

   A. $1.50
   B. $1.20
   C. $1.00
   D. $0.75

7. If Elise buys 8 cans of cat food and uses a coupon that gives her $1.50 off, she will pay less than the regular cost of 6 cans of that cat food. Which of these could be the regular price of one can of cat food?

   A. $0.59
   B. $0.75
   C. $0.89
   D. $1.29

8. On one of Mr. Malcolm's tests, students could score 3 points for each correctly answered multiple-choice question and 15 points for the essay. On that test, every student earned full credit for the essay, and total scores ranged from 60 to 90 points. Which of these is the best description of the number, x, of multiple-choice questions students answered correctly?

   A. $15 < x < 25$
   B. $20 < x < 30$
   C. $45 < x < 75$
   D. $55 < x < 85$

9. On the day that Jane went strawberry picking, each person picked an average of 78 strawberries. The difference between the number of strawberries Jane picked and the average number was more than 12. How many strawberries did Jane pick?

   A. Between 12 and 66 strawberries
   B. Fewer than 12 or more than 78 strawberries
   C. Between 66 and 90 strawberries
   D. Fewer than 66 or more than 90 strawberries

10. Appleton, Bluffton, and Compton are three towns within driving distance of one another and not all on the same line. Starting from Appleton, the difference between the driving time to Bluffton and the driving time to Compton is less than the time it takes to drive from Bluffton to Compton. If it takes 5 hours to drive from Appleton to Bluffton and 2 hours to drive from Bluffton to Compton, what can you say about the time to drive from Appleton to Compton?

    A. Between 2 and 5 hours
    B. Between 2 and 7 hours
    C. Between 3 and 5 hours
    D. Between 3 and 7 hours

Answers

1. **C.** Isolate the variable. First, subtract $10t$ from both sides. Next, add 8 to both sides to isolate the variable. Finally, divide both sides by -1 to solve for t. Remember to reverse the inequality symbol since you're dividing by a negative number:

$$-8+9t>10t-23$$
$$-8-t>-23$$
$$-t>-15$$
$$t<15$$

2. **A.** Isolate the variable. First, subtract $2y$ from both sides, and then add 6 to both sides. Divide both sides by 7 to solve for y. The divisor is positive, so the inequality symbol remains the same.

$$9y-6>2y+15$$
$$7y-6>15$$
$$7y>21$$
$$y>3$$

3. **C.** Rewrite the compound inequality as two inequalities and solve each for b. You can then compress the two solutions into a compound inequality:

$$-7<2b-11<5$$

$$-7<2b-11 \qquad \text{and} \qquad 2b-11<5$$
$$4<2b \qquad\qquad\qquad 2b<16$$
$$2<b \qquad\qquad\qquad b<8$$

$$2<b<8$$

4. **B.** If $|15-3x|>6$, it's possible that $15-3x>6$ or that $15-3x<-6$. Solve each inequality.

$$|15-3x|>6$$

$$15-3x>6 \qquad \text{or} \qquad 15-3x<-6$$
$$-3x>-9 \qquad\qquad\qquad -3x<-21$$
$$x<3 \qquad\qquad\qquad x>7$$

5. **D.** Translate $|5x-3|\le 7$ into $-7\le 5x-3\le 7$, which in turn translates to $-7\le 5x-3$ and $5x-3\le 7$. Solve each inequality for x. You can then compress the two solutions into a compound inequality.

$$|5x-3|\le 7$$
$$-7\le 5x-3\le 7$$

$$-7\le 5x-3 \qquad \text{and} \qquad 5x-3\le 7$$
$$-4\le 5x \qquad\qquad\qquad 5x\le 10$$
$$-\frac{4}{5}\le x \qquad\qquad\qquad x\le 2$$
$$-0.8\le x$$

$$-0.8\le x\le 2$$

6. **B.** Let x = the price of a doughnut. He spent $6x$ for doughnuts + \$1 for a tip. His change was \$10 − (6x + 1) and that was more than \$1 but less than \$2.

$$1 < 10 - (6x + 1) < 2$$
$$1 < 10 - 6x - 1 < 2$$
$$1 < 9 - 6x < 2$$
$$-8 < -6x < -7$$
$$\frac{8}{6} > x > \frac{7}{6}$$
$$1.33 > x > 1.17$$

The price of a doughnut must be between \$1.17 and \$1.33. The correct answer is choice B, \$1.20.

7. **A.** Let x = the regular price of a can of cat food. Translate the information given: $8x - 1.50 < 6x$, so $2x - 1.50 < 0$ and $2x < 1.50$. Therefore $x < 0.75$. The regular price of a can of cat food is less than 75 cents. It cannot be equal to \$0.75, because \$0.75 makes the two sides equal. The correct answer is choice A, \$0.59.

8. **A.** Let x = the number of multiple choice questions answered correctly. $60 < 3x + 15 < 90$, so $45 < 3x < 75$ which simplifies to $15 < x < 25$. Students answered between 15 and 25 multiple-choice questions correctly.

9. **D.** Let x = the number of strawberries Jane picked. $|x - 78| > 12$ Rewrite as a compound inequality and solve.

$$-12 > x - 78 > 12$$

$$-12 > x - 78 \qquad \text{or} \qquad x - 78 > 12$$
$$66 > x \qquad\qquad\qquad\qquad x > 90$$

Either Jane picked fewer than 66 strawberries (and her harvest was below average) or she picked more than 90 strawberries (and was above average).

10. **D.** The difference between the Appleton-to-Bluffton drive, AB, and the Appleton-to-Compton drive, AC, is less than the Bluffton-to-Compton drive, BC, means that the absolute value of $AB - AC < BC$.

$$|AB - AC| < BC$$
$$|5 - x| < 2$$
$$-2 < 5 - x < 2$$
$$-7 < -x < -3$$
$$7 > x > 3$$

The driving time between Appleton and Compton is between 3 and 7 hours.

E. Systems of Linear Equations

A system of equations is a set of two (or more) equations with two (or more) variables. The solution of a system of equations is a set of values that make all the equations in the system true. A system of equations may have one solution, no solution, or infinitely many solutions.

If there's more than one variable in an equation, you usually can't solve for the numerical value of each variable. Solving a system of equations requires that you eliminate all but one variable and solve for the variable remaining. Once you have found the value of one variable, you can substitute to find the other.

Substitution

To solve a system by substitution, choose one equation and isolate one variable. Turn to the other equation and replace the variable with the expression you now know is equivalent. This should give you an equation involving only one variable, which you can solve. When you know the value of one variable, choose one of the original equations, replace the known variable by its value, and solve for the variable remaining.

To solve $\begin{cases} 3x - y = -15 \\ 5x + 2y = -14 \end{cases}$, isolate y in the first equation:

$$3x - y = -15$$
$$-y = -3x - 15 \qquad \text{Subtract } 3x \text{ from both sides to isolate } y.$$
$$y = 3x + 15 \qquad \text{Multiply both sides by } -1 \text{ to make } y \text{ positive.}$$

Replace y with $3x + 15$ in the second equation, and solve for x:

$$5x + 2y = -14$$
$$5x + 2(3x + 15) = -14$$
$$5x + 6x + 30 = -14 \qquad \text{Distribute.}$$
$$11x + 30 = -14 \qquad \text{Combine like terms.}$$
$$11x = -44 \qquad \text{Subtract 30 from both sides to isolate } x.$$
$$x = -4 \qquad \text{Divide both sides by 11.}$$

Now that you know the value of x, substitute that value into one of the original equations to solve for y. Let's use the first equation:

$$3x - y = -15$$
$$3(-4) - y = -15 \qquad \text{Substitute } -4 \text{ for } x \text{ and multiply.}$$
$$-12 - y = -15$$
$$-y = -3 \qquad \text{Add 12 to both sides to isolate } y.$$
$$y = 3 \qquad \text{Multiply both sides by } -1 \text{ to make } y \text{ positive.}$$

The solution of the system is $x = -4$, $y = 3$.

Elimination

The elimination method of solving a system uses addition or subtraction to eliminate one of the variables. If the coefficient of one variable is the same in both equations, subtracting one equation from the other will eliminate that variable. If the coefficients are opposites, adding will eliminate the variable. When you've eliminated one variable, solve and then use substitution to find the value of the other variable.

To solve $\begin{cases} 8a - 2b = 18 \\ 3a + 2b = -7 \end{cases}$, add the equations to eliminate b:

$$8a - 2b = 18$$
$$\underline{3a + 2b = -7}$$
$$11a \quad = 11$$

Solving the equation tells you that $a = 1$. Substitute 1 for a in the second equation, and solve for b:

$$3a + 2b = -7$$
$$3(1) + 2b = -7$$
$$2b = -10$$
$$b = -5$$

Elimination with Multiplication

If neither adding nor subtracting will eliminate a variable, you can multiply one or both equations by a constant to produce matching coefficients. Choose the variable you want to eliminate, and then multiply each equation by the coefficient of that variable from the other equation.

To solve $\begin{cases} 3x + 4y = -34 \\ 2x - 5y = 31 \end{cases}$, make the coefficients of y match by multiplying the first equation by 5 and the

second equation by 4. So,

$$\begin{cases} 5(3x + 4y = -34) \\ 4(2x - 5y = 31) \end{cases} \quad \text{becomes} \quad \begin{cases} 15x + 20y = -170 \\ 8x - 20y = 124 \end{cases}$$

Then add the equations to eliminate y:

$$15x + 20y = -170$$
$$\underline{8x - 20y = \;\; 124}$$
$$23x = -46$$
$$x = -2$$

Substitute for x in one of the equations to solve for y:

$$3x + 4y = -34$$
$$3(-2) + 4y = -34$$
$$-6 + 4y = -34$$
$$4y = -28$$
$$y = -7$$

Practice

Directions: Choose the best answer from the choices provided.

1. Solve: $\begin{cases} y = 2x - 1 \\ x + y = 14 \end{cases}$.

   A. $x = 5, y = 9$
   B. $x = 5, y = 11$
   C. $x = 7.5, y = 6.5$
   D. $x = 15, y = -1$

2. Solve: $\begin{cases} x + y = 4 \\ x - y = 2 \end{cases}$.

   A. $x = 4, y = 2$
   B. $x = 3, y = 1$
   C. $x = 2, y = -4$
   D. $x = 1, y = 3$

3. Solve: $\begin{cases} 2x + y = 1 \\ x - y = -7 \end{cases}$.

   A. $x = -2, y = 9$
   B. $x = -2, y = 5$
   C. $x = -6, y = 1$
   D. $x = 8, y = 1$

4. Solve: $\begin{cases} 2x + y = -5 \\ 3x - y = -10 \end{cases}$.

   A. $x = -3, y = 1$
   B. $x = 1, y = 3$
   C. $x = 3, y = -1$
   D. $x = 5, y = -10$

5. Solve: $\begin{cases} 3x - 2y = -23 \\ 2x + y = 1 \end{cases}$.

   A. $x = 3, y = 16$
   B. $x = -3, y = 7$
   C. $x = -3, y = 2$
   D. $x = 3, y = -5$

6. If 2 doughnuts and 3 muffins cost $4.90 and 6 doughnuts and 1 muffin cost $5.10, find the cost of 1 doughnut and the cost of 1 muffin.

   A. A doughnut costs $0.50 and a muffin costs $1.30.
   B. A doughnut costs $0.50 and a muffin costs $2.10.
   C. A doughnut costs $0.60 and a muffin costs $1.50.
   D. A doughnut costs $0.65 and a muffin costs $1.20.

7. In her campaign for town council, Luisa gave out buttons and stickers. For one campaign event she spent $4.75 for 15 buttons and 20 stickers. For another event, she spent $8.25 for 25 buttons and 40 stickers. Find the cost of 1 button and the cost of 1 sticker.

   A. A button costs $0.13 and a sticker costs $0.14.
   B. A button costs $0.17 and a sticker costs $0.10.
   C. A button costs $0.21 and a sticker costs $0.08.
   D. A button costs $0.25 and a sticker costs $0.05.

8. When arranging travel for field trips, a school can hire a combination of buses and vans. For one trip, the school used 3 buses and 1 van to seat exactly 142 people. On another occasion, they hired 5 buses and 3 vans to seat exactly 246 people. How many seats are in each bus, and how many seats are in each van?

   A. There are 45 seats in each bus and 7 seats in each van.
   B. There are 21 seats in each bus and 8 seats in each van.
   C. There are 17 seats in each bus and 10 seats in each van.
   D. There are 17 seats in each bus and 11 seats in each van.

9. At a sale, all dresses were sold for the same price. There was also one price for all skirts, although a different price than the dresses. Karen bought 3 dresses and 2 skirts and paid $142, while Evelyn bought 1 dress and 3 skirts and paid $101. Find the price of a dress and the price of a skirt.

   A. A dress cost $30 and a skirt cost $26.
   B. A dress cost $32 and a skirt cost $23.
   C. A dress cost $35 and a skirt cost $22.
   D. A dress cost $38 and a skirt cost $21.

10. Mr. Costello's auto shop offers a routine maintenance special for which all tires are the same price and all hoses are the same price. Jeff took his car for service and needed 2 tires and 2 hoses. His bill was $120. Alan's car needed 4 tires and 2 hoses and his bill was $210. Find the price of a tire and the price of a hose.

   A. Tires cost $26 each and hoses cost $34 each.
   B. Tires cost $45 each and hoses cost $15 each.
   C. Tires cost $47 each and hoses cost $11 each.
   D. Tires cost $48 each and hoses cost $12 each.

Answers

1. **A.** Use the first equation to substitute $2x - 1$ for y in the second equation. So, $x + 2x - 1 = 14$ becomes $3x - 1 = 14$. Add 1 to both sides for $3x = 15$. Dividing by 3 gives $x = 5$. Return to the first equation, replacing x with 5. From this, $y = 2(5) - 1 = 9$.

$$
\begin{array}{ll}
\text{Solve for } x: & \text{Solve for } y: \\
x + y = 14 & y = 2x - 1 \\
x + 2x - 1 = 14 & y = 2(5) - 1 \\
3x - 1 = 14 & y = 10 - 1 \\
3x = 15 & y = 9 \\
x = 5 &
\end{array}
$$

2. **B.** Adding the equations eliminates y and leaves $2x = 6$ or $x = 3$. Substituting 3 for x in the first equation yields $3 + y = 4$. Subtract 3 from both sides for $y = 1$.

$$
\begin{array}{ll}
\text{Solve for } x: & \text{Solve for } y: \\
x + y = 4 & x + y = 4 \\
\underline{x - y = 2} & 3 + y = 4 \\
2x \quad = 6 & y = 1 \\
x = 3 &
\end{array}
$$

3. **B.** Add the equations to eliminate y and you have the equation $3x = -6$, so $x = -2$. Substituting -2 for x in the second equation tells you that $-2 - y = -7$ and $y = 5$.

$$
\begin{array}{ll}
\text{Solve for } x: & \text{Solve for } y: \\
2x + y = 1 & x - y = -7 \\
\underline{x - y = -7} & -2 - y = -7 \\
3x \quad = -6 & -y = -5 \\
x = -2 & y = 5
\end{array}
$$

4. **A.** Adding the equations eliminates y and leaves $5x = -15$, or $x = -3$. Substituting -3 for x in the first equation gives you $2(-3) + y = -5$. Then $-6 + y = -5$, and adding 6 to both sides gives $y = 1$.

$$\begin{array}{ll}
\text{Solve for } x: & \text{Solve for } y: \\
2x + y = -5 & 2x + y = -5 \\
\underline{3x - y = -10} & 2(-3) + y = -5 \\
5x \quad\; = -15 & -6 + y = -5 \\
x = -3 & y = 1
\end{array}$$

5. **B.** Multiply the bottom equation by 2: $2(2x + y) = 2(1)$ becomes $4x + 2y = 2$. Adding this transformed version to the top equation eliminates y, leaving $7x = -21$, or $x = -3$. Replacing x with -3 in the first equation gives you $3(-3) - 2y = -23$ or $-9 - 2y = -23$. Add 9 to both sides for $-2y = -14$ and divide by -2 for $y = 7$.

$$\begin{cases} 3x - 2y = -23 \\ 2x + y = 1 \end{cases} \rightarrow \begin{cases} 3x - 2y = -23 \\ 2(2x + y) = 2(1) \end{cases} \rightarrow$$

$$\begin{array}{ll}
\text{Solve for } x: & \text{Solve for } y: \\
3x - 2y = -23 & 3x - 2y = -23 \\
\underline{4x + 2y = 2} & 3(-3) - 2y = -23 \\
7x \quad\; = -21 & -9 - 2y = -23 \\
x = -3 & -2y = -14 \\
& y = 7
\end{array}$$

6. **D.** Let D = the price of a doughnut and M = the price of a muffin. Write the system: $\begin{cases} 2D + 3M = 4.90 \\ 6D + 1M = 5.10 \end{cases}$.

Multiply the top equation by -3; then add the two equations to eliminate D and solve for M.

$$-3(2D + 3M) = -3(4.90) \rightarrow \begin{array}{l} -6D - 9M = -14.70 \\ \underline{6D + 1M = 5.10} \\ -8M = -9.60 \\ M = 1.20 \end{array}$$

Substitute 1.20 for M in $6D + M = 5.10$ and solve for D.

$$\begin{array}{l}
6D + 1M = 5.10 \\
6D + 1(1.20) = 5.10 \\
6D = 3.90 \\
D = 0.65
\end{array}$$

A doughnut costs \$0.65 and a muffin costs \$1.20.

7. **D.** Let B = the cost of a button and S = the cost of a sticker. Write the system: $\begin{cases} 15B + 20S = 4.75 \\ 25B + 40S = 8.25 \end{cases}$.

Multiply the top equation by −2; then add the two equations to eliminate S and solve for B.

$$-2(15B + 20S) = -2(4.75) \quad \rightarrow \quad \begin{aligned} -30B - 40S &= -9.50 \\ 25B + 40S &= 8.25 \\ \hline -5B &= -1.25 \end{aligned}$$

$$-5B = -1.25$$
$$B = 0.25$$

Substitute 0.25 for B and solve for S.

$$15B + 20S = 4.75$$
$$15(0.25) + 20S = 4.75$$
$$3.75 + 20S = 4.75$$
$$20S = 1.00$$
$$S = 0.05$$

Buttons cost $0.25 each and stickers cost $0.05 each.

8. **A.** Let B = the number of seats on a bus and V = the number of seats in a van. Write the system: $\begin{cases} 3B + 1V = 142 \\ 5B + 3V = 246 \end{cases}$. Multiply the top equation by −3 ; then add the two equations to eliminate V and solve for B.

$$-3(3B + 1V) = -3(142) \quad \rightarrow \quad \begin{aligned} -9B - 3V &= -426 \\ 5B + 3V &= 246 \\ \hline -4B &= -180 \end{aligned}$$

$$B = 45$$

Substitute 45 for B and solve for V.

$$3B + 1V = 142$$
$$3(45) + 1V = 142$$
$$135 + V = 142$$
$$V = 7$$

There are 45 seats in each bus and 7 seats in each van.

9. **B.** Let D = the price of a dress and S = the price of a skirt. Write the system: $\begin{cases} 3D+2S=142 \\ 1D+3S=101 \end{cases}$. Multiply

the bottom equation by -3; then add the two equations to eliminate D and solve for S.

$$-3(1D+3S)=-3(101) \quad \rightarrow \quad -3D-9S=-303$$
$$\underline{3D+2S= \quad 142}$$
$$-7S=-161$$
$$S=23$$

Substitute 23 for S and solve for D.

$$1D+3(23)=101$$
$$D+69=101$$
$$D=32$$

Dresses cost \$32 each and skirts cost \$23 each.

10. **B.** Let T = the price of a tire and H = the price of a hose. Write the system: $\begin{cases} 2T+2H=120 \\ 4T+2H=210 \end{cases}$. Subtract
the equations to eliminate H and solve for T.

$$2T+2H=120$$
$$\underline{4T+2H=210}$$
$$-2T \qquad =-90$$
$$T=45$$

Substitute 45 for T and solve for H.

$$2T+2H=120$$
$$2(45)+2H=120$$
$$90+2H=120$$
$$2H=30$$
$$H=15$$

Tires cost \$45 each and hoses cost \$15 each.

F. Polynomials

Polynomials include constants, like 6 or -12, variable terms, like $3x$ or $-7y$, and sums and differences of such terms. A sum or difference of two terms is called a *binomial,* and three terms make a *trinomial.* So, $3x-7$ is a binomial and $4x^2-9x+3$ is a trinomial.

Adding and Subtracting

To add or subtract polynomials, add or subtract like terms and only like terms. The term *like terms* means terms that contain the same variable, raised to the same power. The terms differ only in the numerical coefficient. To add or subtract like terms, add or subtract the coefficients: $9y^2-3y^2=6y^2$.

Parentheses may appear in an algebraic expression to make it clear that one polynomial is to be subtracted from another. In $4x + 3 - (x + 5)$, to subtract the binomial $x + 5$ from the binomial $4x + 3$, distribute the minus sign over all the terms in the parentheses. So, $4x + 3 - (x + 5) = 4x + 3 - x - 5 = 3x - 2$.

Multiplying

Removing parentheses from a variable expression usually involves performing some kind of multiplication.

Distributive

To multiply a single term times a sum or difference, distribute the multiplication to each term of the sum or difference. To simplify $-7x^2(5x^3 - 4x^2 + 8x - 1)$, multiply $-7x^2$ by each of the four terms in the parentheses. Then simplify each term, paying attention to signs:

$$-7x^2(5x^3 - 4x^2 + 8x - 1) = (-7x^2 \cdot 5x^3) - (-7x^2 \cdot 4x^2) + (-7x^2 \cdot 8x) - (-7x^2 \cdot 1)$$
$$= (-35x^5) - (-28x^4) + (-56x^3) - (-7x^2)$$
$$= -35x^5 + 28x^4 - 56x^3 + 7x^2$$

FOIL

To multiply two binomials, use the FOIL rule. The letters in FOIL stand for <u>F</u>irst, <u>O</u>uter, <u>I</u>nner, and <u>L</u>ast, and they refer to the four multiplications that you need to do. So, to multiply $(x + 5)(x - 3)$,

1. Multiply the **first** terms of the binomials: $x \cdot x = x^2$.
2. Multiply the **outer** terms of the binomials: $-3 \cdot x = -3x$.
3. Multiply the **inner** terms of the binomials: $5 \cdot x = 5x$.
4. Multiply the **last** terms of the binomials: $5 \times -3 = -15$.

Combine like terms (usually the inner and the outer):

$$x^2 - 3x + 5x - 15 = x^2 + 2x - 15$$

Factoring

Factoring asks you to go in the opposite direction from multiplication, starting with a single polynomial and rewriting it as the product of two or more factors.

Greatest Common Factor

To factor out a common monomial factor:

1. Determine the largest number that will divide the numerical coefficient of every term.
2. Determine the highest power of the variable that is common to all terms.
3. Place the common factor outside the parentheses.
4. Inside the parentheses, create a new polynomial by dividing each term of the original by the common factor.

To factor $6x^5 - 9x^4 + 27x^3$, first note that the largest number that divides 6, 9, and 27 is 3. The largest power of x common to all terms is x^3. Place the greatest common factor of $3x^3$ in front of a set of parentheses and divide each term of $6x^5 - 9x^4 + 27x^3$ by $3x^3$:

$$\frac{6x^5}{3x^3} = 2x^2 \qquad \frac{-9x^4}{3x^3} = -3x \qquad \frac{27x^3}{3x^3} = 9$$

Place the common factor outside the parentheses, and the simpler polynomial inside:

$$6x^5 - 9x^4 + 27x^3 = 3x^3(2x^2 - 3x + 9)$$

FOIL Factoring

A trinomial of the form $ax^2 + bx + c$ can often, although not always, be factored into the product of two binomials. To factor a trinomial into the product of two binomials:

1. Put the trinomial in standard form: $ax^2 + bx + c$.

2. List pairs of factors for the squared term.

3. List pairs of factors for the constant term.

4. Try different arrangements of these factors, checking with the FOIL rule to see if the inner and outer products can add or subtract to produce the desired middle term.

5. Place signs.

To factor $6x^2 + 13x - 8$, start with factors of $6x^2$ ($6x$ and x or $3x$ and $2x$) and factors of 8 (1 and 8 or 2 and 4.) Don't worry about signs yet. Set up two sets of parentheses and place a pair of factors for the lead term. Try a pair of factors of the last term, and check the inner and outer products to see if they could add or subtract to $13x$:

$(3x\ 1)(2x\ 8)$

Outer: $24x$

Inner: $2x$

$24x$ and $2x$ cannot be added or subtracted to get $13x$, so this is not the correct arrangement of factor pairs. Keep the $3x$ and $2x$ as they are, and reverse the 1 and the 8:

$(3x\ 8)(2x\ 1)$

Outer: $3x$

Inner: $16x$

The inner term of $16x$ and the outer term of $3x$ could make a middle term of $13x$ if the signs are right. To get $+13x$, you'll need $+16x$ and $-3x$. Put a plus sign in front of the 8 and a minus sign in front of the 1, and check by multiplying:

$$(3x + 8)(2x - 1) = 6x^2 - 3x + 16x - 8 = 6x^2 + 13x - 8$$

If the constant term is positive, both signs will be the same as the sign of the middle term, and the inner and outer products will add to the middle term. If the constant term is negative, place the sign of the middle term on the larger of the two products, the opposite sign on the other, and expect the middle term to be the difference of the inner and the outer.

Difference of Squares

The product of two binomials usually produces a trinomial, but in one case the inner and the outer add to 0, leaving only two terms, the difference of squares: $(a + b)(a - b) = a^2 - b^2$. It's wise to memorize this form:

$$(a+b)(a-b)=a^2-b^2$$
$$(x+6)(x-6)=x^2-36$$

Factoring by Grouping

If you are asked to factor an expression with four terms, a technique called *factoring by grouping* may be helpful. It's actually a repeated application of factoring out the greatest common factor. Let's factor $2x^3 + 5x^2 + 6x + 15$.

Divide the four terms into two groups of two: $\underbrace{2x^3+5x^2}_{\text{first group}} \underbrace{+6x+15}_{\text{second group}}$.

Find and factor out the GCF of the first two terms: $x^2(2x + 5) + 6x + 15$.

Find and factor out the GCF of the second two terms: $x^2(2x + 5) + 3(2x + 5)$.

If the same factor appears in both groups (in this case $2x + 5$), factor it out as a common factor:

$$x^2\underbrace{(2x+5)}_{\text{common}}+3\underbrace{(2x+5)}_{\text{common}}=(2x+5)\left[x^2+3\right]$$

Therefore, $2x^3 + 5x^2 + 6x + 15 = (2x + 5)(x^2 + 3)$.

Practice

Directions: Choose the best answer from the choices provided.

1. Simplify: $-4(3t + 2) - (7 - t)$.

   A. $-11t - 15$
   B. $-13t - 15$
   C. $-13t + 1$
   D. $-11t + 1$

2. Simplify: $5t^2(3t - 9)$.

   A. $15t^3 - 45$
   B. $15t^3 - 9$
   C. $15t^3 - 45t^2$
   D. $8t^3 - 14t^2$

3. Simplify: $(5t + 2)(t - 8)$.

   A. $5t^2 - 16$
   B. $5t^2 - 42t - 16$
   C. $5t^2 + 42t - 16$
   D. $5t^2 - 38t - 16$

4. Factor: $x^2 - 9x + 14$.

   A. $(x - 7)(x + 2)$
   B. $(x - 7)(x - 2)$
   C. $(x + 7)(x + 2)$
   D. $(x + 7)(x - 2)$

5. Factor: $9x^2 - y^2$.

   A. $(3x + y)^2$
   B. $(3x - y)^2$
   C. $(3x + y)(3x - y)$
   D. $(9x - y)(x + y)$

6. If you factor both $25t^3 + 15t^2$ and $20t + 12$ by factoring out the greatest common monomial factor, what factor appears in both?

   A. 5
   B. t
   C. $5t$
   D. $5t + 3$

7. Which of these is a correct factoring of $25t^3 + 15t^2 + 20t + 12$?

   A. $9t^2(5t + 3)$
   B. $(5t + 3)(5t^2 + 4)$
   C. $(5t + 3)^2(5t^2 + 4)$
   D. $5t^2(5t + 3) + 4(5t + 3)$

8. Simplify: $(x + 2)^2 - (x + 2)(x - 2)$.

   A. 0
   B. 8
   C. $4x$
   D. $4x + 8$

9. Which of the following is equivalent to $3t(t + 2) - 6(t + 8)$?

   A. $(3t - 6)(t + 10)$
   B. $(3t - 6)(2t + 10)$
   C. $3(t + 4)(t - 4)$
   D. $3(t^2 + 16)$

10. Factor: $3x^2 - 15x - 42$.

   A. $(x - 7)(3x + 2)$
   B. $(3x - 7)(x + 2)$
   C. $3(x - 7)(x + 2)$
   D. Cannot be factored

Answers

1. **A.**

$$-4(3t+2)-(7-t)=-12t-8-7+t$$
$$=-12t+t-8-7$$
$$=-11t-15$$

2. **C.**

$$5t^2(3t-9)=5t^2 \cdot 3t - 5t^2 \cdot 9$$
$$=15t^3 - 45t^2$$

3. **D.**

$$(5t+2)(t-8)=5t^2 - 40t + 2t - 16$$
$$=5t^2 - 38t - 16$$

4. **B.** Basic FOIL factoring solves this problem: $x^2 - 9x + 14 = (x - 7)(x - 2)$.

5. **C.** Factor the difference of squares: $9x^2 - y^2 = (3x + y)(3x - y)$.

6. **D.** $25t^3 + 15t^2 = 5t^2(5t + 3)$ and $20t + 12 = 4(5t + 3)$; therefore, $5t + 3$ appears in both.

7. **B.** Think of this four-term polynomial as two binomials for a moment.

$$25t^3 + 15t^2 + 20t + 12 = (25t^3 + 15t^2) + (20t + 12) = 5t^2(5t + 3) + 4(5t + 3)$$

Because $5t + 3$ appears in both parts, it can be factored out as a common factor.

$$5t^2(5t + 3) + 4(5t + 3) = (5t + 3)(5t^2 + 4)$$

Alternately, you can work through each of the answer choices using multiplication to see which equals $25t^3 + 15t^2 + 20t + 12$.

8. **D.** Multiply and combine like terms:

$$(x+2)^2 - (x+2)(x-2) = x^2 + 4x + 4 - (x^2 - 4)$$
$$= x^2 + 4x + 4 - x^2 + 4$$
$$= 4x + 8$$

Alternately, factor out $x + 2$ as a common factor:

$$(x+2)^2 - (x+2)(x-2) = (x+2)(x+2) - (x+2)(x-2)$$
$$= (x+2)[(x+2) - (x-2)]$$

Then simplify:

$$(x+2)[(x+2) - (x-2)] = (x+2)(x - x + 2 + 2)$$
$$= (x+2)(4)$$
$$= 4x + 8$$

9. **C.** Distribute and combine like terms.

$$3t(t+2) - 6(t+8) = 3t^2 + 6t - 6t - 48$$
$$= 3t^2 - 48$$

Then factor:

$$3t^2 - 48 = 3(t^2 - 16)$$
$$= 3(t+4)(t-4)$$

10. **C.** Factoring $3x^2 - 15x - 42$ looks like a trial-and-error problem, but notice that there is a common factor of 3. Factor that out.

$$3x^2 - 15x - 42 = 3(x^2 - 5x - 14)$$

The rest of the factoring is manageable.

$$3x^2 - 15x - 42 = 3(x^2 - 5x - 14)$$
$$= 3(x-7)(x+2)$$

G. Solving Quadratic Equations

Equations that contain an x^2 term, but no higher powers of the variable, are called *quadratic equations*. Solving them requires some new techniques.

Square Root Method

If a variable expression squared equals a constant term, you can solve by taking the square root of both sides. If you know that $x^2 = 9$, then $x = \pm 3$. If this gives you an irrational result, leave your answer in simplest radical form. To solve $3(x + 1)^2 - 48 = 0$, take these steps:

$$3(x+1)^2 - 48 = 0$$

$$3(x+1)^2 - 48 + 48 = 0 + 48 \qquad \text{Add 48 to both sides.}$$

$$3(x+1)^2 = 48$$

$$\frac{3(x+1)^2}{3} = \frac{48}{3} \qquad \text{Divide both sides by 3.}$$

$$(x+1)^2 = 16$$

$$\sqrt{(x+1)^2} = \sqrt{16} \qquad \text{Take the square root of both sides.}$$

$$x+1 = \pm 4$$

Don't forget that when you take the square root of both sides, you always get the positive and the negative square root. The two possible solutions for x are as follows:

$$x+1 = \pm 4$$

$$x+1 = 4 \qquad \text{or} \qquad x+1 = -4$$

$$x = 3 \qquad\qquad x = -5$$

Factoring

If the product of two numbers is 0, then at least one of the numbers must be 0. That's the key to the most common method of solving a quadratic equation. Put the equation in the form $ax^2 + bx + c = 0$. If you can factor $ax^2 + bx + c$, then at least one of the factors is 0. Create two simple equations by setting the factors equal to 0, and each of those will produce one solution for your quadratic equation.

To solve $3x^2 + 2x - 6 = 2x^2 - 12 - 3x$,

$$3x^2 + 2x - 6 = 2x^2 - 12 - 3x$$

$$3x^2 + 2x - 6 - 2x^2 + 12 + 3x = 2x^2 - 12 - 3x - 2x^2 + 12 + 3x \qquad \text{Bring all the terms to one side to set equal to 0.}$$

$$x^2 + 5x + 6 = 0 \qquad\qquad\qquad \text{Combine like terms.}$$

$$(x+3)(x+2) = 0 \qquad\qquad\qquad \text{Factor the left side.}$$

$$x+3 = 0 \quad \text{or} \quad x+2 = 0$$

$$x = -3 \qquad\qquad x = -2 \qquad\qquad \text{Set each factor equal to 0 and solve for } x.$$

Practice

Directions: Choose the best answer from the choices provided.

1. Solve for x: $x^2 + x = 12$.

   A. $x = -4, x = -3$
   B. $x = 4, x = 3$
   C. $x = -4, x = 3$
   D. $x = 4, x = -3$

2. Solve for x: $x^2 - 7 = 18$.

   A. $x = 7, x = -7$
   B. $x = -1, x = -4$
   C. $x = 2, x = 16$
   D. $x = 5, x = -5$

3. Solve for x: $x(x + 1) = 56$.

   A. $x = 7, x = -8$
   B. $x = -7, x = 8$
   C. $x = 2, x = -28$
   D. $x = 14, x = -4$

4. Solve for x: $(x + 2)^2 = 2x + 4$.

   A. $x = 0, x = 2$
   B. $x = 0, x = -2$
   C. $x = 2, x = -2$
   D. $x = 0, x = -4$

5. Solve for x: $x^2 = 4 + 3x$.

   A. $x = -4, x =$
   B. $x = 4, x = -1$
   C. $x = 3, x = -1$
   D. $x = -3, x = 1$

6. The square of a number plus 8 times the number is 240. What could the number be?

   A. $x = 2\sqrt{58}$
   B. $x = 232$
   C. $x = -20$ or $x = 12$
   D. $x = 20$ or $x = -12$

7. If $x^2 + 16x + 80 = 17$, what is the value of x?

   A. $x = -9$ or $x = -7$
   B. $x = -4$ or $x = -20$
   C. $x = 3$ or $x = -21$
   D. $x = 2$ or $x = 8$

8. If the product of $(x + 11)$ and $(x - 4)$ is 16, find the value of x.

   A. $x = 3$ or $x = -20$
   B. $x = 5$ or $x = 20$
   C. $x = -11$ or $x = 4$
   D. $x = -12$ or $x = 5$

9. The length of a rectangle is 14 inches more than its width. If the area of the rectangle is 312 square inches, what is the width of the rectangle?

   A.   12 inches
   B.   13 inches
   C.   22 inches
   D.   26 inches

10. The height of an object dropped from the top of a building that is 80 feet high is given by the formula $h = 80 - 16t^2$, where h is the height of the object above the ground and t is the time since the object was released. At what time is the object 16 feet above the ground?

    A.   2 seconds after it is released
    B.   4 seconds after it is released
    C.   5 seconds after it is released
    D.   8 seconds after it is released

Answers

1. **C.** Subtract 12 from both sides to set equal to 0 and factor.

$$x^2 + x = 12$$
$$x^2 + x - 12 = 0$$
$$(x+4)(x-3) = 0$$

$$x + 4 = 0 \qquad \text{or} \qquad x - 3 = 0$$
$$x = -4 \qquad\qquad\qquad x = 3$$

2. **D.** Use the square-root method.

$$x^2 - 7 = 18$$
$$x^2 = 25$$
$$\sqrt{x^2} = \sqrt{25}$$
$$x = \pm 5$$

3. **A.** Remember to put this equation in standard form before you try to solve. Even though you see what look like factors, you won't find them useful because the product is not 0.

$$x(x+1) = 56$$
$$x^2 + x = 56$$
$$x^2 + x - 56 = 0$$
$$(x+8)(x-7) = 0$$

$$x + 8 = 0 \qquad \text{or} \qquad x - 7 = 0$$
$$x = -8 \qquad\qquad\qquad x = 7$$

4. **B.** Here again, take the time to get the equation in standard form.

$$(x+2)^2 = 2x + 4$$
$$x^2 + 4x + 4 = 2x + 4$$
$$x^2 + 2x = 0$$
$$x(x+2) = 0$$

$$x = 0 \qquad \text{or} \qquad x + 2 = 0$$
$$x = -2$$

5. **B.** Set equal to 0 and then factor:

$$x^2 = 4 + 3x$$
$$x^2 - 3x - 4 = 0$$
$$(x-4)(x+1) = 0$$

$$x - 4 = 0 \qquad \text{or} \qquad x + 1 = 0$$
$$x = 4 \qquad\qquad\qquad x = -1$$

6. **C.** Let x = the number. "The square of a number plus 8 times the number is 240" translates to $x^2 + 8x = 240$. Move all terms to one side, setting equal to 0, and then factor to solve for x:

$$x^2 + 8x - 240 = 0$$
$$(x + 20)(x - 12) = 0$$

$x + 20 = 0$ 　　　　　 or 　　　　　 $x - 12 = 0$
$x = -20$ 　　　　　　　　　　　　 $x = 12$

Note that the Quadratic Formula is always an option if you're having trouble finding factors.

7. **A.** Remember to collect all terms on one side before trying to solve.

$$x^2 + 16x + 80 = 17$$
$$x^2 + 16x + 63 = 0$$
$$(x + 9)(x + 7) = 0$$

$x + 9 = 0$ 　　　　　 or 　　　　　 $x + 7 = 0$
$x = -9$ 　　　　　　　　　　　　 $x = -7$

8. **D.** "The product of $(x + 11)$ and $(x - 4)$ is 16" translates to $(x + 11)(x - 4) = 16$. FOIL and collect terms on one side before beginning to solve.

$$(x + 11)(x - 4) = 16$$
$$x^2 - 4x + 11x - 44 = 16$$
$$x^2 + 7x - 44 = 16$$
$$x^2 + 7x - 60 = 0$$
$$(x + 12)(x - 5) = 0$$

$x + 12 = 0$ 　　　　　　　　　　 $x - 5 = 0$
$x = -12$ 　　　　　 or 　　　　　 $x = 5$

9. **A.** Let w = the width of the rectangle and $w + 14$ = the length. The area of the rectangle = length × width = $w(w + 14) = 312$. Distribute and collect terms. $w^2 + 14w - 312 = 0$ factors to

$$w^2 + 14w - 312 = 0$$
$$(w + 26)(w - 12) = 0$$

$w + 26 = 0$ 　　　　　 or 　　　　　 $w - 12 = 0$
$w = -26$ 　　　　　　　　　　　　 $w = 12$

The width of a rectangle cannot be negative, so the width is 12 and the length is $12 + 14 = 26$.

10. **A.** Given $h = 80 - 16t^2$, if $h = 16$, you have $16 = 80 - 16t^2$, which simplifies to $16t^2 + 16 = 80$ and $16t^2 = 64$, so $t^2 = 4$ and $t = \pm 2$. The negative value is rejected because you're looking for a time, so the object is 16 feet high 2 seconds after it is released.

H. Rational Expressions

A rational expression is the quotient of two polynomials. To keep the rational expressions in the simplest possible form, you'll want to factor the numerators and denominators and cancel wherever you can.

Simplifying

To simplify a rational expression, factor the numerator and the denominator and cancel any factors that appear in both. To simplify $\dfrac{x^2 - x - 2}{x^2 - 4}$, factor: $\dfrac{x^2 - x - 2}{x^2 - 4} = \dfrac{(x-2)(x+1)}{(x-2)(x+2)}$. The factor $x - 2$ appears in both the numerator and denominator, so it can be canceled, leaving $\dfrac{x+1}{x+2}$.

Multiplying and Dividing

The basic rule for multiplying algebraic fractions is numerator times numerator and denominator times denominator, but you can save time and effort by canceling before multiplying.

To multiply rational expressions:

1. Factor all numerators and denominators.

2. Cancel any factor that appears in both a numerator and a denominator.

3. Multiply numerator times numerator and denominator times denominator.

To divide rational expressions, invert the divisor and multiply.

To divide $\dfrac{x+5}{x^2 + 8x + 15} \div \dfrac{x+5}{x^2 + 6x + 9}$, invert and multiply: $\dfrac{x+5}{x^2 + 8x + 15} \cdot \dfrac{x^2 + 6x + 9}{x+5}$. Factor all numerators and

denominators, cancel, and multiply: $\dfrac{\cancel{(x+5)}}{\cancel{(x+3)}(x+5)} \cdot \dfrac{\cancel{(x+3)}(x+3)}{\cancel{(x+5)}} = \dfrac{(x+3)}{(x+5)}$.

Adding and Subtracting

Adding and subtracting algebraic fractions requires a common denominator. If the fractions have the same denominator, you add or subtract the numerators, and keep the same denominator. Adding the numerators just means combining like terms, but when you subtract, remember that the fraction bar acts like a set of parentheses, so make sure that you change all the signs in the second numerator:

$$\frac{2x+7}{x+5} - \frac{x-8}{x+5} = \frac{2x+7-(x-8)}{x+5}$$
$$= \frac{2x+7-x+8}{x+5}$$
$$= \frac{x+15}{x+5}$$

If the fractions have different denominators, start by factoring the denominators. Use the smallest denominator that contains all the factors in the denominators. Multiply each fraction's numerator and denominator by whatever factors are missing. When the fractions have common denominators, add or subtract the numerators. For subtraction, use parentheses around the second numerator to avoid sign errors. Finally, factor the numerator and denominator and reduce if possible.

To subtract $\dfrac{5x-1}{3x-3} - \dfrac{3x+4}{2x-2}$, factor each denominator:

$$\frac{5x-1}{3(x-1)} - \frac{3x+4}{2(x-1)}$$

The denominators have the factor $x - 1$ in common. The LCD is $3 \times 2(x - 1) = 6(x - 1)$. Transform each fraction by multiplying the first by $\dfrac{2}{2}$ and the second by $\dfrac{3}{3}$:

$$\frac{5x-1}{3(x-1)} \cdot \frac{2}{2} - \frac{3x+4}{2(x-1)} \cdot \frac{3}{3} = \frac{10x-2}{6(x-1)} - \frac{9x+12}{6(x-1)}$$

Put parentheses around the second numerator, as a reminder to change all the signs, and the problem becomes:

$$\frac{10x-2-(9x+12)}{6(x-1)} = \frac{10x-2-9x-12}{6(x-1)}$$

$$= \frac{x-14}{6(x-1)}$$

Practice

Directions: Choose the best answer from the choices provided.

1. Simplify: $\dfrac{x^3 - 4x^2}{x - 4}$.

   A. x
   B. x^2
   C. $x^3 - x$
   D. $x^3 - x^2$

2. Simplify: $\dfrac{x}{3a} - \dfrac{y}{5a}$.

   A. $\dfrac{x-y}{8a}$

   B. $\dfrac{x-y}{15a}$

   C. $\dfrac{5x-3y}{15a}$

   D. $\dfrac{5x-3y}{8a}$

3. Simplify: $\dfrac{7t}{2x^3} \div \dfrac{14t^2}{8x}$.

   A. $\dfrac{98t^3}{16x^4}$

   B. $\dfrac{2}{x^2 t}$

   C. $\dfrac{6tx^2}{7}$

   D. $\dfrac{6}{7x^2 t}$

4. Simplify: $\dfrac{2x-1}{x-7}+\dfrac{3x+5}{x-7}$.

   A. $\dfrac{5x+4}{x-7}$

   B. $\dfrac{5x-6}{x-7}$

   C. $\dfrac{5x+4}{2(x-7)}$

   D. $\dfrac{5x-6}{2(x-7)}$

5. Simplify: $\dfrac{x+3}{x+1}+\dfrac{2x-5}{x-2}$.

   A. $\dfrac{3x^2+4x-1}{(x+1)(x-2)}$

   B. $\dfrac{-x^2+4x-1}{(x+1)(x-2)}$

   C. $\dfrac{3x-2}{(x+1)(x-2)}$

   D. $\dfrac{3x^2-2x-11}{(x+1)(x-2)}$

6. Simplify: $\dfrac{x}{x-3}-\dfrac{5}{x+2}$.

   A. $\dfrac{x^2-3x-13}{(x+2)(x-3)}$

   B. $\dfrac{x^2-3x+15}{(x+2)(x-3)}$

   C. $\dfrac{x^2-3x-15}{(x+2)(x-3)}$

   D. $\dfrac{x^2-3x+17}{(x+2)(x-3)}$

7. Find the difference between $\dfrac{x}{x+1}$ and its reciprocal.

   A. 0

   B. $\dfrac{-2}{x^2}$

   C. $\dfrac{2}{x+1}$

   D. $\dfrac{-2x-1}{x^2+x}$

8. Which of the following is equivalent to $\dfrac{a^2b}{(a^3b)^2}\div\dfrac{a^3b^4}{(ab^5)^3}$?

   A. $\dfrac{b}{a}$

   B. $\dfrac{b^4}{a^3}$

   C. $\dfrac{b^{10}}{a^4}$

   D. $\dfrac{1}{a^4b^{12}}$

9. When $(x-2)$ is divided by $\dfrac{(x^2-4)}{(x+2)}$, which of these is the result?

   A. 1
   B. $4-x^2$
   C. x^2-4
   D. $(x-2)^2$

10. Simplify: $\dfrac{2x+1}{x-3}-\dfrac{x+10}{x+3}$

   A. $\dfrac{x-9}{-6}$

   B. $\dfrac{x^2-27}{(x-3)(x+3)}$

   C. $\dfrac{x^2+33}{(x-3)(x+3)}$

   D. $\dfrac{x^2-2x+33}{(x-3)(x+3)}$

Answers

1. **B.** Factor and cancel: $\dfrac{x^3 - 4x^2}{x - 4} = \dfrac{x^2 \,(\cancel{x - 4})}{\cancel{x - 4}} = x^2$.

2. **C.** Use a common denominator of $15a$:

$$\frac{x}{3a} - \frac{y}{5a} = \frac{x}{3a} \cdot \frac{5}{5} - \frac{y}{5a} \cdot \frac{3}{3}$$
$$= \frac{5x}{15a} - \frac{3y}{15a}$$
$$= \frac{5x - 3y}{15a}$$

3. **B.** Invert and multiply:

$$\frac{7t}{2x^3} \div \frac{14t^2}{8x} = \frac{7t}{2x^3} \cdot \frac{8x}{14t^2}$$
$$= \frac{\cancel{7t}}{x^2 \,\cancel{2x^3}} \cdot \frac{\cancel{8x^4}}{\cancel{14t^2}_{2t}}$$
$$= \frac{4}{2x^2 t}$$
$$= \frac{2}{x^2 t}$$

4. **A.** Add the numerators: $\dfrac{2x - 1}{x - 7} + \dfrac{3x + 5}{x - 7} = \dfrac{2x - 1 + 3x + 5}{x - 7} = \dfrac{5x + 4}{x - 7}$.

5. **D.** $\dfrac{x + 3}{x + 1} + \dfrac{2x - 5}{x - 2} = \dfrac{(x + 3)}{(x + 1)} \cdot \dfrac{(x - 2)}{(x - 2)} + \dfrac{(2x - 5)}{(x - 2)} \cdot \dfrac{(x + 1)}{(x + 1)}$

$$= \frac{x^2 + x - 6 + 2x^2 - 3x - 5}{(x + 1)(x - 2)}$$
$$= \frac{3x^2 - 2x - 11}{(x + 1)(x - 2)}$$

6. **B.** $\dfrac{x}{x - 3} - \dfrac{5}{x + 2} = \dfrac{x(x + 2)}{(x + 2)(x - 3)} - \dfrac{5(x - 3)}{(x + 2)(x - 3)}$

$$= \frac{x^2 + 2x}{(x + 2)(x - 3)} - \frac{(5x - 15)}{(x + 2)(x - 3)}$$
$$= \frac{x^2 + 2x - 5x + 15}{(x + 2)(x - 3)}$$
$$= \frac{x^2 - 3x + 15}{(x + 2)(x - 3)}$$

7. **D.** The reciprocal of $\dfrac{x}{x+1}$ is $\dfrac{x+1}{x}$. Then

$$\frac{x}{x+1} - \frac{x+1}{x} = \frac{(x)(x)}{(x)(x+1)} - \frac{(x+1)(x+1)}{(x)(x+1)}$$

$$= \frac{x^2 - (x^2 + 2x + 1)}{(x)(x+1)}$$

$$= \frac{-2x - 1}{x^2 + x}$$

8. **C.** Invert the divisor and multiply: $\dfrac{a^2 b}{(a^3 b)^2} \div \dfrac{a^3 b^4}{(ab^5)^3} = \dfrac{a^2 b}{(a^3 b)^2} \cdot \dfrac{(ab^5)^3}{a^3 b^4}$. Simplify by removing parentheses:

$\dfrac{a^2 b}{(a^3 b)^2} \cdot \dfrac{(ab^5)^3}{a^3 b^4} = \dfrac{a^2 b}{a^6 b^2} \cdot \dfrac{a^3 b^{15}}{a^3 b^4}$. Use laws of exponents to accomplish the multiplications and divisions:

$\dfrac{a^2 b}{a^6 b^2} \cdot \dfrac{a^3 b^{15}}{a^3 b^4} = \dfrac{a^5 b^{16}}{a^9 b^6} = \dfrac{b^{10}}{a^4}$.

9. **A.** $(x-2) \div \dfrac{(x^2 - 4)}{(x+2)} = \dfrac{(x-2)}{1} \cdot \dfrac{(x+2)}{x^2 - 4}$

$$= \frac{(x-2)^1}{1} \cdot \frac{(x+2)^1}{(x-2)^1 (x+2)^1}$$

$$= \frac{1}{1} = 1$$

10. **C.** $\dfrac{2x+1}{x-3} - \dfrac{x+10}{x+3} = \dfrac{(2x+1)(x+3)}{(x-3)(x+3)} - \dfrac{(x-3)(x+10)}{(x-3)(x+3)}$

$$= \frac{2x^2 + 7x + 3}{(x-3)(x+3)} - \frac{x^2 + 7x - 30}{(x-3)(x+3)}$$

$$= \frac{2x^2 + 7x + 3 - x^2 - 7x + 30}{(x-3)(x+3)}$$

$$= \frac{x^2 + 33}{(x-3)(x+3)}$$

I. Ratio and Proportion

A ratio is a comparison of two numbers by division. If one number is three times the size of another, we say the ratio of the larger to the smaller is "3 to 1." A proportion is a statement that two ratios are equal, as in $\dfrac{1}{3} = \dfrac{2}{6}$. When you're told that the ratio of one number to another is 5:2, you can represent the numbers as $5x$ and $2x$. If two numbers are in ratio 7:3 and their sum is 50, $7x + 3x = 50$, so $10x = 50$ and $x = 5$. Don't forget to find the numbers! So, $7x = 7 \times 5 = 35$ and $3x = 3 \times 5 = 15$.

Cross-Multiplication

In any proportion, the product of the *means* (the two middle numbers) is equal to the product of the *extremes* (the first and last numbers). In the proportion $\frac{5}{8} = \frac{15}{24}$, the product of the means, 8×15, is equal to the product of the extremes, 5×24. Whenever you have two equal ratios, you can cross-multiply. If $\frac{7}{4} = \frac{x}{14}$, cross-multiplying produces $4x = 7 \times 14$. Solving this equation gives $x = 24.5$.

Practice

Directions: Choose the best answer from the choices provided.

1. If $\frac{x}{y} = \frac{3}{5}$, then $y =$

   A. $\frac{5x}{3}$

   B. $\frac{3x}{5}$

   C. $\frac{15}{x}$

   D. $\frac{x}{15}$

2. In the senior class, the ratio of boys to girls is 7:8. If there are 300 students in the senior class, how many are girls?

   A. 15
   B. 20
   C. 140
   D. 160

3. If $\frac{3}{5} = \frac{x}{70}$, find x.

   A. 116.7
   B. 42
   C. 14
   D. 4.2

4. The ratio of peppermints to lemon drops in Ms. Heller's candy bowl is 5:7. If she adds 100 peppermints, the ratio will become 10:7. How many lemon drops are in the bowl?

   A. 100
   B. 110
   C. 120
   D. 140

5. The ratio of station wagons to sedans sold at Mr. Corning's dealership is 6:5. If Mr. Corning sold 22 cars last month, how many were sedans?

   A. 10
   B. 11
   C. 12
   D. 20

6. If $\frac{5x - 23}{x} = \frac{12}{7}$, find x.

   A. $x = 1$
   B. $x = 5$
   C. $x = 7$
   D. $x = 12$

7. If $\frac{x - 3}{3x} = \frac{x + 3}{5x}$, find x.

   A. $x = 0$
   B. $x = \sqrt{3}$
   C. $x = 12$
   D. No solution

8. An artist mixes a shade of green paint that combines 5 parts blue paint to 3 parts yellow. If he needs 50 grams of the green paint, how many grams of yellow paint will he use?

   A. 6.25 g
   B. 18.75 g
   C. 30.0 g
   D. 31.25 g

9. A polling organization selected a group of 100 people made up of 51 women and 49 men, and then decided to expand the group to 120 people. If they want the final ratio of women to men to be equal to 1, what should the ratio of women to men in the additional members be?

   A. 9:11
   B. 11:9
   C. 49:51
   D. 51:49

10. In baseball, batting averages are usually recorded as decimals, but are calculated as the ratio of hits to times at bat. If two players, Chris and Jack, both have a batting average of "200," the ratio of their hits to their times at bat converts to the decimal 0.200. Jack has 10 hits and 50 at-bats and Chris has 12 hits and 60 at-bats. If each of these players gets 2 hits in the next 5 at-bats, which of the following is true?

    A. Their batting averages remain exactly the same, at 0.200.
    B. Both batting averages increase to 0.215.
    C. Both batting averages increase to 0.218.
    D. Jack's batting average increases to 0.218 and Chris' increases to 0.215.

Answers

1. **A.** If $\dfrac{x}{y} = \dfrac{3}{5}$, cross-multiplying gives you $5x = 3y$. Dividing by 3, you have $y = \dfrac{5x}{3}$.

2. **D.** $7x + 8x = 300$, so $15x = 300$, and $x = 20$. Therefore, there are $7 \times 20 = 140$ boys and $8 \times 20 = 160$ girls.

3. **B.** Cross-multiply for $5x = 210$ and solve to get $x = 42$.

4. **D.** The current proportion is $P:L = 5:7$. If she adds 100 peppermints, it will become $(P + 100):L = 10:7$. According to the original proportion, $7P = 5L$. Then using the second proportion, cross-multiply to get $7P + 700 = 10L$, and replace $7P$ with $5L$. $5L + 700 = 10L$, so $700 = 5L$, and $L = 140$.

5. **A.** $6x + 5x = 22$, so $11x = 22$ and $x = 2$. This means Mr. Corning sold 12 station wagons and 10 sedans.

6. **C.** Cross-multiply $\dfrac{5x - 23}{x} = \dfrac{12}{7}$ to get $35x - 161 = 12x$, and then subtract $35x$ from both sides. Next, divide both sides by -23 to solve for x:

$$\frac{5x - 23}{x} = \frac{12}{7}$$
$$35x - 161 = 12x$$
$$35x - 161 - 35x = 12x - 35x$$
$$-161 = -23x$$
$$\frac{-161}{-23} = \frac{-23x}{-23}$$
$$x = 7$$

223

7. **C.** Cross-multiplying $\dfrac{x-3}{3x} = \dfrac{x+3}{5x}$ gives you $5x^2 - 15x = 3x^2 + 9x$. Collect like terms to get $2x^2 - 24x = 0$.

   Factor out $2x$ and set each factor equal to zero.

$$\frac{x-3}{3x} = \frac{x+3}{5x}$$
$$5x^2 - 15x = 3x^2 + 9x$$
$$2x^2 - 24x = 0$$
$$2x(x-12) = 0$$

$$2x = 0 \qquad \text{or} \qquad x - 12 = 0$$
$$x = 0 \qquad\qquad\qquad x = 12$$

   Reject $x = 0$ because it would make the denominators equal 0. Therefore, $x = 12$.

8. **B.** If the ratio of blue to yellow paint is 5:3, let $5x$ = the number of grams of blue paint and $3x$ = the number of grams of yellow paint. The total of 50 g of paint is formed by adding, so $5x + 3x = 50$. Simplify to get $8x = 50$, and divide to get $x = 6.25$ g. The amount of blue paint is $5(6.25) = 31.25$ g, and the amount of yellow paint is $3(6.25) = 18.75$ g.

9. **A.** Let W = the number of women needed and $20 - W$ = the number of men. The desired ratio is

   $\dfrac{51+W}{49+20-W} = 1$, which means $\dfrac{51+W}{69-W} = \dfrac{1}{1}$ or $51 + W = 69 - W$. Add W to both sides to get $51 + 2W = 69$. Subtract 51 to get $2W = 18$, and divide to get $W = 9$ women. The ratio of women to men in the additional group should be 9:11.

10. **D.** Both players start with a batting average of 0.200 because $\dfrac{10}{50} = \dfrac{12}{60} = 0.200$. However, when the

    ratios are adjusted for 2 hits in the next 5 at-bats, $\dfrac{12}{55} \neq \dfrac{14}{65}$. Instead, $\dfrac{12}{55} = 0.21\overline{8}$ and $\dfrac{14}{65} = 0.2153....$

    Therefore, Jack's batting average increases to 0.218 and Chris' increases to 0.215.

J. Solving Rational Equations

Some equations that involve algebraic fractions can be solved by cross-multiplying, like a proportion. If the equation is two equal fractions, or if it can easily be simplified to two equal fractions, then you can cross-multiply. If it's more complicated, multiply through the equation by the common denominator.

Start by factoring each of the denominators, and determine the LCD of all the fractions. Multiply both sides of the equation by the LCD, distributing if necessary, and cancel. All denominators should disappear.

To solve $\dfrac{4}{x+1} + \dfrac{2}{3} = \dfrac{5}{3x+3}$, first recognize that the denominator $3x + 3$ factors to $3(x + 1)$. Then, multiply each term of the equation by $3(x + 1)$. Distribute and cancel to eliminate all the denominators:

$$3\cancel{(x+1)}\,\frac{4}{\cancel{x+1}} + 3(x+1)\frac{2}{\cancel{3}} = 3\cancel{(x+1)}\cdot\frac{5}{\cancel{3(x+1)}}$$

$$12 + 2(x+1) = 5$$

$$12 + 2x + 2 = 5$$

$$2x = -9$$

$$x = -4.5$$

When you solve rational equations, be careful not to say that a value that makes the denominator 0 is a solution. They'll pop up sometimes, but they're called *extraneous solutions,* and you ignore them.

Practice

Directions: Choose the best answer from the choices provided.

1. Solve for x: $\dfrac{x}{16} = \dfrac{4}{x}$.
   - **A.** $x = 8, x = -8$
   - **B.** $x = 8, x = 0$
   - **C.** $x = 4, x = 16$
   - **D.** $x = 4, x = -16$

2. Solve for x: $\dfrac{5}{x} - \dfrac{3}{2x} = \dfrac{1}{2}$.
   - **A.** $x = 2$
   - **B.** $x = 4$
   - **C.** $x = 7$
   - **D.** $x = 13$

3. Solve for x: $\dfrac{x}{x-1} + \dfrac{12}{x-1} = \dfrac{6}{x-1}$.
   - **A.** $x = -12$
   - **B.** $x = -6$
   - **C.** $x = 6$
   - **D.** $x = 12$

4. Solve for x: $\dfrac{x+4}{x-5} = \dfrac{x-2}{x+3}$.
   - **A.** No solution
   - **B.** $x = 2$
   - **C.** $x = 0$
   - **D.** $x = -\dfrac{1}{7}$

5. Solve for x: $\dfrac{x+1}{4} - \dfrac{3}{x} = \dfrac{1}{2}$.
   - **A.** $x = -4, x = 3$
   - **B.** $x = 4, x = -3$
   - **C.** $x = 6, x = -2$
   - **D.** $x = 2, x = -6$

6. Solve for x: $\dfrac{x+4}{x-2} - \dfrac{x+4}{x-4} = \dfrac{-1}{6}$.
   - **A.** $x = 20$ or $x = -2$
   - **B.** $x = 10$ or $x = -4$
   - **C.** $x = -10$ or $x = 4$
   - **D.** $x = -2\dfrac{1}{4}$

7. Solve for x: $\dfrac{x-5}{2x+3} - \dfrac{x-2}{x-1} = \dfrac{-3x}{5(x-1)}$.
   - **A.** $x = 1$ or $x = 19$
   - **B.** $x = 1$ or $x = 30$
   - **C.** $x = 1$ or $x = 31$
   - **D.** $x = 5$ or $x = 11$

8. If it takes H hours to complete a task, the part of the task that can be completed in 1 hour is $\dfrac{1}{H}$. It takes Marianna 3 hours to prepare a presentation for the board, but Janine can complete the presentation in 2 hours. If they work together, each doing part of the job, how long will it take to complete the presentation?

A. $\dfrac{1}{5}$ hour

B. $\dfrac{5}{6}$ hour

C. 1 hour

D. $1\dfrac{1}{5}$ hours

9. Elise can do all of the weeding in her garden in 60 minutes. If her brother, Mark, helps her, the job gets done in 40 minutes. How long would it take Mark to do the weeding alone?

A. 120 minutes
B. 100 minutes
C. 90 minutes
D. 20 minutes

10. If Ali and Stephanie work together, they can get all their books packed in 2 hours and 24 minutes. Working alone, Ali takes 2 hours longer than Stephanie working alone. How long does it take Stephanie to pack all the books?

A. 5 hours
B. 4 hours
C. 3 hours
D. 2 hours

Answers

1. **A.** Cross-multiply for $x^2 = 64$, and take the square root of both sides to get $x = \pm 8$.

2. **C.** Multiply through by $2x$:

$$2x\left(\frac{5}{x}-\frac{3}{2x}\right)=2x\left(\frac{1}{2}\right)$$
$$\frac{10x}{x}-\frac{6x}{2x}=\frac{2x}{2}$$
$$10-3=x$$
$$7=x$$

3. **B.** Multiply through by $x - 1$:

$$(x-1)\left(\frac{x}{x-1}\right)+(x-1)\left(\frac{12}{x-1}\right)=(x-1)\left(\frac{6}{x-1}\right)$$
$$x+12=6$$
$$x=-6$$

4. **D.** Cross-multiply:

$$\frac{x+4}{x-5} = \frac{x-2}{x+3}$$
$$(x+4)(x+3) = (x-5)(x-2)$$
$$x^2 + 7x + 12 = x^2 - 7x + 10$$
$$7x + 12 = -7x + 10$$
$$14x = -2$$
$$x = \frac{-2}{14}$$
$$x = -\frac{1}{7}$$

5. **B.** Multiply through by $4x$: $4x\left(\frac{x+1}{4} - \frac{3}{x}\right) = 4x\left(\frac{1}{2}\right)$, then clear the parentheses, and place in standard

form. Then factor to find the two possible solutions for x:

$$\cancel{4}x\left(\frac{x+1}{\cancel{4}}\right) - 4\cancel{x}\left(\frac{3}{\cancel{x}}\right) = \overset{2}{\cancel{4}}x\left(\frac{1}{\cancel{2}}\right)$$
$$x^2 + x - 12 = 2x$$
$$x^2 - x - 12 = 0$$
$$(x-4)(x+3) = 0$$

$$x - 4 = 0 \qquad \text{or} \qquad x + 3 = 0$$
$$x = 4 \qquad\qquad\qquad\qquad x = -3$$

6. **A.** Subtract the rational expressions first to simplify the left side:

$$\frac{x+4}{x-2} - \frac{x+4}{x-4} = \frac{(x+4)(x-4) - (x-2)(x+4)}{(x-2)(x-4)}$$
$$= \frac{x^2 - 16 - (x^2 + 2x - 8)}{x^2 - 6x + 8}$$
$$= \frac{x^2 - 16 - x^2 - 2x + 8}{x^2 - 6x + 8}$$
$$= \frac{-2x - 8}{x^2 - 6x + 8}$$

Then set the simplified left side equal to the original right side and cross-multiply:

$$\frac{-2x - 8}{x^2 - 6x + 8} = \frac{-1}{6}$$
$$-12x - 48 = -x^2 + 6x - 8$$

Collect terms on one side and factor to solve:

$$x^2 - 18x - 40 = 0$$
$$(x - 20)(x + 2) = 0$$

$$x - 20 = 0 \qquad \text{or} \qquad x + 2 = 0$$
$$x = 20 \qquad\qquad\qquad x = -2$$

7. **D.** Notice that two of the rational expressions have a common factor in their denominators. Add $\dfrac{x-2}{x-1}$ to both sides to make the equation $\dfrac{x-5}{2x+3} = \dfrac{-3x}{5(x-1)} + \dfrac{x-2}{x-1}$. Do the addition on the right side, then cross-multiply and solve:

$$\frac{x-5}{2x+3} - \frac{x-2}{x-1} + \frac{x-2}{x-1} = \frac{-3x}{5(x-1)} + \frac{x-2}{x-1}$$

$$\frac{x-5}{2x+3} = \frac{-3x}{5(x-1)} + \frac{5(x-2)}{5(x-1)}$$

$$\frac{x-5}{2x+3} = \frac{-3x+5x-10}{5(x-1)}$$

$$\frac{x-5}{2x+3} = \frac{2x-10}{5x-5}$$

$$(x-5)(5x-5) = (2x+3)(2x-10)$$

$$5x^2 - 30x + 25 = 4x^2 - 14x - 30$$

$$x^2 - 16x + 55 = 0$$

$$(x-5)(x-11) = 0$$

$$x - 5 = 0 \qquad\qquad \text{or} \qquad\qquad x - 11 = 0$$
$$x = 5 \qquad\qquad\qquad\qquad\qquad x = 11$$

8. **D.** Let x = the number of hours it takes Marianna and Janine to do the job working together, and therefore $\dfrac{1}{x}$ is the part of the job they can do in 1 hour working together. In 1 hour working alone, Marianna can do $\dfrac{1}{3}$ of the job. In 1 hour working alone, Janine can do $\dfrac{1}{2}$ of the job. In 1 hour working together, they do $\dfrac{1}{3} + \dfrac{1}{2} = \dfrac{1}{x}$ of the job.

$$\frac{1}{3} + \frac{1}{2} = \frac{1}{x}$$

$$\frac{2}{6} + \frac{3}{6} = \frac{1}{x}$$

$$\frac{5}{6} = \frac{1}{x}$$

Cross-multiply to get $5x = 6$, and divide to get $x = \dfrac{6}{5} = 1\dfrac{1}{5}$ hours or 1 hour and 12 minutes.

9. **A.** Let M = the number of minutes it takes Mark to do the job. In 1 minute, Elise does $\frac{1}{60}$ of the job and Mark does $\frac{1}{M}$ of the job. Together they can do $\frac{1}{60} + \frac{1}{M} = \frac{1}{40}$. Solve for M.

$$\frac{1}{60} + \frac{1}{M} = \frac{1}{40}$$

$$\frac{M+60}{60M} = \frac{1}{40}$$

$$40(M+60) = 60M$$

$$40M + 2,400 = 60M$$

$$2,400 = 20M$$

$$120 = M$$

10. **B.** If Ali and Stephanie working together can do the whole packing job in 2 hours and 24 minutes, you'll need to either convert that to a mixed number of hours or to a number of minutes. Other measurements are in hours, so write 2 hours and 24 minutes as $2\frac{24}{60} = 2\frac{2}{5} = \frac{12}{5}$ hours. Then in 1 hour, they complete $\frac{1}{\left(\frac{12}{5}\right)} = \frac{5}{12}$ of the job. Let $\frac{1}{S}$ represent the part Stephanie does in 1 hour and $\frac{1}{S+2}$ the part Ali does in does in 1 hour. Together they do $\frac{1}{S} + \frac{1}{S+2}$. Solve the equation $\frac{1}{S} + \frac{1}{S+2} = \frac{5}{12}$ by multiplying both sides by the common denominator $12S(S + 2)$.

$$[12S(S+2)]\left(\frac{1}{S} + \frac{1}{S+2}\right) = [12S(S+2)]\left(\frac{5}{12}\right)$$

$$\left[12S(S+2)\right]\frac{1}{S} + \left[12S(S+2)\right]\frac{1}{S+2} = \left[12S(S+2)\right]\left(\frac{5}{12}\right)$$

$$12(S+2) + 12S = 5S(S+2)$$

$$12S + 24 + 12S = 5S^2 + 10S$$

$$24S + 24 = 5S^2 + 10S$$

$$0 = 5S^2 + 10S - 24S - 24$$

$$0 = 5S^2 - 14S - 24$$

$$0 = (5S+6)(S-4)$$

$$5S + 6 = 0 \quad \text{or} \quad S - 4 = 0$$

$$5S = -6 \qquad\qquad S = 4$$

$$S = -\frac{6}{5}$$

$$\text{reject}$$

It takes Stephanie 4 hours to pack all the books alone.

K. Linear Equations

A single equation with two variables has infinitely many solutions, each of which is a pair of numbers, (x, y). Each ordered pair of numbers that solves the equation can be represented by a point in the coordinate plane.

Slope

The slope of a line tells whether the line is rising or falling, and how quickly. Slope can be expressed as the ratio of rise to run—that is, the amount of vertical change to the amount of horizontal change. If two points on the line are (x_1, y_1) and (x_2, y_2), then the slope, m, of the line is $m = \dfrac{y_2 - y_1}{x_2 - x_1}$. The slope of the line through the points $(-4, -4)$ and $(7, 3)$ is $m = \dfrac{y_2 - y_1}{x_2 - x_1} = \dfrac{3 - (-4)}{7 - (-4)} = \dfrac{7}{11}$.

A horizontal line has a slope of 0. The slope of a vertical line is undefined. We say a vertical line has no slope.

Equation of a Line

There are several forms for the equation of a line. Slope-intercept form is most useful for graphing, and point-slope form is most useful for writing the equation.

Slope-Intercept Form

The slope-intercept form of a linear equation is $y = mx + b$, where m is the slope and b is the y-intercept, the point at which the line crosses the y-axis. If the slope and y-intercept of a line are known, you can write the equation simply by putting these numbers into the correct positions. The equation of a line with a slope of -5 and a y-intercept of $(0, 2)$ is $y = -5x + 2$.

Point-Slope Form

The point-slope form $y - y_1 = m(x - x_1)$ is used to write the equation of a line with slope m through the point (x_1, y_1). To find the equation of the line through the points $(2, 5)$ and $(-7, 23)$, use the slope formula to find the slope from the two points:

$$m = \frac{y_2 - y_1}{x_2 - x_1} = \frac{23 - 5}{-7 - 2} = \frac{18}{-9} = -2$$

Using $(2, 5)$ and the slope $m = -2$, point-slope form becomes $y - 5 = -2(x - 2)$. You can simplify to slope-intercept form if you want: $y = -2x + 9$.

Parallel and Perpendicular Lines

Parallel lines have the same slope, but if two lines are perpendicular, their slopes will be negative reciprocals—that is, they'll be numbers that multiply to -1, like -2 and $\dfrac{1}{2}$, or $\dfrac{3}{4}$ and $-\dfrac{4}{3}$.

To find the equation of a line through the point $(-1, 3)$ parallel to $y = -2x + 5$, use the slope of $y = -2x + 5$, or -2. The equation of a line through the point $(-1, 3)$ with slope $m = -2$ is $y - 3 = -2(x - (-1))$ or $y - 3 = -2(x + 1)$. In slope-intercept form, it's $y = -2x + 1$.

To find the equation of a line through the point $(-1, 3)$ perpendicular to $y = -2x + 5$, use a slope of $\frac{1}{2}$ and the point $(-1, 3)$. Then $y - 3 = \frac{1}{2}(x - (-1))$ simplifies to $y = \frac{1}{2}x + \frac{7}{2}$.

Practice

Directions: Choose the best answer from the choices provided.

1. Find the slope of a line perpendicular to $y = x - 4$.

   A.   1
   B.   −1
   C.   −4
   D.   4

2. Which of the following is the equation of a line with a slope of −3 and a y-intercept of 7?

   A. $y = 7x - 3$
   B. $y = 3x - 7$
   C. $y = -3x + 7$
   D. $y = -7x + 3$

3. Find the equation of a line through the point $(1, 1)$ and parallel to $y = 5x - 7$.

   A. $y = 5x - 4$
   B. $y = -5x - 6$
   C. $y = 0.2x - 6$
   D. $y = -0.2x - 1$

4. Which of the following is the equation of a vertical line?

   A. $y = 9$
   B. $y = 9x$
   C. $x + y = 9$
   D. $x = 9$

5. The slope of $\overline{ST}$ is −3. If S is the point $(4, -8)$ and T is $(-8, y)$, find y.

   A.   2
   B.   28
   C.   −14
   D.   26

6. Find the equation in point-slope form of a line perpendicular to $y = \frac{3}{4}x - 2$ that passes through the point $(-3, 5)$.

   A. $y - 5 = -\frac{3}{4}(x + 3)$
   B. $y - 5 = -\frac{4}{3}(x + 3)$
   C. $y + 3 = -\frac{3}{4}(x - 5)$
   D. $y + 5 = -\frac{4}{3}(x - 3)$

7. Line segment $\overline{AB}$ has endpoints $A\,(6, -1)$ and $B\,(-2, 5)$ and midpoint $(2, 2)$. The line $4x - 3y = 2$ intersects $\overline{AB}$. Which of the following is true?

   A. $4x - 3y = 2$ is the perpendicular bisector of $\overline{AB}$.
   B. $4x - 3y = 2$ is perpendicular to $\overline{AB}$ but does not pass through the midpoint of $\overline{AB}$.
   C. $4x - 3y = 2$ passes through the midpoint of $\overline{AB}$ but is not perpendicular to $\overline{AB}$.
   D. $4x - 3y = 2$ is not perpendicular to $\overline{AB}$ and does not pass through the midpoint of $\overline{AB}$.

8. Which of the following lines is perpendicular to the line that connects (0, 5) to (5, 0)?

   A. $y = x$
   B. $y = -x$
   C. $y = 5x$
   D. $y = 5$

9. Which of these is a horizontal line that passes through the y-intercept of $y = 7 - 3x$?

   A. $x = -3$
   B. $y = -3$
   C. $x = 7$
   D. $y = 7$

10. If a line has a slope of $-\frac{3}{5}$ and an x-intercept at (10, 0), what is its y-intercept?

   A. $(0, -6)$
   B. $(0, -3.3)$
   C. $(0, 6)$
   D. $(0, 10)$

Answers

1. **B.** The slope of the given line is 1. The slope of a line perpendicular to the given line would be −1, since perpendicular lines have slopes that are negative reciprocals.

2. **C.** Use the slope-intercept form $y = mx + b$ and replace m with −3 and b with 7: $y = -3x + 7$.

3. **A.** The slope of $y = 5x - 7$ is 5, so the new line should also have a slope of 5. Use the point-slope form and plug in 5 for m, 1 for x_1, and 1 for y_1. Then $y - 1 = 5(x - 1)$ becomes $y - 1 = 5x - 5$ or $y = 5x - 4$.

4. **D.** A vertical line has an equation of the form $x = $ a constant; therefore, only choice D, $x = 9$, could be the equation of a vertical line.

5. **B.** Use the slope formula and replace m with −3, x_2 with 4, y_2 with −8, x_1 with −8, and y_1 with y:

$$m = \frac{y_2 - y_1}{x_2 - x_1}$$

$$-3 = \frac{-8 - y}{4 - (-8)}$$

Simplify and cross-multiply:

$$-3 = \frac{-8 - y}{12}$$

$$-36 = -8 - y$$

$$y - 36 = -8$$

$$y = 28$$

6. **B.** A line perpendicular to $y = \frac{3}{4}x - 2$ has a slope of $-\frac{4}{3}$ and passes through the point (−3, 5), so it has the equation $y - 5 = -\frac{4}{3}(x + 3)$.

7. **A.** If $4x - 3y = 2$ passes through the midpoint, then (2, 2) will be a solution of the equation. $4(2) - 3(2) = 8 - 6 = 2$ is true, so $4x - 3y = 2$ does pass through the midpoint of $\overline{AB}$. The slope of $\overline{AB}$ is $m = \dfrac{y_2 - y_1}{x_2 - x_1} = \dfrac{5 + 1}{-2 - 6} = \dfrac{6}{-8} = -\dfrac{3}{4}$.

To find the slope of $4x - 3y = 2$, transform the equation to slope-intercept form: $-3y = -4x + 2$ and $y = \dfrac{-4}{-3}x + \dfrac{2}{-3}$ or $y = \dfrac{4}{3}x - \dfrac{2}{3}$, which has a slope of $\dfrac{4}{3}$. The slopes are negative reciprocals, so the line is the perpendicular bisector of $\overline{AB}$.

8. **A.** The line that connects (0, 5) to (5, 0) will have a slope of $m = \dfrac{y_2 - y_1}{x_2 - x_1} = \dfrac{0 - 5}{5 - 0} = -1$. A line perpendicular to this will have a slope of 1. Choice A is correct. Choice B has the same slope, so it is parallel. Choice C will intersect the line, but it is neither parallel nor perpendicular. Choice D is a horizontal line.

9. **D.** The y-intercept of $y = 7 - 3x$ is (0, 7). A horizontal line passing through this point has the equation $y = 7$, so choice D is correct. Lines of the form $x = $ a constant are vertical lines, so choice A and choice C are incorrect. Choice B is a horizontal line, but it does not pass through the y-intercept of the given line.

10. **C.** If a line has a slope of $-\dfrac{3}{5}$ and an x-intercept at (10, 0), it has the equation $y - 0 = -\dfrac{3}{5}(x - 10)$ or $y = -\dfrac{3}{5}x + 6$. The y-intercept of the line is (0, 6).

Chapter 13

Mathematics Knowledge: Geometry

The geometry on the Mathematics Knowledge section of the AFQT focuses on crucial, useable ideas. The questions are about relationships you can use to calculate lengths or angle measures.

A. Angles

An angle is made of two rays or segments that meet at a point, called the *vertex*. It's important to remember that the length of the sides has no effect on the size of the angle. Angles are measured by the amount of rotation, like the hinge on a door. The wider the door is opened, the bigger the angle.

In geometry, angles are measured in degrees and classified by size. A full rotation—all the way around the circle—is 360°. Two angles with equal measurements are said to be *congruent*. The symbol for congruent is ≅.

Angles	
Type of Angle	**Measure of Angle**
Acute angle	Between 0° and 90°
Right angle	90°
Obtuse angle	Greater than 90° but less than 180°
Straight angle	180°

Complementary Angles

Two angles whose measurements total to 90° are called *complementary angles*. If two angles are complementary, each is the complement of the other. Complementary angles don't have to be *adjacent*—that is, they don't have to have the same vertex and share a side. They simply have to have measurements that add to 90°. But if they are adjacent, then together they'll form a right angle. To find the complement of an angle of 25°, subtract from 90°. So, 90° − 25° = 65°.

Supplementary Angles

Two angles whose measurements total to 180° are called *supplementary angles*. If two angles are supplementary, each is the supplement of the other. Like complementary angles, supplementary angles don't have to be adjacent. But if supplementary angles are adjacent, they form a *straight angle*: the sides that they don't share make a line. To find the supplement of an angle of 32°, subtract from 180°. So, 180° − 32° = 148°.

Vertical Angles

When two lines intersect, four angles are formed. Each pair of angles across the X from one another is a pair of vertical angles. Vertical angles are always the same size. In the following figure, if ∠1 measures 53°, the measure of ∠3 is also 53°.

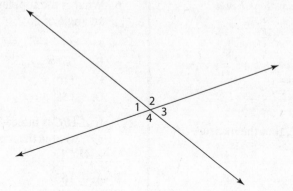

Linear Pairs

When a pair of adjacent angles has exterior sides that form a line, they're called a *linear pair*. Linear pairs are always supplementary. In the preceding figure, ∠1 and ∠4 form a linear pair. They have the same vertex, they share a side, and their exterior sides form a line. Since they're a linear pair, they're supplementary, so the measure of ∠4 is 180° − 53° = 127°.

Angle Bisectors

A line that cuts an angle into two angles of equal size is called an *angle bisector*. A bisector divides the angle into two pieces, each of which is half the original.

Practice

Directions: Choose the best answer from among the choices provided.

Use the following figure for questions 1 and 2.

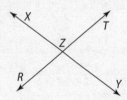

1. If ∠*TZX* measures 93°, find the measure of ∠*XZR*.

    A. 3°
    B. 46.5°
    C. 87°
    D. 93°

2. If ∠*TZX* measures 93°, find the measure of ∠*RZY*.

    A. 3°
    B. 46.5°
    C. 87°
    D. 93°

3. If ∠*A* measures 42°, what is the measure of the complement of ∠*A*?

    A. 42°
    B. 48°
    C. 84°
    D. 138°

4. Find the supplement of an angle of 15°.

    A. 15°
    B. 30°
    C. 75°
    D. 165°

5. If $\overline{YW}$ bisects ∠*XYZ* and ∠*XYZ* measures 86°, find the measure of ∠*XYW*.

    A. 4°
    B. 43°
    C. 86°
    D. 94°

6. What is the supplement of the complement of an angle of 25°?

    A. 25°
    B. 65°
    C. 115°
    D. 155°

7. If ∠*ABC* is bisected by $\overline{BD}$ and m∠*ABD* is 37°, what is the measure of the supplement of ∠*ABC*?

    A. 16°
    B. 53°
    C. 74°
    D. 106°

8. If ∠*RST* and ∠*TSU* form a linear pair and the measure of ∠*RST* is twice the measure of ∠*TSU*, what is m∠*TSU*?

    A. 30°
    B. 60°
    C. 90°
    D. 120°

9. Line $\overline{AB}$ and line $\overline{CD}$ intersect at point *P*. If m∠*APC* = 58°, find the measure of ∠*BPD*.

    A. 32°
    B. 58°
    C. 122°
    D. 148°

10. ∠*WXY* and ∠*YXZ* form a linear pair. If ∠*WXY* measures 48° less than twice the measure of ∠*YXZ*, what is the measure of the complement of ∠*YXZ*?

    A. 14°
    B. 76°
    C. 104°
    D. 152°

Answers

1. **C.** $\angle XZR$ and $\angle TZX$ are a linear pair and, therefore, supplementary. If $\angle TZX$ measures 93°, the measure of $\angle XZR$ is 180° – 93° = 87°.

2. **D.** $\angle RZY$ and $\angle TZX$ are vertical angles, so their measures are equal. If $\angle TZX$ measures 93°, $\angle RZY$ measures 93°.

3. **B.** The complement of $\angle A$ = 90° – 42° = 48°.

4. **D.** The supplement of an angle of 15° = 180° – 15° = 165°.

5. **B.** If $\overrightarrow{YW}$ bisects $\angle XYZ$ and $\angle XYZ$ measures 86°, the measure of $\angle XYW$ will be half of 86°, or 43°.

6. **C.** The supplement of the complement of an angle of 25° is the supplement of 90° – 25° = 65°. The supplement of 65° is 180° – 65° = 115°.

7. **D.** If $\angle ABC$ is bisected by $\overrightarrow{BD}$ and m$\angle ABD$ is 37°, then m$\angle ABC$ = 2m$\angle ABD$ = 2(37°) = 74°. The measure of the supplement of $\angle ABC$ is 180° – 74° = 106°.

8. **B.** If $\angle RST$ and $\angle TSU$ form a linear pair, they are supplementary, and if the measure of $\angle RST$ is twice the measure of $\angle TSU$, m$\angle RST$ + m$\angle TSU$ = 2m$\angle TSU$ + m$\angle TSU$ = 3m$\angle TSU$ = 180°. Therefore m$\angle TSU$ = 60°.

9. **B.** If line $\overleftrightarrow{AB}$ and line $\overleftrightarrow{CD}$ intersect at point P, vertical angles are formed. $\angle APC$ and $\angle BPD$ are a pair of vertical angles. If m$\angle APC$ = 58°, m$\angle BPD$ = 58° because vertical angles are congruent.

10. **A.** $\angle WXY$ and $\angle YXZ$ form a linear pair and therefore are supplementary. If $\angle WXY$ measures 48° less than twice the measure of $\angle YXZ$, m$\angle WXY$ + m$\angle YXZ$ = (2m$\angle YXZ$ – 48°) + m$\angle YXZ$ = 180°. Simplifying, 3m$\angle YXZ$ – 48° = 180°, so 3m$\angle YXZ$ = 228° and m$\angle YXZ$ = 76°. The measure of the complement of $\angle YXZ$ is 90° – 76° = 14°.

B. Lines

Angles are one basic building block of geometry. The other is the class of objects that include lines, rays, and segments.

Lines and Segments

A *line* has infinite length. A *line segment* is a portion of a line between two endpoints. You can measure the length of a line segment. Two line segments that have the same length are congruent.

Midpoints and Bisectors

The *midpoint* of a line segment is a point on the segment that divides it into two pieces of equal size. Any line, ray, or segment that passes through the midpoint of a segment is a *bisector* of the segment.

Parallel Lines

Lines that are always the same distance apart and, therefore, never intersect are called *parallel lines*. The symbol for parallel is ‖. When a pair of parallel lines is cut by another line, called a *transversal,* eight angles are formed. Different pairs from this group of eight are named in different ways.

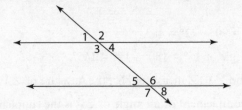

In the figure above, here are the different kinds of angles:

- **Corresponding angles:** ∠1 and ∠5, ∠2 and ∠6, ∠3 and ∠7, ∠4 and ∠8. If the lines are parallel, as they are in the figure above, each pair of corresponding angles is congruent. If the lines are not parallel, you can still describe the angles in these positions with the names of corresponding angles, but they will not have the same measurements.
- **Alternate interior angles:** ∠3 and ∠6, ∠4 and ∠5. If the lines are parallel, each pair of alternate interior angles is congruent.
- **Alternate exterior angles:** ∠1 and ∠8, ∠2 and ∠7. If the lines are parallel, each pair of alternate exterior angles is congruent.

Add the fact that ∠1 and ∠2 are supplementary, and it becomes possible to assign each of the angles created when parallel lines are cut by a transversal one of two measurements. If ∠1, ∠4, ∠5, and ∠8 all measure $n°$, then ∠2, ∠3, ∠6, and ∠7 measure $(180 - n)°$.

Perpendicular Lines

Perpendicular lines are lines that intersect at right angles. The symbol for *is perpendicular to* is ⊥. All right angles are congruent because all right angles measure 90°.

A line that passes through the midpoint of a segment and is perpendicular to the segment is a perpendicular bisector. Every point on the perpendicular bisector is equidistant from the endpoints of the segment it bisects. As shown in the figure at the top of the next page, if $\overleftrightarrow{CD}$ is the perpendicular bisector of $\overline{AB}$, $EA = EB$, $CA = CB$, $DA = DB$, and for any point P on $\overleftrightarrow{CD}$, $PA = PB$.

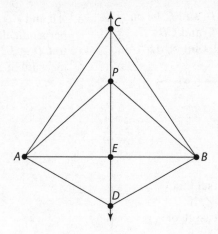

Practice

Directions: Choose the best answer from among the choices provided.

Refer to the following figure for questions 1 and 2
$\overrightarrow{PQ} \parallel \overrightarrow{RT}$.

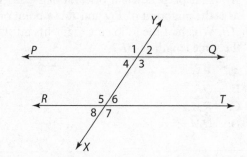

1. If ∠3 measures 112°, what is the measure of ∠5?

   A. 53°
   B. 68°
   C. 112°
   D. 127°

2. If ∠1 measures 127°, what is the measure of ∠8?

   A. 53°
   B. 68°
   C. 112°
   D. 127°

3. $\overleftrightarrow{AB} \parallel \overleftrightarrow{CD}$ and $\overleftrightarrow{PQ}$ is a transversal that intersects $\overleftrightarrow{AB}$ at R and $\overleftrightarrow{CD}$ at T. If ∠PRB and ∠RTD are corresponding angles and ∠PRB measures 32°, find the measure of ∠QTD.

   A. 32°
   B. 58°
   C. 64°
   D. 148°

4. M is the midpoint of $\overline{XY}$. If XM = 3 cm, what is the length of $\overline{XY}$?

   A. 3 cm
   B. 4 cm
   C. 5 cm
   D. 6 cm

5. If $\overleftrightarrow{AB}$ is the perpendicular bisector of $\overline{XY}$ and $\overline{AX}$ is 7 cm long, how long is $\overline{AY}$?

   A. 3.5 cm
   B. 7 cm
   C. 10.5 cm
   D. 14 cm

6. Five points, labelled A, B, C, D, and E, lie on a line. $AB = 8$, $CD = 3$, $AE = 6$, and $CB = 7$. Which of the points is the midpoint of $\overline{AB}$?

   A. C
   B. D
   C. E
   D. None of these

7. $\overrightarrow{RS} \parallel \overrightarrow{XY}$ and $\overrightarrow{AB}$ is a transversal that intersects $\overrightarrow{RS}$ at T and $\overrightarrow{XY}$ at Z. If $m\angle RTA = 73°$, what is the measure of $\angle XZB$?

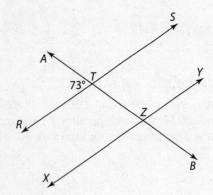

   A. 17°
   B. 90°
   C. 107°
   D. 163°

8. $\overleftrightarrow{AB}$ and $\overleftrightarrow{CD}$ intersect at E, but are not perpendicular. However, $\overrightarrow{FG}$ is perpendicular to $\overleftrightarrow{CD}$ at E. If $m\angle AED = 72°$, what is the measure of $\angle AEF$?

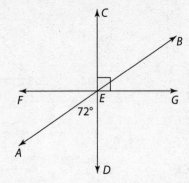

   A. 18°
   B. 72°
   C. 90°
   D. 108°

9. $\overrightarrow{AB}$ is the perpendicular bisector of $\overline{PQ}$. M is the midpoint of $\overline{PQ}$ and R is a point on $\overrightarrow{AB}$. Which of the following segments must be the same length as $\overline{PR}$?

   A. $\overline{PM}$
   B. $\overline{QR}$
   C. $\overline{RM}$
   D. $\overline{QM}$

10. Parallel lines $\overleftrightarrow{AB}$ and $\overleftrightarrow{CD}$ are cut by transversal $\overline{XY}$ at R and S, respectively. All of the following are pairs of corresponding angles EXCEPT

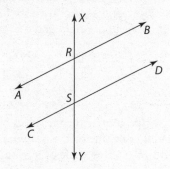

A. $\angle ARX$ and $\angle CSR$
B. $\angle XRB$ and $\angle RSD$
C. $\angle CSY$ and $\angle ARS$
D. $\angle DSY$ and $\angle BRX$

Answers

1. **C.** $\angle 3$ and $\angle 5$ are alternate interior angles, so their measurements are equal. If $\angle 3$ measures 112°, $\angle 5$ also measures 112°.

2. **A.** $\angle 1$ and $\angle 8$ are not congruent, so they'll be supplementary. If $\angle 1$ measures 127°, $\angle 8$ measures $180° - 127° = 53°$.

3. **D.** $\angle RTD$ and $\angle QTD$ will be supplementary, so $\angle QTD = 180° - 32° = 148°$.

4. **D.** If M is the midpoint of $\overline{XY}$, $\overline{XM}$ and $\overline{MY}$ are equal in length, and each is half of $\overline{XY}$. If $XM = 3$ cm, $\overline{XY}$ measures 6 cm.

5. **B.** If $\overleftrightarrow{AB}$ is the perpendicular bisector of $\overline{XY}$, $\overline{AX}$ and $\overline{AY}$ are equal in length. If $\overline{AX}$ is 7 cm long, $\overline{AY}$ is also 7 cm.

6. **B.** The distance from A to B is 8 units. If $AB = 8$, the midpoint will lie 4 units from A and 4 units from B. Use the given information to determine the distances between the points: $CD = 3$, $AE = 6$, and $CB = 7$.

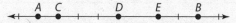

   $AE = 6$ tells you that the distance from A to E is 6 units and that puts E too far from A to be the midpoint. $CB = 7$ means C is 7 units from B, which is also too far to be the midpoint. $CD = 3$ places point D 4 units from A and 4 units from B. D is the midpoint of $\overline{AB}$.

7. **C.** If $\overrightarrow{RS} \parallel \overline{XY}$ and m$\angle RTA = 73°$, each of the angles formed by the transversal will be either congruent to $\angle RTA$ or supplementary to it. $\angle XZB$ will be supplementary to $\angle RTA$, so m$\angle XZB = 180° - 73° = 107°$ because $\angle RTA$ and $\angle XZB$ are exterior angles on the same side of the transversal.

8. **A.** $\angle AED$ and $\angle AEF$ together form one of the right angles created by the perpendicular lines. If m$\angle AED = 72°$, its complement measures $90° - 72° = 18°$. The measure of $\angle AEF$ is 18°.

9. **B.** Every point on the perpendicular bisector of $\overline{PQ}$ is equidistant from P and Q. R is a point on $\overleftrightarrow{AB}$, the perpendicular bisector, so the distance from P to R must be the same as the distance from Q to R. $PR = QR$.

10. **D.** As shown in the provided figure, $\angle ARX$ and $\angle CSR$ are corresponding angles, one from each vertex, both on the upper left. $\angle XRB$ and $\angle RSD$ are both upper right. $\angle CSY$ and $\angle ARS$ are both lower left, one at each vertex. $\angle DSY$ and $\angle BRX$ are one at each vertex, but one is upper right and one is lower right. $\angle DSY$ and $\angle BRX$ are not corresponding angles.

C. Triangles

A triangle is a polygon with three sides and three angles. In any triangle, the sum of the measures of the three angles is 180°. An exterior angle of a triangle is formed by extending one side of the triangle, and is supplementary to the interior angle at the same vertex. The measure of an exterior angle of a triangle is equal to the sum of the two remote interior angles.

In $\triangle ABC$ below, m$\angle A = 43°$, m$\angle B = 28°$, and side $\overline{AC}$ is extended through C to D. The exterior angle of the triangle at C is equal to m$\angle A$ + m$\angle B$, so m$\angle BCD = 43° + 28° = 71°$. You could also calculate the measure of $\angle BCA$ (180° − 43° − 28° = 109°), and since $\angle BCD$ is supplementary to $\angle BCA$, it'll be 180° − 109° = 71°.

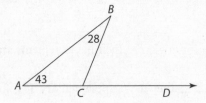

Classifying Triangles

Triangles are classified by their sides and by their angles.

Classified by Sides	
Type of Triangle	**Description**
Scalene	All sides are different lengths.
Isosceles	Two sides are equal.
Equilateral	All sides are equal.

Classified by Angles	
Type of Triangle	**Description**
Acute	All angles are acute.
Right	One angle is a right angle.
Obtuse	One angle is obtuse.

In scalene triangles, all three angles are different sizes. Isosceles triangles have two equal angles at each end of the side that is a different length. Equilateral triangles are equiangular: All three angles are 60°.

Special Line Segments

An *altitude* is a line or segment from a vertex perpendicular to the opposite side. In an isosceles triangle, the altitude drawn from the vertex angle to the base bisects the base and the vertex angle. In $\triangle ABC$, $\overline{AB} \cong \overline{BC}$, $\overline{BD}$ is an altitude, and $\angle ABD$ measures 16°. $\angle ABD$ is part of the vertex angle. Since we know that an altitude from the vertex of an isosceles triangle bisects the vertex angle, $\angle ABD$ is exactly half of the vertex angle. With a vertex angle of 32° and two congruent base angles, you can calculate that each base angle is half of 180° − 32° = 148°. Half of 148° is 74°. Each base angle of the triangle is 74°.

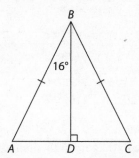

A *median* of a triangle is a line segment that connects a vertex of the triangle to the midpoint of the opposite side. A median divides the triangle into two triangles of equal area.

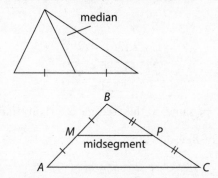

A segment that joins the midpoints of two sides of a triangle is called a *midsegment* of the triangle. A midsegment of a triangle is parallel to the third side and half as long. In $\triangle ABC$, M is the midpoint of side $\overline{AB}$ and P is the midpoint of side $\overline{BC}$. $\overline{MP}$ connects the midpoints of two sides of the triangle, so it's a midsegment. If the length of $\overline{MP}$ is 18 cm, the length of $\overline{AC}$ is 36 cm.

Triangle Inequality

In any triangle, the sum of the lengths of any two sides will be greater than the length of the third. Put another way, the length of any side of a triangle is less than the sum of the other two sides but more than the difference between them.

Gretchen lives 5 miles from the library and 2 miles from school. If Gretchen's house, the library, and the school are the vertices of a triangle, then the distance from the library to school must be greater than 5 − 2 and less than 5 + 2, so the distance is between 3 and 7 miles.

Pythagorean Theorem

A right triangle contains one right angle, and the side opposite the right angle is called the *hypotenuse*. The other two sides that form the right angle are called *legs*. The Pythagorean theorem states that in any right triangle, the square of the hypotenuse is equal to the sum of the squares of the other two sides. Most people remember it in symbolic form. If the legs of the right triangle are a and b and the hypotenuse is c, then $a^2 + b^2 = c^2$.

To find the length of the hypotenuse of a right triangle whose legs measure 5 yards and 12 yards, use the Pythagorean theorem:

$$a^2 + b^2 = c^2$$
$$5^2 + 12^2 = c^2$$
$$25 + 144 = c^2$$
$$169 = c^2$$
$$13 = c$$

Working the other way, the converse of the Pythagorean theorem can tell you whether a triangle is a right triangle or not. Start with $a^2 + b^2 = c^2$ and plug in the length of the longest side for c and the lengths of the other two sides for a and b. If, after you simplify, the statement is true, the triangle is a right triangle because it fits the Pythagorean theorem. Here's a check for a triangle with sides of 15, 36, and 39:

$$a^2 + b^2 = c^2$$
$$(15)^2 + (36)^2 = (39)^2$$
$$225 + 1,296 = 1,521$$
$$1,521 = 1,521$$

Both sides of the equation turn out the same, so this triangle is a right triangle.

Now check for a triangle with sides of 8, 9, and 20:

$$a^2 + b^2 = c^2$$
$$(8)^2 + (9)^2 = (20)^2$$
$$64 + 81 = 400$$
$$145 \neq 400$$

This triangle is not a right triangle because $145 \neq 400$. But there's actually a little bit more information here. When you test the sides to see if you have a right triangle and discover you don't, look at which side is larger. If $a^2 + b^2 < c^2$, as it is in this example, the triangle contains an obtuse angle. If $a^2 + b^2 > c^2$, then all the angles are acute.

Pythagorean Triples

Sets of three whole numbers that fit the Pythagorean theorem are called *Pythagorean triples*. Common Pythagorean triples are 3-4-5 and 5-12-13 but there are others. Multiples of Pythagorean triples are also Pythagorean triples, so 6-8-10 and 25-60-65 also fit the Pythagorean theorem.

Practice

Directions: Choose the best answer from among the choices provided.

Use the following figure for questions 1 and 2.

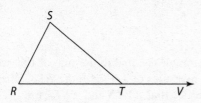

1. If ∠*VTS* measures 120° and ∠*TRS* measures 40°, find the measure of ∠*RST*.

   A. 40°
   B. 60°
   C. 80°
   D. 120°

2. If *RT* = *TS* and ∠*STR* measures 50°, find the measure of ∠*S*.

   A. 25°
   B. 50°
   C. 65°
   D. 130°

3. *P, Q,* and *R* are the midpoints of sides $\overline{AB}$, $\overline{BC}$, and $\overline{AC}$, respectively. If *AB* = 20 cm, *BC* = 24 cm, and *AC* = 30 cm, find the perimeter of Δ*PQR*.

   A. 20 cm
   B. 24 cm
   C. 30 cm
   D. 37 cm

4. Placidville is 43 miles from Aurora, and Aurora is 37 miles from Lake Grove. Which of the following could be the distance from Placidville to Lake Grove?

   A. 5 miles
   B. 28 miles
   C. 85 miles
   D. 108 miles

5. Δ*RST* is a right triangle with right angle at *R*. If *RS* = 12 and *RT* = 16, find the length of $\overline{TS}$.

   A. 18
   B. 20
   C. 24
   D. 28

6. Δ*ABC* is an acute triangle with *AB* = 8 cm and *BC* = 6 cm. Which of these could NOT be the length of $\overline{AC}$?

   A. 4 cm
   B. 6 cm
   C. 8 cm
   D. 10 cm

7. In Δ*RST*, *RS* = 13 inches and altitude $\overline{SX}$ measures 5 inches. What is the length of $\overline{RX}$?

   A. 5 inches
   B. 12 inches
   C. 13 inches
   D. 26 inches

8. Δ*XYZ* is an isosceles triangle with a vertex angle that measures 50°. Which of the following best describes Δ*XYZ*?

   A. Acute triangle
   B. Right triangle
   C. Obtuse triangle
   D. Equiangular triangle

9. In equilateral triangle $\triangle ABC$, $AC = 12$ cm. Find the length of altitude $\overline{BD}$.

   A. 6 cm
   B. $6\sqrt{3}$ cm
   C. 12 cm
   D. $12\sqrt{3}$ cm

10. In $\triangle XYZ$, $XY = 17$ cm and $YZ = 11$ cm. The length of $\overline{XZ}$ CANNOT be

   A. 7 cm
   B. 11 cm
   C. 23 cm
   D. 31 cm

Answers

1. **C.** $\angle VTS$ is an exterior angle of the triangle, and the exterior angle is equal to the sum of the two remote interior angles. So, $\angle VTS$ is equal to the sum of the measures of $\angle TRS$ and $\angle RST$. Therefore, $\angle RST$ is equal to $120° - 40° = 80°$. Alternately, you might notice that $\angle VTS$ and $\angle STR$ are supplementary, so $\angle STR$ measures $180° - 120° = 60°$. The three interior angles of the triangle must add to $180°$, so $\angle RST$ must measure $80°$.

2. **C.** If $RT = TS$, then $\angle R$ and $\angle S$ are the same size. Since $\angle STR$ measures $50°$, there are $180° - 50° = 130°$ left for those two angles, so each measures $65°$.

3. **D.** The sides of $\triangle PQR$ are all midsegments of $\triangle ABC$, so they measure half of the sides of $\triangle ABC$. The perimeter of $\triangle PQR = 10 + 12 + 15 = 37$ cm.

4. **B.** If the three cities are arranged in a triangle, the distance from Placidville to Lake Grove will be greater than $43 - 37$ and less than $43 + 37$, or between 6 and 80.

5. **B.** Use the Pythagorean theorem, with $a = 12$ and $b = 16$:

$$a^2 + b^2 = c^2$$
$$12^2 + 16^2 = c^2$$
$$144 + 256 = c^2$$
$$400 = c^2$$
$$20 = c$$

The length of $\overline{TS}$ is 20.

6. **D.** If $\triangle ABC$ is an acute triangle with $AB = 8$ cm and $BC = 6$ cm, the triangle inequality says that the third side will be between $8 - 6 = 2$ cm and $8 + 6 = 14$ cm, but that is not sufficient to narrow the choices. The triangle is acute, so the converse of the Pythagorean theorem may be helpful. In an acute triangle, $a^2 + b^2 > c^2$, where c is the longest side. If the unknown side is the longest, set up as follows and solve for c:

$$6^2 + 8^2 > c^2$$
$$36 + 64 > c^2$$
$$100 > c^2$$
$$10 > c$$

The unknown side would have to be less than 10. Therefore, 10 cm could NOT be the length of $\overline{AC}$.

7. **B.** Altitude $\overline{SX}$ is perpendicular to $\overline{RT}$ at X, so $\overline{RS}$, $\overline{SX}$, and $\overline{RX}$ form a right triangle. If $RS = 13$ inches and altitude $\overline{SX}$ measures 5 inches, use the Pythagorean theorem:

$$a^2 + b^2 = c^2$$
$$5^2 + b^2 = 13^2$$
$$25 + b^2 = 169$$
$$b^2 = 169 - 25$$
$$b^2 = 144$$
$$b = 12$$

The length of $\overline{RX}$ is 12 inches.

8. **A.** ΔXYZ is an isosceles triangle with a vertex angle that measures 50°, so the base angles each measure 65°: $180 - 50 = 130$, and $130 \div 2 = 65$. ΔXYZ has three acute angles, and so it is an acute triangle.

9. **B.** In equilateral triangle ΔABC, the altitude is the perpendicular bisector of the base, creating two right triangles.

If $AC = 12$ cm, then $AB = BC = 12$ cm because the triangle is equilateral. AB is the hypotenuse of the right triangle ADB that is formed and $AD = 6$. Using the Pythagorean theorem,

$$a^2 + b^2 = c^2$$
$$6^2 + b^2 = 12^2$$
$$36 + b^2 = 144$$
$$b^2 = 144 - 36$$
$$b^2 = 108$$
$$b = \sqrt{108}$$
$$b = \sqrt{36 \cdot 3}$$
$$b = 6\sqrt{3}$$

The length of altitude $\overline{BD}$ is $6\sqrt{3}$.

10. **D.** In ΔXYZ, $XY = 17$ cm and $YZ = 11$ cm. The triangle inequality says length of $17 - 11 < \overline{XZ} < 17 + 11$, so $6 < \overline{XZ} < 28$ and $\overline{XZ}$ cannot be 31.

D. Quadrilaterals

The term *quadrilateral* denotes any four-sided figure, but most of the attention falls on the members of the parallelogram family, which includes *parallelograms, rhombuses, rectangles,* and *squares*. All members of the parallelogram family have two pairs of parallel sides. A *trapezoid* is a quadrilateral with one pair of parallel sides and one pair of nonparallel sides. Any quadrilateral can be divided, by drawing a diagonal, into two triangles. The interior angles of a triangle total 180°, so the interior angles of a quadrilateral have measurements that total 2(180°) or 360°.

Parallelograms

A *parallelogram* is a quadrilateral with two pairs of opposite sides parallel. In a parallelogram, opposite sides are congruent, that is, the same length, opposite angles are congruent, which means they have the same measurement, and consecutive angles are supplementary, adding to 180°. Drawing one diagonal in a parallelogram divides it into two congruent triangles. The word *congruent*, when applied to a triangle or a figure with more than three sides, means exactly the same shape and size. When both diagonals are drawn, the diagonals bisect each other.

A *rhombus* is a parallelogram with four equal sides. Because the rhombus is a parallelogram, it has all the properties of a parallelogram. In addition, the diagonals of a rhombus are perpendicular to one another. The diagonals of a rhombus also bisect the angles of the rhombus.

A *rectangle* is a parallelogram with four right angles. Because the rectangle is a parallelogram, it has all the properties of a parallelogram. Its angles are all right angles, so they're all congruent and any pair is supplementary. The diagonals of a rectangle bisect each other and the diagonals are congruent.

A *square* is a parallelogram that is both a rhombus and a rectangle. The square has all the properties of the parallelogram, the rhombus, and the rectangle.

In square *ABCD*, the diagonals intersect at *E*. Since the square is a rectangle, diagonals are congruent and bisect each other. If $BE = 8$ cm, $AE = EC = BE = ED = 8$ cm. Since the square is a rhombus, the diagonals are perpendicular and create four identical isosceles right triangles. The side of the square is the hypotenuse of each right triangle.

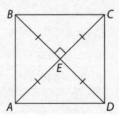

You can use the Pythagorean theorem to find the length of the hypotenuse and, thus, the length of the side of the square:

$$a^2 + b^2 = c^2$$
$$8^2 + 8^2 = c^2$$
$$64 + 64 = c^2$$
$$128 = c^2$$

Take the square root of 128 and simplify the radical to find *c*: $c = \sqrt{128} = \sqrt{64 \cdot 2} = \sqrt{64}\sqrt{2} = 8\sqrt{2}$ cm. Therefore, each side of the square measures $8\sqrt{2}$ cm.

Trapezoids

A *trapezoid* is a quadrilateral with one pair of parallel sides. In trapezoids, the parallel sides are called the *bases*, and the nonparallel sides are called *legs*.

If the nonparallel sides of a trapezoid are congruent, the trapezoid is an *isosceles trapezoid*. In an isosceles trapezoid, base angles are congruent and diagonals are congruent.

The line segment joining the midpoints of the nonparallel sides is called the *midsegment* of the trapezoid. The midsegment is parallel to the bases, and its length is the average of the lengths of the bases.

Practice

Directions: Choose the best answer from among the choices provided.

1. If *MNOP* is a rhombus with sides 5 cm long, and diagonal $\overline{MO}$ measures 8 cm, find the length of diagonal $\overline{PN}$.

   A.   5 cm
   B.   6 cm
   C.   7 cm
   D.   8 cm

2. Find the length of a diagonal of a rectangle if its sides measure 15 cm and 20 cm.

   A.   15 cm
   B.   18 cm
   C.   20 cm
   D.   25 cm

3. *ABCD* is a trapezoid with $\overline{BC} \parallel \overline{AD}$. If *BC* = 14 inches and the midsegment of the trapezoid measures 18 inches, find *AD*.

   A.   22 inches
   B.   20 inches
   C.   18 inches
   D.   16 inches

4. If *ABCD* is an isosceles trapezoid, with ∠*A* measuring 48°, find the measure of ∠*C*.

   A.   24°
   B.   48°
   C.   96°
   D.   132°

5. A rectangle has a side of 15 inches and a diagonal of 39 inches. Find the length of the other side.

   A.   48 inches
   B.   36 inches
   C.   24 inches
   D.   12 inches

6. Line segments $\overline{AB} \parallel \overline{CD}$ and transversals $\overline{BC}$ and $\overline{AD}$ are drawn. ∠*ABD* measures 57°. Which of the following is enough additional information to assure that *ABCD* is a parallelogram?

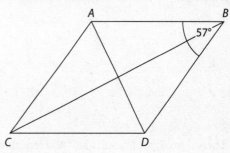

   A.   m∠*DAB* = 123°
   B.   m∠*BAC* = 123°
   C.   m∠*ADC* = 57°
   D.   m∠*DAB* = 57°

7. In trapezoid *PQRS*, the midpoint of $\overline{PQ}$ is *M* and the midpoint of $\overline{RS}$ is *N*. Midsegment $\overline{MN}$ measures 14 inches and $\overline{PS}$ is 22 inches. What is the length of $\overline{QR}$?

   A.   6 inches
   B.   14 inches
   C.   18 inches
   D.   22 inches

8. *ABCD* is an isosceles trapezoid with m∠*A* = 36°. Base $\overline{BC}$ is extended through point *C* to point *E* and $\overline{ED}$ is drawn. In order for $\overline{ED}$ to be parallel to $\overline{AB}$, what must be the measure of ∠*CDE*?

   A.   36°
   B.   60°
   C.   108°
   D.   144°

9. Square $ABCD$ has diagonals $\overline{AC}$ and $\overline{BD}$ that intersect at point E. Which best describes ΔCED?

   A. Equilateral triangle
   B. Isosceles right triangle
   C. Right triangle but not isosceles
   D. Isosceles triangle but not right

10. $PQRS$ is a trapezoid with $\overline{QR} \parallel \overline{PS}$. $PS > QR$. $\overline{PQ}$ and $\overline{RS}$ are extended and meet at point T. If m$\angle QPS = 43°$ and m$\angle PTS = 94°$, which of the following is true?

   A. ΔQTR is a right triangle.
   B. The measure of $\angle TQR$ is $60°$.
   C. $PQRS$ is an isosceles trapezoid.
   D. ΔPTS is an equilateral triangle.

Answers

1. **B.** Diagonals $\overline{MO}$ and $\overline{PN}$ bisect each other, creating a right triangle with a hypotenuse of 5 cm, and a leg equal to half of diagonal $\overline{MO}$, or 4 cm. Use the Pythagorean theorem to find the length of $\overline{PN}$:

$$a^2 + b^2 = c^2$$
$$a^2 + 4^2 = 5^2$$
$$a^2 + 16 = 25$$
$$a^2 = 9$$
$$a = 3$$

The value of a represents half the length of $\overline{PN}$, so the diagonal is 6 cm long.

2. **D.** Use the Pythagorean theorem with $a = 15$ and $b = 20$ to find c:

$$a^2 + b^2 = c^2$$
$$15^2 + 20^2 = c^2$$
$$225 + 400 = c^2$$
$$625 = c^2$$
$$\sqrt{625} = c^2$$
$$25 = c$$

Alternatively, you may recognize that 15 and 20 are 5×3 and 5×4, so the Pythagorean triple would be completed by 5×5, or 25.

3. **A.** The midsegment of the trapezoid is half the sum of the lengths of the bases, so if the midsegment is 18, the bases must total 36. $BC = 14$, so $AD = 36 - 14 = 22$.

4. **D.** In isosceles trapezoid $ABCD$, base angles are congruent. That means that if $\angle A$ measures $48°$, then there is a second angle measuring $48°$ and two other angles, each of which measures $180° - 48° = 132°$. Since $\angle A$ and $\angle C$ are opposite each other, they'll be supplementary. So, m$\angle C = 132°$.

5. **B.** If a rectangle has a side of 15 inches and a diagonal of 39 inches, you can find the other side with the Pythagorean theorem:

$$a^2 + b^2 = c^2$$
$$a^2 + 15^2 = 39^2$$
$$a^2 + 225 = 1,521$$
$$a^2 = 1,296$$
$$a = \sqrt{1,296}$$
$$a = 36$$

Alternatively, you can recognize that 15 is 3 × 5 and 39 is 3 × 13, and spot the 5, 12, 13 Pythagorean triple. The other side of the rectangle will be 3 × 12, or 36 inches.

6. **B.** To be certain that $ABCD$ is a parallelogram, you need to know that $\overline{AC}$ is parallel to $\overline{BD}$. The simplest way to do that is to show that $\angle ABD$ and $\angle BAC$, consecutive interior angles, are supplementary. Knowing that m$\angle BAC$ = 123° is sufficient.

7. **A.** The length of the midsegment is the average of the lengths of the bases, so $MN = \dfrac{PS + QR}{2}$. Solve for the length of $\overline{QR}$:

$$MN = \frac{PS + QR}{2}$$
$$14 = \frac{22 + QR}{2}$$
$$28 = 22 + QR$$
$$6 = QR$$

8. **C.** Because $ABCD$ is an isosceles trapezoid, m$\angle ADC$ = m$\angle A$ = 36°. In order for $\overline{ED}$ to be parallel to $\overline{AB}$, m$\angle ADE$ must equal 144° so that it and $\angle A$ are supplementary. $\angle ADC$ is part of $\angle ADE$ and measures 36°, so $\angle CDE$ must measure 144° – 36° = 108°.

9. **B.** The diagonals of a square are perpendicular, bisect each other, and bisect the angles at the vertices of the square. The triangle $\triangle CED$ is a right triangle. Its acute angles each measure 45° and have legs half the length of the diagonal. $\triangle CED$ is an isosceles right triangle.

10. **C.** $\overline{PQ}$ and $\overline{RS}$, extended to meet at point T, form a triangle. If m$\angle QPS$ = 43° and m$\angle PTS$ = 94°, then m$\angle TSP$ = 180° – (43° + 94°) = 180° – 137° = 43°. Choice A cannot be correct because a triangle cannot contain both a right angle and a 94° angle. The measure of $\angle TQR$ is equal to m$\angle QPS$ because $\overline{QR} \parallel \overline{PS}$ and those angles are corresponding angles; therefore, choice B is not correct. Choice D is incorrect because none of the angles in $\triangle PTS$ measure 60°. That leaves choice C, which is correct because the equal base angles indicate that the trapezoid is isosceles.

E. Perimeter and Area

Perimeter

The perimeter of a polygon is the distance all the way around the figure. You can generally find the perimeter by simply adding all the sides, but there are a few shortcuts:

- perimeter of a rectangle: $P = 2l + 2w$ (where l stands for length and w stands for width)
- perimeter of a square: $P = 4s$ (where s = the length of one side)

Area

The area, or space enclosed by a polygon, can sometimes be calculated by simple formulas, and at other times an area can be broken down into sections whose areas can be calculated by a formula.

Parallelograms

The area of a parallelogram is found by multiplying the base times the height: $A = bh$. The height must be measured as the perpendicular distance between the bases. Don't confuse the side with the height. Since a rectangle is a parallelogram, its area is also base times height. But since the adjacent sides of the rectangle are perpendicular, the length and width are the base and the height, so the formula for the area of a rectangle is $A = lw$. In a square, all sides are the same length, so the formula for the area of a square is also $A = lw$ or $A = s^2$.

Triangles

Every triangle is half of some parallelogram, so the area of a triangle is half the product of the base and the height: $A = \frac{1}{2}bh$. If the area of a triangle is 88 square feet, and the base is 16 feet, you can find the height of the triangle by putting the known values into the formula:

$$A = \frac{1}{2}bh$$

$$88 = \frac{1}{2}(16)h$$

$$88 = 8h$$

$$11 = h$$

Trapezoids

If you draw a diagonal in a trapezoid, you create two triangles. The area of one triangle is half the top base times the height, and the area of the other triangle is half the bottom base times the height. Therefore, the area of a trapezoid is equal to the areas of the two triangles added together, or $\frac{1}{2}b_1h + \frac{1}{2}b_2h$, which can be simply written as $A = \frac{1}{2}h(b_1 + b_2)$. Because the length of the midsegment of a trapezoid, the line segment that connects the midpoints of the nonparallel sides, is equal to half the sum of the bases, you can also think of the area formula as $A = h \cdot \frac{1}{2}(b_1 + b_2) = h \cdot$ length of the midsegment. If the area of a trapezoid is 40 cm^2 and the bases are 3 cm and 5 cm, you can find the height by substituting into the formula:

$$A = \frac{1}{2}h(b_1 + b_2)$$

$$40 = \frac{1}{2}h(3 + 5)$$

$$40 = \frac{1}{2}(8h)$$

$$40 = 4h$$

$$10 = h$$

Practice

Directions: Choose the best answer from among the choices provided.

1. Find the area of trapezoid *ABCD* if the midsegment measures 18 cm and the height is 6 cm.

   A. 24 cm²
   B. 27 cm²
   C. 54 cm²
   D. 108 cm²

2. A parallelogram has a base of 12 inches. If its area is 96 square inches, find the height of the parallelogram.

   A. 8 inches
   B. 16 inches
   C. 42 inches
   D. 84 inches

3. The legs of a right triangle have lengths of 12 cm and 16 cm. Find the area of the triangle.

   A. 192 cm²
   B. 96 cm²
   C. 48 cm²
   D. 36 cm²

4. The length of a rectangle is 2 more than 3 times its width. If the perimeter of the rectangle is 60 cm, what is the area?

   A. 659.75 cm²
   B. 420 cm²
   C. 210 cm²
   D. 161 cm²

5. The base of a triangle is twice its height. If the area is 64 square inches, what is the length of the base?

   A. 4 inches
   B. 8 inches
   C. 16 inches
   D. 32 inches

6. The length of a rectangle is 6 inches more than its width. If the area of the rectangle is 55 square inches, find the length.

   A. 5 inches
   B. 6 inches
   C. 11 inches
   D. 17 inches

7. The midsegment of a trapezoid measures 18 inches and the trapezoid has an area of 216 square inches. What is the height of the trapezoid?

   A. 6 inches
   B. 12 inches
   C. 18 inches
   D. 24 inches

8. The perimeter of a rectangle is 40 cm. If the length and width are both whole numbers, which of these could NOT be the area of the rectangle?

   A. 36 cm²
   B. 75 cm²
   C. 100 cm²
   D. 169 cm²

9. The perimeter of isosceles $\triangle ABC$ is 80 meters and its height, drawn from the vertex angle, is 12 meters. If the area of the triangle is 218.4 square meters, find the length of one of the congruent legs.

   A. 21.8 meters
   B. 36.4 meters
   C. 43.6 meters
   D. 105.8 meters

10. The area of trapezoid $ABCD$ is 240 square inches. If a rectangle is drawn with the same height as trapezoid $ABCD$ and with a base equal in length to the midsegment of $ABCD$, what is the area of that rectangle?

   A. 120 in²
   B. 240 in²
   C. 360 in²
   D. 480 in²

Answers

1. **D.** The area of a trapezoid is half the height times the sum of the bases. The length of the midsegment is equal to half the sum of the bases, so the area is equal to the length of the midsegment times the height, or $18 \times 6 = 108$ cm².

2. **A.** The area of a parallelogram is base times height, so the height is equal to the area divided by the base: $96 \div 12 = 8$ inches.

3. **B.** In a right triangle, since the legs are perpendicular to each other, the lengths of the legs can be used as the base and the height. The area of the triangle is half the base times the height, and half of $12 \cdot 16$ is 96 square cm.

4. **D.** If the length of a rectangle is 2 more than 3 times its width, the length can be expressed as $2 + 3w$. The perimeter is $2l + 2w$ or $2(2 + 3w) + 2w = 60$ cm, so $4 + 6w + 2w = 60$. Simplifying, $4 + 8w = 60$ and $8w = 56$ tells you that $w = 7$. Substituting back, you can find that $l = 2 + (3 \times 7) = 23$, and since the length and width of the rectangle are 23 and 7, the area is $23 \times 7 = 161$ cm².

5. **C.** If $b = 2h$, the area of the triangle becomes $A = \frac{1}{2}bh = \frac{1}{2}(2h)h = h^2$. If the area is 64, the height is 8. Since the base of this triangle is twice its height, the base is 16 inches.

6. **C.** Let w = the width of the rectangle and $w + 6$ = the length. Since $A = lw$, $55 = w(w + 6)$. Solve for w:

$$w(w+6) = 55$$
$$w^2 + 6w = 55$$
$$w^2 + 6w - 55 = 0$$
$$(w+11)(w-5) = 0$$

$$(w+11) = 0 \qquad \text{or} \qquad (w-5) = 0$$
$$w = -11 \qquad\qquad\qquad w = 5$$

Reject $w = -11$ because a width cannot be negative. Therefore, the length $= 5 + 6 = 11$ inches.

7. **B.** The area of a trapezoid is $A = \frac{1}{2}(b_1 + b_2)h$. Recall that $\frac{1}{2}(b_1 + b_2)$ is the length of the midsegment, so the area can be found by multiplying the length of the midsegment times the height. Therefore, $18h = 216$ and $h = 12$ inches. The height of the trapezoid is 12 inches.

8. **D.** If the perimeter of a rectangle is 40 cm and both the length and width are whole numbers, then $l + w = 20$ and the possible values (l, w) are $(1, 19)$, $(2, 18)$, $(3, 17)$, $(4, 16)$, $(5, 15)$, $(6, 14)$, $(7, 13)$,

(8, 12), (9, 11), and (10, 10). It is not necessary to look further because (11, 9) will have the same area as (9, 11) and so on. Choice A is possible (2, 18), as are choices B (5, 15) and C (10, 10). No area larger than 100 square centimeters is possible, so choice D, at 169 cm², is correct.

9. **A.** Because $\triangle ABC$ is isosceles, the perimeter is $2x + y = 80$. Drawing the height from the vertex angle creates two right triangles with hypotenuse of 12 meters, one leg that measures x and another that measures $\frac{1}{2}y$.

$$A = \frac{1}{2}bh$$
$$218.4 = \frac{1}{2}y(12)$$
$$218.4 = 6y$$
$$36.4 = y$$

That means $2x + 36.4 = 80$ and $2x = 43.6$. The length of one of the congruent legs is $x = 21.8$ meters.

10. **B.** The area of trapezoid $ABCD$ is equal to the length of the midsegment times the height, which is 240 square inches. If a rectangle is drawn with the same height as trapezoid $ABCD$ and with a base equal in length to the midsegment of $ABCD$, the area of that rectangle is equal to the area of the trapezoid.

F. Polygons

While most of the attention is focused on triangles and quadrilaterals, there are polygons with more than four sides. You should know their names and some general properties they share. Like triangles and quadrilaterals, other polygons take their names from the number of sides they have.

Types of Polygons	
Number of Sides	**Name of Shape**
3	Triangle
4	Quadrilateral
5	Pentagon
6	Hexagon
7	Heptagon
8	Octagon

Properties

Polygons are *convex* if every diagonal you can draw stays inside the polygon. The pentagon on the left is convex. The octagon on the right is not.

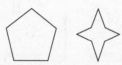

The total of the measures of the three angles in a triangle is 180°. Since any convex quadrilateral divides into two triangles when you draw a diagonal, the total of the four angles in a convex quadrilateral is 360°. If a convex polygon with more than three sides is divided into triangles by drawing all the possible diagonals from a single vertex, there are $n-2$ triangles, each with angles totaling 180°. Therefore, the sum of the interior angles of any convex polygon can be found with the formula: sum of interior angles = $180°(n-2)$, where n is the number of sides. If the polygon is *regular* (that is, all sides congruent and all angles congruent), then the measure of any one interior angle can be found by dividing the total measure by the number of angles.

If you want to find the measure of one interior angle of a regular pentagon, start by finding the total. A pentagon has five sides, so drawing all the diagonals from one vertex will create three triangles. The total of the measures of the five interior angles of a pentagon is 180 × 3, or 540°. The pentagon is regular, so all the angles are the same size. Divide 540° by 5 to find that each angle is 108°.

If you extend one side at each vertex of the polygon, as shown below, so that you create one exterior angle at each vertex, the sum of the exterior angles will be 360°. It doesn't matter how many sides the polygon has. The total of the measurements of one exterior angle at each vertex is always 360°.

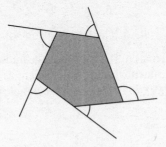

Practice

Directions: Choose the best answer from among the choices provided.

1. Find the sum of the interior angles of an octagon.

   A. 540°
   B. 720°
   C. 900°
   D. 1,080°

2. Find the sum of the exterior angles of a pentagon.

   A. 180°
   B. 360°
   C. 540°
   D. 720°

3. Find the measure of one interior angle of a regular hexagon.

   A. 60°
   B. 120°
   C. 180°
   D. 360°

4. If the total of the measures of the interior angles in a regular polygon is 1,260°, what is the measure of one interior angle?

   A. 180°
   B. 140°
   C. 126°
   D. 90°

5. Find the measure of one exterior angle of a regular pentagon.

   A. 72°
   B. 108°
   C. 180°
   D. 360°

6. How many distinct diagonals can be drawn in a pentagon?

   A. 3
   B. 5
   C. 10
   D. 20

7. Find the measure of one exterior angle of a regular hexagon.

   A. 60°
   B. 90°
   C. 120°
   D. 180°

8. Find the difference between the total of the measures of the interior angles of a pentagon and the total of its exterior angles.

   A. 30°
   B. 60°
   C. 90°
   D. 180°

9. What is the measure of one interior angle of a regular 20-sided polygon?

   A. 18°
   B. 162°
   C. 180°
   D. 200°

10. The ratio of the measure of one exterior angle of a regular pentagon to the measure of one exterior angle of a regular decagon is

   A. 1:2
   B. 2:1
   C. 3:4
   D. 4:3

Answers

1. **D.** The sum of the interior angles of an octagon is $180°(8 − 2) = 180°(6) = 1,080°$.

2. **B.** The sum of the exterior angles of a pentagon—or any polygon—is 360°.

3. **B.** The total of the interior angles of a hexagon is $180°(6 − 2) = 180°(4) = 720°$. Since the polygon is regular, divide by 6 to find that the measure of one angle is 120°.

4. **B.** If n is the number of sides and the total of the interior angles is $180°(n − 2) = 1,260°$, you can divide 1,260 by 180 to find that $n − 2$ must equal 7, and therefore $n = 7 + 2 = 9$. The regular polygon has 9 sides. Since the polygon is regular, divide the total of the interior angles by 9 to find that the measure of one angle is 140°.

5. **A.** The total of the exterior angles of a pentagon is 360°. Since the pentagon is regular, all the exterior angles are the same size, so you can divide by 5. Each exterior angle is 72°.

6. **B.** A pentagon has five vertices. From any one vertex, you can draw to two other vertices. That would create 10 diagonals, but not all are distinct. The diagonal from A to C, for example, is the same as the diagonal from C to A. There are 5 distinct diagonals in a pentagon.

7. **A.** The six exterior angles of a regular hexagon total 360° and are of equal size. Therefore, one exterior angle measures 60°: $360° ÷ 6 = 60°$.

8. **D.** The total of the measures of the interior angles of a pentagon is $180°(5 − 2) = 180°(3) = 540°$. The total of the exterior angles is 360°. $540° − 360° = 180°$.

9. **B.** The total of the measures of the interior angles of a 20-gon is $180°(20 - 2) = 180°(18) = 3,240°$. Each of the 20 interior angles of a regular 20-gon measures $3,240° ÷ 20 = 162°$.

10. **B.** One exterior angle of a regular pentagon measures $360° ÷ 5 = 72°$. Each exterior angle of a regular decagon measures $360° ÷ 10 = 36°$. The ratio is $72°:36°$, or $2:1$.

G. Congruence and Similarity

Geometry is interested in relationships between polygons as well as their individual properties. Congruence and similarity are the two fundamental relationships.

The word *congruent* is used to mean *having the same measurement* when talking about segments or angles. The symbol for congruent is $≅$, so when we write $∠A ≅ ∠B$, we're saying those two angles have the same measurement. But when triangles or other polygons are said to be congruent, we mean that all their measurements are the same. Each of the sides in one triangle is the same length as a side in the other, and each of the angles in one triangle has the same measurement as an angle in the other triangle. More than that, the parts are arranged in such a way that the two triangles are exactly the same size and shape; they are copies of each other. If we write $∆ABC ≅ ∆XYZ$, we're saying $AB = XY$, $BC = YZ$, $AC = XZ$, $∠A ≅ ∠X$, $∠B ≅ ∠Y$, and $∠C ≅ ∠Z$.

Congruence

Triangles are *congruent* if they're the same shape and the same size. Since the size of the angles controls the shape of the triangle, angles are congruent. The length of the sides controls size, so sides are congruent. When the congruent triangles are named, the order in which the vertices are listed tells you what matches up. If you're told that $∆ABC ≅ ∆RTS$, the $∠A ≅ ∠R$, $∠B ≅ ∠T$, and $∠C ≅ ∠S$. Following the order of the letters again, $\overline{AB} ≅ \overline{RT}$, $\overline{BC} ≅ \overline{TS}$, and $\overline{AC} ≅ \overline{RS}$.

What's most likely to show up in problems on the AFQT is that all the sides and all the angles that correspond are congruent. Suppose $∆ABC ≅ ∆YXZ$ and $\overline{BC}$ measures 6 inches. $\overline{BC} ≅ \overline{XZ}$, so $\overline{XZ}$ also measures 6 inches.

Similarity

Triangles are *similar* if they are the same shape, but not necessarily the same size. Similar triangles are enlargements or reductions of each other, with all sides expanded or compressed proportionally. The symbol for *is similar to* is $\sim$. (You may notice that $\sim$ is part of the symbol for congruent, $≅$, in which the $\sim$ says same shape, and the $=$ says same size.) Congruent figures are both the same shape and same size, while similar figures are the same shape but proportional in size, not the same size.

Corresponding angles are congruent and corresponding sides are in proportion. Just as the order in which the vertices of congruent triangles are named tells you what matches up, so the order in which similar triangles are named tells you which angles are the same size and which sides are in proportion. If you know that $∆RST \sim ∆MPN$, that tells you that $∠R ≅ ∠M$, $∠S ≅ ∠P$, and $∠T ≅ ∠N$. It also lets you know that the proportion is $\dfrac{RS}{MP} = \dfrac{ST}{PN} = \dfrac{RT}{MN}$. If $∆ABC \sim ∆XYZ$ and $XZ = 4$ inches, $XY = 7$ inches, and $AB = 21$ inches, you can find the length of $\overline{AC}$ by setting up the proportion $\dfrac{AB}{XY} = \dfrac{BC}{YZ} = \dfrac{AC}{XZ}$. Working with the given

lengths, $\dfrac{AB}{XY} = \dfrac{21}{7} = \dfrac{AC}{4}$. Notice that you can simplify $\dfrac{21}{7} = \dfrac{AC}{4}$ to $3 = \dfrac{AC}{4}$ and then multiply both sides by

4 to solve: $AC = 12$ inches. If you don't recognize that you can simplify first, you can solve by cross-multiplying:

$$\frac{21}{7} = \frac{AC}{4}$$
$$21 \cdot 4 = 7AC$$
$$84 = 7AC$$
$$12 = AC$$

Area and Perimeter in Congruent and Similar Triangles

Congruent triangles are copies of one another and so will have identical areas and identical perimeters. Similar triangles have sides that are in proportion, and their perimeters will be in the same proportion. If the ratio of corresponding sides reduces to 3:5, the ratio of the perimeters will be 3:5. Because the area is found by multiplying two dimensions, each of which is enlarged in the same proportion, the ratio of the areas of similar triangles is the square of the ratio of the sides. Therefore, if the ratio of the sides is 3:5, then the ratio of the areas is 9:25.

Suppose $\triangle CAT \sim \triangle DOG$, $\dfrac{AT}{OG} = \dfrac{5}{12}$, and the area of $\triangle DOG$ is 72 in.[2]. $\dfrac{\text{Area of } \triangle CAT}{\text{Area of } \triangle DOG} = \left(\dfrac{5}{12}\right)^2 = \dfrac{25}{144}$. You know the area of $\triangle DOG$, so plug that in, and solve:

$$\frac{\text{Area of } \triangle CAT}{72} = \frac{25}{144}$$
$$\text{Area of } \triangle CAT = \overset{1}{\cancel{72}}\left(\frac{25}{\cancel{144}_2}\right)$$
$$= \frac{25}{2}$$
$$= 12\frac{1}{2}, \text{ or } 12.5 \text{ in.}^2$$

Practice

Directions: Choose the best answer from among the choices provided.

1. $\triangle ABC \cong \triangle RST$, and $AB = 12$ cm, $BC = 18$ cm, and $AC = 20$ cm. Find the length of $\overline{RT}$.

   A. 12 cm
   B. 16 cm
   C. 18 cm
   D. 20 cm

2. $\triangle MNP \sim \triangle XYZ$ and $MN = 12$ inches, $NP = 8$ inches, and $XY = 18$ inches. Find the length of $\overline{YZ}$.

   A. 8 inches
   B. 12 inches
   C. 16 inches
   D. 18 inches

3. $\triangle ARM \sim \triangle LEG$, $RM = 9$ inches, $AM = 15$ inches, and $EG = 21$ inches. Find the length of $\overline{LG}$.

   A. 15 inches
   B. 21 inches
   C. 27 inches
   D. 35 inches

4. If $\triangle ARM \sim \triangle LEG$, $RM = 9$ inches, $EG = 21$ inches, and the perimeter of $\triangle ARM$ is 24 inches, find the perimeter of $\triangle LEG$.

   A. 24 inches
   B. 56 inches
   C. 72 inches
   D. 168 inches

5. If $\triangle ARM \sim \triangle LEG$, $RM = 9$ inches, $EG = 21$ inches, and the area of $\triangle LEG$ is 98 in.², find the area of $\triangle ARM$.

   A. 9 in.²
   B. 18 in.²
   C. 49 in.²
   D. 98 in.²

6. In $\triangle ABC$, $AB = 27$ cm and $BC = 36$ cm. In $\triangle RST$, $RS = 42$. If $\triangle ABC \sim \triangle RST$, find the length of $\overline{ST}$.

   A. $18\dfrac{2}{3}$ cm
   B. $31\dfrac{1}{2}$ cm
   C. 51 cm
   D. 56 cm

7. $\triangle XYZ \cong \triangle RST$. If $XY = 93$ meters, $YZ = 87$ meters, and $RT = 100$ meters, find the length of $\overline{RS}$.

   A. 13 meters
   B. 87 meters
   C. 93 meters
   D. 100 meters

8. $\triangle JKL$ has sides of 35 cm, 84 cm, and 91 cm. $\triangle NMO$ has a longest side of 65 cm. If $\triangle JKL \sim \triangle NMO$, what is the length of the shortest side of $\triangle NMO$?

   A. 25 cm
   B. 35 cm
   C. 58 cm
   D. 60 cm

9. $\triangle ABC \cong \triangle XYZ$. $\overline{AB}$ is 6 meters longer than $\overline{BC}$, and $\overline{AC}$ is twice the length of $\overline{AB}$. If the perimeter of $\triangle XYZ$ is 42 meters, find the length of $\overline{YZ}$.

   A. 6 meters
   B. 15 meters
   C. 18 meters
   D. 21 meters

10. In $\triangle RST$, m$\angle R = 54°$ and m$\angle S =$ m$\angle T$. If $\triangle RST \sim \triangle EFG$, find the measure of $\angle E$.

   A. 45°
   B. 54°
   C. 63°
   D. 72°

Answers

1. **D.** If $\triangle ABC \cong \triangle RST$, $RT = AC = 20$ cm.

2. **B.** If $\triangle MNP \sim \triangle XYZ$, $\dfrac{MN}{XY} = \dfrac{NP}{YZ}$, so $\dfrac{12}{18} = \dfrac{8}{YZ}$. Cross-multiply and solve:

$$\frac{12}{18} = \frac{8}{YZ}$$
$$12YZ = 18 \cdot 8$$
$$12YZ = 144$$
$$YZ = 12$$

3. **D.** If $\triangle ARM \sim \triangle LEG$, $\dfrac{RM}{EG} = \dfrac{AM}{LG}$, so $\dfrac{9}{21} = \dfrac{15}{LG}$. Simplify and then cross-multiply and solve:

$$\frac{\overset{3}{\cancel{9}}}{\underset{7}{\cancel{21}}} = \frac{15}{LG}$$

$$3LG = 7 \cdot 15$$

$$3LG = 105$$

$$LG = 35$$

4. **B.** If the triangles are similar in a ratio of 9:21 = 3:7, then the ratio of the perimeters is also 3:7. If the perimeter of $\triangle ARM$ is 24 inches, then the perimeter of $\triangle LEG$ can be found by solving $\dfrac{24}{P} = \dfrac{3}{7}$:

$$\frac{24}{P} = \frac{3}{7}$$

$$3P = 24 \cdot 7$$

$$3P = 168$$

$$P = 56$$

5. **B.** If the triangles are similar in a ratio of 9:21 = 3:7, then the ratio of the areas is $3^2 : 7^2 = 9:49$. Set up the proportion $\dfrac{A}{98} = \dfrac{9}{49}$ and cross-multiply to solve:

$$\frac{A}{98} = \frac{9}{49}$$

$$49A = 98 \cdot 9$$

$$49A = 882$$

$$A = 18$$

6. **D.** If $\triangle ABC \sim \triangle RST$, then $\dfrac{AB}{RS} = \dfrac{BC}{ST} = \dfrac{AC}{RT}$. Using the first two ratios, simplify and then cross-multiply to solve:

$$\frac{\overset{9}{\cancel{27}}}{\underset{14}{\cancel{42}}} = \frac{36}{ST}$$

$$9ST = 14 \cdot 36$$

$$9ST = 504$$

$$ST = 56$$

7. **C.** If $\triangle XYZ \cong \triangle RST$, $RS = XY$, so $RS = 93$ meters.

8. **A.** If $\triangle JKL \sim \triangle NMO$, corresponding sides are in proportion, so the ratio of the longest side of $\triangle JKL$ to the longest side of $\triangle NMO$, 91:65, should be the same as the ratio of the shortest sides, 35:x. Solve $\dfrac{91}{65} = \dfrac{35}{x}$ by simplifying and then cross-multiplying:

$$\frac{\overset{7}{\cancel{91}}}{\underset{5}{\cancel{65}}} = \frac{35}{x}$$

$$7x = 5 \cdot 35$$

$$7x = 175$$

$$x = 25$$

9. **A.** Let x = the length of $\overline{BC}$, $x + 6$ = the length of $\overline{AB}$, and $2(x + 6)$ = the length of $\overline{AC}$. Because $\triangle ABC \cong \triangle XYZ$, $AB = XY$, $BC = YZ$, $AC = XZ$, and the two triangles have the same perimeter. Therefore, $x + (x + 6) + 2(x + 6) = 42$. Combine like terms and solve for x:

$$x + (x + 6) + 2(x + 6) = 42$$
$$x + x + 6 + 2x + 12 = 42$$
$$4x + 18 = 42$$
$$4x = 24$$
$$x = 6$$

The length of $\overline{YZ}$ = the length of $\overline{BC}$ = 6 meters.

10. **B.** If $\triangle RST \sim \triangle EFG$, $m\angle E = m\angle R$, so $m\angle E = 54°$.

H. Circles

A circle is the set of all coplanar points at a fixed distance, called the *radius,* from a given point, called the *center.* An *arc* is a portion of a circle, a curve cut from a circle. A *minor arc* is an arc of less than 180° and is named by giving its endpoints with an arc symbol over the top, for example, $\overset{\frown}{AB}$. A *major arc* is an arc of more than 180° and is named by giving one endpoint, some point on the major arc, and the other endpoint, with the arc symbol on top, as in $\overset{\frown}{AZB}$.

Angles

The angles in and around circles have many shapes and many names, but all of them fall into one of four categories, as detailed in the table on the next page. Each category has a particular location for its vertex and a particular rule for its measurement. For all of the categories, the measurement of the angle depends on the measurement of its *intercepted arc* or arcs, the section of the circle cut off by the sides of the angle as they intersect the circle. The arcs are measured in degrees, with 360° being a full rotation or full circle.

In circle O (see the following figure), $\overline{OA}$ and $\overline{OB}$ are radii and $\overline{AC}$ and $\overline{BC}$ are chords. If $\angle AOB$ measures 50°, $\overset{\frown}{AB}$ is also 50° because a central angle has the same measure as its intercepted arc. $\overset{\frown}{AB}$ is the intercepted arc for both central angle $\angle AOB$ and inscribed angle $\angle ACB$. The measure of the inscribed angle is half the measure of the intercepted arc, so $m\angle ACB = 25°$.

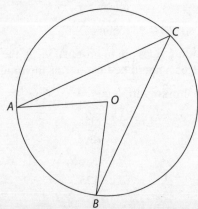

Suppose chords $\overline{PQ}$ and $\overline{RT}$ intersect at point S. If $\overparen{PR}$ is 70° and $\overparen{TQ}$ is 20°, $\angle PSR$ and $\angle TSQ$ are vertical angles. $\angle PSR$ intercepts $\overparen{PR}$ and $\angle TSQ$ intercepts $\overparen{TQ}$. The measure of these angles is half the sum of those arcs. Average the measurements $\dfrac{70° + 20°}{2}$ to find that angles $\angle PSR$ and $\angle TSQ$ measure 45° each.

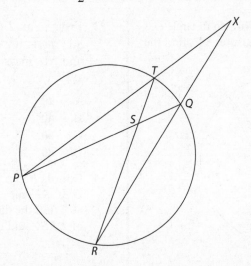

In the figure above, $\angle PTR$ has its vertex on the circle, and its sides are chords. This is an inscribed angle and its measurement is half the measure of the intercepted arc $\overparen{PR}$. If $\overparen{PR}$ is 70°, then $\angle PTR$ measures 35°.

The angle whose vertex is outside the circle, $\angle X$, or to give it its full name, $\angle PXR$, has a measurement equal to half of the difference between its two intercepted arcs. One arc is $\overparen{TQ}$, where the sides of the angle first meet the circle, and the other is $\overparen{PR}$, where the sides touch the other side of the circle. The measure of

$$\angle PXR = \frac{1}{2}\left(\overparen{PR} - \overparen{TQ}\right) = \frac{1}{2}(70° - 20°) = \frac{1}{2}(50°) = 25°.$$

Angles		
Location of Vertex	**Measure of the Angle Equals**	**Angle Name**
At the center	Measure of the intercepted arc	Central angle
On the circle	Half the measure of the intercepted arc	Inscribed angle
Inside the circle (like $\angle PSR$ in the figure above)	Half the sum of the measures of the intercepted arcs	
Outside the circle (like $\angle X$ in the figure above)	Half the difference of the measures of the intercepted arcs	

Practice

Directions: Choose the best answer from among the choices provided.

1. Chords $\overline{DU}$ and $\overline{UG}$ are drawn in circle O. If central angle $\angle DOG$ measures 84°, find the measure of $\angle DUG$.

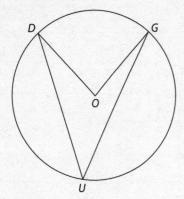

   A. 21°
   B. 42°
   C. 63°
   D. 84°

2. Chords $\overline{XY}$ and $\overline{VW}$ intersect inside the circle at T. $\widehat{XW} = 160°$ and $\widehat{VY} = 30°$. Find the measure of $\angle XTV$.

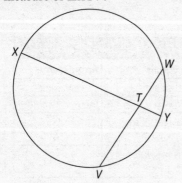

   A. 30°
   B. 85°
   C. 95°
   D. 170°

3. From point T outside the circle, secants $\overline{TSR}$ and $\overline{TUV}$ are drawn. $\widehat{RV}$ measures 100° and $\widehat{SU}$ measures 20°. Find the measure of $\angle T$.

   A. 20°
   B. 40°
   C. 60°
   D. 80°

4. Chords $\overline{RS}$, $\overline{SV}$, and $\overline{VU}$ are drawn in circle O. If $\widehat{RV}$ measures 100° and $\widehat{SU}$ measures 80°, find the difference between the measure of $\angle RSV$ and the measure of $\angle SVU$.

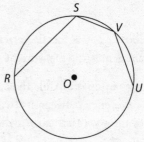

   A. 10°
   B. 20°
   C. 40°
   D. 60°

5. Two tangents are drawn to circle O from point P outside the circle. One touches the circle at point A and the other at point B, dividing the circle into two arcs that measure 220° and 140°. Find the measure of $\angle P$.

   A. 40°
   B. 70°
   C. 110°
   D. 140°

6. In circle O, inscribed angle $\angle ABC$ measures 48°. What is the measure of central angle $\angle AOC$?

   A. 24°
   B. 48°
   C. 90°
   D. 96°

7. From point P outside circle O, tangent $\overline{PS}$ is drawn and touches the circle at S. Secant $\overline{PR}$ crosses the circle at Q and R. Chord $\overline{ST}$ crosses $\overline{PR}$ at V. Arc $\widehat{QS}$ measures 44° and $\widehat{TR}$ measures 56°. If $m\angle RPS = 20°$, find $m\angle TSP$.

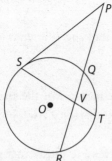

Figure not drawn to scale

   A. 50°
   B. 90°
   C. 110°
   D. 116°

8. Two tangents from point P touch the circle at A and B. C is a point on $\widehat{AB}$. If $\widehat{AB}$ measures 75°, find the measure of $\angle ACB$.

   A. 37.5°
   B. 75°
   C. 105°
   D. 142.5°

9. $\overline{PQ}$ and $\overline{RT}$ are chords in circle O that intersect at point S inside the circle. If $\widehat{PR}$ measures 94° and $\widehat{TQ}$ measures 82°, find $m\angle PST$.

   A. 82°
   B. 88°
   C. 92°
   D. 94°

10. Central angle $\angle AOB$ is a right angle and D is a point on $\widehat{AB}$. $\overline{DC}$ and $\overline{DE}$ are drawn so that $\overline{DC} \perp \overline{AO}$ and $\overline{DE} \perp \overline{OB}$. What is the measure of $\widehat{CE}$?

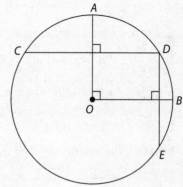

   A. 45°
   B. 90°
   C. 180°
   D. 270°

Answers

1. **B.** If central angle $\angle DOG$ measures 84°, then the measure of $\overset{\frown}{DG}$ is 84°, and inscribed angle $\angle DUG$ measures half of 84°, or 42°.

2. **B.** The arcs whose measurements are given are the arcs that are used to find the measure of $\angle XTW$ or $\angle YTV$. The measure of $\angle XTW = \frac{1}{2}\left(\overset{\frown}{XW} + \overset{\frown}{VY}\right) = \frac{1}{2}(160° + 30°) = \frac{190°}{2} = 95°$. The angle you're looking for is supplementary to $\angle XTW$, so $\angle XTV$ measures $180° - 95° = 85°$.

3. **B.** $\angle T$ has its vertex outside the circle, so its measure is half the difference of the intercepted arcs: $m\angle T = \frac{1}{2}(100 - 20) = \frac{80}{2} = 40°$.

4. **A.** $\angle RSV$ is an inscribed angle equal to half of $\overset{\frown}{RUV}$, so $\frac{1}{2}(360° - 100°) = \frac{1}{2}(260°) = 130°$. $\angle SVU$ is also inscribed and equal to half of $\overset{\frown}{SRU}$, or $\frac{1}{2}(360° - 80°) = \frac{1}{2}(280°) = 140°$. The difference is $140° - 130° = 10°$.

5. **A.** The vertex is outside the circle, so the measure of the angle is half the difference of the arcs. The measure of $\angle P$ is $\frac{1}{2}(220 - 140) = \frac{1}{2}(80) = 40°$.

6. **D.** Inscribed angle $\angle ABC$ intercepts $\overset{\frown}{AC}$ and is equal to half the measure of the arc. If the inscribed angle measures 48°, then the arc measures 2(48°) = 96°. The central angle $\angle AOC$ also intercepts $\overset{\frown}{AC}$ and is equal to the measure of the arc, so $m\angle AOC = 96°$.

7. **C.** First find the measure of $\angle PVS$, which along with $\angle RVT$ is equal to the average of $\overset{\frown}{TR}$ and $\overset{\frown}{QS}$. $m\angle PVS = \frac{44° + 56°}{2} = \frac{100°}{2} = 50°$. In $\triangle PVS$, $m\angle RPS = 20°$ and $m\angle PVS = 50°$, leaving 110° for the measure of $\angle PSV$. Since $m\angle PSV = m\angle TSP$, $m\angle TSP$ is also 110°.

8. **D.** If $\overset{\frown}{AB}$, the minor arc between A and B, measures 75°, then the major arc around the other way is the rest of the circle, so measures $360° - 75° = 285°$. The measure of $\angle ACB$ is half of that major arc, or $\frac{1}{2}(285°) = 142.5°$.

9. **C.** First find the measure of $\angle PSR$ or $\angle QST$, each of which is equal to the average of the measures of $\overset{\frown}{PR}$ and $\overset{\frown}{TQ}$. $m\angle PSR = m\angle QST = \frac{94° + 82°}{2} = \frac{176°}{2} = 88°$. Then $\angle PST$ is supplementary to $\angle PSR$, so $m\angle PST = 180° - 88° = 92°$.

10. **C.** Central angle $\angle AOB$ is a right angle, so $\overset{\frown}{AB}$ measures 90°. Drawing $\overline{DC} \perp \overline{AO}$ and $\overline{DE} \perp \overline{OB}$ creates a rectangle, which means that $\angle CDE$ is also a right angle. $\angle CDE$ is an inscribed angle with its vertex on the circle, so its measure is half of the intercepted arc, $\overset{\frown}{CE}$. Arc $\overset{\frown}{CE}$ measures 180°.

Circumference and Area

The circumference of a circle is the distance around the circle. The formula for the circumference of a circle is $C = 2\pi r = \pi d$, where r is the radius of the circle, d is the diameter of the circle, and π is a constant approximately equal to 3.14159. The area of a circle is the product of π and the square of the radius: $A = \pi r^2$.

If the circumference of a circle is 32π cm, the diameter is 32 cm and the radius is 16 cm. The area is $A = \pi r^2 = \pi(16)^2 = 256\pi$ cm^2.

Arc Length and Area of a Sector

When a central angle is drawn in a circle, it cuts off a section of the circle—a wedge, like a piece of pie, called a *sector*—and it intercepts an *arc*, a portion of the circumference. The length of the arc is a fraction of the circumference of the circle, and the area of the sector is a fraction of the area of the circle. The particular fraction is the measure of the central angle over 360.

Suppose the area of the sector defined by a central angle of 72° is 5π square inches. The fraction of the circle cut off by a central angle of 72° is $\frac{72}{360} = \frac{1}{5}$. So the 5π square inches is $\frac{1}{5}$ of the area of the circle. The area of the circle must be 25π, which means the radius of the circle is 5 inches. The circumference of the circle will be 10π, but the angle intercepts an arc whose length is $\frac{1}{5}$ of that circumference or 2π.

Practice

Directions: Choose the best answer from among the choices provided.

1. Find the circumference of a circle if the radius is 11 inches.

    A. 11π inches
    B. 22π inches
    C. 121π inches
    D. 484π inches

2. Find the circumference of a circle whose area is 36π square inches.

    A. 12π inches
    B. 18π inches
    C. 36π inches
    D. 72π inches

3. The circumference of a circle is 40π cm. Find its area.

    A. 20π cm^2
    B. 40π cm^2
    C. 400π cm^2
    D. 1600π cm^2

4. Find the area of a sector defined by a 60° central angle, if the circumference of the circle is 24π cm.

    A. 6π cm^2
    B. 12π cm^2
    C. 24π cm^2
    D. 48π cm^2

5. Find the length of the arc intercepted by a 40° central angle, if the radius of the circle is 18 cm.

    A. 81π cm
    B. 18π cm
    C. 9π cm
    D. 4π cm

6. In a circle of radius 12 inches, $\overset{\frown}{AB}$ has a length of 4π inches. What is the measure of central angle $\angle AOB$?

    A. 30°
    B. 60°
    C. 90°
    D. 120°

7. If a sector defined by a central angle of 60° has an area of 24π square inches, what is the radius of the circle?

   A. 6 inches
   B. 10 inches
   C. 12 inches
   D. 24 inches

8. A central angle of 45° intercepts an arc that is 2π units long. What is the area of the sector?

   A. 2π square units
   B. 8π square units
   C. 16π square units
   D. 64π square units

9. Find the circumference of a circle in which a 90° central angle defines a sector with an area of 64π square units.

   A. 8π units
   B. 16π units
   C. 32π units
   D. 64π units

10. In a circle with a radius of 3 inches, a central angle intercepts an arc that measures π inches. What is the measure of the central angle?

    A. 15°
    B. 30°
    C. 45°
    D. 60°

Answers

1. **B.** $C = 2\pi r$, so the circumference is 22π inches.

2. **A.** If $A = \pi r^2 = 36\pi$, the radius of the circle is 6 inches, so the circumference is 12π inches.

3. **C.** $C = \pi d = 40\pi$ cm, so the diameter must be 40 cm and the radius 20 cm. Therefore, the area of the circle is $\pi(20)^2 = 400\pi$ cm^2.

4. **C.** If the circumference is 24π cm, the diameter is 24 cm, the radius is 12 cm, and the area of the circle is $\pi(12)^2 = 144\pi$ cm^2. A 60° central angle is $\dfrac{60}{360} = \dfrac{1}{6}$ of the circle, so the area of the sector will be $\dfrac{1}{6} \cdot 144\pi = 24\pi$ cm^2.

5. **D.** If the radius is 18 cm, the diameter is 36 cm and the circumference is 36π. The length of the arc intercepted by a 40° central angle is $\dfrac{40}{360} = \dfrac{1}{9}$ of the circumference, or $\dfrac{1}{9} \cdot 36\pi = 4\pi$.

6. **B.** If the radius is 12 inches, the circumference $= 2\pi r = 2\pi(12) = 24\pi$ inches. The length of the arc is 4π inches, or $\dfrac{\overset{1}{\cancel{4\pi}}}{\underset{6}{\cancel{24\pi}}} = \dfrac{1}{6}$ of the circumference. That means that the central angle $\angle AOB$ must contain $\dfrac{1}{\underset{1}{\cancel{6}}} \times \overset{60}{\cancel{360}}° = 60°$.

7. **C.** Let A represent the area of the circle. Then $\dfrac{60°}{360°} \times A = \dfrac{1}{6} \times A = 24\pi$, and, therefore, the area of the circle is $6(24\pi) = 144\pi$. The area of the circle is $A = \pi r^2$, so $144\pi = \pi r^2$ means that $r^2 = 144$ and $r = 12$ inches.

8. **B.** If $\dfrac{45°}{360°} \times C = \dfrac{1}{8} \times C = 2\pi$, then the circumference is 16π units. The circumference is $2\pi r = 16\pi$, so $2r = 16$ and $r = 8$ units. The area of the sector is $\dfrac{45°}{360°} \times A = \dfrac{1}{8} \times \pi r^2 = \dfrac{1}{8} \times \pi (8)^2 = 8\pi$ square units.

9. **C.** If a 90° angle defines a sector with an area of 64π square units, then $\dfrac{90°}{360°} \times \pi r^2 = \dfrac{1}{4} \times \pi r^2 = 64\pi$, which means that $\pi r^2 = 256\pi$. Therefore, $r^2 = 256$ and $r = 16$ units. Then $C = 2\pi r = 2\pi(16) = 32\pi$ units.

10. **D.** Let a = the measure of the central angle. $\dfrac{a}{360°} \times 2\pi(3) = \pi$, so $\dfrac{a}{360°} \times 6\pi = \pi$. Therefore, $\dfrac{a}{360°} = \dfrac{1}{6}$, and $a = 60°$.

I. Solids

Traditionally, the term *solids* refers to figures that are three-dimensional, but they don't necessarily have to be solid, as in "filled."

A *prism* is a three-dimensional figure with two identical parallel polygons as bases and other polygons as flat sides. The shape of the bases gives the prism its name, as in triangular prism or square prism.

A *cylinder* has two identical parallel bases, which are circles, at either end of a curved surface that is a rolled rectangle.

A *pyramid* has a polygon as its base, surrounded by triangles that meet at a single point. The shape of the base gives the pyramid its name, as in triangular pyramid or square pyramid.

A *cone* has a circular base surrounded by a smooth curving surface that tapers to a point.

Surface Area

To find the surface area of a prism or a cylinder, find the area of each surface and add them all together. The surface area of a rectangular solid, for example, is made up of six rectangles: top and bottom, front and back, left and right. The surface area of a cylinder is the total of the areas of the two circles at the ends plus the area of the rectangle that forms the sides. (Think about a label on a can.)

Surface area of a rectangular solid: $S.A. = 2lw + 2lh + 2wh$

Surface area of a cylinder: $S.A. = 2\pi r^2 + 2\pi rh$

To find the surface area of a cylinder with diameter and height both equal to 4 cm, remember that if the diameter is 4 cm, the radius is 2 cm, and the area of each of the top and bottom circles is 4π cm². The circumference is 4π cm, and since the height is 4 cm, the area of the "label"—the lateral area—is 16π cm². The total surface area is made up of the two circles and the lateral area, or $2(4\pi) + 16\pi = 8\pi + 16\pi = 24\pi$ cm².

Volume

If the sides are perpendicular to the base, the volume of a prism or a cylinder is equal to the area of its base times its height. The volume of a pyramid or cone is one-third of the product of the base area and the height. Volume is measured in cubic units.

Volume of a prism: $V = Bh$, where B is the area of the base and h is the height of the prism. The area of the base will be found by different rules, depending on its shape.

Volume of a cylinder: $V = \pi r^2 h$, where r is the radius of the circular base and h is the height of the cylinder.

Volume of a pyramid: $V = \frac{1}{3} Bh$, where B is the area of the base and h is the height of the pyramid.

The area of the base will be found by different rules, depending on its shape.

Volume of a cone: $V = \frac{1}{3} \pi r^2 h$, where r is the radius of the circular base and h is the height of the cone.

To find the volume of a square prism 4 inches high, whose base edges are 6 inches long, first find that the area of the base is 36 square inches. Multiply that by the height of 4 inches, and the volume is 144 cubic inches.

Practice

Directions: Choose the best answer from among the choices provided.

1. A can is made in the shape of a cylinder with a radius of 4 inches and a height of 10 inches. In square inches, how much metal will be needed to make the can?

   A. 400π in.^{2}
   B. 112π in.^{2}
   C. 56π in.^{2}
   D. 40π in.^{2}

2. A rectangular prism is constructed with a base that is a square with a side of 10 cm. If the prism is 20 cm high, find its volume.

   A. 200 cm^3
   B. 400 cm^3
   C. 2,000 cm^3
   D. 4,000 cm^3

3. Find the volume of a cylinder with a radius of 2 cm and a height of 8 cm.

   A. 6π cm^3
   B. 16π cm^3
   C. 32π cm^3
   D. 64π cm^3

4. Find the surface area of a cube whose volume is 27 cm^3.

   A. 9 cm^2
   B. 18 cm^2
   C. 27 cm^2
   D. 54 cm^2

5. Find the height of a square pyramid with a volume of 108 cm^3 and a base edge of 9 cm.

   A. 2 cm
   B. 4 cm
   C. 8 cm
   D. 12 cm

6. Find the surface area of a cylinder with a radius of 6 cm and a height of 12 cm.

   A. 72π cm^2
   B. 144π cm^2
   C. 180π cm^2
   D. 216π cm^2

7. Find the volume of a square prism with an edge of 4 inches and a height of 15 inches.

   A. 60 in.^{3}
   B. 64 in.^{3}
   C. 240 in.^{3}
   D. 900 in.^{3}

8. A square prism and a square pyramid have the same base, a square with a perimeter of P cm and an area of B cm². The square prism has a height of 20 cm, but in the square pyramid each of the triangles that tip into the point has a height of 20 cm. Find the difference between the surface areas of the two solids.

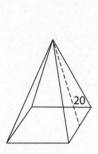 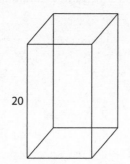

A. B
B. $10P$
C. $B + 10P$
D. $B - 10P$

9. A triangular prism with a base area of 12 square units has a volume of 228 units³. If a square prism is the same height but has a square base 4 units on a side, what is the volume of the square prism?

A. 228 units³
B. 288 units³
C. 304 units³
D. 307 units³

10. A cylinder has a height of 32 cm and a volume of 1,152π cm³. The height must be reduced to 18 cm, but the volume must remain the same. By how much should the radius increase?

A. 2 cm
B. 8 cm
C. 14 cm
D. 64 cm

Answers

1. **B.** The metal needed to make the can is the surface area of the cylinder. Each of the two circular bases has an area of 16π. The curved surface of the can unrolls to a rectangle whose base is the circumference of the circular base, 8π, and whose height is 10. The total surface area is $2 \times 16\pi + 80\pi = 32\pi + 80\pi = 112\pi$ in.².

2. **C.** The area of the base is 100 cm², and the volume is equal to the area of the base times the height, so the volume is 2,000 cm³.

3. **C.** Volume of the cylinder is area of the base times the height, so $4\pi \times 8 = 32\pi$ cm³.

4. **D.** If the volume of the cube is 27 cm³, its edge is 3 cm. It has six identical faces, each with an area of 9 cm², so the total surface area is 54 cm².

5. **B.** The volume is $V = \frac{1}{3}bh$, and the area of the base will be 81 cm², since the edge is 9 cm. So, $108 = \frac{1}{3} \cdot 81 \cdot h$ means that $108 = 27h$ and $h = 4$ cm.

6. **D.** $S.A. = 2\pi r^2 + 2\pi rh = 2\pi(6)^2 + 2\pi(6)(12) = 72\pi + 144\pi = 216\pi$ cm².

7. **C.** $V = Bh = (4)(4)(15) = 16 \times 15 = 240$ in.³.

8. **C.** The square prism has a surface area of $2B + 20P$. The square pyramid has a surface area of $B + \frac{1}{2}(20)P = B + 10P$. The difference between the two surface areas is $(2B + 20P) - (B + 10P) = B + 10P$.

9. **C.** The triangular prism has a volume of $Bh = 12h = 228$ units^3, so $h = 19$ units. The square prism also has a height of 19 units, and a base area of $4^2 = 16$ units^2, so it has a volume of $16 \times 19 = 304$ units^3.

10. **A.** Currently, the cylinder has a height of 32 cm and a volume of $1,152\pi$ cm^3, which means that $V = \pi r^2 h$ becomes $1,152\pi = \pi r^2(32)$. Solving for r, $1,152 = 32r^2$ and $r^2 = \dfrac{1,152}{32} = 36$. That gives a current radius of 6 cm. If the height is reduced to 18 cm, but the volume must remain the same, $V = \pi r^2 h$ becomes $1,152\pi = \pi r^2(18)$ and $r^2 = \dfrac{1,152}{18} = 64$, so $r = 8$ cm. The radius should increase by 2 cm.

Chapter 14

Mathematics Knowledge: Trigonometry

Trigonometry is based on similar triangle relationships, and since calculators are not permitted on the AFQT, questions are likely to be about the principles of trigonometry or based on special right triangles.

A. Special Right Triangles

When an altitude is drawn in an equilateral triangle, it divides the triangle into two congruent right triangles. Each of these smaller triangles is a 30°-60°-90° triangle. The hypotenuse of the 30°-60°-90° triangle is the side of the original equilateral triangle. The side opposite the 30° angle is half of the hypotenuse. By the Pythagorean theorem, the side opposite the 60° angle is half the hypotenuse times $\sqrt{3}$. If the hypotenuse of a 30°-60°-90° triangle is 20 cm, the side opposite the 30° angle is 10 cm and the side opposite the 60° angle is $10\sqrt{3}$ cm.

If the altitude of an equilateral triangle is $7\sqrt{3}$ cm and you want to find the perimeter of the equilateral triangle, remember that the altitude divides the equilateral triangle into two 30°-60°-90° triangles. The altitude is the side opposite the 60° angle, so the side opposite the 30° angle is 7 cm, and the hypotenuse is 14 cm. Three sides, each 14 cm long, make the perimeter 42 cm.

In an isosceles right triangle, the two legs are of equal length. By the Pythagorean theorem, the hypotenuse is equal to the side times the square root of 2. A 45°-45°-90° right triangle has two legs of equal length and a hypotenuse equal to a leg times $\sqrt{2}$.

To find the diagonal of a square whose area is 225 square inches, realize that if the area of the square is 225 square inches, the side of the square is $\sqrt{225}$, or 15 inches. The diagonal is the hypotenuse of an isosceles right triangle, so its length is $\sqrt{15^2 + 15^2} = \sqrt{225 \cdot 2} = 15\sqrt{2}$.

30°-60°-90°	The hypotenuse is the side opposite the right angle: h. The side opposite the 30° angle is half as long as the hypotenuse: $\frac{1}{2}h$. The side opposite the 60° angle is half the hypotenuse $\times \sqrt{3}$: $\frac{1}{2}h\sqrt{3}$.	
45°-45°-90°	The legs are the sides opposite the 45° angles: ℓ. The hypotenuse, opposite the 90° angle, is the length of a leg $\times \sqrt{2}$: $\ell\sqrt{2}$.	

Practice

Directions: Choose the best answer for each question from the choices provided.

1. Find the hypotenuse of an isosceles right triangle with a leg 4 inches long.

   A.   4 inches

   B. $4\sqrt{2}$ inches

   C. $4\sqrt{3}$ inches

   D. $8\sqrt{3}$ inches

2. Find the shorter leg of a $30°-60°-90°$ right triangle with a hypotenuse of 18 cm.

   A.   9 cm

   B. $9\sqrt{2}$ cm

   C. $9\sqrt{3}$ cm

   D. $18\sqrt{3}$ cm

3. Find the side of a square with a diagonal of 8 cm.

   A. $4\sqrt{2}$ cm

   B. $4\sqrt{3}$ cm

   C. $8\sqrt{2}$ cm

   D. $8\sqrt{3}$ cm

4. Find the longer leg of a $30°-60°-90°$ right triangle with a hypotenuse of 8 inches.

   A.   4 inches

   B. $4\sqrt{2}$ inches

   C. $4\sqrt{3}$ inches

   D. $8\sqrt{3}$ inches

5. Find the diagonal of a square with an area of 64 square inches.

   A.   8 inches

   B. $8\sqrt{2}$ inches

   C. $8\sqrt{3}$ inches

   D. $64\sqrt{2}$ inches

6. An altitude is drawn in an equilateral triangle. If the area of the equilateral triangle is $36\sqrt{3}$ square inches, what is the perimeter of the equilateral triangle?

   A. $6\sqrt{3}$ inches

   B.   12 inches

   C. $24\sqrt{3}$ inches

   D.   36 inches

7. In square $ABCD$, point E is the midpoint of side $\overline{AD}$. Diagonal $\overline{BD}$ and segment $\overline{BE}$ are drawn. If $\overline{BD}$ measures $8\sqrt{2}$ cm, what is the area of $\triangle BED$?

   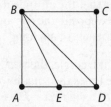

   A. 16 cm^2

   B. 32 cm^2

   C. $32\sqrt{2}$ cm^2

   D. $64\sqrt{2}$ cm^2

8. Point P and point S lie on side $\overline{AC}$ of equilateral triangle $\triangle ABC$ so that $AP = SC$. Square $PQRS$ is drawn. Point Q lies on $\overline{AB}$ and point R falls on $\overline{BC}$. If the area of square $PQRS$ is 9 square units, what is the length of $\overline{AB}$?

   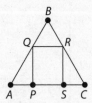

   A. $2\sqrt{3}$

   B. $6\sqrt{3}$

   C. $3+2\sqrt{3}$

   D. $6+\sqrt{3}$

9. In square $WXYZ$, diagonal $\overline{WY}$ is drawn. Point V lies on side $\overline{YZ}$ and $\overline{WV}$ is drawn, dividing $\angle YWZ$ so that m$\angle VWZ = 2$m$\angle YWV$. If $\overline{YZ}$ measures 12 cm, find the area of $\triangle WYV$.

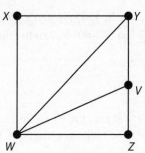

W   Z

Figure not drawn to scale

A. 36 cm^2

B. $48\sqrt{3}$ cm^2

C. $48\sqrt{6}$ cm^2

D. $72 - 24\sqrt{3}$ cm^2

10. $\triangle ABC$ is a 30°-60°-90° right triangle with hypotenuse $\overline{AC}$ measuring 12 cm. $\triangle RST$ is a 45°-45°-90° right triangle with hypotenuse $\overline{RT}$ also measuring 12 cm. If the triangles are positioned so that $\overline{AC}$ and $\overline{RT}$ coincide, what is the area of quadrilateral $ABCS$?

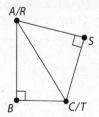

A. 18

B. 36

C. $18\sqrt{3} + 36$

D. $36\sqrt{6}$

Answers

1. **B.** The hypotenuse of an isosceles right triangle will be the length of a leg $\times \sqrt{2}$, so a leg will be $4\sqrt{2}$.

2. **A.** The shorter leg of a 30°-60°-90° right triangle will sit opposite the 30° angle and will measure half the hypotenuse, so 9 cm.

3. **A.** The diagonal of the square will be the hypotenuse of a 45°-45°-90° right triangle, so its measure will be a side $\times \sqrt{2}$, which means the side is equal to the diagonal divided by $\sqrt{2}$.
So, $\dfrac{8}{\sqrt{2}} = \dfrac{8}{\sqrt{2}} \cdot \dfrac{\sqrt{2}}{\sqrt{2}} = \dfrac{8\sqrt{2}}{2} = 4\sqrt{2}$.

4. **C.** The longer leg of a 30°-60°-90° right triangle will be the leg opposite the 60° angle. It will measure half the hypotenuse $\times \sqrt{3}$, or $4\sqrt{3}$.

5. **B.** The diagonal divides the square into two congruent isosceles right triangles (45°-45°-90°), so the length of the diagonal is a side $\times \sqrt{2}$. If the area is 64 square inches, the side is 8 inches. The diagonal is $8\sqrt{2}$ inches.

6. **D.** The area of a triangle is $A = \dfrac{1}{2}bh$, and because the altitude divides the equilateral triangle into two 30°-60°-90° right triangles, we can say that $h = \dfrac{1}{2}b\sqrt{3}$. Then $A = \dfrac{1}{2}bh = \dfrac{1}{2}b\left(\dfrac{1}{2}b\sqrt{3}\right) = \dfrac{1}{4}b^2\sqrt{3} = 36\sqrt{3}$. Divide both sides of $\dfrac{1}{4}b^2\sqrt{3} = 36\sqrt{3}$ by $\sqrt{3}$ and solve $\dfrac{1}{4}b^2 = 36$: $b^2 = 36 \times 4 = 144$ and $b = 12$. Each side of the equilateral triangle measures 12 inches, so the perimeter is $3 \times 12 = 36$ inches.

7. **A.** If diagonal $\overline{BD}$ measures $8\sqrt{2}$ cm in square $ABCD$, it creates two isosceles right triangles that each have the sides of the square as their legs. Each of those legs is 8 cm. Point E is the midpoint of side $\overline{AD}$, so $AE = ED = 4$ cm. $\triangle BED$ has base $\overline{ED}$, which measures 4 cm, and height equal to the side of the square. $A = \dfrac{1}{2}bh = \dfrac{1}{2}(4)(8) = \dfrac{1}{2}(32) = 16$ cm^2.

8. **C.** Because $PQRS$ is a square with an area of 9, $PQ = QR = RS = SP = 3$. Then $AC = AP + PS + SC = AP + 3 + SC$. Remember, $AP = SC$, so $AC = 3 + 2(AP)$. $\triangle APQ$ is a 30°-60°-90° right triangle. $\overline{PQ}$ is the side opposite the 60° angle, and $PQ = 3 = \dfrac{1}{2}(AQ)\sqrt{3}$. Therefore,

$$AP = \dfrac{1}{2}(AQ) = \dfrac{3}{\sqrt{3}} = \dfrac{3 \cdot \sqrt{3}}{\sqrt{3} \cdot \sqrt{3}} = \dfrac{3\sqrt{3}}{3} = \sqrt{3} \text{ and } AC = 3 + 2(AP) = 3 + 2\sqrt{3}.$$

9. **D.** $\triangle WYZ$ is a 45°-45°-90° right triangle. If m$\angle VWZ = 2$m$\angle YWV$, let m$\angle YWV = x$ and m$\angle VWZ = 2x$. Then $x + 2x = $ m$\angle YWZ$, which is 45°. Solving $3x = 45°$ tells you that m$\angle YWV = 15°$ and m$\angle VWZ = 30°$, so $\triangle WVZ$ is a 30°-60°-90° right triangle, with $WZ = 12 = \dfrac{1}{2}(WV)\sqrt{3}$ so $WV = \dfrac{24}{\sqrt{3}} = \dfrac{24\sqrt{3}}{3} = 8\sqrt{3}$ and $VZ = 4\sqrt{3}$. The area of $\triangle WYV$ is equal to the area of $\triangle WYZ$ minus the area of $\triangle WVZ$.

$$\text{Area of } \triangle WYV = \text{Area of } \triangle WYZ - \text{Area of } \triangle WVZ$$

$$= \dfrac{1}{2}(WZ)(YZ) - \dfrac{1}{2}(WZ)(VZ)$$

$$= \dfrac{1}{2}(12)(12) - \dfrac{1}{2}(12)\left(4\sqrt{3}\right)$$

$$= \dfrac{1}{2}(144) - \dfrac{1}{2}\left(48\sqrt{3}\right)$$

$$= 72 - 24\sqrt{3}$$

10. **C.** The area of $ABCS = $ the area of $\triangle ABC + $ the area of $\triangle RST = \dfrac{1}{2}(AB)(BC) + \dfrac{1}{2}(RS)(ST)$. The legs of $\triangle ABC$ will be 6 and $6\sqrt{3}$, and although we don't know which is AB and which is BC, that won't matter for the calculation. The legs of $\triangle RST$ are both $6\sqrt{2}$.

$$\dfrac{1}{2}(AB)(BC) + \dfrac{1}{2}(RS)(ST) = \dfrac{1}{2}(6)\left(6\sqrt{3}\right) + \dfrac{1}{2}\left(6\sqrt{2}\right)\left(6\sqrt{2}\right)$$

$$= \dfrac{1}{2}\left(36\sqrt{3}\right) + \dfrac{1}{2}(36)(2)$$

$$= 18\sqrt{3} + 36$$

B. Similar Right Triangles

Two right triangles, each with an acute angle of 25°, are similar. In fact, all right triangles containing an angle of 25° are similar. If you think of all the right triangles that contain an angle of 25° as the 25° family, you can start to talk about characteristics of the family. In any right triangle in this family, the ratio of the side opposite the 25° angle to the hypotenuse will always be the same, and the ratios of other pairs of sides will remain constant throughout the family. If you were to look instead at the 32° family—all right triangles containing a 32° angle—the ratio of opposite side to hypotenuse would be different from the ratio for the 25° family, but it would be the same for every triangle in the 32° family. Trigonometry takes advantage of that fact and gives a name to each of the possible ratios.

If the three sides of the right triangle are labeled as (1) the hypotenuse, (2) the side opposite a particular acute angle, A, and (3) the side adjacent to the acute angle A, six different ratios are possible.

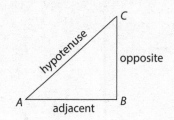

$$\sin(A) = \frac{\text{opposite}}{\text{hypotenuse}} \qquad \csc(A) = \frac{\text{hypotenuse}}{\text{opposite}}$$

$$\cos(A) = \frac{\text{adjacent}}{\text{hypotenuse}} \qquad \sec(A) = \frac{\text{hypotenuse}}{\text{adjacent}}$$

$$\tan(A) = \frac{\text{opposite}}{\text{adjacent}} \qquad \cot(A) = \frac{\text{adjacent}}{\text{opposite}}$$

If you look at the special right triangles, you can tell the value of the ratios for the 30°-60°-90° family and the values for the 45°-45°-90° family. It's worthwhile to commit these to memory because they're the values most likely to show up in problems.

The 30°-60°-90° Family		
Sine	**Cosine**	**Tangent**
$\sin(30°) = \dfrac{1}{2}$	$\cos(30°) = \dfrac{\sqrt{3}}{2}$	$\tan(30°) = \dfrac{\sqrt{3}}{3}$
$\sin(60°) = \dfrac{\sqrt{3}}{2}$	$\cos(60°) = \dfrac{1}{2}$	$\tan(60°) = \sqrt{3}$

The 45°-45°-90° Family		
Sine	**Cosine**	**Tangent**
$\sin(45°) = \dfrac{\sqrt{2}}{2}$	$\cos(45°) = \dfrac{\sqrt{2}}{2}$	$\tan(45°) = 1$

Practice

Directions: Choose the best answer from among the choices provided.

Use the following figure for questions 1–5.

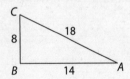

1. Find sin(*A*).

   A. $\dfrac{4}{9}$

   B. $\dfrac{4}{7}$

   C. $\dfrac{7}{9}$

   D. $\dfrac{7}{4}$

2. Find cos(*A*).

   A. $\dfrac{4}{9}$

   B. $\dfrac{4}{7}$

   C. $\dfrac{7}{9}$

   D. $\dfrac{7}{4}$

3. Find tan(*A*).

   A. $\dfrac{4}{9}$

   B. $\dfrac{4}{7}$

   C. $\dfrac{7}{9}$

   D. $\dfrac{7}{4}$

4. Find sin(*C*).

   A. $\dfrac{4}{9}$

   B. $\dfrac{4}{7}$

   C. $\dfrac{7}{9}$

   D. $\dfrac{7}{4}$

5. Find tan(*C*).

   A. $\dfrac{4}{9}$

   B. $\dfrac{4}{7}$

   C. $\dfrac{7}{9}$

   D. $\dfrac{7}{4}$

6. In isosceles right triangle $\triangle ABC$, m∠*A* = m∠*C*. What is the value of tan∠*A*?

   A. $\sqrt{2}$

   B. $\dfrac{\sqrt{2}}{2}$

   C. $\dfrac{\sqrt{3}}{2}$

   D. 1

For questions 7 and 8, use right triangle $\triangle RST$, with RS = 35 cm and ST = 84 cm.

7. In $\triangle RST$, find $\sin\angle T$.

    A. $\dfrac{5}{12}$

    B. $\dfrac{5}{13}$

    C. $\dfrac{12}{13}$

    D. $\dfrac{12}{5}$

8. In $\triangle RST$ described above, find $\cos\angle T$

    A. $\dfrac{5}{12}$

    B. $\dfrac{5}{13}$

    C. $\dfrac{12}{13}$

    D. $\dfrac{12}{5}$

For questions 9 and 10, use right triangle $\triangle ABC$ with $\overline{AB} \perp \overline{BC}$, AB = 68 inches and AC = 85 inches.

9. Find $\tan\angle C$.

    A. $\dfrac{3}{5}$

    B. $\dfrac{3}{4}$

    C. $\dfrac{4}{5}$

    D. $\dfrac{4}{3}$

10. Find $\cos\angle C$.

    A. $\dfrac{3}{5}$

    B. $\dfrac{3}{4}$

    C. $\dfrac{4}{5}$

    D. $\dfrac{5}{3}$

Answers

1. **A.** From the point of view of $\angle A$, the opposite side is $\overline{BC}$, the adjacent side is $\overline{AB}$, and the hypotenuse is $\overline{AC}$, so $\sin(A) = \dfrac{\text{opposite}}{\text{hypotenuse}} = \dfrac{8}{18} = \dfrac{4}{9}$.

2. **C.** The opposite side is $\overline{BC}$, the adjacent side is $\overline{AB}$, and the hypotenuse is $\overline{AC}$, so $\cos(A) = \dfrac{\text{adjacent}}{\text{hypotenuse}} = \dfrac{14}{18} = \dfrac{7}{9}$.

3. **B.** The opposite side is $\overline{BC}$, the adjacent side is $\overline{AB}$, and the hypotenuse is $\overline{AC}$, so $\tan(A) = \dfrac{\text{opposite}}{\text{adjacent}} = \dfrac{8}{14} = \dfrac{4}{7}$.

4. **C.** From the point of view of $\angle C$, the opposite side is $\overline{AB}$, the adjacent side is $\overline{BC}$, and the hypotenuse is $\overline{AC}$, so $\sin(C) = \dfrac{\text{opposite}}{\text{hypotenuse}} = \dfrac{14}{18} = \dfrac{7}{9}$.

5. **D.** The opposite side is $\overline{AB}$, the adjacent side is $\overline{BC}$, and the hypotenuse is $\overline{AC}$, so $\tan(C) = \dfrac{\text{opposite}}{\text{adjacent}} = \dfrac{14}{8} = \dfrac{7}{4}$.

6. **D.** $\tan \angle A = \dfrac{\text{opposite}}{\text{adjacent}} = \dfrac{BC}{AB}$. Because the triangle is isosceles with right $\angle B$, $AB = BC$,

so $\tan \angle A = \dfrac{BC}{AB} = 1$.

7. **B.** First find the length of $\overline{RT}$. If $RS = 35 = 7 \times 5$ and $ST = 84 = 7 \times 12$, it is highly likely that this is a multiple of the Pythagorean triple 5-12-13. You could use the Pythagorean theorem to investigate whether 84 is the hypotenuse, but that produces a leg length that is an irrational number slightly larger than 76, and the answer choices suggest the length of $\overline{RT}$ is an integer. Using the 5-12-13 triple, multiplied by 7, the legs are 35 and 84 and the hypotenuse is $7 \times 13 = 91$.

$\sin \angle T = \dfrac{\text{opposite}}{\text{hypotenuse}} = \dfrac{RS}{RT} = \dfrac{35}{91} = \dfrac{5}{13}$.

8. **C.** $\cos \angle T = \dfrac{\text{adjacent}}{\text{hypotenuse}} = \dfrac{ST}{RT} = \dfrac{84}{91} = \dfrac{12}{13}$

9. **D.** If $\overline{AB} \perp \overline{BC}$, then $\angle B$ is a right angle, $\overline{AB}$ and $\overline{BC}$ are the legs, and $\overline{AC}$ is the hypotenuse. $AB = 68$

$= 4 \times 17$ and hypotenuse $AC = 85 = 5 \times 17$, so $BC = 3 \times 17 = 51$. $\tan \angle C = \dfrac{\text{opposite}}{\text{adjacent}} = \dfrac{AB}{BC} = \dfrac{68}{51} = \dfrac{4}{3}$.

10. **A.** $\cos \angle C = \dfrac{\text{adjacent}}{\text{hypotenuse}} = \dfrac{BC}{AC} = \dfrac{51}{85} = \dfrac{3}{5}$

C. Solving for the Sides of Triangles

With the six trig ratios, it's possible to solve for any unknown side of the right triangle, if another side and an acute angle are known, or to find the angle if two sides are known. Unfortunately, you can't use a calculator on the AFQT, so you can expect that any trig questions you encounter will be based on the special right triangles.

To find a missing side, look at the known angle, the known side, and the missing side, and determine which ratio they form. Start with the definition of the ratio, fill in the information you know, and solve for the missing side.

If, in right triangle ABC, hypotenuse $\overline{AC}$ is 6 cm long and $\angle A$ measures 30°, you can find the length of the shorter leg by remembering that you have a 30°-60°-90° triangle.

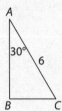

The known side is the hypotenuse, and the shorter leg will be opposite the 30° angle. Opposite and

hypotenuse make the sin ratio: $\sin(30°) = \dfrac{BC}{AC} = \dfrac{x}{6}$ and $\sin(30°) = \dfrac{1}{2}$, so $\dfrac{x}{6} = \dfrac{1}{2}$ and $x = 3$. The shorter leg is

3 cm long.

To find a missing angle, you'll need to have those common values from the special right triangles committed to memory. Determine what ratio can be formed from the two known sides, set up the ratio, and reduce it to simplest form.

If you want to find the measure of $\angle R$ in right triangle RST, and you know that leg $\overline{RS}$ is 18 cm long and hypotenuse $\overline{RT}$ is 36 cm long, set up the ratio of the lengths of $\overline{RS}$ and $\overline{RT}$, $\frac{18}{36}$ or $\frac{1}{2}$.

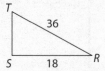

That ratio would be $\sin(T)$ or $\cos(R)$. You're looking for the measure of $\angle R$, so use $\cos(R)$ equal to $\frac{1}{2}$, which means $\angle R$ measures 60°.

There are two expressions often used in problems that may need a little bit of explanation. If you begin at point A and look up to the top of an object in the distance—let's call the object $\overline{BC}$—then the horizontal (the ground) and the object $\overline{BC}$ form the legs of a right triangle, and your line of sight to the top of the object is the hypotenuse. The *angle of elevation* is the angle at A between the horizontal and your line of sight.

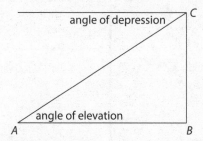

If, instead of being down on the ground, you start at the top of the object we called $\overline{BC}$, and you look down at point A, the angle of depression is the angle between the horizontal and your line of sight down to A. You may notice that the *angle of depression* is equal to the angle of elevation.

Practice

Directions: Choose the best answer from among the choices provided.

1. $\triangle ABC$ is an isosceles right triangle with right angle B. If $\overline{AB}$ measures 20 inches, find the length of the hypotenuse.

   A. 10 inches

   B. $10\sqrt{2}$ inches

   C. $10\sqrt{3}$ inches

   D. $20\sqrt{2}$ inches

2. $\triangle ABC$ is a 30°-60°-90° right triangle, with right angle at B. If hypotenuse $\overline{AC}$ measures 28 cm and $\overline{BC}$ measures $14\sqrt{3}$ cm, find the measure of $\angle C$.

   A. 30°

   B. 45°

   C. 60°

   D. 90°

3. In right triangle $\triangle RST$, $\angle S$ is a right angle and $RT = 24$ feet. If $\angle T$ measures 30°, find the length of $\overline{RS}$.

   A. 12 feet

   B. $12\sqrt{3}$ feet

   C. 24 feet

   D. $24\sqrt{3}$ feet

4. In right triangle $\triangle PQR$, $PQ = 24$ cm, $QR = 10$ cm, and $RP = 26$ cm. Find $\tan(P)$.

   A. $\dfrac{5}{13}$

   B. $\dfrac{12}{13}$

   C. $\dfrac{5}{12}$

   D. $\dfrac{12}{5}$

5. Given $\triangle XYZ$, with $\angle Y$ a right angle, and hypotenuse $\overline{XZ}$ equal to 42 inches, if $\sin(X) = \dfrac{\sqrt{3}}{2}$, find the length of side $\overline{YZ}$.

   A. 21 inches

   B. $21\sqrt{2}$ inches

   C. $21\sqrt{3}$ inches

   D. $42\sqrt{2}$ inches

6. From a point 100 meters from the foot of a building, the angle of elevation is 62°. Which best describes the height of the building?

   A. $100 \cdot \sin(62°)$

   B. $100 \cdot \cos(62°)$

   C. $100 \cdot \tan(62°)$

   D. $\dfrac{100}{\tan(62°)}$

7. From a scenic lookout point on a cliff known to be 2,000 feet above the valley floor, you spot a hot-air balloon about to launch from the valley floor. If the angle of depression from your location to the balloon is 40°, how far from the base of the cliff is the balloon?

   A. $2{,}000 \cdot \tan(40°)$

   B. $\dfrac{2{,}000}{\tan(40°)}$

   C. $2{,}000 \cdot \sin(40°)$

   D. $\dfrac{\sin(40°)}{2{,}000}$

8. A cherry tree in bloom is growing on a hill. To get a photo of the tree, you move away from the tree, lower on the hill, until your camera is level with the base of the tree and the angle of elevation from your camera to the top of the tree is 30°. If T is the approximate height of the tree, which best describes your distance from the base of the tree?

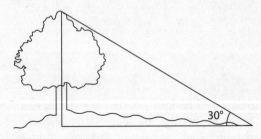

   A. $T \tan(30°)$

   B. $T \sin(30°)$

   C. $\dfrac{\cos(30°)}{T}$

   D. $\dfrac{T}{\tan(30°)}$

Questions 9 and 10 refer to attempts to determine the length of an oval reservoir. Let *x* = the length of the reservoir.

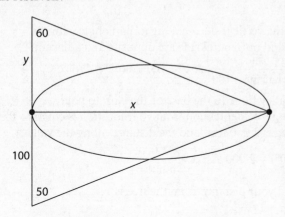

9. If you stand 100 yards due south of one edge of the reservoir, you would need to turn through an angle of 50° to see to the other edge. Which of these would calculate the length of the reservoir?

   A. $x = 100 \tan(50°)$ yards

   B. $x = 100 \sin(50°)$ yards

   C. $x = \dfrac{100}{\sin(50°)}$ yards

   D. $x = \dfrac{\tan(50°)}{100}$ yards

10. Your classmate chooses a point due north of the edge of the reservoir and finds an angle of 60° to the other edge. Which of the following represents your classmate's distance from the edge of the reservoir?

    A. $\dfrac{x}{\tan 70°}$ yards

    B. $\dfrac{100}{\tan 50°}$ yards

    C. $100 \tan(110°)$ yards

    D. $\dfrac{x}{\tan 60°}$ yards

Answers

1. **D.** If $\triangle ABC$ is an isosceles right triangle, then both acute angles measure 45°. The known side is a leg, and the missing side is the hypotenuse, so you can make $\sin(A) = \dfrac{20}{x} = \dfrac{\sqrt{2}}{2}$. Cross-multiplying, you find that $\sqrt{2}x = 40$, so $x = \dfrac{40}{\sqrt{2}} \cdot \dfrac{\sqrt{2}}{\sqrt{2}} = \dfrac{40\sqrt{2}}{2} = 20\sqrt{2}$.

2. **A.** If $\triangle ABC$ is a 30°-60°-90° right triangle, with hypotenuse $\overline{AC}$ and side $\overline{BC}$ adjacent to $\angle C$, then $\cos(C) = \dfrac{\text{adjacent}}{\text{hypotenuse}} = \dfrac{BC}{AC} = \dfrac{14\sqrt{3}}{28} = \dfrac{\sqrt{3}}{2}$. If $\cos(C) = \dfrac{\sqrt{3}}{2}$, C must equal 30°.

3. **A.** $\overline{RT}$ is the hypotenuse of this 30°-60°-90° right triangle. The side opposite the 30° angle is half the hypotenuse. So, $RS = 12$.

4. **C.** You know that the hypotenuse must be the longest side, so the right angle is at Q. So, $\tan(P) = \dfrac{\text{opposite}}{\text{adjacent}} = \dfrac{QR}{PQ} = \dfrac{10}{24} = \dfrac{5}{12}$.

5. **C.** If $\sin(X) = \dfrac{\text{opposite}}{\text{hypotenuse}} = \dfrac{YZ}{XZ} = \dfrac{YZ}{42} = \dfrac{\sqrt{3}}{2}$, you can cross-multiply to find that $2 \cdot YZ = 42\sqrt{3}$ and $YZ = 21\sqrt{3}$.

6. **C.** If a right triangle is drawn with the building as the vertical side, making a right angle with the horizontal side along the ground, the vertical side and horizontal side are opposite and adjacent, respectively, to the angle of elevation. $\tan(62°) = \dfrac{\text{opposite}}{\text{adjacent}} = \dfrac{x}{100}$, so $x = 100 \tan(62°)$, choice C.

7. **B.** Draw a right triangle from the balloon on the valley floor to the base of the cliff, to your observation point, and back to the balloon. The angle of depression from your location is equal to the angle of elevation from the balloon. The vertical leg is 2,000 feet, and the distance along the valley floor is x. $\tan(40°) = \dfrac{\text{opposite}}{\text{adjacent}} = \dfrac{2,000}{x}$, so $x \tan(40°) = 2,000$ and $x = \dfrac{2,000}{\tan(40°)}$.

8. **D.** The vertical side opposite the 30° angle is T, and your distance from the tree is x. $\tan(30°) = \dfrac{\text{opposite}}{\text{adjacent}} = \dfrac{T}{x}$, so $x \tan(30°) = T$ and $x = \dfrac{T}{\tan(30°)}$.

9. **A.** Let the length of the reservoir be one leg of a right triangle, making a right angle with the leg that is your distance south of the edge. $\tan(50°) = \dfrac{x}{100}$, so $x = 100 \tan(50°)$.

10. **D.** Let y = your classmate's distance from the reservoir edge. Your classmate's equation would be $\tan(60°) = \dfrac{x}{y}$, so $x = y \tan(60°)$ and $y = \dfrac{x}{\tan(60°)}$.

Chapter 15
Mathematics Knowledge: Probability and Statistics

People are quick to talk about chance and odds, but they often don't stop to calculate probabilities. Finding the probability of an event requires counting all the ways it can happen and all the other things that can happen, so start with techniques of counting.

A. Quick Counting

The probability that something *will* happen is based on the number of things that *can* happen. Sometimes a lot of things can happen, and you need to be able to count them quickly.

Basic Counting Principle

If you were asked about the probability of a particular number coming up when you roll a die, you'd want to know how many sides the die had (and what numbers were printed on it). If you were asked about the probability of pulling a certain two-card combination from a standard deck of 52 cards, you would want to know how many different ways there are to pull two cards. In some situations, like the die, you can quickly list all the possible outcomes, but listing all the two-card combinations you could possibly draw would take too long. When it's too difficult, or too time-consuming, to list all the possibilities, the counting principle provides a convenient alternative.

The basic counting principle says to:

1. **Create a space for each choice that needs to be made or thing that needs to happen.**

2. **Fill each slot with the number of options you have for making that choice or the number of ways that thing can happen.**

3. **Multiply the numbers you've entered to find the total number of ways your choices can be made or the events can happen.**

If Susan has four skirts, seven blouses, and three jackets, and all these pieces coordinate, the number of different outfits, each consisting of skirt, blouse, and jacket, that Susan can create can be found with the basic counting principle. Susan must choose three items of clothing, so you need three slots:

$$(\_)(\_)(\_)$$

There are four options for the skirt, seven options for the blouse, and three options for the jacket, so:

$$(4)(7)(3)$$

Multiply the numbers you've entered to find the total number of ways your choices can be made:

$$(4)(7)(3) = 84 \text{ different outfits}$$

Permutations and Combinations

A *permutation* is an arrangement of items in which order matters. If you were asked, for example, how many different ways John, Martin, and Andrew could finish a race, the order they finish in would matter, so you would want all the permutations of these three names.

A *combination* is a group of objects in which the order *doesn't* matter. If you were asked to select a team of 5 students to represent your class of 20 students, the order in which you chose the 5 would not matter, so the number of different teams would be the combinations of 20 students taken 5 at a time.

There are formulas for the number of permutations and the number of combinations, but they can be scary-looking. Here's the permutation formula:

$$_nP_t = \frac{n!}{(n-t)!}$$

And here's the combination formula:

$$_nC_t = \frac{n!}{(n-t)!\,t!}$$

In each of these formulas, $n!$ means the product of the whole numbers from n down to 1. The number of permutations of five things taken three at a time is

$$_5P_3 = \frac{5!}{(5-3)!} = \frac{5\times4\times3\times\cancel{2}\times1}{\cancel{2}\times1} = 60$$

The number of combinations of five things taken three at a time is

$$_5C_3 = \frac{5!}{(5-3)!3!} = \frac{5\times4\times\cancel{3}\times\cancel{2}\times\cancel{1}}{(2\times1)(\cancel{3}\times\cancel{2}\times\cancel{1})} = \frac{20}{2} = 10$$

Most questions are simple enough not to require a formula, however. In these cases, you can adapt the basic counting principle. For example, in how many different ways can John, Martin, and Andrew finish a race? The order matters here. There are three choices for the first-place finisher, leaving two choices for second place, and one for third, so $(3)(2)(1) = 6$. That's the number of permutations.

Your class of 20 students is asked to select a team of 5 to represent the class. How many different teams are possible? Order doesn't matter in this one, so if you just did $(20)(19)(18)(17)(16)$, you'd have a much larger number than you need, because you'd be counting all the different orders in which you could pick the same five people. Five people can be arranged in $5\cdot4\cdot3\cdot2\cdot1$ different orders, so you want $\dfrac{20\times19\times18\times17\times16}{5\times4\times3\times2\times1}$. That's still a huge number: 15,504.

Practice

Directions: Choose the best answer from among the choices provided.

1. A test consists of six questions. Each student is required to choose five of these questions to answer and omit the remaining question. How many different subsets of questions could be chosen?

   A. 2
   B. 5
   C. 6
   D. 30

2. There are 10 contestants in a talent competition. Prizes will be awarded for first, second, and third places. How many different choices are possible for the top three finishers?

   A. 30
   B. 120
   C. 720
   D. 1,000

3. A pizza shop has eight toppings available and offers thick or thin crust. Determine the number of different two-topping pizzas available.

   A. 16
   B. 28
   C. 56
   D. 112

4. In how many ways can you answer a five-question multiple-choice test if each question has four choices?

   A. 4
   B. 5
   C. 20
   D. 1,024

5. At a ceremony, five people are to be seated in a row on the stage. How many different seatings are possible?

   A. 5
   B. 25
   C. 120
   D. 3,125

Use this information for questions 6 and 7.

Your new job requires you to dress for work in either black or khaki pants, and a polo shirt that is white, black, or red.

6. How many distinct uniforms are possible?

   A. 4
   B. 5
   C. 6
   D. 7

7. How many distinct uniforms are possible if all black is not acceptable?

   A. 4
   B. 5
   C. 6
   D. 7

8. A student's schedule includes classes in art, music, English, math, history, Spanish, science, and physical education, but only five of those meet on any given day. How many distinct combinations of five classes are possible?

   A. 56
   B. 120
   C. 1,344
   D. 6,720

9. If a word contains duplicate letters and it is impossible to distinguish between them, the number of distinct arrangements is reduced. The letters in BOAT can be arranged in 24 distinct ways. How many distinct arrangements are possible with the letters in BOOT?

   A. 6
   B. 8
   C. 12
   D. 24

10. A committee is to be formed to include two members from each of the four classes in the high school. The freshman class nominated four possible members, the sophomore class six, the junior class five, and the senior class five. How many different committees are possible?

   A. 41
   B. 600
   C. 9,000
   D. 144,000

Answers

1. **C.** There are five choices to make from six options, and order doesn't matter. That means
$$_6C_5 = \frac{6 \times 5 \times 4 \times 3 \times 2}{5 \times 4 \times 3 \times 2 \times 1} = \frac{6 \times \cancel{5} \times \cancel{4} \times \cancel{3} \times \cancel{2}}{\cancel{5} \times \cancel{4} \times \cancel{3} \times \cancel{2} \times 1} = \frac{6}{1} = 6.$$

2. **C.** There are 10 choices for first place, leaving 9 for second, and 8 for third, and order matters, so $_{10}P_3 = 10 \times 9 \times 8 = 720$.

3. **C.** When you're choosing the two toppings, order doesn't matter, so there are $_8C_2 = \frac{8 \times 7}{2 \times 1} = \frac{56}{2} = 28$

   possibilities, but remember that you also have two crusts to choose from, so 28 × 2 = 56.

4. **D.** Five questions, with four choices for each, means 4 × 4 × 4 × · 4 × 4 = 1,024.

5. **C.** You're arranging five people in order. That's $_5P_5 = 5! = 5 \times 4 \times 3 \times 2 \times 1 = 120$.

6. **C.** You have two choices for pants and three for shirts. 2 × 3 = 6.

7. **B.** Of the six possible uniforms in question 6, only one is unacceptable, so there are 5 possible uniforms.

8. **A.** There are eight types of classes, but only five slots to fill. The question asks for combinations; the order is not significant. $_8C_5 = \frac{8 \times 7 \times 6 \times \cancel{5 \times 4 \times 3 \times 2 \times 1}}{\cancel{(5 \times 4 \times 3 \times 2 \times 1)}(3 \times 2 \times 1)} = \frac{\overset{4}{\cancel{8}} \times 7 \times \overset{2}{\cancel{6}}}{\underset{1}{\cancel{3}} \times \underset{1}{\cancel{2}} \times 1} = 56$.

9. **C.** The letters in BOAT can be arranged in 24 distinct ways: $_4P_4 = 4! = 4 \times 3 \times 2 \times 1 = 24$. When A is changed to O, BOAT becomes BOOT, but BAOT also becomes BOOT. BATO becomes BOTO, but BOTA becomes BOTO as well. The number of distinct arrangements is cut in half, because arrangements of BOAT where A precedes O and those where O precedes A both change to the same O preceding O arrangement. The number of distinct arrangements is $\frac{_4P_4}{2!} = \frac{4!}{2!} = \frac{4 \times 3 \times \cancel{2 \times 1}}{\cancel{2 \times 1}} = 12$ because there are 4 letters taken 4 at a time but 2 are identical.

10. **C.** Possible ways to choose freshman are $_4C_2 = \frac{4!}{2!2!} = \frac{4 \times 3 \times \cancel{2 \times 1}}{2 \times 1 \times \cancel{2 \times 1}} = 6$. There are
$_6C_2 = \frac{6!}{2!4!} = \frac{6 \times 5 \times \cancel{4 \times 3 \times 2 \times 1}}{2 \times 1 \times \cancel{4 \times 3 \times 2 \times 1}} = 15$ ways to choose sophomores, $_5C_2 = \frac{5!}{2!3!} = \frac{5 \times 4 \times \cancel{3 \times 2 \times 1}}{2 \times 1 \times \cancel{3 \times 2 \times 1}} = 10$

ways to choose juniors, and $_5C_2 = 10$ ways to choose seniors. There are 6 choices of freshmen, 15 of sophomores, 10 of juniors, and 10 of seniors. There are $6 \times 15 \times 10 \times 10 = 9,000$ ways to choose the committee.

B. Probability

The probability of an event is a number between 0 and 1 that indicates how likely the event is to happen. An impossible event has a probability of 0. An event with a probability of 1 is certain to happen.

Simple Probability

The probability of an event is the number of successes divided by the number of possible outcomes. The probability of choosing the ace of spades from a standard deck of 52 cards is $\frac{1}{52}$, while the probability of choosing any ace is $\frac{4}{52} = \frac{1}{13}$.

Probability of Compound Events

If two events are independent, the probability of both occurring is the product of the probability of the first event times the probability of the second event. Be sure to think about whether the first event affects the probability of the second.

Suppose a card is drawn from a standard deck of 52 cards, recorded, and replaced in the deck. The deck is shuffled and a second card is drawn. The probability that both cards are hearts is

$P(\text{heart}) \times P(\text{heart}) = \frac{13}{52} \times \frac{13}{52} = \frac{1}{4} \times \frac{1}{4} = \frac{1}{16}$. Since the first card drawn is replaced before the second draw, the probability of drawing a heart on the second try is the same.

If the first card is not returned to the deck before the second card is drawn, the probability of the first card being a heart is $\frac{13}{52} = \frac{1}{4}$, but the probability of drawing a heart on the second try is $\frac{12}{51} = \frac{4}{17}$ because there are 12 hearts left among the 51 remaining cards. The probability of drawing two hearts without replacement is $\frac{1}{4} \times \frac{4}{17} = \frac{1}{17}$, slightly less than with replacement.

The probability that one event or another will occur is the probability that the first will occur plus the probability that the second will occur, minus the probability that both occur. Suppose a card is drawn at random from a standard deck. What is the probability that the card is either an ace or a heart? The probability that the card is an ace is $\frac{4}{52} = \frac{1}{13}$. The probability that it is a heart is $\frac{13}{52} = \frac{1}{4}$. One card, however—the ace of hearts—fits into both categories, so it gets counted twice. To eliminate that duplication, subtract $\frac{1}{52}$. The probability that the card is an ace or a heart is $\frac{4}{52} + \frac{13}{52} - \frac{1}{52} = \frac{16}{52} = \frac{4}{13}$.

Practice

Directions: Choose the best answer from among the choices provided.

1. If a card is selected at random from a standard deck of 52 cards, what is the probability that it is either a queen or a king?

   A. $\dfrac{1}{26}$

   B. $\dfrac{2}{13}$

   C. $\dfrac{1}{4}$

   D. $\dfrac{1}{169}$

2. A bag contains 20 marbles, of which 10 are red, 2 are white, and 8 are blue. What is the probability that a marble selected at random will be blue?

   A. $\dfrac{1}{2}$

   B. $\dfrac{1}{10}$

   C. $\dfrac{2}{5}$

   D. $\dfrac{1}{5}$

3. A box contains 12 socks, of which 6 are black and 6 are brown. If two socks are chosen at random, what is the probability that they are not the same color?

   A. $\dfrac{1}{6}$

   B. $\dfrac{1}{2}$

   C. $\dfrac{6}{11}$

   D. $\dfrac{7}{11}$

4. Find the probability of choosing a red ace from a standard deck of 52 cards.

   A. $\dfrac{1}{52}$

   B. $\dfrac{1}{26}$

   C. $\dfrac{1}{13}$

   D. $\dfrac{1}{4}$

5. A fair die, numbered 1 through 6, is rolled. Find the probability that the die shows an even number.

   A. $\dfrac{1}{6}$

   B. $\dfrac{1}{3}$

   C. $\dfrac{1}{2}$

   D. $\dfrac{2}{3}$

Use this information for questions 6 through 8.

Each time a computer is started, a log-in screen appears. The background of this screen is a photo chosen at random from a folder that contains three landscape photos, five family photos, and two photos of pets.

6. What is the probability that the next log-in will display a pet photo?

   A. $\dfrac{1}{5}$

   B. $\dfrac{3}{10}$

   C. $\dfrac{1}{2}$

   D. $\dfrac{7}{10}$

7. What is the probability that the next log-in background will NOT be a landscape photo?

   A. $\dfrac{3}{10}$

   B. $\dfrac{1}{2}$

   C. $\dfrac{7}{10}$

   D. $\dfrac{4}{5}$

8. What is the probability that the next log-in background is a family photo or a pet photo?

   A. $\dfrac{3}{10}$

   B. $\dfrac{1}{2}$

   C. $\dfrac{7}{10}$

   D. $\dfrac{4}{5}$

Use this information for questions 9 and 10.

A slot machine has three wheels, each of which displays one of 12 symbols at random.

9. What is the probability that on a random spin all three wheels will display the same symbol?

   A. $\dfrac{1}{12}$

   B. $\dfrac{1}{4}$

   C. $\dfrac{1}{144}$

   D. $\dfrac{1}{1,728}$

10. What is the probability that on a random spin all three wheels will display stars?

   A. $\dfrac{1}{12}$

   B. $\dfrac{1}{4}$

   C. $\dfrac{1}{144}$

   D. $\dfrac{1}{1,728}$

Answers

1. **B.** There are four queens and four kings, so eight successes out of 52 cards: $\frac{8}{52} = \frac{2}{13}$.

2. **C.** There are 8 blue marbles: $\frac{8}{20} = \frac{2}{5}$.

3. **C.** The probability that the first sock chosen is black will be $\frac{6}{12} = \frac{1}{2}$. The probability that the second sock chosen is brown will be $\frac{6}{11}$, because there are 6 brown socks left among the remaining 11 socks. So the probability of drawing black and then brown is $\frac{1}{2} \times \frac{6}{11} = \frac{3}{11}$. But the probability of drawing brown and then black is also $\frac{3}{11}$, so the probability of getting two different colors is $\frac{3}{11} + \frac{3}{11} = \frac{6}{11}$.

4. **B.** There are four aces, but only two are red, so $\frac{2}{52} = \frac{1}{26}$.

5. **C.** There are three even numbers (2, 4, and 6) out of six, so $\frac{3}{6} = \frac{1}{2}$.

6. **A.** There are $3 + 5 + 2 = 10$ photos that may appear. The probability that the next one is a pet photo is $\frac{\text{number of pet photos}}{\text{number of photos}} = \frac{2}{10} = \frac{1}{5}$.

7. **C.** The probability that the next background WILL be a landscape is $\frac{\text{number of landscapes}}{\text{number of photos}} = \frac{3}{10}$, so the probability that it WILL NOT be a landscape is $1 - \frac{3}{10} = \frac{7}{10}$.

8. **C.** The probability that the next screen will be a family photo or a pet photo is the probability that it is a family photo plus the probability that it is a pet photo: $\frac{5}{10} + \frac{2}{10} = \frac{7}{10}$.

9. **C.** It does not matter what symbol is displayed, as long as all three are the same. Put another way, you're looking for the probability that the second and third wheels will display the same symbol as the first wheel. The probability that the second wheel matches the first is $\frac{1}{12}$, and the probability that the third wheel matches the first is $\frac{1}{12}$. You need both, so $\frac{1}{12} \times \frac{1}{12} = \frac{1}{144}$.

10. **D.** The probability that the first wheel will display a star is $\frac{1}{12}$. The probability that the second wheel will display a star is $\frac{1}{12}$, and the probability that the third wheel will display a star is $\frac{1}{12}$. All three are necessary, so $\frac{1}{12} \times \frac{1}{12} \times \frac{1}{12} = \frac{1}{1,728}$.

C. Mean, Median, and Mode

Statistics are numbers that represent collections of data or information. They help us to draw conclusions about the data.

One of the ways you can represent a set of data is by giving an average of the data. There are three different averages in common use:

- **Mean:** The *mean* is the number most people think of when you say "average." The mean is found by adding all the data items and dividing by the number of items. If the data set is large, this can be a nasty calculation. ***Remember:*** The mean is the average with the mean, nasty arithmetic.

- **Median:** The *median* is the middle value when a set of data has been ordered from smallest to largest or largest to smallest. ***Remember:*** The median is that strip of grass in the middle of the highway. If there is an even number of data points, and two numbers seem to be in the middle, the mean of those two is the median.

- **Mode:** The phrase *a la mode* really doesn't mean "with ice cream." It means "according to the fashion." The *mode* is the most fashionable value, the one that occurs most often.

Practice

Directions: Choose the best answer from among the choices provided.

1. Find the mean of set A if $A = \{32, 34, 36, 38\}$.
   A.   33
   B.   34
   C.   35
   D.   36

2. Find the median of set B if $B = \{33, 34, 35, 36, 37, 38, 39\}$.

   A.   33
   B.   34
   C.   35
   D.   36

3. Find the mode of set C if $C = \{31, 32, 33, 33, 35\}$.

   A.   31
   B.   32
   C.   33
   D.   35

4. Set $D = \{2, 2, 3, 4, 5\}$ and set $E = \{1, 3, 5, 5\}$. Find the mean of the medians of sets D and E.

   A.   3
   B.   3.5
   C.   4
   D.   4.5

5. Ten high school students were asked how much money they were carrying. The responses were $5, $16, $25, $18.50, $7, $5, $1.50, $3, $12, and $9. Find the difference between the mean and the median values.

   A. $2.20
   B. $8
   C. $10.20
   D. $12.20

Use this information for questions 6 and 7.

A survey of 100 commuters asked them about their typical daily travel time. The responses are summarized in the table below, organized by the mode of transportation they chose.

Number of People	Mode of Transportation	Average Travel Time for This Group	Number of People × Average Travel Time
43	train	57 minutes	2,451
38	bus	38 minutes	1,444
11	car	45 minutes	495
8	bicycle	15 minutes	120
Total: 100 people			**Total:** 4,510 minutes

6. What is the best estimate, to the nearest minute, of average travel time for the whole group of 100 commuters?

   A. 8
   B. 36
   C. 39
   D. 45

7. Which of these statements best describes the median travel time for the group of 100 commuters?

   A. The median travel time is 42.5 minutes.
   B. The median travel time is 38 minutes.
   C. The median travel time is 45 minutes.
   D. The grouping of data makes it difficult to determine the median travel time.

Use this information for questions 8 through 10.

Information about the ages of senators in the 115th United States Congress is organized in the table below.

Age Range	Number of Senators in that Range	Lowest Age × Number of Senators
85–89	1	85
80–84	6	480
75–79	6	450
70–74	12	840
65–69	19	1,235
60–64	21	1,260
55–59	14	770
50–54	9	450
45–49	10	450
40–44	2	80

8. In what range is the median age of the senators?

   A. 55 to 59
   B. 60 to 64
   C. 65 to 69
   D. 70 to 74

9. When the mean age is found using all 100 ages, the mean age is 63 years. When the mean is found using this grouped data and the lowest age in each group as the class mark, which of these statements is true?

   A. The mean age in this calculation is higher than 63.
   B. The mean age in this calculation is equal to 63.
   C. The mean age in this calculation is lower than 63.
   D. The mean age in this calculation is lower than 60.

10. Which of these statements about the mode is most accurate?

   A. The range that occurs most often is 60 to 64.
   B. The range that occurs most often is 65 to 69.
   C. There are two modes: 60 to 64 and 65 to 69.
   D. There is no mode.

Answers

1. **C.** 32 + 34 + 36 + 38 = 140. Divide by 4 to find that the mean is 35.

2. **D.** The numbers {33, 34, 35, 36, 37, 38, 39} are already in order, so find the middle value. The median is 36.

3. **C.** The mode is the most common value, 33.

4. **B.** The median of set D = {2, 2, 3, 4, 5} is 3, and the median of set E = {1, 3, 5, 5} is midway between 3 and 5, so it's 4. The mean of 3 and 4 is 3.5.

5. **A.** First, put the numbers in order:

    $1.50 $3 $5 $5 $7 $9 $12 $16 $18.50 $25

    The median is midway between $7 and $9, so the median is $8.

    To find the mean, add the numbers: 1.5 + 3 + 5 + 5 + 7 + 9 + 12 + 16 + 18.5 + 25 = 102. Divide by the number of responses, 10, to get a mean of $10.20. The difference between the mean and the median is $10.20 – $8 = $2.20.

6. **D.** According to the table, 43 people averaged 57 minutes for a total of 2,451 minutes spent on trains, 38 people averaged 38 minutes for a total of 1,444 minutes on buses, 11 people averaged 45 minutes for a total of 495 minutes in cars, and 8 people averaged 15 minutes for a total of 120 minutes on bicycles. The 100 commuters spent a total of 2,451 + 1,444 + 495 + 120 = 4,510 minutes traveling. 4,510 ÷ 100 = 45.1 minutes on average, or 45 minutes when rounded to the nearest minute.

7. **D.** Finding the median requires putting all 100 times in order and averaging the 50th and 51st times. Because of the grouping, the 100 times are not available. Average times are known, and therefore total time can be calculated, but individual times cannot be identified. The average train commuter time was 57 minutes, but one individual might travel for 12 minutes and another for over an hour.

8. **B.** The median age is the average of the 50th and 51st ages, so add the number of senators in each range until you reach or pass 50: 1 + 6 + 6 + 12 + 19 + 21 = 65 (or working up from the bottom, 2 + 10 + 9 + 14 + 21 = 56). The 50th and 51st ages fall in the interval with 21 senators: 60 to 64 years of age.

9. **C.** To use grouped data to find the mean, multiply the number of senators in an age range times the class mark, the number representing the range. In this case, the lowest age in the range is used. Those products appear in the last column of the table. Add the products. 85 + 480 + 450 + 840 + 1,235 + 1,260 + 770 + 450 + 450 + 80 = 6,100. Divide by 100 senators and the mean age is 61 years. The mean age calculated using grouped data is lower than the mean of 63 found using individual ages, probably because the lowest age in the range was used as a class mark.

10. **A.** The age range in which the most senators fall is 60 to 64. Because of grouping, you cannot say which one age is most common. There might be twelve senators who are 60, two who are 61, two who are 62, two who are 63, and three who are 64, and it might be the case that all 10 of the senators in the 45–49 range are 45. That kind of detail is lost because of grouping. It is only possible to say which age range is most popular.

You'll need 1 hour and 24 minutes to complete the Practice Test. The AFQT Practice Test consists of four sections:

Section Number	Section	Number of Questions	Time
1	Arithmetic Reasoning	30	36 minutes
2	Word Knowledge	35	11 minutes
3	Paragraph Comprehension	15	13 minutes
4	Mathematics Knowledge	25	24 minutes

Section 1: Arithmetic Reasoning

Time: 36 minutes—30 questions

Directions: These questions can be answered using basic arithmetic. No calculators are permitted. Choose the best answer for each question from the four choices presented.

1. A case of 12 cans of soda costs $5.40. What is the cost of one can?

   A. 43.5¢
   B. 44¢
   C. 45¢
   D. 45.5¢

2. Jeff committed to studying for 4 hours for his midterm. If he has been studying for 185 minutes, how many minutes of studying does he have left?

   A. 5
   B. 25
   C. 55
   D. 181

3. A shipment of 500 water bottles is delivered, and 20 are immediately removed and distributed to the office staff. The remainder of the bottles is equally divided and shipped to three stores. How many bottles does each store receive?

   A. 173
   B. 167
   C. 160
   D. 25

4. How long will it take to drive 420 miles at 60 mph?

   A. 8 hours
   B. 7 hours
   C. 6 hours
   D. 5 hours

5. $6\frac{3}{8} \times 5\frac{1}{3} =$

   A. $30\frac{1}{8}$

   B. 34

   C. $3\frac{7}{8}$

   D. $11\frac{17}{24}$

6. All the following are true EXCEPT

   A. $0.038 < 0.308$
   B. $0.0308 < 0.308$
   C. $0.0038 < 0.0308$
   D. $0.3008 < 0.0308$

7. A train travels 432 miles in 6 hours. At that rate, how far will it travel in 11 hours?

   A. 235 miles
   B. 792 miles
   C. 864 miles
   D. 2,160 miles

8. On a map, 1 inch represents 5 miles. If two cities are 238 miles apart, how far apart do they appear on the map?

   A. 21 inches
   B. 47.6 inches
   C. 238 inches
   D. 1,190 inches

9. The train makes the 40-mile trip from Alphatown to Betaville in 37 minutes. John can drive on a road parallel to the train tracks at 50 mph. How much longer would it take to drive between the two towns than it would to take the train?

   A. 3 minutes
   B. 10 minutes
   C. 11 minutes
   D. 13 minutes

10. A refrigerator originally priced at $800 is on sale for $600. By what percent has the price of the refrigerator been reduced?

    A. 20%
    B. 25%
    C. 60%
    D. 75%

11. Alina wins a lottery prize and puts $\frac{3}{8}$ of her prize money into her savings account. If she saves $450, how much was the lottery prize?

    A. $168.75
    B. $1,200
    C. $1,350
    D. $3,600

12. Each week, Chime puts half of his paycheck aside to pay bills and then puts one-fifth of his paycheck in his savings account. If Chime's weekly paycheck is $550, how much money does he have left after bills and savings?

    A. $165
    B. $275
    C. $385
    D. $440

13. Magdalena bought several shares of stock in a small company for $350. She held the stock for a year and then sold it for $1,050. What was the percent increase in Magdalena's investment?

    A. $33\frac{1}{3}\%$
    B. 50%
    C. 200%
    D. 300%

14. When rounded to the nearest hundredth, 4,739.9374 is equal to

    A. 4,700
    B. 4,739.9
    C. 4,739.93
    D. 4,739.94

15. A savings account pays 4 percent simple interest per year. You deposit $300 and, a year later, interest is added to your account. You then deposit an additional $200 and leave the account undisturbed for another year. How much interest will be added to your account at the end of the second year?

    A. $20.48
    B. $20
    C. $12
    D. $8

16. A grocer buys rolls from the local baker for $4 a dozen and sells them for 50¢ per roll. If he sells 8 dozen rolls per day, what is his daily profit?

    A. $16
    B. $12
    C. $8
    D. $4

17. A lecture hall is designed to seat 250 students. If designers estimate that 12 percent of the population is left-handed, how many left-handed desks should be installed?

    A. 12
    B. 24
    C. 30
    D. 37

18. The staff of an office is made up of 36 men and 24 women. What percentage of the staff is female?

    A. 66.7%
    B. 60%
    C. 40%
    D. 24%

19. Jesse and Jane start from the same rest stop on the interstate, but they drive in opposite directions. If Jesse drives at 55 mph and Jane drives at 60 mph, how far apart will they be after 3 hours?

    A. 15 miles
    B. 165 miles
    C. 180 miles
    D. 345 miles

20. 30 percent of what number is 60?

    A. 18
    B. 20
    C. 180
    D. 200

21. The furlong is a measurement of distance sometimes used in horse racing. A furlong is $\frac{1}{8}$ of a mile, and a mile is 5,280 feet. How many feet are there in 5 furlongs?

    A. 8,448
    B. 3,300
    C. 1,056
    D. 660

22. Mr. Singh earns $12.20 an hour for the first 40 hours he works in a week, and $1\frac{1}{2}$ times that for any hours beyond 40. What will his salary be in a week when he works 43 hours?

    A. $488.90
    B. $542.90
    C. $786.90
    D. $668

23. If you can walk a mile in 12 minutes, how long will it take you to walk a quarter-mile?

    A. 3 minutes
    B. 9 minutes
    C. 15 minutes
    D. 48 minutes

24. Jennifer earns $6 per hour plus 2 percent commission on everything she sells. Last week, she worked 40 hours and sold $1,820 of merchandise. How much did she earn for the week?

    A. $36.40
    B. $240.80
    C. $276.40
    D. $364

25. Alan chooses a suit that sells for $350, but it is on sale for 20 percent off. What is the sale price?

    A. $280
    B. $330
    C. $343
    D. $370

26. If you buy a coffeemaker for $63.79 and pay with a $100 bill, how much change will you receive?

    A. $47.21
    B. $37.79
    C. $37.21
    D. $36.21

27. Betsy left home at 9:30 a.m. and arrived at her grandmother's home, 153 miles away, at 12:30 p.m., without stopping along the way. How fast was she driving, on average?

    A. 50 mph
    B. 51 mph
    C. 52 mph
    D. 53 mph

28. Alex is assigned 479 pages of reading for a history course. If he can read 30 pages a day, on what day will he complete the assignment?

    A. 14th day
    B. 15th day
    C. 16th day
    D. 17th day

29. A baseball team had 4, 7, 6, and 13 hits in their first four games. How many total hits did they record?

    A. 17
    B. 20
    C. 26
    D. 30

30. If a baseball player had a batting average percentage of .290 and he had 300 at-bats, how many hits did he have?

    A. 10
    B. 29
    C. 87
    D. 97

IF YOU FINISH BEFORE TIME IS CALLED, CHECK YOUR WORK ON THIS SECTION ONLY. DO NOT WORK ON ANY OTHER SECTION IN THE TEST.

Section 2: Word Knowledge

Time: 11 minutes—35 questions

Directions: Select the word or phrase that is nearest in meaning to the italicized word.

1. A synonym for *banish* is

    A. punish
    B. demand
    C. oust
    D. reprimand

2. *Credulous* most nearly means

    A. gullible
    B. latent
    C. ridiculous
    D. genetic

3. A synonym for *barrier* is

    A. catalyst
    B. obstruction
    C. credential
    D. vehicle

4. The old manuscript was difficult for the professor to *decipher*.

    A. delineate
    B. decode
    C. develop
    D. design

5. A synonym for *deleterious* is

    A. innocent
    B. omitted
    C. harmful
    D. brilliant

6. Expecting hours of tedious reading, I was pleasantly surprised by the *brevity* of the report.

    A. detail
    B. harshness
    C. briefness
    D. sarcasm

7. David always tried to *emulate* his older brother.

    A. praise
    B. ignore
    C. imitate
    D. reject

8. *Streamline* most nearly means

    A. to adjust readily
    B. to make more efficient
    C. to make more complex
    D. to increase in volume

9. A synonym for *pugnacious* is

    A. weary
    B. indifferent
    C. reckless
    D. argumentative

10. After the budget was defeated, the department was forced to *retrench*.

    A. expand
    B. cut back
    C. dissolve
    D. find funding

11. Trying to *elucidate* the baffling theory, the professor reviewed it slowly and thoroughly.

    A. inspect
    B. contradict
    C. clarify
    D. mollify

12. *Mobilize* most nearly means

    A. assemble
    B. stabilize
    C. delete
    D. overcome

13. *Jeopardy* most nearly means

   A. danger
   B. quiz
   C. humor
   D. envy

14. A synonym for *avarice* is

   A. amiability
   B. greed
   C. adventure
   D. confidence

15. *Intrepid* most nearly means

   A. courageous
   B. gloomy
   C. indirect
   D. supportable

16. Negotiations were halted when both sides felt they had reached a *stalemate.*

   A. decision
   B. denial
   C. mandate
   D. impasse

17. After the first snowball was thrown, the twins felt they had to *retaliate.*

   A. regain territory
   B. strike back
   C. call it even
   D. back away

18. *Seclusion* most nearly means

   A. conflagration
   B. circumspection
   C. ending
   D. isolation

19. A synonym for *inevitable* is

   A. unforgiveable
   B. unfortunate
   C. unavoidable
   D. undeliverable

20. By traveling up the steep mountain, the troops were able to *elude* the enemy.

   A. capture
   B. delude
   C. entrap
   D. escape

21. The *audacious* plan worked, much to the surprise of everyone who doubted it.

   A. daring
   B. clumsy
   C. complicated
   D. tentative

22. The biologist was excited to find that the fish was *extant.*

   A. extinct
   B. living
   C. huge
   D. unique

23. The *fallacious* account was filled with inaccuracies and exaggerations.

   A. wordy
   B. official
   C. disappointing
   D. misleading

24. The young recruit was reprimanded for his *impulsive* actions.

   A. violent
   B. reckless
   C. incompetent
   D. mean

25. *Manipulate* most nearly means

   A. handle
   B. pull
   C. ignore
   D. misuse

26. A synonym for *fretful* is

    A. bland
    B. noisy
    C. worried
    D. rapid

27. *Exotic* most nearly means

    A. unknown
    B. unforgiveable
    C. uninteresting
    D. unusual

28. *Pervasive* most nearly means

    A. widespread
    B. previous
    C. insignificant
    D. demeaning

29. Experts were called in to *assess* the damage from the earthquake.

    A. contain
    B. fix
    C. document
    D. evaluate

30. A synonym for *bog* is

    A. hill
    B. swamp
    C. cave
    D. geyser

31. *Jovial* most nearly means

    A. cheerful
    B. energetic
    C. gloomy
    D. remote

32. A synonym for *meander* is

    A. retreat
    B. roam
    C. revise
    D. redesign

33. A synonym for *ally* is

    A. supporter
    B. teacher
    C. enemy
    D. leader

34. A synonym for *confidential* is

    A. routine
    B. aimless
    C. tardy
    D. secret

35. *Ingenuity* most nearly means

    A. calmness
    B. moderation
    C. inventiveness
    D. promptness

IF YOU FINISH BEFORE TIME IS CALLED, CHECK YOUR WORK ON THIS SECTION ONLY. DO NOT WORK ON ANY OTHER SECTION IN THE TEST.

Section 3: Paragraph Comprehension

Time: 13 minutes—15 questions

Directions: Read each passage below and answer the questions based on what is stated in or implied by the information in the passage.

Question 1 is based on the following passage.

DNA, or deoxyribonucleic acid, is the hereditary material in humans and almost all other organisms. Nearly every cell in a person's body has the same DNA. Most DNA is located in the cell nucleus (where it is called nuclear DNA), but a small amount of DNA can also be found in the mitochondria. The information in DNA is stored as a code made up of four chemical bases: adenine (A), guanine (G), cytosine (C), and thymine (T). Human DNA consists of about 3 billion bases, and more than 99 percent of those bases are the same in all people. The order, or sequence, of these bases determines the information available for building and maintaining an organism, similar to the way in which letters of the alphabet appear in a certain order to form words and sentences.

1. According to the passage,

   A. All living organisms have the same four bases in their DNA in exactly the same order.
   B. Human beings have equal amounts of nuclear DNA and mitochondrial DNA.
   C. Hereditary information in human beings is determined by each person's DNA.
   D. Adenine, guanine, cytosine, and thymine are organized in human DNA in alphabetical order.

Question 2 is based on the following passage.

The Appalachian Trail is a continuous footpath that runs from Maine to Georgia. The trail is about 2,160 miles long and passes through 14 states. To do the complete walk, most hikers take between five and seven months. While it isn't necessary to be an experienced backpacker, the hike should be undertaken only by those in fairly good physical condition.

2. The passage best supports which of the following statements?

   A. No one has attempted to do the complete 2,160-mile hike.
   B. An experienced backpacker can complete the entire Appalachian Trail in less than six weeks.
   C. It is possible for a person to walk on a continuous footpath through at least 12 states.
   D. It is impossible for disabled hikers to complete the 2,160-mile hike.

Questions 3 and 4 are based on the following passage.

The America of Civil War days was a country without transcontinental railroads, without telephones, without European cables, or wireless stations, or automobiles, or electric lights, or skyscrapers, or million-dollar hotels, or trolley cars, or a thousand other conveniences and comforts of what we call our American civilization. The cities of that period, with their unpaved streets; their dingy, flickering gaslights; their ambling horse-cars; and their hideous slums, seemed appropriate settings for the unformed social life and the rough-and-ready political methods of American democracy. The railroads, with their fragile iron rails, their little wheezy locomotives, their wooden bridges, their unheated coaches, and their kerosene lamps, fairly typified the prevailing frontier business and economic organization.

3. The author's main purpose in writing this passage is to

    A. suggest that the Civil War was the lowest point in the history of the United States

    B. summarize the events leading up to and continuing after the Civil War

    C. characterize a period in the development of the American society

    D. contrast the frontier spirit that characterized the early history of the United States with selfish and impersonal, modern attitudes

4. The author of this passage would agree that

    A. The state of democracy in America has declined since the period immediately following the Civil War.

    B. During the Civil War, railroads played an important role in transporting troops and supplies to the front.

    C. Americans, as a whole, tend to regard comforts and conveniences as necessities rather than luxuries.

    D. The America of the Civil War period is dramatically different from the country we live in today.

Question 5 is based on the following passage.

According to the U.S. Department of Health and Human Services, an estimated 1,700 young people between the ages of 18 and 24 die in alcohol-related accidents each year. In an effort to limit underage drinking, parents, educators, community activists, and concerned young people have formed coalitions to increase educational programs, encourage parents to dialogue with their children, and build peer support for alcohol abstinence. The alcohol industry asserts that it is onboard with the campaign to stem the surge of teen drinking.

5. The author of this passage would agree that

    A. Very little is being done in schools to cut down on alcohol abuse.

    B. Alcohol use among people between the ages of 18 and 24 should be curbed.

    C. Since the alcohol industry has joined forces with parents and educators, underage drinking has significantly declined.

    D. The only way to solve the problems associated with drinking and driving is to raise the driving age to 21.

Question 6 is based on the following passage.

Tropical weather is basically hot and humid because this part of the earth that is close to the equator receives more solar radiation than it re-radiates back to space. There is also abundant rainfall in the tropics due to the rising air created by the sun's heating. During certain periods, thunderstorms can occur every day. Nevertheless, the tropics still receive a lot of sunshine. When this sunshine is combined with the excessive rainfall, together they provide ideal growing conditions.

6. From this passage it is reasonable to assume that

    A. Water is far more important than sunshine in growing crops.
    B. A good choice of location to plant crops is land near the equator.
    C. Many fruits and vegetables need cool, dry evenings to ripen.
    D. Thunderstorms are often harmful to agriculture.

Question 7 is based on the following passage.

Curling, a team sport that is somewhat similar to bowling and shuffleboard, originated in Scotland. To play, two teams of four players each take turns sliding heavy, polished granite stones down lanes of slick ice toward the house, the target. As the stone slides down the ice, two sweepers with brooms sweep the ice in front of the stone to guide it toward the target.

7. According to this passage,

    A. Curling can be played only in Scotland.
    B. Sweepers can block the other team's stones as they slide down the ice.
    C. Each team consists of two players who get four chances to hit the house.
    D. The path of the stone can be altered by the actions of team members after it has been thrown.

Question 8 is based on the following passage.

A hybrid car is a passenger vehicle that is powered by two sources: an internal combustion engine powered by gasoline and an electric motor. The gas engine and the electric motor work together to provide power to the car. The brakes in these cars generate kinetic energy to recharge the electric motor. In addition to their fuel economy, hybrid cars have lower polluting emissions than cars powered by gasoline alone.

8. From this passage, it is reasonable to assume that

    A. In just a few years, gas-powered cars will become as out-of-date as the horse and buggy.
    B. The high cost of electricity makes hybrid vehicles too expensive for most consumers.
    C. Car shoppers who are concerned about harmful pollutants in the atmosphere are likely to purchase a hybrid vehicle.
    D. Hybrid vehicles are popular with consumers because they have a lower sticker price than traditional vehicles.

Question 9 is based on the following passage.

Mount Rushmore, a monument to four American presidents, is located in the Black Hills of South Dakota. It was based on an idea conceived by Doane Robinson, who wanted to create a site that would attract visitors from all over to South Dakota. Robinson hired a sculptor, Gutzon Borglum, to design the monument. Borglum carved 60-foot-high faces of George Washington, Thomas Jefferson, Abraham Lincoln, and Theodore Roosevelt on the side of the mountain. It took Borglum 14 years to complete the work; the monument was dedicated on October 31, 1941. Approximately 2 million people visit the site each year.

9. Based on the information in this passage, it is reasonable to assume that

    A.   The actual work on the carving of Mount Rushmore began in 1914.

    B.   Since the completion of Mount Rushmore, more than 5 million tourists have visited the site.

    C.   The original plan called for five presidents, but there was not enough space.

    D.   Doane Robinson conceived the design of Mount Rushmore and sculpted an inspiring monument.

Question 10 is based on the following passage.

Great triumphs and historic firsts highlight women's initial foray into national political office. Four years after Jeannette Rankin of Montana was elected to the House of Representatives in 1916, women won the right to vote nationally, with the ratification of the 19th Amendment in 1920. Rebecca Felton of Georgia became the first woman to serve in the U.S. Senate in 1922.

10. All of the following can be inferred from this passage EXCEPT

    A.   Jeannette Rankin was the first woman to be elected to Congress.

    B.   To be elected to the Senate, it isn't necessary for a candidate to be a member of the House of Representatives.

    C.   Jeannette Rankin's victory was a direct result of passage of the 19th Amendment.

    D.   Both men and women were able to vote for Rebecca Felton.

Question 11 is based on the following passage.

A *cam,* a sliding or rotating piece in a mechanism, is used to convert a rotating motion into a linear motion (or vice versa). The cam is often used as part of a rotating wheel or a shaft (as in a camshaft). Because the wheel is often irregularly shaped or the hole through which the shaft is placed is off-center, the cam can act as a lever and deliver pulses of power.

11. It can be inferred from this passage that

    A.   A cam must be irregularly shaped to provide a rotating motion.

    B.   It is mechanically possible to transform one form of motion into another form.

    C.   The power of the camshaft is obtained from pulses of electricity generated by linear motion.

    D.   When the hole in a cam is placed off-center, the cam will rotate in a regular circular motion.

Question 12 is based on the following passage.

When measuring the economic health of the nation, economists use a variety of statistics. One of the most closely observed statistics is the consumer price index (CPI). Economists use the CPI to estimate the average cost of purchasing necessary goods and services for a "typical" urban household. It is computed by filling an imaginary basket with the products that this family might buy in a given period of time. By tracking the CPI, economists can calculate the rate of inflation.

12. The author's main point in this passage is that

    A. Families that can't afford to buy sufficient goods must rely on the CPI for assistance.

    B. When calculating the CPI, economists factor in a typical farm family and a typical city family.

    C. If the rate of inflation is 4 percent, the cost of consumer goods has decreased by at least that amount.

    D. The CPI is useful to economists who study trends in the financial stability of the nation.

Question 13 is based on the following passage.

The global positioning system (GPS) relies on a group of more than 20 satellites that are orbiting the earth at any given time. Each of these satellites orbits the earth twice each day. To calculate the position of a car, for example, the GPS first locates four satellites and then figures out its own distance from each one. By a process called *trilateration,* the GPS can use the intersection of three distances to pinpoint the location of the car.

13. According to the passage, which of the following is the correct order of events?

    A. The GPS trilaterates, then calculates its distance from the car, and then measures the distance to the sun.

    B. The GPS measures its distance from earth, then measures its distance from four satellites, and then calculates its position on earth.

    C. The GPS finds four satellites, then calculates its distance from each, and then trilaterates its position on earth.

    D. The satellites locate the GPS, which then measures the distance between the satellites and then trilaterates its own position on earth.

Question 14 is based on the following passage.

There was a steaming mist in all the hollows, and it had roamed in its forlornness up the hill, like an evil spirit, seeking rest and finding none. A clammy and intensely cold mist, it made its slow way through the air in ripples that visibly followed and overspread one another, as the waves of an unwholesome sea might do. It was dense enough to shut out everything from the light of the coach-lamps but these its own workings, and a few yards of road; and the reek of the labouring horses steamed into it, as if they had made it all.

14. Which of the following best describes the author's tone in this excerpt?

    A. mildly irritated

    B. mysteriously ominous

    C. gleefully malicious

    D. melancholy

Question 15 is based on the following passage.

The Olympic Games, a major international athletic competition, originated in Greece in the 8th century B.C. The ancient games included traditional sports, along with hand-to-hand combat and chariot races. For unknown reasons, the competitions ended, and the games were not revived until the 19th century. The modern Olympic Games are held in different venues every two years, with summer games alternating with winter games. Athletes come from all over the world to compete, living together, playing against each other, and sharing their cultures.

15. Based on the passage, it can be inferred that

    A. Because of their historic importance, the Olympic Games are held in Greece every two years.

    B. The Olympic Games are an outstanding opportunity for cultural exchange.

    C. During the 18th century, the Olympic Games were not held due to ongoing wars in Europe.

    D. The next Olympic Games will reintroduce some ancient sports such as chariot racing and hand-to-hand combat.

IF YOU FINISH BEFORE TIME IS CALLED, CHECK YOUR WORK ON THIS SECTION ONLY. DO NOT WORK ON ANY OTHER SECTION IN THE TEST.

Section 4: Mathematics Knowledge

Time: 24 minutes—25 questions

Directions: Each of the following questions has four possible answer choices. Choose the best answer for each question. No calculators are permitted.

1. Find the area of a square that measures 12 feet on a side.

   A. 24 ft.^{2}
   B. 48 ft.^{2}
   C. 96 ft.^{2}
   D. 144 ft.^{2}

2. Find the circumference of a circle with a radius of 3 yards.

   A. 6π yards
   B. 9π yards
   C. 18π yards
   D. 81π yards

3. Which of the following statements is NOT true?

   A. The square of a positive number is positive.
   B. The square of a negative number is positive.
   C. The square of 0 is 0.
   D. The square of a number is always larger than the number.

4. Jennifer's average for the first three tests of the term is 86 percent. Her final exam will count as two tests. What must she score on the final exam to average 90 percent for the term?

   A. 92
   B. 94
   C. 96
   D. 98

5. George drove from Baltimore to Charlotte, a distance of 420 miles. The next day, he drove from Charlotte to Norfolk, a distance of 310 miles. On the third day, he drove from Norfolk back to Baltimore. If the total trip was 960 miles, how far is Baltimore from Norfolk?

   A. 230 miles
   B. 540 miles
   C. 650 miles
   D. 730 miles

6. Which of the following statements is true of an equilateral triangle?

   A. The base and height of the triangle are the same length.
   B. All three angles have the same measure.
   C. The triangle contains an obtuse angle.
   D. The length of the base is an even number.

7. What is the value of y if $y = -3x + 5$ and $x = -4$?

   A. -2
   B. -7
   C. 17
   D. 7

8. $4.51 \times 10^5 =$

   A. 4.5100000
   B. 451
   C. 451,000
   D. 225.5

9. Solve for x: $\dfrac{x}{4} - 7 = -3$.

   A. 40
   B. 16
   C. 2.5
   D. 1

10. Which of the following is NOT a prime number?

   A. 31
   B. 41
   C. 51
   D. 61

11. Find the value of $(x+4)\left(\dfrac{x}{2}\right)^3$ when $x = 6$.

   A. 54
   B. 108
   C. 270
   D. 1,080

12. $(t^5)^2 =$

   A. $7t$
   B. $10t$
   C. t^7
   D. t^{10}

13. The sum of two consecutive numbers is 69. Find the smaller number.

   A. 33
   B. 34
   C. 35
   D. 36

14. At a certain time of day, a 3-foot pole casts a 4-foot shadow. At the same time, a flagpole casts a 36-foot shadow. How tall is the flagpole?

   A. 27 feet
   B. 36 feet
   C. 45 feet
   D. 48 feet

15. Evaluate $\dfrac{4x-3y}{2x^2+y} - xy^2$ when $x = 2$ and $y = -1$.

   A. $\dfrac{-3}{7}$
   B. -5
   C. $\dfrac{-1}{3}$
   D. 3

16. Ashton is 30 miles north of Benton and 40 miles west of Columbus. Find the distance from Benton to Columbus.

   A. 10 miles
   B. 50 miles
   C. 70 miles
   D. 120 miles

17. $\sqrt{12(147)} =$

   A. 42
   B. 84
   C. 98
   D. 126

18. Which of the following is the square of an odd number?

   A. 1,296
   B. 1,369
   C. 1,444
   D. 1,764

19. Twice a number reduced by three more than the number results in six. Find the number.

   A. 9
   B. 4.5
   C. 3
   D. 0

20. The product of –3.2 and 7.9, rounded to the nearest tenth, is

   A. –25.2
   B. 25.2
   C. –25.3
   D. 25.3

21. $x^2 - 9 =$

   A. $(x-3)^2$
   B. $(x+3)^2$
   C. $-(x+3)^2$
   D. $(x-3)(x+3)$

22. If a 3-×-5-inch photograph is enlarged so that its longer side is 10 inches long, the shorter dimension of the photo will be

    A. $3\frac{1}{3}$ inches

    B. 6 inches

    C. 8 inches

    D. 10 inches

23. If $\dfrac{x-5}{3} = 7$, then $x =$

    A. 4
    B. 9
    C. 26
    D. 36

24. The area of a right triangle whose legs measure 10 inches and 8 inches is

    A. 80 in.²
    B. 40 in.²
    C. 20 in.²
    D. 6 in.²

25. A bag contains 12 marbles. Three are red, five are blue, and four are white. If one marble is chosen at random, what is the probability that it is NOT white?

    A. $\dfrac{1}{4}$

    B. $\dfrac{1}{3}$

    C. $\dfrac{2}{3}$

    D. $\dfrac{3}{4}$

IF YOU FINISH BEFORE TIME IS CALLED, CHECK YOUR WORK ON THIS SECTION ONLY. DO NOT WORK ON ANY OTHER SECTION IN THE TEST.

Answer Key

Section 1: Arithmetic Reasoning

1. C	7. B	13. C	19. D	25. A
2. C	8. B	14. D	20. D	26. D
3. C	9. C	15. A	21. B	27. B
4. B	10. B	16. A	22. B	28. C
5. B	11. B	17. C	23. A	29. D
6. D	12. A	18. C	24. C	30. C

Section 2: Word Knowledge

1. C	8. B	15. A	22. B	29. D
2. A	9. D	16. D	23. D	30. B
3. B	10. B	17. B	24. B	31. A
4. B	11. C	18. D	25. A	32. B
5. C	12. A	19. C	26. C	33. A
6. C	13. A	20. D	27. D	34. D
7. C	14. B	21. A	28. A	35. C

Section 3: Paragraph Comprehension

1. C	4. D	7. D	10. C	13. C
2. C	5. B	8. C	11. B	14. B
3. C	6. B	9. B	12. D	15. B

Section 4: Mathematics Knowledge

1. D	6. B	11. C	16. B	21. D
2. A	7. C	12. D	17. A	22. B
3. D	8. C	13. B	18. B	23. C
4. C	9. B	14. A	19. A	24. B
5. A	10. C	15. A	20. C	25. C

Answer Explanations

Section 1: Arithmetic Reasoning

1. **C.** $5.40 ÷ 12 cans = 45¢ per can. Since all the answer choices are similar, you know the cost is at least 40¢ per can. So, 40 × 12 = $4.80, but $5.40 is an additional 60¢. That 60¢ represents 5¢ per can. (*See Chapter 6, Section E.*)

2. **C.** Multiplication is generally easier than division, so change 4 hours to minutes: 4 × 60 = 240 minutes. If he has been studying for 185 minutes, he needs to study for an additional 240 − 185 = 55 minutes. (*See Chapter 6, Sections C and D; Chapter 5, Section C.*)

3. **C.** Removing 20 leaves 500 − 20 = 480 to be distributed to the three stores. So, 480 ÷ 3 = 160 bottles. (*See Chapter 6, Section E.*)

4. **B.** 420 miles ÷ 60 mph = 7 hours. (*See Chapter 6, Section E.*)

5. **B.** Convert the mixed numbers to improper fractions, then simply and multiply to solve:
$$6\frac{3}{8} \times 5\frac{1}{3} = \frac{48+3}{8} \times \frac{15+1}{3} = \frac{\overset{17}{\cancel{51}}}{\cancel{8}} \times \frac{\overset{2}{\cancel{16}}}{\cancel{3}} = 34$$. (*See Chapter 7, Section D.*)

6. **D.** To compare easily, place each pair of numbers one under another, with the decimal points aligned, and annex zeros if the numbers don't have the same number of digits. Then you can ignore decimal points and leading zeros and compare as though they were whole numbers. The upper number is smaller in each case except choice **D.** (*See Chapter 6, Section A.*)

   A. $\begin{matrix} 0.038 \\ 0.308 \end{matrix} \rightarrow \begin{matrix} 38 \\ 308 \end{matrix}$

   B. $\begin{matrix} 0.0308 \\ 0.3080 \end{matrix} \rightarrow \begin{matrix} 308 \\ 3,080 \end{matrix}$

   C. $\begin{matrix} 0.0038 \\ 0.0308 \end{matrix} \rightarrow \begin{matrix} 38 \\ 308 \end{matrix}$

   D. $\begin{matrix} 0.3008 \\ 0.0308 \end{matrix} \rightarrow \begin{matrix} 3,008 \\ 308 \end{matrix}$

7. **B.** You can find the speed of the train in miles per hour, and then multiply by 11 hours, or you can do this problem with proportional thinking. Use short division to divide 432 miles ÷ 6 hours = 72 mph. Multiply that by 11 hours, using the shortcut for multiplying by 11, and you get 792 miles. (*See Chapter 6, Sections D and E.*)

8. **B.** If two cities are 238 miles apart, and each 5 miles is represented by 1 inch, divide $238 \div 5 = 47.6$ inches. (*See Chapter 6, Section E.*)

9. **C.** Driving 40 miles at 50 mph will take $\frac{4}{\cancel{5}} \times \cancel{60}^{12} = 48$ minutes, and 40 miles $\div \frac{50 \text{ miles}}{\text{hour}} = \frac{4}{5}$ hour. The drive will take $48 - 37 = 11$ minutes longer by car. (*See Chapter 5, Section C; Chapter 7, Section D.*)

10. **B.** The refrigerator that originally cost \$800 was reduced \$200, to sell for \$600. The reduction of \$200 is $\frac{200}{800} = \frac{1}{4} = 25$ percent. (*See Chapter 5, Section E.*)

11. **B.** \$450 is $\frac{3}{8}$ of her prize money, so divide $\$450 \div \frac{3}{8} = {}^{150}\cancel{450} \times \frac{8}{\cancel{3}} = \$1,200$. Or use mental math: \$450 is $\frac{3}{8}$ of her prize money, so \$150 is $\frac{1}{8}$ of the prize, and $\$150 \times 8 = \$800 + \$400 = \$1,200$ is the whole prize. (*See Chapter 7, Section E.*)

12. **A.** He earmarks $\frac{1}{2} + \frac{1}{5} = \frac{5+2}{10} = \frac{7}{10}$, so he has $\frac{3}{10}$ left, and $\frac{3}{\cancel{10}} \times 55\cancel{0} = 3 \times 55 = 3 \times 5 \times 11 = 15 \times 11 = 165$.

    Or you can work through the money amounts. Half of \$550 goes to pay bills, leaving \$275. He saves $\frac{1}{5}$ of his salary, or \$110, leaving \$165. (*See Chapter 7, Sections B and D.*)

13. **C.** The increase in the price of the stock was $\$1,050 - \$350 = \$700$. Percent increase is $\frac{\text{increase}}{\text{original}}$ expressed as a percent, so $\frac{700}{350} = 2$, or 200%. (*See Chapter 5, Section C; Chapter 6, Sections C and E.*)

14. **D.** To round to the nearest hundredth, the second place to the right of the decimal point, look to the thousandth place, the third place to the right. In 4,739.9374, the thousandth place contains a 7, so round the hundredths digit up and drop the remaining places. $4,739.9374 \approx 4,739.94$. (*See Chapter 6, Section A.*)

15. **A.** Begin with the original deposit of \$300 and add 4 percent interest, or \$12. (Four percent is 4 for each 100, and you have three hundreds, so $3 \times 4 = 12$.) At the end of the first year, the balance is \$312. Add the additional \$200 to bring the balance to \$512. At the end of the second year, interest is calculated as 4 percent of \$512, which is $\$512 \times 0.04 = \$20.48$. (*See Chapter 5, Section D.*)

16. **A.** Eight dozen rolls is $8 \times 12 = 96$ rolls. At 50¢ per roll, they will bring in income of \$48. (Fifty cents is half of a dollar, so think half of 96.) They were purchased for \$4 a dozen, or $8 \times 4 = \$32$. Income minus cost is $\$48 - \$32 = \$16$. (*See Chapter 6, Sections C and D.*)

17. **C.** Twelve percent of the 250 desks should be left-handed. Multiply $0.12 \times 250 = 30$. Do the multiplication mentally by thinking 12 for every hundred, and you have 200 and half a hundred, so $12 + 12 + 6 = 30$. Or think 10 percent of 250 is 25, and 2 percent of 250 is 2×2.5 or 5, so $25 + 5 = 30$. (*See Chapter 6, Section D.*)

18. **C.** Twenty-four women out of a total staff of $36 + 24 = 60$ people is $\frac{24}{60} = \frac{4}{10} = 40\%$. (*See Chapter 6, Section E.*)

19. **D.** If Jesse and Jane drive in opposite directions at 55 mph and 60 mph, respectively, then each hour they move 55 + 60 = 115 miles farther apart. If they do this for 3 hours, they'll be 3 × 115 = 345 miles apart. (*See Chapter 6, Sections B and D.*)

20. **D.** Realize that 30 percent of 100 is 30, and you want 60, so double the 100. 30 percent of 200 will be 60. (*See Chapter 5, Section C.*)

21. **B.** One-eighth of a mile is $\frac{1}{8} \times 5,280$ feet $= \frac{5,280}{8} = \frac{1,320}{2} = 660$ feet, so each furlong is 660 feet. Multiply 660 by 5 to find that 5 furlongs is 3,300 feet. (*See Chapter 5, Section C; Chapter 7, Section D.*)

22. **B.** If he works 43 hours, he earns $12.20 an hour for the first 40 hours and $1\frac{1}{2}$ times $12.20 per hour for the additional 3 hours. So, $12.20 × 40 = $488 and $1\frac{1}{2} \times \$12.20 \times 3 = \frac{3}{2} \times \cancel{12.20}^{6.10} \times 3 = 9 \times 6.10 = \$54.90$.

Add $488 + $54.90 to find that his total earnings are $542.90. (*See Chapter 5, Section F; Chapter 7, Section D.*)

23. **A.** A quarter of the distance should take a quarter of the time, so if you can walk a mile in 12 minutes, you can walk a quarter mile in 12 ÷ 4 = 3 minutes. (*See Chapter 6, Section E.*)

24. **C.** Jennifer's base salary was $6 per hour × 40 hours = $240. Commission was 2 percent of $1,820, which is $1,820 × 0.02 = $36.40. (You can just multiply by 2 and move the decimal point two places left.) Add salary plus commission to find total earnings: $240 + $36.40 = $276.40. (*See Chapter 5, Section F.*)

25. **A.** Twenty percent off on a $350 purchase is 2 × (0.10 × 350) = 2 × 35 = 70. He saves $70 on the suit, so $350 – $70 = $280. (*See Chapter 5, Section D.*)

26. **D.** Find $100 – $63.79 mentally by making change. You'll need $0.01 to make $63.80, then $0.20 to make $64, $6 to make $70, and another $30 to make $100. So, $0.01 + $0.20 + $6 + $30 = $36.21. (*See Chapter 6, Section C.*)

27. **B.** Betsy traveled 153 miles in 3 hours: 153 ÷ 3 = 51 mph. (*See Chapter 6, Section E.*)

28. **C.** 479 pages ÷ 30 pages a day is best estimated by rounding 479 to 480 and then dividing: 480 ÷ 30 = 48 ÷ 3 = 16 days. If you choose to do the division of 479 ÷ 30, you get $15.9\overline{6}$ as shown below, which would round to 16.

$$
\begin{array}{r}
15.9\overline{6} \\
30\overline{)479.00} \\
\underline{30} \\
179 \\
\underline{150} \\
290 \\
\underline{270} \\
200 \\
\underline{180} \\
20
\end{array}
$$

The division tells you that after 15 days he has read 450 pages and has 29 pages left to read. He will complete those on the 16th day. (*See Chapter 6, Section E.*)

29. **D.** 4 + 7 + 6 + 13 = (4 + 6) + (7 + 13) = 10 + 20 = 30 hits. (*See Chapter 6, Section A.*)

30. **C.** Batting average is number of hits divided by number of times at bat, so $\dfrac{\text{hits}}{\text{at-bats}} = \dfrac{x}{300} = 0.290$. Multiply $0.290 \times 300 = 87$ hits. (*See Chapter 6, Section D.*)

Section 2: Word Knowledge

All the words in questions 1–35 are included in Chapter 9, Section C.

1. **C.** *Banish* (verb) means to kick someone out or to oust.

2. **A.** *Credulous* (adjective) means gullible. (The root *cred* means belief.) (*See also Chapter 8, Section B.*)

3. **B.** A *barrier* (noun) is a barricade or an obstruction.

4. **B.** *Decipher* (verb) means to make sense of or to decode.

5. **C.** *Deleterious* (adjective) means harmful.

6. **C.** *Brevity* (noun) means briefness.

7. **C.** *Emulate* (verb) means to copy or imitate.

8. **B.** *Streamline* (verb) means to make more efficient.

9. **D.** *Pugnacious* (adjective) means tending to fight or argumentative. (The root *pug* means fight.) (*See also Chapter 8, Section B.*)

10. **B.** *Retrench* (verb) means to cut back.

11. **C.** *Elucidate* (verb) means to make clear.

12. **A.** *Mobilize* (verb) means to rally, organize, or assemble.

13. **A.** *Jeopardy* (noun) means danger.

14. **B.** *Avarice* (noun) means greed.

15. **A.** *Intrepid* (adjective) means brave or courageous.

16. **D.** A *stalemate* (noun) is a deadlock or impasse.

17. **B.** *Retaliate* (verb) means to even the score or to strike back.

18. **D.** *Seclusion* (noun) means isolation.

19. **C.** *Inevitable* (adjective) means unavoidable.

20. **D.** *Elude* (verb) means to avoid capture or to escape.

21. **A.** *Audacious* (adjective) means bold or daring.

22. **B.** *Extant* (adjective) means living or in existence. (It is the opposite of *extinct*.)

23. **D.** *Fallacious* (adjective) means misleading or illogical.

24. **B.** *Impulsive* (adjective) means acting on impulse or reckless.

25. **A.** *Manipulate* (verb) means to control or handle.

26. **C.** *Fretful* (adjective) means worried.

27. **D.** *Exotic* (adjective) means foreign or unusual.

28. **A.** *Pervasive* (adjective) means widespread.

29. **D.** *Assess* (verb) means to appraise or evaluate.

30. **B.** A *bog* (noun) is a swamp. (The word *bog* can also be used as part of a verb, such as *bog down,* which means to get stuck or slowed down.)

31. **A.** *Jovial* (adjective) means cheerful.

32. **B.** *Meander* (verb) means to wander aimlessly or roam.

33. **A.** An *ally* (noun) is a friend or supporter. (When *ally* is used as a verb, it means to form a mutually supportive connection.)

34. **D.** *Confidential* (adjective) means secret.

35. **C.** *Ingenuity* (noun) means cleverness or inventiveness.

Section 3: Paragraph Comprehension

See Chapter 10, Sections A and B, and Chapter 11, Section B, for assistance with questions 1–15.

1. **C.** According to the first sentence of the passage, DNA determines hereditary information, choice C. Choice A is inaccurate; the passage states that the order of the bases is individual and determines the characteristics of the organism. Choice B is inaccurate; most DNA is in the nucleus. The passage doesn't state that the bases are arranged in alphabetical order, merely that bases can be rearranged like letters of the alphabet, so choice D is not correct.

2. **C.** The passage states that the Appalachian Trail is a continuous footpath through 14 states, which makes choice C correct. There is no evidence in the passage to support choices A, B, and D. In fact, they're all inaccurate.

3. **C.** The passage gives a general overview of America during the Civil War period, choice C. The author doesn't suggest that this period was a low point (choice A), nor does he discuss post–Civil War America (choice B). He doesn't contrast the frontier spirit with modern attitudes, so choice D is incorrect.

4. **D.** The only generalization that can be supported with evidence from the passage is that today's America is very different from the America of the Civil War period, choice D. There is no indication that the state of democracy has declined (choice A) or that the railroads played an important role in transporting troops (choice B). Choice C may be a true statement, but it isn't supported by the passage.

5. **B.** It is clear that the author of this passage would agree that alcohol use among people between the ages of 18 and 24 should be curbed, choice B. The passage indicates that educational programs are in place, so choice A is incorrect. Choice C may be true, but the passage offers no evidence to support this assertion. Choice D is off-topic.

6. **B.** The last sentence of the passage supports choice B, planting crops near the equator is a good choice. Choice A can't be supported by this passage. Choice C is irrelevant. The harmful nature of thunderstorms (choice D) is not discussed in the passage.

7. **D.** Only choice D, the path of the stone can be altered by the actions of team members after it has been thrown, can be supported by the passage. Choice A is inaccurate (and silly). The sweepers don't block the stone, so choice B is incorrect. The team consists of four players, so choice C is incorrect.

8. **C.** Because hybrids have lower polluting emissions, it is reasonable to assume that car shoppers who are concerned about pollution will be attracted to them, choice C. Choice A makes a broad generalization that isn't based on reasonable evidence. Choice B is not addressed in the passage. The passage doesn't discuss the price of the hybrid vehicles, so choice D is not a reasonable assumption.

9. **B.** Because the passage states that more than 2 million people visit Mount Rushmore each year, it is reasonable to assume that more than 5 million tourists have visited the site since it was completed in 1941. Choices A and C are not based on any information stated in the passage. Choice D is incorrect; Gutzon Borglum, not Doane Robinson, was the sculptor.

10. **C.** Since women couldn't vote in national elections until the ratification of the 19th Amendment in 1920 and Rankin was elected in 1916, choice C can't be inferred from the passage. Choice A is directly stated in the passage. Choice B is true; the passage states that Rebecca Felton was elected to the Senate. Nowhere does it imply that she was first elected to the House of Representatives. Choice D can be logically implied because Felton's election took place after the ratification of the 19th Amendment.

11. **B.** The passage indicates that the cam converts rotating motion into linear motion, so choice B is correct. Choice A is not accurate; according to the passage, a cam may be irregularly shaped, but it doesn't have to be. Choice C is incorrect because the linear motion doesn't create electricity. Choice D is inaccurate.

12. **D.** Choice D correctly states the main point of the passage: The CPI is useful to economists who study trends in the financial stability of the nation. Choice A is not supported by information in the passage. Choice B is inaccurate; only a typical urban family is used to calculate the CPI. Choice C is not supported by information in the passage.

13. **C.** Based on the information in the passage, only choice C is in the correct order: The GPS finds four satellites, then calculates its distance from each, and then trilaterates its position on earth. Choices A, B, and D are all in the incorrect order.

14. **B.** The author describes a scene that is both mysterious and ominous. The passage contains no irritation (choice A) or malice (choice C). You might be tempted by choice D, but the author has created a tone of vaguely threatening mystery rather than sadness.

15. **B.** Choice B, the Olympic Games are an outstanding opportunity for cultural exchange, can be inferred from the last sentence of the passage. Choice A is inaccurate. Choice C may be true, but it is not alluded to in the passage. Choice D is not supported by the passage.

Section 4: Mathematics Knowledge

1. **D.** The area of a square is the length of a side, squared, so $12^2 = 144$ ft.^{2} (*See Chapter 13, Section E.*)

2. **A.** The circumference of a circle is the product of π and the diameter, or $2\pi r$. The radius is 3 yards, so the circumference is $2 \times \pi \times 3 = 6\pi$ yards. (*See Chapter 13, Section H.*)

3. **D.** It's true that the square of a positive number is positive (choice A) and the square of a negative number is also positive (choice B) because when two numbers with the same sign are multiplied, the result is positive. Zero squared is 0, so choice C is true. However, choice D, the square of a number is always larger than the number, is NOT a true statement. For any number less than 0 or larger than 1, the square is larger than the original number, but for 0 and 1, the square is equal to the number, and for fractions between 0 and 1, the square is smaller than the number; for example, $\left(\dfrac{1}{2}\right)^2 = \dfrac{1}{4}$. Therefore, choice D is the correct answer. (*See Chapter 12, Section C.*)

4. **C.** If Jennifer's average on three tests is 86 percent, then her total score is 86 × 3 = 258. Since the exam counts as two tests, her final grade is the equivalent of averaging five tests. To average 90 percent on five tests, she would need a total of 5 × 90 = 450 points, which means she needs 450 – 258 = 192 additional points. Divide 192 by 2 to find the grade she needs on the exam: 192 ÷ 2 = 96. (*See Chapter 15, Section C.*)

5. **A.** Baltimore to Charlotte plus Charlotte to Norfolk is 420 miles + 310 miles = 730 miles. Since the total trip is 960 miles, the distance from Norfolk to Baltimore is 960 – 730 = 230 miles. (*See Chapter 13, Section C.*)

6. **B.** By definition, an equilateral triangle has three sides of equal length, but every equilateral triangle is also equiangular—all three angles have the same measure, choice B. Since all the angles measure 60°, the triangle does not contain an obtuse angle (choice C). The base and height of an equilateral triangle are not the same length (choice A). The height, measured perpendicular to the base, will be shorter than the sides. Equilateral triangles come in all sizes, so it's not possible that the length of the base is an even number for every equilateral triangle (choice D). (*See Chapter 13, Section C.*)

7. **C.** $y = -3x + 5 = -3(-4) + 5 = 12 + 5 = 17$. (*See Chapter 12, Sections C and K.*)

8. **C.** $4.51 \times 10^5 = 4.51 \times 10 \times 10 \times 10 \times 10 \times 10 = 4.51 \times 100,000 = 451,000$. Or you can just remember that 4.51×10^5 means to move the decimal point five places to the right. So, $4.51 \times 10^5 = 4.\underline{51000} = 451,000$. (*See Chapter 12, Section C.*)

9. **B.** You need to isolate x. First, add 7 to both sides, and then multiply both sides by 4:

$$\frac{x}{4} - 7 = -3$$
$$\frac{x}{4} = 4$$
$$x = 16$$

(*See Chapter 12, Section D.*)

10. **C.** Prime numbers are numbers that have no factors other than themselves and 1, so you're looking for an answer choice that is divisible by some other number. All the answer choices are odd, so none of them is divisible by 2. Check for divisibility by 3 by adding the digits; if the sum of the digits is a multiple of 3, the number is divisible by 3. The sum of the digits of 31 is 4 (which is not divisible by 3), of 41 is 5 (which is not divisible by 3), and of 51 is 6, which is divisible by 3 and, therefore, not prime. (*See Chapter 12, Section A.*)

11. **C.** Substitute 6 for x and solve:

$$(x+4)\left(\frac{x}{2}\right)^3 = (6+4)\left(\frac{6}{2}\right)^3$$
$$= 10(3)^3$$
$$= 10(27)$$
$$= 270$$

(*See Chapter 12, Section C.*)

12. **D.** When a power is raised to a power, the exponents are multiplied: $(t^5)^2 = t^{(5)(2)} = t^{10}$. (*See Chapter 12, Section C.*)

13. **B.** Represent the two consecutive numbers as x and $x + 1$. The sum of x and $x + 1$ is $2x + 1$ and that equals 69. To solve, isolate x by subtracting 1 from both sides and then dividing both sides by 2:

$$2x + 1 = 69$$
$$2x = 68$$
$$x = 34$$

(See Chapter 12, Section D.)

14. **A.** In each case, the pole and its shadow form the legs of a right triangle with the sun's rays as the hypotenuse. Since the two shadows occur at the same time of day, the angle of the sun is the same, and so the triangles are similar. The proportion $\dfrac{\text{pole}}{\text{shadow}} = \dfrac{\text{pole}}{\text{shadow}}$ can be solved to find the height of the flagpole:

$$\frac{3}{4} = \frac{x}{36}$$
$$\frac{3}{{}_1\cancel{4}}(\cancel{36}^{\,9}) = \frac{x}{36}(36)$$
$$27 = x$$

(See Chapter 14, Section B.)

15. **A.** Replace x with 2 and y with –1. Next, simplify powers and remove unnecessary parentheses. Perform the multiplications. Simplify the numerator and denominator of the fraction, change the 2 to a fraction with a denominator of 7, and then subtract:

$$\frac{4x - 3y}{2x^2 + y} - xy^2 = \frac{4(2) - 3(-1)}{2(2)^2 + (-1)} - (2)(-1)^2$$
$$= \frac{4(2) - 3(-1)}{2(4) - 1} - (2)(1)$$
$$= \frac{8 + 3}{8 - 1} - 2$$
$$= \frac{11}{7} - 2$$
$$= \frac{11}{7} - \frac{14}{7}$$
$$= \frac{-3}{7}$$

(See Chapter 12, Section C.)

16. **B.** If you sketch the locations described, you'll see that Ashton, Benton, and Columbus are the vertices of a right triangle, and the distance from Benton to Columbus is the hypotenuse. Use the Pythagorean theorem to find the answer:

$$a^2 + b^2 = c^2$$
$$30^2 + 40^2 = c^2$$
$$900 + 1{,}600 = c^2$$
$$2{,}500 = c^2$$
$$\sqrt{2{,}500} = c$$
$$50 = c$$

Or, you can recognize this as a Pythagorean triple, noting that since 30 and 40 are multiples of 3 and 4, the hypotenuse will be a corresponding multiple of 5; therefore, the distance is 50. (*See Chapter 13, Section C.*)

17. **A.** Multiplying 12×147 is not likely to be helpful. Instead, factor each of the numbers, looking for factors that are perfect squares:

$$\sqrt{12(147)} = \sqrt{4 \cdot 3(147)}$$
$$= \sqrt{4 \cdot 3(3 \cdot 49)}$$
$$= \sqrt{4 \cdot 9 \cdot 49}$$
$$= \sqrt{4}\sqrt{9}\sqrt{49}$$
$$= 2 \cdot 3 \cdot 7$$
$$= 42$$

(*See Chapter 12, Section B.*)

18. **B.** Odd numbers end in 1, 3, 5, 7, or 9, so their squares will end in the same digits that occur at the end of 1^2, 3^2, 5^2, 7^2, and 9^2. So, $1^2 = 1$, $3^2 = 9$, $5^2 = 25$, $7^2 = 49$, and $9^2 = 81$. That means that the square of an odd number will end in 1, 9, or 5. Only 1,369 could be the square of an odd number. It is the square of 37. (*See Chapter 12, Sections A and B.*)

19. **A.** The sentence *Twice a number reduced by three more than the number results in six* translates to $2x - (x + 3) = 6$. Remove the parentheses by distributing the negative in front of the parentheses, and then combine like terms. Add 3 to both sides to isolate x.

$$2x - (x + 3) = 6$$
$$2x - x - 3 = 6$$
$$x - 3 = 6$$
$$x = 9$$

(*See Chapter 12, Section D; Chapter 5, Section B.*)

20. **C.** The product is the result of multiplication. A quick estimate ($-3 \times 8 = -24$) eliminates the two positive answer choices. Once you know your answer is negative, you simply need to multiply 3.2 and 7.9 to determine which of the remaining choices is correct. To multiply 3.2 and 7.9, you can think of the problem as $(3 + 0.2)(7 + 0.9)$ and FOIL:

$$(3+0.2)(7+0.9) = 21+2.7+1.4+0.18$$
$$= 23.7+1.58$$
$$= 25.28$$

Remember: In the original problem, 3.2 is negative, so your answer is actually –25.28, and –25.28 will round to –25.3. (*See Chapter 12, Sections A and F.*)

21. **D.** Factor the difference of squares as the sum and difference of the same two terms:

$$x^2 - 9 = x^2 - 3^2$$
$$= (x-3)(x+3)$$

(*See Chapter 12, Section F.*)

22. **B.** One dimension of the 3-×-5-inch photo is doubled, so that the longer side becomes 10 inches. Therefore, the other dimension should be doubled as well, and $2 \times 3 = 6$ inches. (*See Chapter 13, Section G.*)

23. **C.** Multiply both sides by 3, and then add 5 to both sides:

$$\frac{x-5}{3} = 7$$
$$x - 5 = 21$$
$$x = 26$$

(*See Chapter 12, Section D.*)

24. **B.** The area of a triangle is $\frac{1}{2}bh$, and in a right triangle the legs can be used as base and height because they're perpendicular. So, $A = \frac{1}{2}bh = \frac{1}{2}(10)(8) = 40$ square inches. (*See Chapter 13, Section E.*)

25. **C.** Four of the marbles are white, so eight are not white: $\frac{8}{12} = \frac{2}{3}$. (*See Chapter 15, Section B.*)